Lars Ewald/Sture Westman

Data-communication

Data networks, protocols and design

Translated by: A.G. McK. Nicholl

Studentlitteratur

Chartwell-Bratt Ltd

This books was first published in Swedish 1983. The title of the original editim: Datakommunikation. Datanät, protokoll och design.

Translated by A.G. McK. Nicholl
Cover art: Kjeld Brandt

Printed in Sweden
Studentlitteratur, Lund
ISBN 91-44-23981-5 (Studentlitteratur)
ISBN 0-86238-092-8 (Chartwell-Bratt)

1 2 3 4 5 6 7 8 9 10 | 1991 90 89 88

Contents

Preface

"Once you are in communications,
you will never be out of it"

Data communication is, as many know, a very comprehensive subject. In addition, it is the area within the realms of data processing where the rate of development will accelerate during the rest of the 1980's. Most people will be affected by data communication in one form or another.

This book, which is an introduction, aims to give a general knowledge of data communication without going too deeply into the subject. Terms which the well informed tend to "throw around" are presented in this book in a more easily-understood form. The contents may be regarded to some extent as a reference book, while at the same time dealing, among other things, with the technology, the protocols and the types of network which exist today.

This book is intended primarily for students, both at universities and colleges, and also for vocational trainees in data processing. The intention is also for it to be useful to those studying on thir own, whether they have been working in DP for some years or whether they are just curious to get an insight into the "jungle" of data communication. Finally we hoped that this book will prove its worth as a reference book for those who are already working in this area.

The chapters of the book are completely independent of one another, and so they don't need to be read in order. Some of the chapters (3,13) are more theoretical, but with judicious skimming it is possible to choose the sections according to previous knowledge and interest. Chapter 7 contains a general orientation into the architectures which some suppliers have chosen as the basis for their networks. The material was obtained from manuals and handbooks which the suppliers made available.

Some may think that a small number of products or suppliers have received disproportionate space in the book. For practical reasons, however, it has been necessary to select some out.

We pass on our warm thanks to all suppliers who helped us with booklets, information material, pictures and manuals, and those people who read through and approved the material.

Stockholm,
February 1983

Lars Ewald *Sture Westman*

1 Introduction to data communication

In the middle of the 1960's, nearly all data processing was centralised. Most jobs were run on a large and powerful host computer, either by batch processing or directly (on-line) via a terminal. Batch processing means that the jobs were collected through the day and fed into the computer at night for processing. The output from the run was distributed the following day to the users, who nearly all worked close to the computer. The terminals were connected up and controlled by the central computer, and used most for questions and answers and for the input and output of data. Data communication and networks had not yet made their breakthrough.

Databases and transaction processing were techniques which as yet were not available to the users. The machines and all the peripheral equipment which the computer needed for its processing were expensive, but the salary costs were lower than today. The advantages of large installations were gained by assembling machines and DP staff together at one place.

Figure 1.1 shows a centralised computer system where the computer is responsible for all the processing and storage of data at one and the same site.

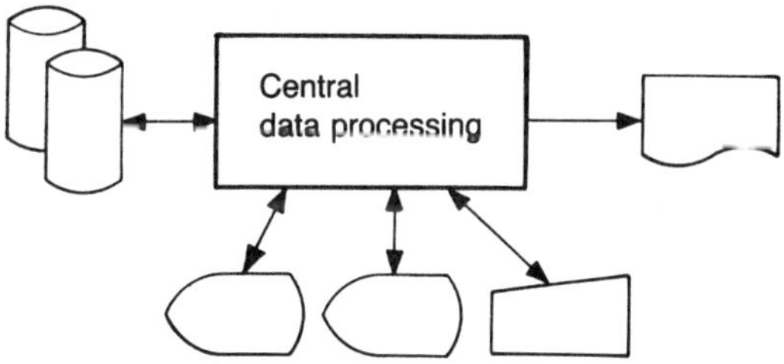

Figure 1.1 Centralised computer system

Time passed, and the machines became cheaper, thanks to the rapid developments of electronics. This trend, together with the increased salary costs, meant that it became more and more worthwhile to invest in machines which saved work. One step towards a decentralised solution was to move the data processing out to the users. This could be done by taking into account the developments, primarily in the area of communications. Special computers, communication computers ('front ends') off-loaded the central computer by taking care of all the communication traffic between the user terminals and the host computer. The results were faster processing, better sharing of capacity and greater reliability than the earliest terminal systems.

By the middle of the 1970's, the performance of computers in comparison with their price had improved so much that it was worth in some cases carrying out data processing locally. With the aid of small processors in the terminals, the users could pre-process data locally before it was sent over to the central computer for further processing. The development of software, however, did not keep pace with the rapid technical development and the possibilities it brought with it.

The computer suppliers also began to offer their customers the possibility of connecting together different types of terminal and several computers in a general data network with unified overall control (IBM – SNA Systems Network Architecture; Honeywell Bell – DSA Distributed Systems Architecture, etc). Figure 1.2 shows a distributed network.

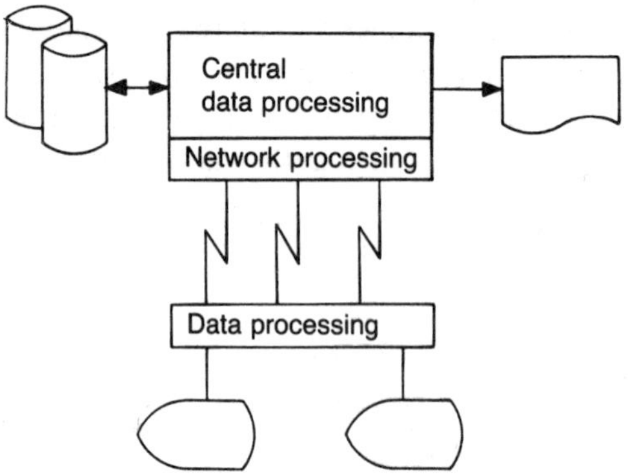

Figure 1.2 Distributed network

Distributed computer systems provide standard functions for local storage and handling of databases. Similar functions are provided locally for data processing to those provided centrally. The local system can function on its own, but also in connection with the central computer. At the same time, it can form part of a total network with other central and local computer systems. Not only computers are connected to these networks, but also terminals of different types. Figure 1.3 is a development of the previous Figure, and shows a distributed data processing system.

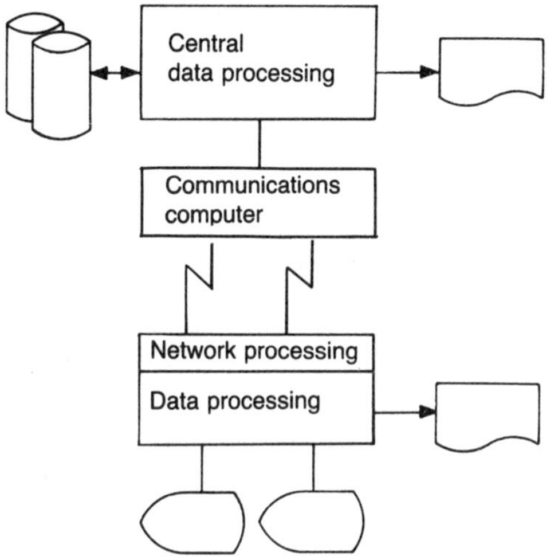

Figure 1.3 Distributed data processing

Now in the middle of the 1980's much is happening on the hardware side, and particularly in the microcomputer area. At the same time, software is coming through to load in and use on the new computer systems. Because of this, it has become simpler to build and control a distributed system with a large number of units geographically widespread throughout the country. The critical points concerning the use of these systems are databases, data security and data communication. A distributed system requires special rules for how the distributed databases and applications programs are to work together. Some of the requirements are

- The ability to move programs between the computers in the system
- Well-defined routines for development of programs and applications
- Flexible access to information
- The ability to move data between different systems
- Security in all types of files and records

The architecture used in networks usually follows the concepts of the computer supplier. Connections are usually lines, but the Swedish telephone administration Televerket's new data transfer service DATEX, the general data network, will be of importance in the future.

Software for the future distributed systems must be considerably more comprehensive than that needed to control central systems. It will have to be possible to access, update, copy and move data and files from one place in a system to another. It must be possible to carry out de-bugging, corrections and alterations without upsetting the system. All this must not mean that the system becomes too complicated to use, as the users' experience of computers is generally less in a distributed system than in today's centralised systems.

Every workstation acts like a link in a chain, and not as isolated individuals with no contact with the outside world. Everyone must be able to have access to data and resources from other systems.

In the first place, this sets high demands on the software when the system is designed. The hardware perhaps comes in second place, depending on the point-to-point functions one needs in the system. It all has then to be connected together in a network suitable for the geographical spread of the workplaces. Figure 1.4 shows a distributed database system.

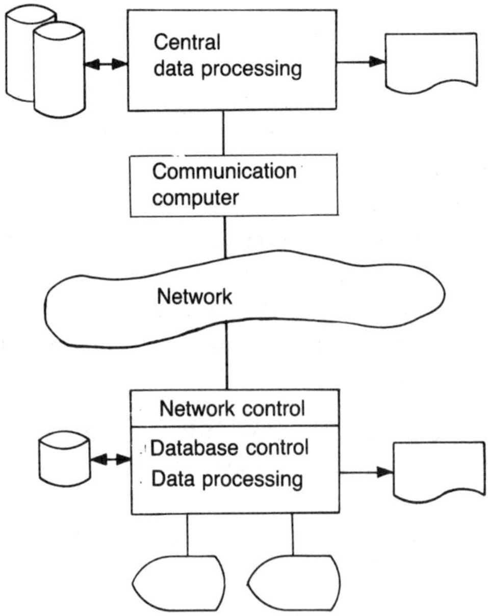

Figure 1.4 Distributed database system

The rapid developments in the data processing area during the last few years make it difficult for many users to choose correctly from among all the system solutions on offer. Users must not be blinded by the very latest equipment, but must be able to choose from what is available in line with their needs.

Development will go on, very rapidly in certain areas – somewhat slower in others. The changes must, however, be made within the framework of what the user is able to handle. The equipment one has invested in must not become old-fashioned overnight, or make practically everyone redundant.

2 Cables and wires

2.1 Introduction

The telephone network in Sweden is very widespread and well-designed for today's needs. In 1986 there were 6 million subscriber lines.

The telephone network does not consist solely of what is known as the public network, i e the installations administered by Televerket, the Swedish Telephone Company; the national railways, defence and industry also have large telephone networks.

When telephone systems were first developed, only solid, airborne lines were used. The cross-talk problems were solved by interchanging or transposition, a system whereby the positions of the cables were systematically changed over on the insulators on the telegraph poles. The telephone network then grew to such an extent that the solid wire system took up too much room. Cables were developed in which the cross-talk problem was solved by twinning of the cable pairs.

2.2 Cable construction

A telephone cable consists of a number of insulated wires, or leads, enclosed within a cover (mantle). The wires are usually made of copper drawn out to a thread of a specific diameter.

The wires are given an insulating covering, usually a plastic coating sprayed around them. Paper is also used for insulation, where a strip of paper is bound in a spiral around the wire.

The thickness and evenness of the insulation determine the capacitance of the cable. In order to allow identification of the wires, their insulation is made in different colours or given other distinctive markings, such as stripes. The insulated wires are twinned or twisted together into pairs and are then called leads.

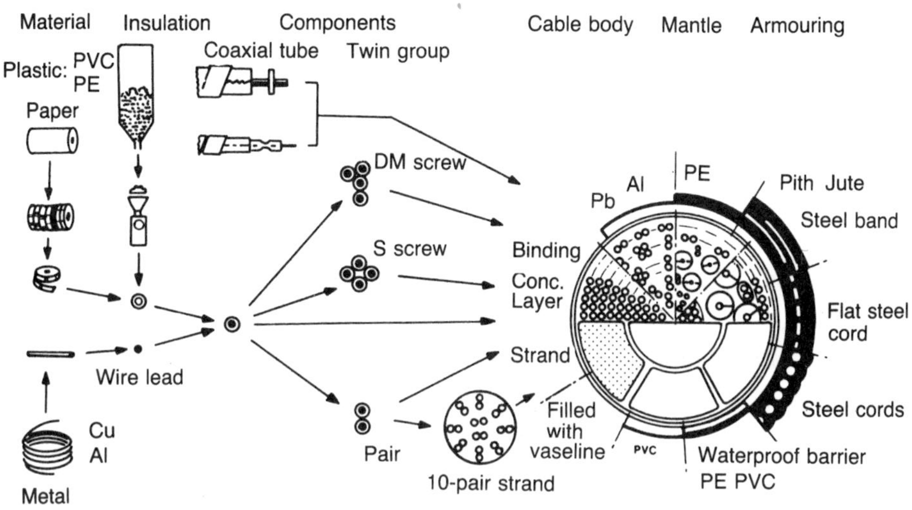

Figure 2.1 Cable construction

Telephone cables are often standardised in terms of numbers of pairs and lead diameter. The number of pairs varies from 1 to 2 400.

The most common wire diameters used are 0.4, 0.5, 0.6 and 0.7 mm. The outer diameter of the cable can vary from a few millimetres up to 100 millimetres.

Telephone cables are also constructed of other types of leads, such as coaxial tubes and optical fibres.

2.3 Coaxial cables

A coaxial cable consists of an inner lead surrounded by a tube-shaped outer lead, with insulation between which holds the inner lead centered. It is a double conductor, with the centre as one lead and the concentric surrounding mantle forming the other one.

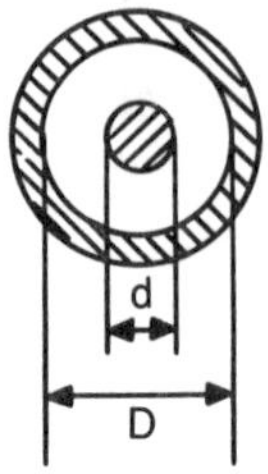

Figure 2.2 Coaxial cable

Coaxial cables are used for transmission at very high frequencies.

Where the coaxial cables are used in broad band systems, the dielectric consists mainly of air.

Both the outer and the inner leads are made of copper. It is common to call this type of concentric lead a 'tube'. Two such tubes are used for a broad band system, one for transmission in each direction. Figure 2.3 shows a section of a coaxial cable, which contains two tubes (for two broad band systems), and their associated control and service lines.

Figure 2.3 Coaxial cable with two pairs of tubes

2.4 Optical fibres

Optical fibre cables – the transmission medium of tomorrow – where information is transmitted by means of light in transparent leads, are at the present time under intensive development.

Optical fibres have many interesting characteristics, including small physical dimensions, and hence small mass, and above all the ability to transfer enormous amounts of information. Theoretically it is possible to carry more telephone conversations simultaneously down a single fibre than there are people on the earth.

The signal transfer in an optical fibre is done by means of electromagnetic waves of the same type as in normal metal wires, but at very much higher frequencies of the order of 300 THz ($=300\times10^{12}$Hz). This frequency range includes the visible spectrum, hence the term 'optical'.

The technology will be of great importance in the areas of

- telecommunication
- data communication
- video transmission
- military and space
- process industries

The advantages of fibre optics

- wide bandwidth
- complete electrical insulation
- immune to short-circuiting
- no spark generation
- cannot be overheard ('tapped')
- reliable and insensitive to interference
- small dimensions
- low cost

The disadvantages of fibre optics

- lack of international standards
- reliability of the light source
- ageing characteristics of the fibres

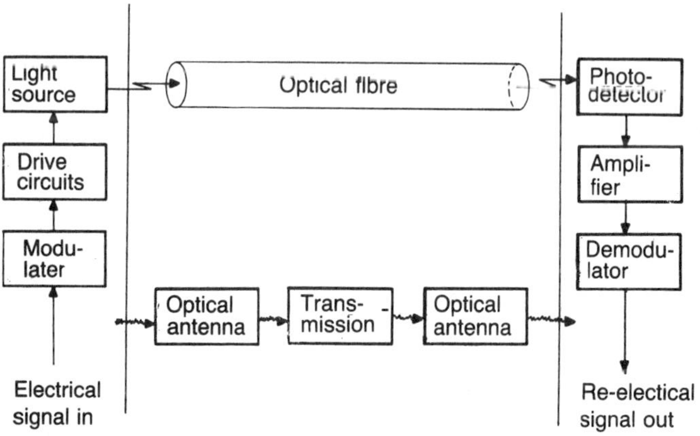

Figure 2.4 Optical communications link

The most important characteristics of an optical conductor are best described with the aid of some diagrams.

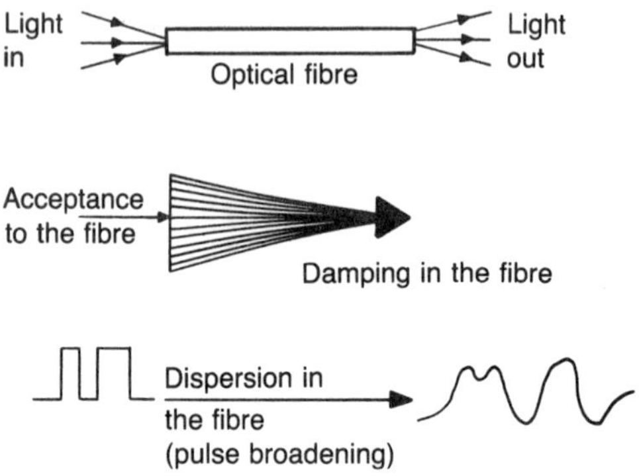

Figure 2.5 Optical fibre, attenuation in the fibre and pulse broadening

The acceptance angle of the fibre, θ, is measured in degrees, and gives the maximum angle at which light is accepted by the fibre.

Attenuation in fibres is commonly expressed in dB/km, and is a measure of how much of the optical signal gets lost in the fibre.

Dispersion (pulse broadening) in a fibre is given as ns/km, and is a measure of the time difference between the light rays taking the shortest and the longest route respectively through the fibre.

Optical conductors

An optical fibre may consist of a core made, for example, of quartz glass, surrounded by a material (the cladding) with a lower refractive index than the core, and a protective outer coating of, for example, plastic.

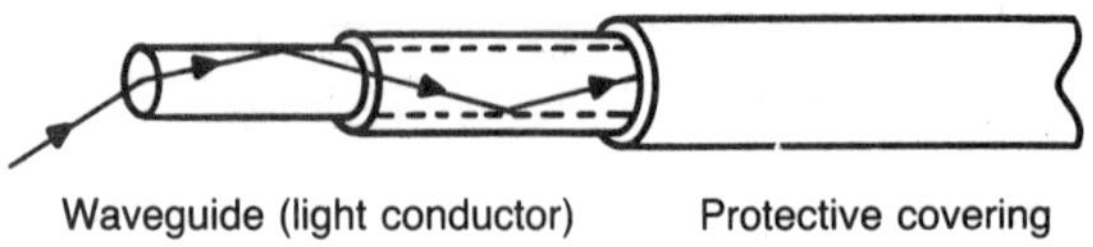

Figure 2.6 Optical conductor

Waveguides

A simplified optical diagram may clarify how transmission is effected. There is a total inward reflection of light at the boundary between the core and the cladding.

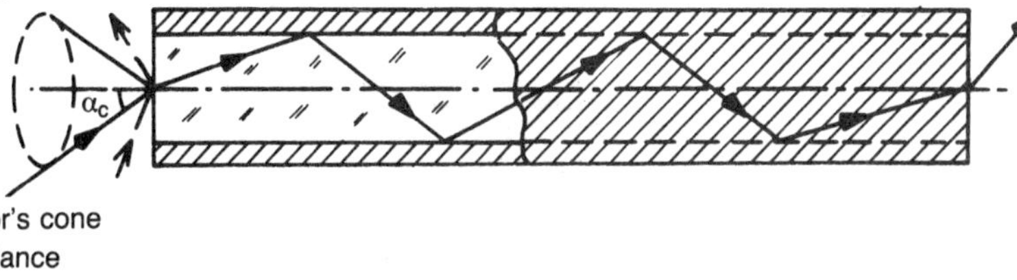

Figure 2.7 Waveguide (conductor)

The definition of the numerical aperture is:

$N.A. = \sin\alpha_c = (n^2_{core} - n^2_{cladding})^{1/2}$, where α_c is the limiting angle for light acceptance.

There are three types of waveguide, differing in the ratio of refractive indices of the core and the cladding.

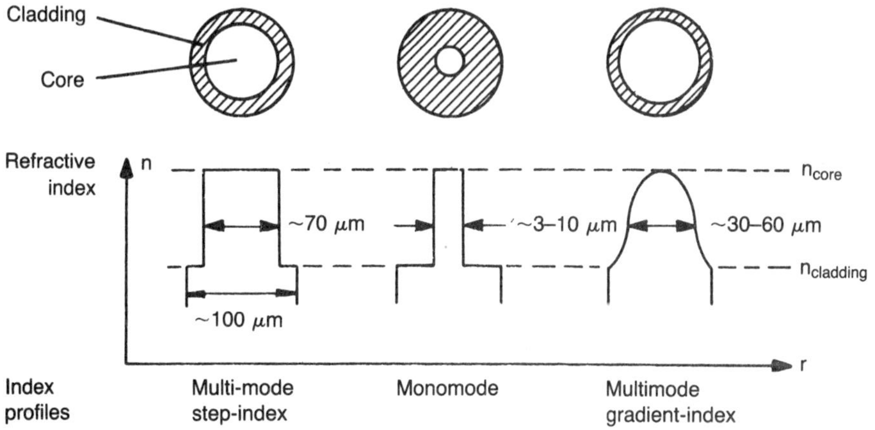

Figure 2.8 Different types of waveguide

The light source

The task of the light source is to transfer the light corresponding to our electrical signal to the fibre as efficiently as possible.

The main types of light sources used are light-emitting diodes (LED) and laser diodes (injection laser, semiconductor laser).

Figure 2.9 shows the principles of how a LED and a laser diode function.

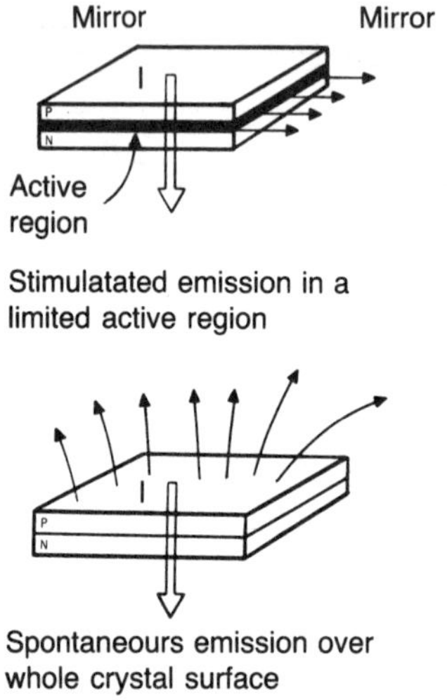

Figure 2.9 Principles of light-emitting diode and laser diode

For both these components, the light produced (optical effect) is dependent upon the current I (drive current) through the component.

The relationship between drive current and optical effect (output) is shown in Figure 2.10.

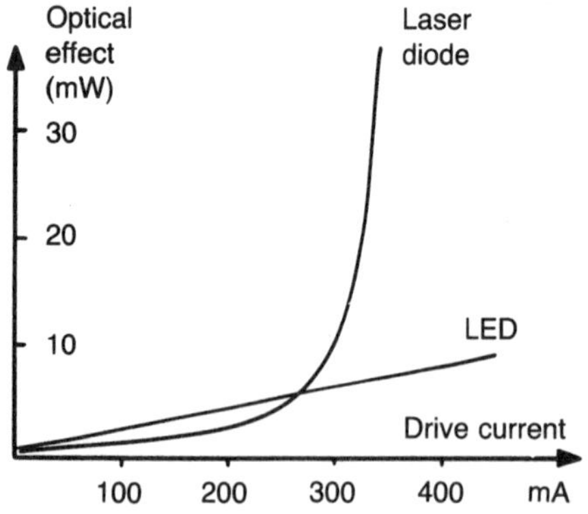

Figure 2.10 Optical effect (ouput) as a function of drive current for laser diode and light emitting diode

The detector

The detector in the opto-electronic system has up till now been the simplest component with the fewest limitations as to speed, length of life, etc, so there has been relatively little emphasis on their further development.

Current detectors used in opto-electronic systems are mainly photodiodes, PIN diodes and Avalanche Photo Diodes (APD's).

All photodiodes work reverse-biased, and let through a current in the reverse direction according to the amount of light falling on them.

Figure 2.11 shows the crystal structure, equivalent circuit digram and the IO diagram for an ordinary photodiode.

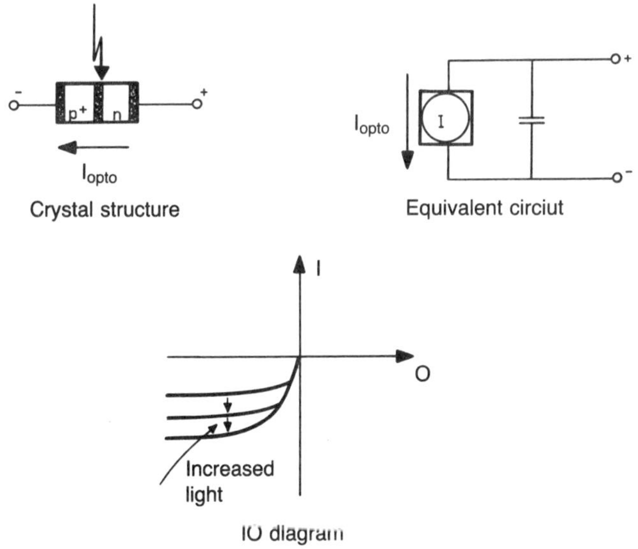

Figure 2.11 Principles of the photodiode

In the PIN diode, the sensitivity and speed are increased by inserting an 'I region' (Intrinsic, undoped) between the P and N regions, which are highly doped. This means that the light-sensitivite P–N junction is increased by the whole length of the I region.

The name PIN diode comes directly from the crystal structure in the diode.

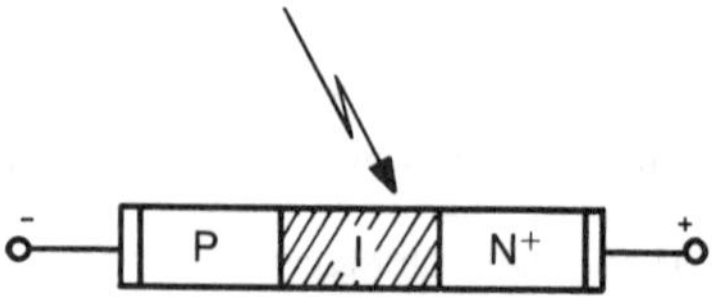

Figure 2.12 PIN diode

The avalanche diode, which in principle looks like a PIN diode, gives an amplification of 100–200 on detection by means of avalanche break-through and ionisation; they are often used on long-distance systems, therefore, where the optical effect may be so low that a PIN diode is not sufficiently sensitive.

A great disadvantage of the avalanche diode is that it requires a bias voltage of several hundred volts to work satisfactorily.

3 Conductor theory

3.1 Two-terminal-pair networks

The term 'two-terminal-pair network' is used for an impedance network, a pair of conductors or an amplifier which has pairs of input and output leads. It can be likened to a 'black box' wich contains an unknown number of impedances or amplifier functions.

Figure 3.1 Two-terminal-pair network

Where the network contains only impedances, it is said to be passive. The power fed in is higher than the output power. If it contains any form of amplifier, the network is said to be active. In the latter case, the attenuation is negative. A two-terminal-pair network can be linear or non-linear; if it only contains impedances it is linear, and non-linear if it contains, for example, diodes. This chapter deals only with linear networks.

The impedance measured at a certain frequency at the input will vary with the impedance with which the output is loaded. The maximum and minimum values then represent the short-circuit and open-circuit values.

3.2 Characteristics and matching

In communications technology, the component networks often have to be matched. The matching should be carried out so that the greatest amount of power possible is transferred from network to network. The impedance of a telephone lead (network), which is taken into account when matching, is known as the wave impedance, characteristic impedance or commonest characteristic. If the open-circuit (Zo) and short-circuit (Zs) impedances are measures in one direction, the characteristic Z is defined as:

$$Z=\sqrt{Zo \cdot Zk}$$

Where the network is not symmetrical, the characteristics are different for the input and the output sides.

In order to explain the concepts of characteristic and damping, let's take an example of the simplest type of two-terminal pair network. Figure 3.2 shows a purely resistive parallel resistance Rp and a series resistor Rs.

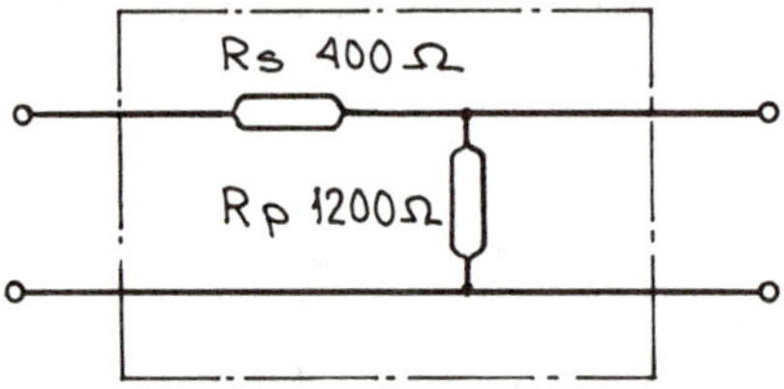

Figure 3.2 Simple two-terminal pair network

By choosing 'pure' resistances we can do the calculations using simple direct-current relationships. Measured from the left-hand side, we get an open-circuit resistance of:

$$Zo1=Rs+Rp=400+1200=1600 \text{ Ohms}$$

If we short-circuit the output side, measurement of the resistance on the input side will give

$$Zk1=Rs=400 \text{ Ohms}$$

So:

$$Z1=\sqrt{Zo1 \cdot Zk1}=\sqrt{1600 \cdot 400}=800 \text{ Ohms}$$

The corresponding measurements from the output side give:

$$Zo2=Rp=1200 \text{ Ohms}$$

$$Zk2=\frac{Rs \cdot Rp}{Rs+Rp}=\frac{1200 \cdot 400}{1600}=300 \text{ Ohms}$$

So the characteristic from the right-hand side becomes:

$$Z2=\sqrt{Zo2 \cdot Zk2}=\sqrt{1200 \cdot 300}=600 \text{ Ohms}$$

If the two-terminal pair is to be connected into a network, the network on the left must have an impedance of 800 ohms and the one on the right an impedance of 600 ohms if they are to be correctly matched. If several such networks are to be connected up in series, the connecting ends of each two-terminal pair network must have the same characteristic impedances. In Figure 3.3, the network has been connected up to generator G which has an internal resistance Ra of 800 ohms. A load Rb of 600 ohms has been connected at the output side.

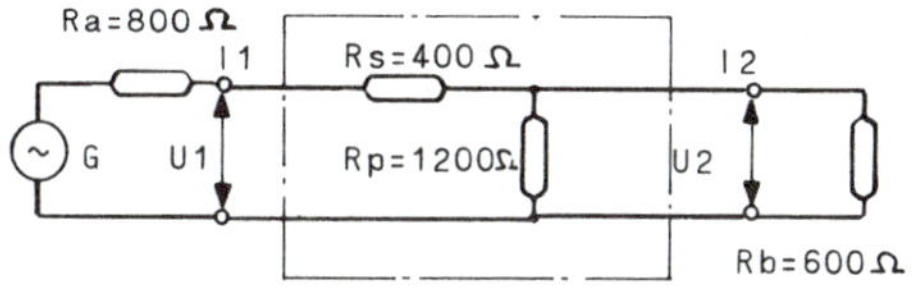

Figure 3.3 Two-terminal pair network with generator and load

If G and Ra are disconnected, the input impedance consists of series resistor Rs which in turn is series-connected to parallel resistors Rp and Rb:

$$Z1=Rs+\frac{Rp \cdot Rb}{Rp+Rb}=400+\frac{1200 \cdot 600}{1200+600}=800 \text{ Ohms}$$

If the load resistance Rb is removed, the impedance measured from the right-hand side is:

$$Z2=\frac{Rp(Rs+Ra)}{Rp+Rs+Ra}=\frac{1200(400+800)}{1200+400+800}=600 \text{ Ohms}$$

which agrees with previous working.

So Figure 3.3 consists of three matched sections, the generator G with its international resistance, the two-terminal pair network (e g cable run) and a load resistance Rb.

Take the case where the power source delivers a voltage of U1 volts, which produces a current I1 amperes (amps) in the network, and where after attenuation the load Rb has a voltage U2 across it and a current I2 through it.

The voltage drop across Rp is Rp(I1–I2), and the voltage drop across Rb is Rb.I2, but both are equal to U2; it follows that:

$$(I1-I2) \cdot Rp=Rb \cdot I2 \text{ or}$$

$$\frac{I2}{I1-I2}=\frac{Rp}{Rb}\ ; \qquad \frac{I1-I2}{I2}=\frac{Rp}{Rb}$$

$$\frac{I1}{I2}-1=\frac{Rb}{Rp}\ ; \qquad \frac{I1}{I2}=1+\frac{Rb}{Rp}\ ; \qquad 1+\frac{600}{1200}=1.5$$

The voltage drop across Rs is $U1-U2=I1 \cdot Rs$, and U2 is

$$U2=I2 \cdot Rb$$

Putting these two equations together we get:

$$\frac{U1-U2}{U2}=\frac{I1 \cdot Rs}{I2 \cdot Rp}$$

$$\frac{U1}{U2}=1+\frac{I1 \cdot Rs}{I2 \cdot Rb}=1+1.5 \cdot \frac{400}{600}=2$$

The ratio of powers becomes:

$$\frac{P1}{P2}=\frac{U1 \cdot I1}{U2 \cdot I2}=2 \cdot 1.5=3$$

The current, voltage and power have thus been attenuated in the ratio 1.5:1, 2:1, 3:1.

In this example the current, voltage and power have been attenuated to different extents. Measurements in practice, therefore, have been standardised at 600 ohms. In the example, Z1 is not equal to Z2.

3.3 Attenuation and its measurement units

When calculating currents, voltages and power, it is usual to compare these quantities with reference units or reference levels. This is also the case with transmission media, where the current, voltage and power on the output side are compared with those on the input side. The relationship between these units therefore gives a measure of the damping or amplification of the transmission medium. Rather than using the relationships between the units and their reference levels directly, it is often more practical to use the logarithms of the numbers in question in calculations. This has the advantage that the amplifications of cascaded amplifier stages can just be added together to give the overall amplification. With very large levels of amplification or damping, it is also practical to calculate with logarithms instead of using the ratios between units.

Using the decade system, the ratios of damping and amplification are expressed as logarithms to the base 10, or

$$\log \frac{P1}{P2}$$

The unit for this system is the Bel. It is more common to use units of a tenth of a Bel, called a decibel (dB)

$$A=10 \log \frac{P1}{P2} \text{ dB}$$

But $P1=\frac{(U1)^2}{R1}$ and $P2=\frac{(U2)^2}{R2}$

giving

$$A=10 \log \left(\frac{U1}{U2}\right)^2 \cdot \frac{R1}{R2} \text{ dB}$$

If the resistances are equal, then

$$A=20 \log \frac{U1}{U2} \text{ dB or } A=20 \log \frac{I1}{I2} \text{ dB}$$

In the natural logarithmic system, attenuation or amplification are expressed as half the logarithm of the ratio between powers. The units of the system are called nepers (N). This gives:

$$A=\frac{1}{2} \ln \frac{P1}{P2} \text{ neper}$$

$$A=\ln \frac{U1}{U2} \text{ neper;} \quad A=\ln \frac{I1}{I2} \text{ neper}$$

The decade and natural systems are linearly related, so that

1 dB=0.1151 neper
1 neper=8.686 dB

The natural system is commonly used for relating units of power to a fixed reference level. In communications technology, a reference level of 1 mW in an impedance of 600 ohms is used. The term 'level' then refers to the power by which it exceeds the reference level, given in either nepers or decibels.

In the example given

$$A=10 \log \frac{U1\ I1}{U2 \cdot I2}=10 \log 3=4.77 \text{ dB}$$

$$A=0.115 \cdot 4.77=0.549 \text{ neper}$$

3.4 Technical aspects of transmission

We will take the case of a lead, as shown in Figure 3.4, with a length S, and which has its far end loaded with an impedance Zb. A voltage Uo is applied to the near end, which results in currents of Io at the near end and Is at the far end. The impedance has a voltage of Us across it. At a certain distance x from the near end, the current is therefore Ix and the voltage Ux. Clearly, one should be able to use simple electrical laws for calculating the currents and voltages; however, this is not the case in practice. There are four quantities which affect a lead from the point of view of transmission, which are known as the primary parameters. Other quantities, the secondary parameters of the lead, can be determined from its primary parameters.

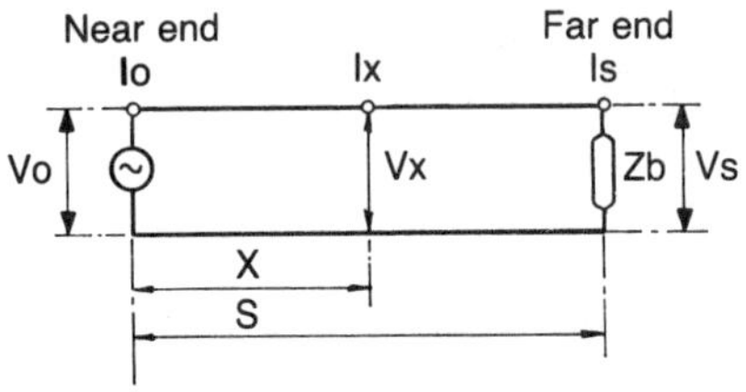

Figure 3.4 Telephone lead with generator and load

The primary parameters are:

r = resistance per unit length
l = inductance per unit length
g = conductance per unit length
c = capacitance per unit length

Resistance r

The DC resistance r_o for a copper conductor with a resistivity of 1.73×10^{-8} ohms/m and diameter d is

$$r_o = \frac{44.0}{d^2} \text{ ohms/km (double lead)}$$

The resistance increases by about 0.4% per degree rise in temperature. The AC resistance differs somewhat from the DC value due to the so-called skin effect, which occurs because at high frequencies the current is concentrated near the outside of the wire. At audio frequencies, r can as a rule be taken as $=r_0$. At 100 MHz, however, the current is concentrated in the outer layer of the conductor to a depth of only 7 μm. The result is, of course, a higher resistance, which is one of the reasons why cables exhibit higher attenuation at higher frequencies.

Inductance l

Inductance is a measure of the magnetic field produced by a current in a wire. The equation for this is:

$$l=0.1+0.92\times 10 \log \frac{2a}{d} \text{ mH/km}$$

where

d=conductor diameter in mm
a=distance apart of lead centres

The first term is the internal inductance of the leads, arising from the magnetic field inside the leads due to the current being present over the whole cross-section. When the current is concentrated towards the outside of the lead at very high frequencies, this term tends towards zero.

The second term is the external inductance, arising from the magnetic field between the leads.

The inductance for a normal twin cable at speech frequencies is about 0.7 mH/km.

Conductance g

The insulation conductance, i e the derived measure using direct current, lacks practical meaning in terms of transmission. Nevertheless, much notice is taken of it, where its size is indirectly a good measure of the conductor's function. Insulation is normally measured with DC in the range 100–500 V. The result is expressed as conductance in μS/km or as resistance in GΩ/m or MΩ/km. Values of 5 000 GΩ m or more are typical.

From the point of view of transmission, the important losses are those via the dielectric. The relevant equations are:

$$g=\omega \cdot \text{ctg} \cdot \delta=2\pi f \cdot \text{ctg} \cdot \delta$$

where

δ =loss angle
ω=2πf rad/s

If $tg\delta$ is frequency-dependent, g will then be proportional to frequency. This is approximately true for PE insulation, where $tg\delta \approx 0.0003$. On the other hand, $tg\delta$ is both considerably larger for paper insulation, and frequency dependent. So, for example, $tg\delta$ in a paper-insulated cable is about 0.003 at 800 Hz and about 0.015 at 100 kHz, assuming the insulation is dry. Dampness in paper insulation rapidly leads to high losses.

Capacitance c

The equation for the capacitance of a twin unscreened cable is:

$$c=\frac{12.1\ \varepsilon}{10\log\frac{2a}{d}} \quad \text{if } 2a \gg d$$

where

ε=the relative dielectric constant
a=the distance between the centres of the wires in mm
d=the diameter of the wires in mm

In a cable, the above formula is only of limited validity because of other leads and the mantle. Other empirical formulae have been developed on the basis of experience, such as:

$$c=\frac{k}{\log_e[1.346\ (2\frac{D}{d}-1)]}$$

where

k =55 for paper insulation
k =66 homogeneous PE+air
k =59 for cellular PE+air
k =66 for cellular PE+vaseline
D=diameter of insulation
d =wire diameter

The effective relative dielectric constants are approximately

1.3–1.45	for paper insulation
1.9–2.0	for homogeneous PE+air
1.9–2.0	for cellular PE+vaseline
3	for EKKX-type PVC-cable

Secondary parameters

From the four primary parameters, a new set of parameters can be calculated which perhaps describe better the behaviour of the cable in practice, ie.

Z=the characteristic impedance of the cable (image impedance)
$\gamma = \alpha + j\beta$=the complex propagation constant
α=the attenuation constant
β=the phase constant

and the following relationship is obtained:

$$\gamma = \alpha + j\beta = \sqrt{(r + j\omega l)\,(g + j\omega c)}$$

Impedance Z

The impedance or the Characteristic is the impedance found across the end of an infinitely long lead. For a considerable section of such a lead, the relationship between voltage and current is constant:

$$Z = \frac{U}{I}$$

In practice, one aims for the same conditions which can be obtained by putting the same load across the far end of the cable as the internal impedance of the transmitter.

$$Z = \sqrt{\frac{r + j\omega l}{g + j\omega c}} \text{ (ohm)}$$

In the general case, Z is complex, i.e. it has a resistive and a reactive component.

Impedance Z (at low frequencies)

At low frequencies, $j\omega l$ can as a rule be neglected in comparison with r, and g is negligible compared with $j\omega c$, so that we get:

$$Z \text{ (low frequency)} = \sqrt{\frac{r}{j\omega c}} = (1 - j)\sqrt{\frac{r}{2\omega c}}$$

Impedance Z (at high frequencies)

At high frequencies, r can be ignored. g is also negligible here if the cable has good insulation, i e,

$$Z\text{ (high frequency)}=\sqrt{\frac{j\omega l}{j\omega c}}=\sqrt{\frac{1}{c}}$$

Here Z is real, while at low frequencies the phase angle of Z is $-\frac{\pi}{4}$.

Attenuation constants and phase constants

If a voltage Vx is applied to the near end of a conductor, it will be attenuated as it goes along the conductor. Figure 3.5 shows an exponentially attenuated outgoing voltage wave at a certain instant. Because of the inductance and capacitance of the lead, the voltage is subjected to a phase shift along the lead relative to the applied voltage. As time progresses, the curve is displaced within the tangential exponential lines in the positive x-direction. A similarly-constructed curve also applies to the outgoing current wave. Where the characteristic of the lead usually has a negative phase angle, the current graph precedes the voltage graph.

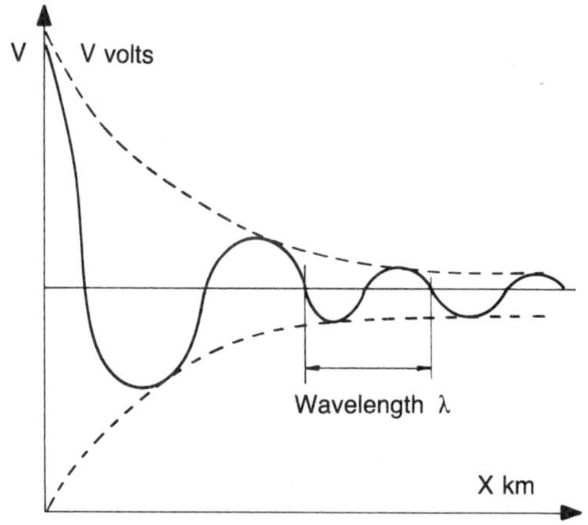

Figure 3.5 Attenuated wave

If the applied voltage is

$$U=\hat{U}\cdot\sin\omega t$$

the voltage at a distance X from the end will be:

$$U_x=\hat{U}e^{\alpha x}\cdot\sin(\omega t\cdot\beta x)$$

where

α=attenuation constant per unit length (nepers/km)
β=phase constant per unit length (radians/km)

If at a certain instant the voltage Ux is zero, and x is increased by a distance x′, the current returns to zero after a time t′, chosen so that $\omega t'-\beta x'=0$. The propagation speed of the wave is then

$$v=\frac{x'}{t'}=\frac{\omega}{\beta}$$

At high frequencies the propagation speed in a smooth lead is almost at the speed of light, $3 \cdot 10^8$ m/s. In cables, the speed at higher frequencies is the speed of light divided by $\sqrt{8}$. At lower frequencies the propagation speed is lower.

In Figure 3.5 the periodicity of the waves is 2π. The distance between two points on a conductor where the voltage and the current have the same phase,

$$\beta x=2\pi$$

is known as the conductor's wavelength for the frequency in question. If the wavelength is denoted by λ,

$$\lambda=\frac{2\pi}{\beta}$$

In one second the voltage and current curves cover a distance equal to the frequency times the wavelength:

$$v=\frac{\omega}{2\pi}\cdot\lambda$$

or, as mentioned earlier,

$$v=\frac{\omega}{\beta}$$

For cable conductors within the audible spectrum,

$$\alpha=\sqrt{\frac{\omega rc}{2}}$$

$$\beta\approx\sqrt{\frac{\omega rc}{2}}$$

At higher frequencies,

$$\alpha=\frac{1}{2}\cdot\sqrt{\frac{c}{\iota}}+\frac{\alpha}{2}\sqrt{\frac{\iota}{c}}$$

$$\beta=\omega\sqrt{\iota\cdot c}$$

3.5 Hyperbolic functions

In order to be able to solve the so-called telegraph equations if the primary parameters are known, we must make use of hyperbolic functions. The derivations of these functions will not be discussed here.

$$\sinh x = \frac{e^x - e^{-x}}{2}$$

$$\cosh x = \frac{e^x + e^{-x}}{2}$$

$$\tanh x = \frac{e^x - e^{-x}}{e^x + e^{-x}} = \frac{(e^{2x} - 1)}{(e^{2x} + 1)}$$

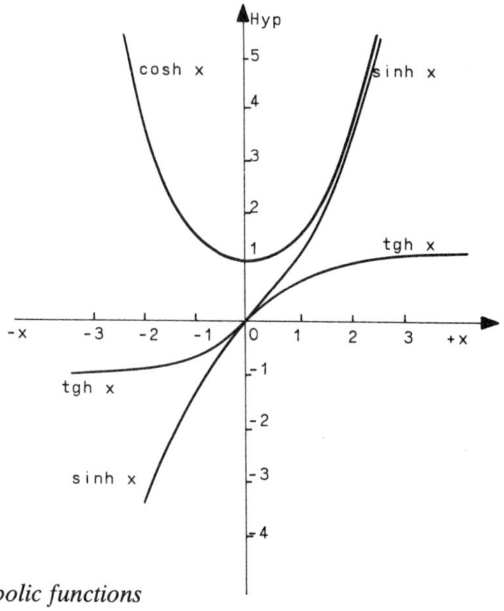

Figure 3.6 Hyperbolic functions

3.6 Network model for telephone lines

We have mentioned earlier the factors which affect transmission along a conductor, which we called primary parameters. Leading on from this, we can now convert the appearance of the conductor into its equivalent network, in other words the way in which the conductor behaves in practice. Thus, every little section of conductor consists of an infinite number of inductances in series with resistances. In parallel with the conductor there are an infinite number of capacitances and conductances.

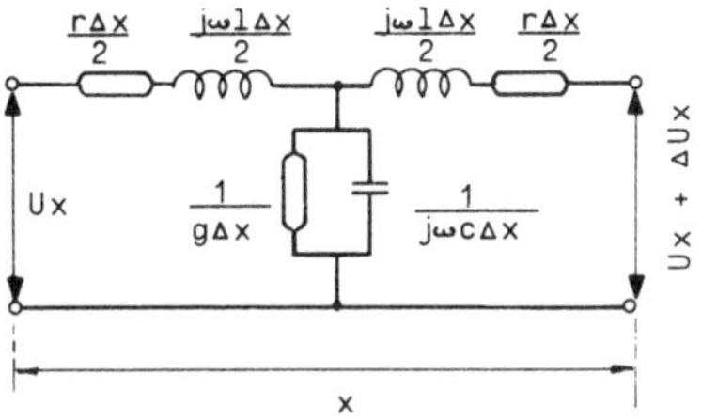

Figure 3.7 Equivalent network model of telephone lines

Let's consider the conductor to be divided up into an infinite number of pieces Δx. In the determination of the equations defining the voltage Ux and the current Ix at a distance x from the near end of the conductor, x is the independent variable. This is increased by a distance Δx, whereupon the voltage and current 'increase' by ΔUx and ΔIx respectively, although these additions are in reality negative, because both the voltage and the current are attenuated. The derivations of the equations, which are generally known as the telegraph equations for determining the input impedance of conductors, and the current and voltage at the far end, will not be given in this book.

3.7 Attenuator units

Within telephone technology one often needs to be able to attenuate a current and voltage wave. The device used is a resistive network. These consist of resistances whose attenuation and characteristics are independent of frequency.

Such networks can be of π or T configurations. In the calculation of the characteristics and attenuation, it is practical to treat the two types of filter separately.

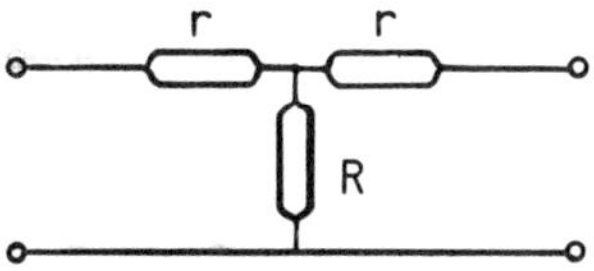

Figure 3.8 T-network

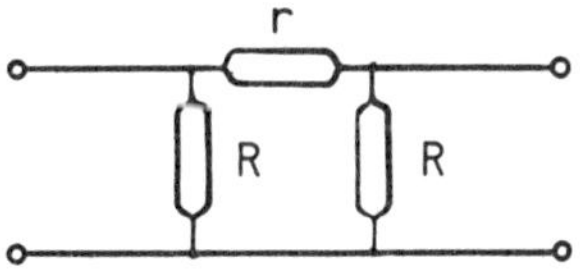

Figure 3.9 π-network

3.8 Filters

The term filter applies to a four-pole with the characteristic that current and voltage waves falling within a certain frequency range are transmitted either with minimal attenuation, or else with very considerable attenuation. The frequency range where the attenuation of the filter is small is called the pass-band, and the region of very strong attenuation is known as the rejection band. The pass and rejection bands are separated by the limit frequencies of the filter. Filters may be divided into four types according to the relative positions of the pass and rejection bands:

Low-pass filters have a pass band from zero frequency up to the limiting frequency, and thereafter a rejection band.

High pass filters have a passband upwards from the limiting frequency, and a rejection band below it.

The band pass filter has a pass band between two limiting frequencies, with rejection bands on either side of them.

The band rejection filter rejects signals between the two limiting frequencies, with pass bands on either side of the rejection region.

3.9 Factors affecting data transmission quality on telephone networks

CCITT have produced methods for making measurements of the quality of data transmission over telephone lines. These methods start by determining the effect of interference and distortion, and giving acceptable limits.

The factors measured are:

- attenuation (loss)
- attenuation distortion
- group delay
- noise
- phase jitter
- phase hits
- frequency shifts
- gain hits
- dropouts

We shall just look briefly here at what is hidden behind these terms, and how they can be measured in different cases.

Attenuation

Attenuation results in a reduction of the signal amplitude as it progresses along the line. It is determined by measuring the amplitudes at the sender and the receiver at a fixed frequency, commonly 800 Hz.

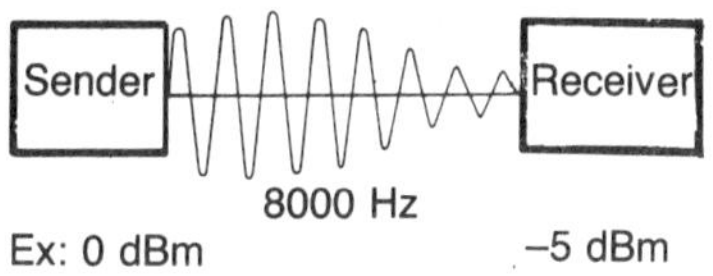

Figure 3.10 Attenuated wave

Attenuation distortion

Attenuation distortion is a measure of the attenuation at frequencies other than the measurement frequency.

The attenuation is measured over the whole of the frequency spectrum, and the attenuation at the fixed frequency (say 800 Hz) is used as reference.

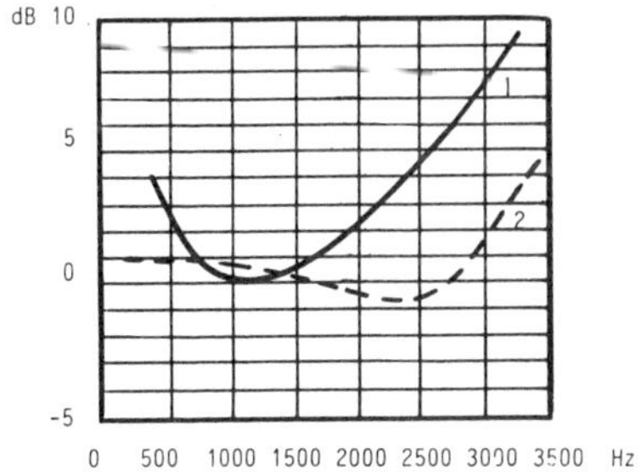

Figure 3.11 Attenuation distortion as a function of frequency
1) Typical attenuation distortion curve (measurement frequency here is 1000 Hz)
2 Attenuation distortion when an equalizer is used

Propagation time distortion

Propagation time distortion is defined as the ratio of relative phase shift and the given frequency shift $(\frac{\Delta\theta}{\Delta f})$.

Group delay is much more interesting from the point of view of transmission than absolute phase shift. Because the ear is slow we seldom notice phase shifts, but in data communication they can be disastrous.

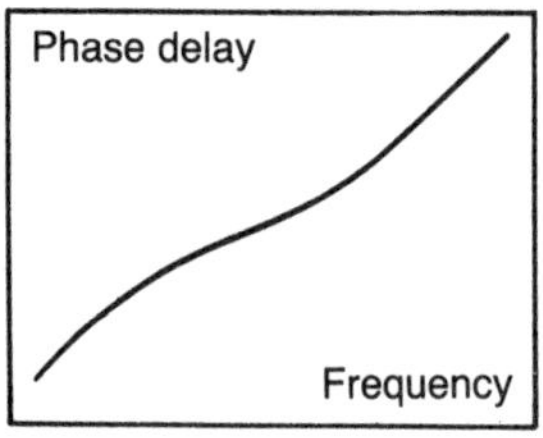

Figure 3.12 Phase delay

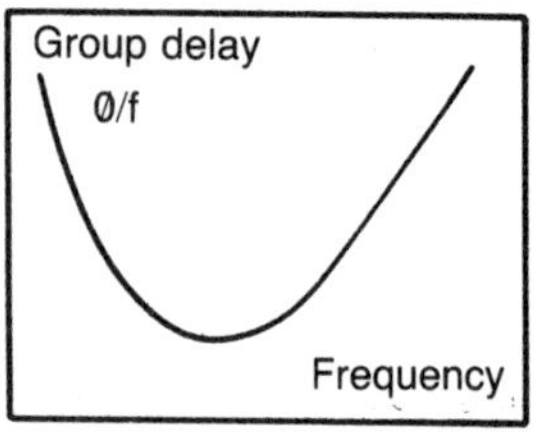

Figure 3.13 Group delay

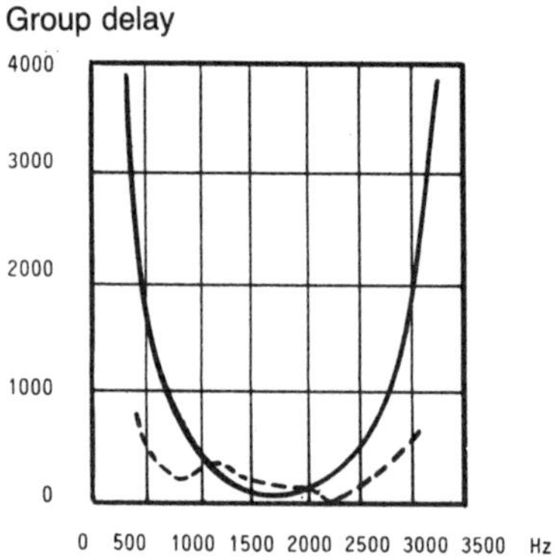

Figure 3.14 Propagation time as a function of frequency
1) Typical group delay curve
2) With equalizer

Attenuation distortion and propagation time are compensated in the modem with the aid of an equalizer, either automatic or manual.

Noise

Noise sets a limit on the weakest signal which can be amplified. Noise is a physical effect, and of course an undesired phenomenon. Two types of noise are differentiated: thermal noise and semiconductor noise. Thermal noise arises from temperature changes in circuits. The effective value of the total noise voltage from a resistor is:

$$Ub=\sqrt{4\,k \cdot T \cdot R \cdot B}$$

where:

k = Boltzmann's constant = $1.38 \cdot 10^{-23}$ Ws/K
T = absolute temperature
R = resistance
B = bandwidth of the amplifier (Hz).

Thermal noise is by nature "white noise", which arises because charging up at randomly varying rates brings about random voltage variations, as shown in Figure 3.17.

Semiconductor noise arises from the particulate nature of the current. Such noise is described variously as shot noise and current partition noise, and is characteristically white noise.

Noise factor

The noise factor is a measure of the freedom of a signal from interference.

$$\text{Noise factor} = S/N = \frac{\text{signal power}}{\text{noise power}}$$

During the passage of a signal through an amplifier the S/N ratio deteriorates. As a measure of the amplification of the S/N, the concept of the noise factor is used; this is measured in dB and is termed Fb.

$$Fb = \frac{(S/N)\ \text{in}}{(S/N)\ \text{out}} = 10 \cdot \log_{10} \frac{(S/N)\ \text{in}}{(S/N)\ \text{out}}\ \text{dB}$$

Background noise usually consists of white noise (measured with a psophometer). Impulse noise consists of short-lasting pulses with a high amplitude. Background noise mainly produces randomly-occurring errors, while impulse noise usually causes a burst of errors.

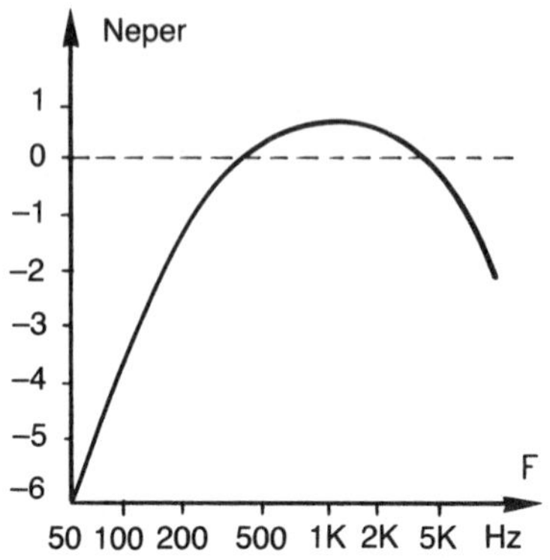

Figure 3.15 Weighting factor in nepers as a function of frequency for filters in a psophometer

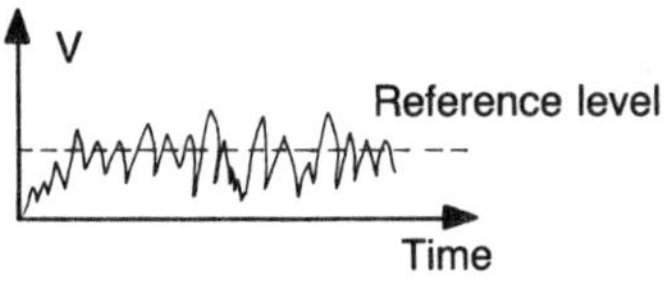

Figure 3.16 Noise

Phase jitter

Phase jitter consists of constant phase changes. It has a serious effect on modems which work with phase-shift modulation. Jitter is often caused by frequency multiplexers, or by network interference from microwave transmission apparatus.

Phase jitter can be measured by sending a 1020 Hz signal down a line, and analysing the jitter components at the receiving end at frequencies up to 300 Hz.

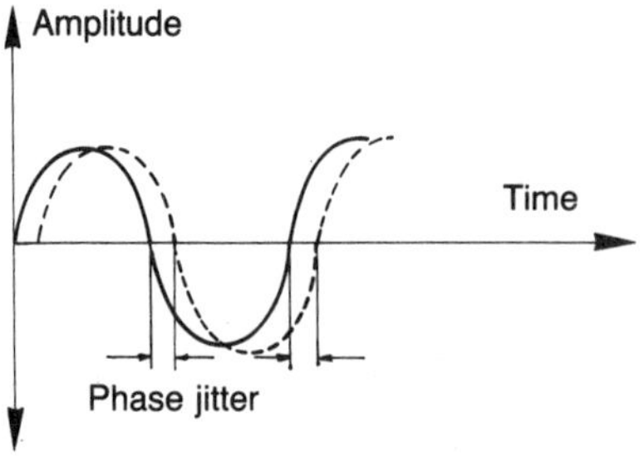

Figure 3.17 Phase jitter

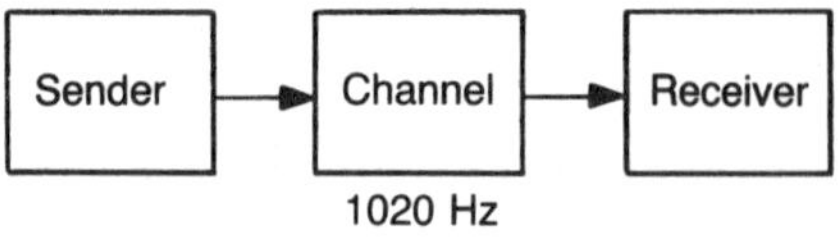

Figure 3.18 Method of measuring phase jitter

Phase hits

Phase hits are sudden changes in phase angle. They are measured by counting up all the hits which exceed a set threshold level in a certain time, usually 15 minutes.

Frequency shift

Differences in frequency between sender and receiver may be due to defective synchronisation between the oscillators in the transmitter and the receiver.

Drop-outs

Drop-outs consist of short-duration breaks in transmission.

Echo

Because it is impossible to achieve perfect matching in cross-overs, e g in connections, this gives a reflection which gives rise to an echo. In speech transmission this can be suppressed, but in data transmission (in both directions, duplex), this is not possible.

Cross-talk

Cross-talk is an undersirable phenomenon in telephone cables, where a signal "leaks across" from the line it is being sent down to other lines running alongside. Cross-talk can be 'understandable', i e one can hear one's neighbour's conversation, or 'incomprehensible', where one only hears an undefinable interference.

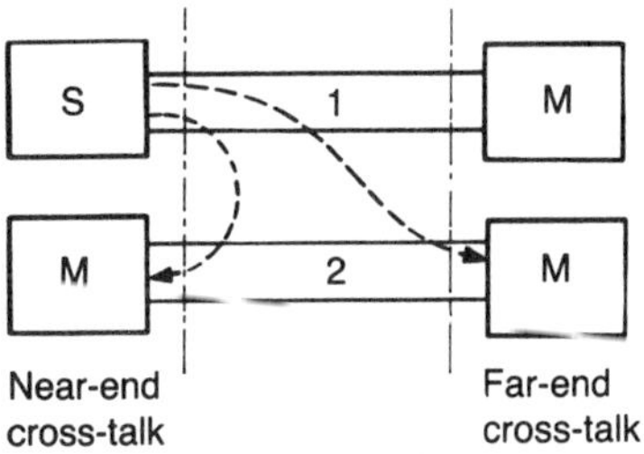

Figure 3.19 The connection between near-end and far-end cross-talk

One can distinguish between near-end cross-talk, where cross-talk occurs between transmitter and receiver at the same end of the line, and far-end cross-talk with the receiver at the opposite end from the transmitter.

Cross-talk is generally caused by connections between wires not being completely symmetrical relative to one another. It can be capacitative, inductive or resistive in nature. At low frequencies capacitative coupling dominates, and one can talk in terms of capacitative unbalance or capacitance unbalance.

At high frequencies, inductive coupling becomes more important, and also coupling via the mantle or screen. It is thus important to keep inductive coupling and earth balancing down in cables carrying higher frequencies.

4 Data communication

4.1 Introduction

Data communication is used today over very large areas, from transferring simple alarm and status signals to the transmission of large amounts of data in complex systems.

Data communication means the transmission of information in the form of data between a sender and a receiver.

Figure 4.1 shows the basic elements in a data communication system, from the sender, which can be a person or a machine, via a data transmitter which converts the data to the correct form, a transmission part, responsible for the purely physical transfer of signals to a data receiver, which splits up the received data signals and reproduces them in their original form for the recipient.

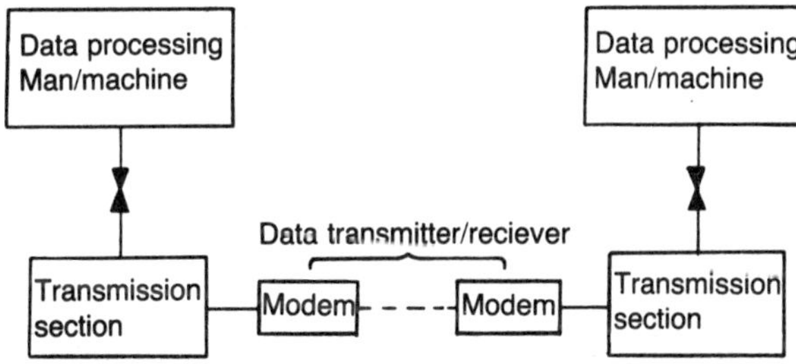

Figure 4.1 The parts of a data communication system

Information can generally be transferred in both directions. What is called "data transmitter" here may be a simple matching unit designed for a certain type of transmission, usually wholly under hardware control, or else in a large modern data communication system it may be a computer, a communications processor or "front-end processor", which is software controlled and which has a high level of flexibility and suitability for different types of transmission.

The commonest unit for data transmission speed is bits/second. Data speed in bits/second can be obtained by multiplying the baud rate by $\log_2 n$, where n is the number of distinguishable characters in the signal during one signal element.

The transmission rate in characters/second can be obtained most simply by dividing the baud rate by the number of bits in the character set used.

For example: 9 600 baud ≈ 960 characters/second.

Figure 4.2 shows the areas of responsibility in data communication.

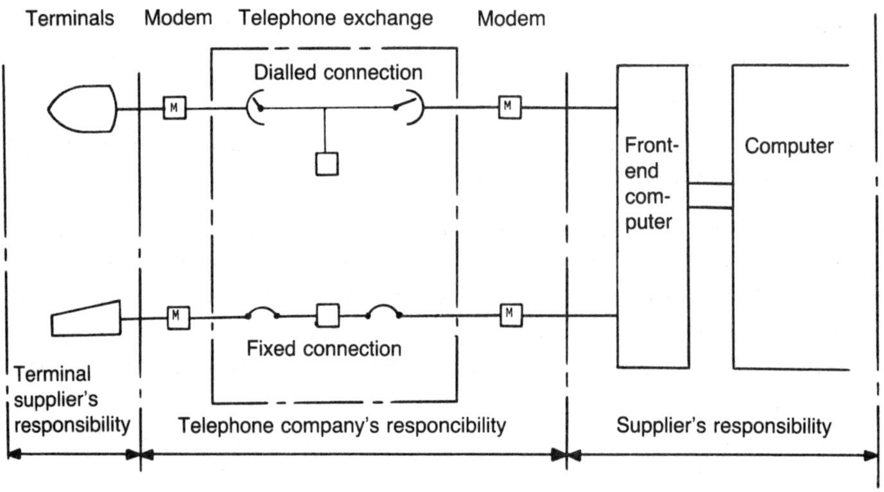

Figure 4.2 Areas of responsibility in data communication

4.2 Standards for data communication

Standardisation of telecommunications of different types is needed in the first place for connection of subscribers' equipment to the telephone networks. As in most cases the network is controlled by some central administration, (Televerket in Sweden) it is natural for the standardisation work to have been tightly controlled by such authorities over a long period.

International communication between the national networks has been a further powerful factor towards standardisation, mainly regarding conventions for signalling between networks.

Figure 4.3 shows this information flow between some of the existing standards organisations.

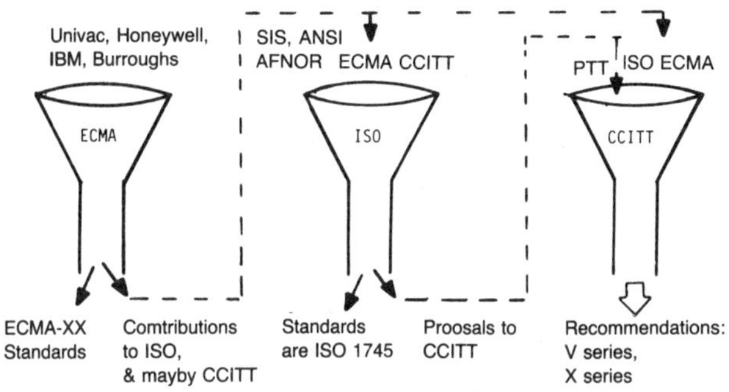

Figure 4.3 Standardisation organisations

ECMA =European Computer Manufacturers' Association
ISO =International Standards Organisation
CCITT =Comité Consultatif International Télégraphique et Téléphonique

The following groups are among those which are members of the ISO

- ANSI =USA
- BSI =Great Britain
- AFNOR =France
- SIS =Sweden
- DIN =Germany

The internationally standardised interface is determined by CCITT, which is a committee of the ITU (International Telecommunications Union), which in its turn is an agency of the United Nations. Every four years, CCITT produces a new edition of the recommendations on which they were unanimous. Different editions have different colours. Data transmission is dealt with in CCITT vol VIII:1 and 2, Data Transmission, where the first part of the volume contains recommendations for data transfer on the telephone network, and the second for data transmission in data networks (V and X recommendations respectively).

There follow some of the recommendations which CCITT have distributed.

Selection of CCITT X and V recommendations

Selection of X-series recommendations: General data networks

X.1 Description of speed classifications in public data networks.

X.2 Descriptions of additional facilities.

X.3 How asynchronous equipment must convert the data flow in order to work on a "packet-switching" network.

X.20 Interface functions for connection of asynchronous data equipment designed for use on the general asynchronous data network.

X.20 bis Interface functions for connection of asynchronous data equipment designed for use on the telephone network.

X.21 Interface functions for connection of synchronous data equipment designed for use on the general synchronous data network.

X.21 bis Interface functions for connection of synchronous data equipment specifically designed for use on the telephone network.

X.22 Gives specifications for a multiplexed interface between DTE and DCE for user classes 3–6 (600–9600 bits/sec).

X.24 Definitions for interface circuits in data terminal equipment designed for use on the public data network.

X.25 Interface functions for the connection of data terminal equipment to the "packet-switching" services.

X.26, X.27 Electrical characteristics of interface circuits.

X.50 Specifies multiplexing structure in networks using 8 bits, i.e. 6 data bits and 2 control bits.

X.51 Specifies multiplexing structure in networks using 10 bits, i.e. 8 data bits and 2 control bits. This format is used in the Scandinavian public data network (DATEX).

X70, X71 Specifies signal procedures over international connections.

X.95 Description of network parameters.

X.96 Description of call progress/status signals.

Selection of V-series recommendations: Data transfer over telephone and telex networks

V.10, V.11	Electrical characteristics for interface circuits.
V.21	Interface functions and line signals for 200 bits/s modems.
V.23	Interface functions and line signals for 600/1200 bits/s modems.
V.24	Definitions for interface circuits between data terminal equipment and circuit-terminating equipment, i e modems. For further information, see Chapter 13.
V.25	Interface procedures etc for automatic dialling and/or answering equipment.
V.26	Interface functions and line signals on 2400 bits/s modems for use on 4-wire leased lines.
V.26 bis	Interface functions and line signals on 1200/2400 bits/s modems used on general telephone lines.
V.27	Interface functions and line signals for 4800 bit/s modems used on leased lines.
V.27 ter	Interface functions and line signals for 4800 bits/s modems on the general telephone network.
V.28	Electrical characteristics for interface circuits.
V.29	Interface functions and line signals for 9600 bit/s modems on leased lines.
V.35	Interface functions and line signals for 48 kbits/s modems on leased broad-band (60–108kHz) circuits.

V.21

$\leqslant$200 bits/s (300) on dialled or leased line.

- Full duplex possible (2 FDM channels)
- Frequency modulation
- Carrier frequencies: 1080 Hz Channel 1
  1750 Hz Channel 2
- $\Delta f = 100$ Hz $F_{A_1} = 1080 + 100 = 1180$ Hz $\rightarrow$ "0"
  $F_{Z_1} = 1080 - 100 = 980$ Hz $\rightarrow$ "1"

- Synchronous or asynchronous transmission
- a) When both channels are used for simultaneous transmission (full duplex), channel 1 is used for the caller's data and channel 2 for the data of the one called.
  b) Where one channel is used for data transmission and the other for check signals, service signals etc, channel 1 is used for transmitting data from the caller's end, regardless of the direction in which the data is transmitted.

V.23

≤600/1200 bits/s, dialled or leased line

- Frequency modulation
- Asynchronous or synchronous transmission
- Secondary channel (backward channel) ≤75 bits/s for error checking

	Fo	F_Z("1")	F_A("0")
• Modulation:			
• Mode 1: ≤600 bit/s	1500 Hz	1300 Hz	1700 Hz
• Mode 2: ≤1200 bit/s	1700 Hz	1300 Hz	2100 Hz
• Secondary channel: ≤75 bit/s		390 Hz	450

- Mode 1 is used, for example, in long lines.

V.24

Deals with the connections pins in the interface between the data terminal equipment (DTE) and the data circuit-terminating equipment (DCE) – usually a modem. See Chapter 13.

V.26

2400/1200 bits/s *dialled* connection

- Carrier frequency, modulation and coding follow recommendation V.26 alternative B (2400 bit/s).
- Possibility of using reduced data transmission speed, 1200 bit/s, as 'fall back'.

Differential	2-phase modulation
0	+90°
1	+270°

- Synchronisation – see V.21.

- Modem must contain a fast equaliser.

2400 bit/s *leased* connection, *4-wire*

- Full duplex
- 4-phase modulation
- Synchronous transmission
- Secondary channel ≤75 bit/s as option in both transmission directions
- Carrier frequency 1800±1 Hz
- The data stream is divided into groups of 2 bits (DIBIT)
- 1200 bits/s

V.27

4800 bits/s *leased* line

- Half or full duplex
- Synchronous transmission
- Secondary channel ≤75 bits/s (see V.23) in each direction
- Carrier frequency 1800 Hz
- Differential 8-phase modulation, TRIBIT (→ 1600 bits/s)

Tribit	Phase shift
001	0°
000	45°
010	90°
011	135°
111	180°
110	225°
100	270°
101	315°

- Synchronisation: During the time interval between OFF and ON on pin 105 and between OFF and ON on 106 (20±3 ms or 50±20 ms), a signal is sent at repeated 180° phase displacement corresponding to a continuous '1' signal) for 9±1 ms, followed by the sending of a signal which one gets when one feeds the scrambler with 1's, until 106 has gone from OFF to ON.

- The modem must contain a self-synchronising scrambler/descrambler which uses the polynomial $1+X^{-6}+X^{-7}$, with extra protection for repeated patterns of 1, 2, 3, 4, 6, 9 and 12 bits.
- A *manually* adjustable equaliser to compensate for amplitude and group delay distortion.

V.27 bis

4800 bits/s *leased* line

- Full of half duplex on 4-wire leased line. Half duplex on 2-wire
- Modulation, see V.27
- Reduced speed at 2400 bits/s. 4-phase modulation according to V.26 alt. A (1200 bits/s)
- Automatic self-adjusting equaliser
- Synchronisation: During the time interval between OFF and ON on pin 105 and OFF to ON on 106, synchronisation signals are sent to enable searching for the correct carrier, set the AGC (Automatic Gain Control) correctly, set up time synchronisation, set the equaliser and synchronise the scrambler. Two times are specified:
  a) 50 ms for good 4-wire lines
  b) 708 ms for 2-wire and poor 4-wire lines
- As the modem is equipped with an automatic adaptive equaliser and can work on 2-wire lines, it is also possible to use it on the public telephone network for dialled connections.

V.27 ter

4800/2400 bits/s *dialled* connections

- For essential details, see V.27 bis.

V.29

9600 bits/s *leased* lines

- Fall-back to 7200 and 4800 bits/s
- Full or half duplex

- Carrier frequency 1700 Hz
- Automatic adaptive equaliser
- Allows multiplex functioning for up to four channels
- Combined amplitude and phase modulation for quadbit (4 bit) QAM (quadrature amplitude modulation)
- QAM

  Q1 Q2 Q3 Q4 quadbits
- The relative amplitude is determined by Q and the absolute phase position of the signal element. The absolute phase position is established upon synchronisation.
- Bits Q2, Q3 and Q4 determine the differential phase shift (see V.27)
- If the modem should, for example, lose information on the absolute phase position, a new synchronisation must be demanded.

4.3 Synchronous and asynchronous transmission

"Synchrony" is pure Greek to many. It is in fact a Greek word, meaning 'in time with'. Two periodic waves are synchronous if they have exactly the same frequency and pass through the origin in the same direction at the same time.

We also use the term synchrony within data communications. Synchrony between equipment at the transmitting and the receiving ends. In order to achieve synchrony and correct the phase differences which occur in the periodic wave between sender and receiver, the phase at the receiving end must be able to be corrected. The equipment at the receiving end commonly checks this at every changeover between zero and one in the signal received. Correction is made when the time deviation measured oversteps a certain predetermined value. There is synchrony where the phase difference between the two periodic waves is zero, or also if the phase difference between the transmitter and receiver is constant.

Asynchronous transmission

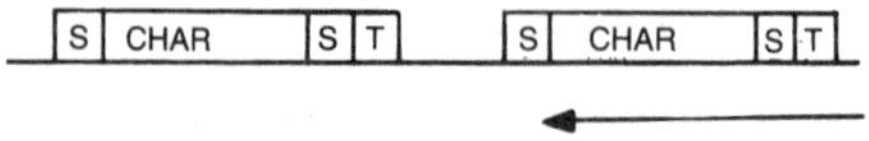

Figure 4.4 Asynchronous transmission

In *asynchronous* transmission, a character can come at any time. When no character is being sent, the line is in the idle condition. With this type of transmission, synchronisation is maintained during the sending of the character. The sender's end can do his transmission character by character without being tied to any form of synchrony.

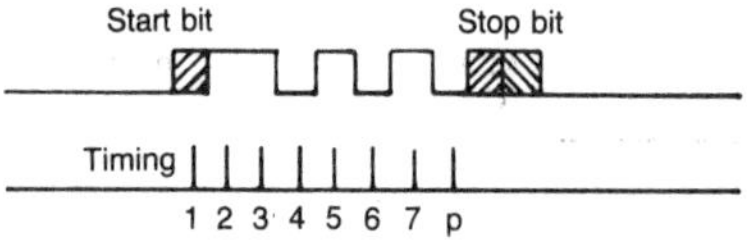

Figure 4.5

Transmission begins with a start bit. The receiving equipment then knows that a character is being sent and that the first bit carrying information can be expected within a certain time interval. When all the bits in the character have been transmitted, this part of the transmission is finished off with a stop bit.

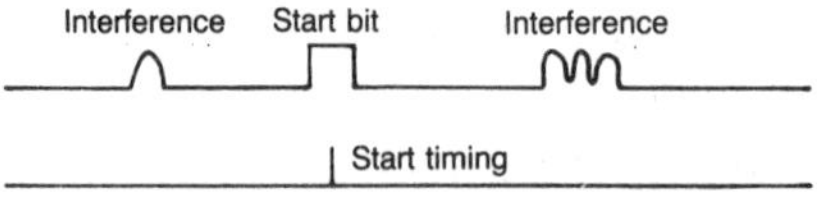

Figure 4.6

In order to avoid starting to receive on interference signals, the signal must be high for at least 46% of the duration of a normal bit. Higher transmission speeds therefore involve a greater risk of starting the receiving clock at the wrong moment.

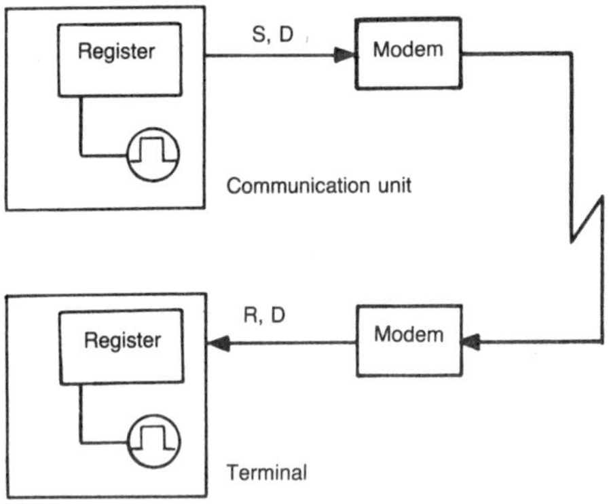

Figure 4.7 Positioning of the clocks

In asynchronous transmission, however, data is sent character by character. There has to be a gap between each character. This means that the actual transmission speed is lower. For example, at 1200 bits/s, the practical transmission rate for ASCII text is 120 characters/second and not 150 (i e about 80% of the theoretical maximum).

Synchronous transmission

Figure 4.8

Synchronous transmission always starts with the sending of a character at a specific point in time. When no transmission is in progress, "idle" characters (hex FF) are normally "sent".

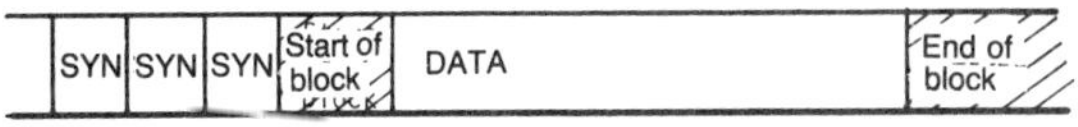

Figure 4.9
In synchronous transmission the whole block is sent, and the terminal/computer is synchronised at the beginning of this block. The clock in the modem then gives time pulses during the whole transmission.

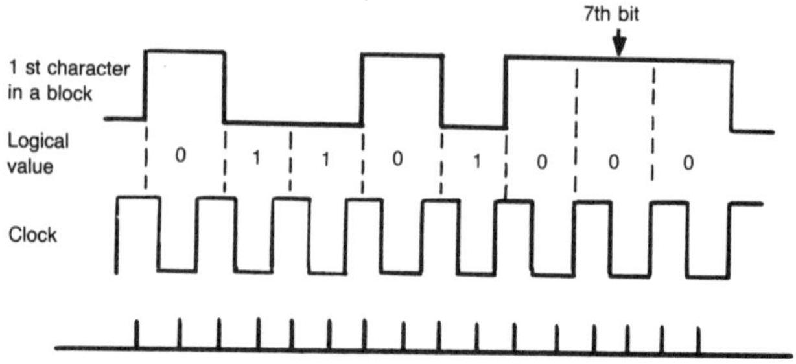

Figure 4.10

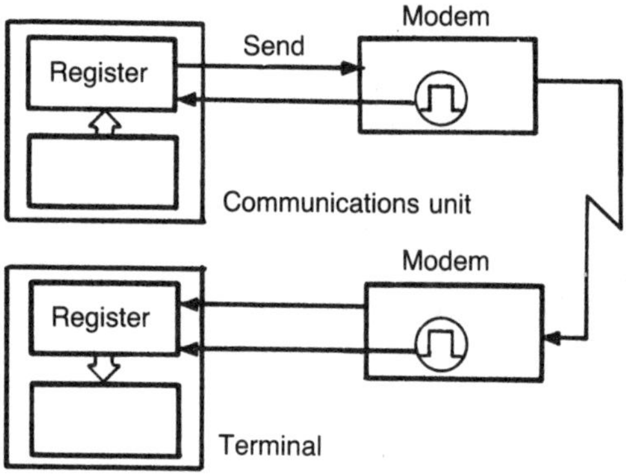

Figure 4.11 Positioning of the clocks

For normal synchronous transmission the ASCII alphabet (7 bits) is used, plus one parity bit. During the transmission both the "lateral" and the "longitudinal" parity are checked.

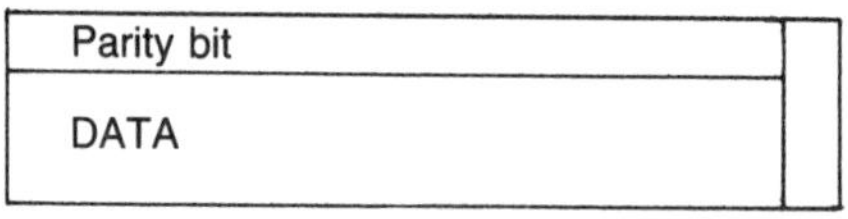

Figure 4.12

The EBCDIC alphabet is used mainly in IBM environments for the transmission of binary data, using 8 bits with no parity bit but with two CRC characters at the end of each block.

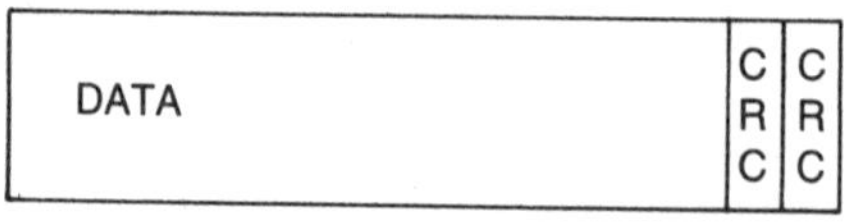

Figure 4.13

A synchronous system needs more expensive equipment than an asynchronous system. On the other hand, more characters can be transmitted per time unit for the same line speed using a synchronous system. This is because start and stop bits do not have to be sent with every character. Synchronous systems are best suited for transmission of large amounts of data where the sender and receiver are far apart. It is a question in this case of making the maximal use of the line in order to keep costs down.

4.4 Telex

The word "telex" is an abbreviation of "*tele*printer *ex*change".

Telex uses a special type of connection known as "Current Modulation".

Transmission is always asynchronous, and at 50 bits/second.

The equipment provided by Telecom administrations for each subscriber consists of a teleprinter and connection device. In addition, some 80% of subscribers have a paper tape punch/reader for receiving and auto-sending.

The connection procedure when calling another subscriber is briefly as follows:

- The subscriber operates the call switch, and a lamp lights to acknowledge it.
- When calling a Swedish subscriber from within Sweden, for example, a four- or five-digit number is then dialled on the connection apparatus. When the connection is made, the teleprinter motor starts up.
- When calling a foreign subscriber, a two-digit number is first dialled to the international exchange. When connection has been made here, the teleprinter motor starts, and the required country and subscriber numbers are entered via the keyboard. As confirmation that the connection has been made, the subscriber's telex name is printed out using key ↑ D.

As the telex name usually contains the subscriber's number, it can easily be checked that connection has been made to the correct subscriber. When calling a subscriber, the telex name stored in the teleprinter must be requested separately by sending a special character (WRU) ↑ D.

Transmission of characters between teleprinters is done using five-bit codes according to CCITT's alphabet No.2. By using two combinations, letter shift and numeric shift, to specify letters or numbers/special characters respectively, a total of 51 characters can be obtained. Each character thus consists of the five pulses for the character, and additional start and stop pulses. With a nominal pulse length of 20 ms, telexing speed is 50 bits/s, corresponding to 400 characters/minute.

There are currently about 1.6 million telex sets around the world, of which Sweden has just over 19.000.

4.5 Teletex

The Swedish Telecom is now supplying a new standardised text communication serivce – Teletex. This service is now available. The development of Teletex terminals is a joint operation of Swedish Philips AB and Telephon AB LM Ericsson.

This service has been developed with the eventual aim of replacing telex. The service itself includes terminals, networks and maintenance. It can be used for:

- producing messages
- text communication
- archiving messages.

Messages are produced on terminals working in local mode, or by transferring data from one's own central computer to the central "database" of the terminal. Editing and correction are supported by the word/text processing facilities.

The network is exclusive to Teletex subscribers, and works at a transmission rate of 2400 bits/s, i e 240 cps or 10 seconds/A4 page. (The corresponding time for telex is 5 mins/page). Traffic can be exchanged between all subscribers connected to the Teletex network. One important aspect of Teletex is the ability to talk to telex. The necessary conversion will be carried out automatically in special centres in the Teletex network.

The Teletex terminal

The terminal includes VDU, keyboard, printer and a control unit with its own memory. The unit also contains secondary memory in the form of floppy discs. In the future, the floppy discs will probably be replaced by hard discs. The unit also holds a communications adapter. Three types of screen will be available, depending on whether it is intended for word/text processing:

- a small one, with 1–8 lines
- a normal one with 24 lines
- A4 size, with about 70 lines.

The printer speed is 25–100 characters/s. The text being worked on is stored in a memory, while documents and operating programs are stored on floppy disc. The capacity of a floppy disc is approximately 125 A4 pages. The programs are stored on a separate floppy disc, and contain different modules for:

- communication
- word/text processing
- text handbook
- combination of text and addresses from file.

The terminals also offer an internal interface for locally-placed units, such as an extended individual or office-wide database or a local computer. In this case, the interface must be designed so that the terminal and the local computers can communicate. This should then mean that the program fetches data from the central database and sends it to the Teletex terminal. From here communication can now take place to the desired receiver.

The terminal contains a device to return the name, to allow checking that the correct receiver has been connected. The communications procedure works in blocks with a checking program and re-transmission of incorrect bocks (this is not available with telex).

The Teletex terminal solves the problem of calling subscribers, which for the moment is not possible to as great an extent as on the computer side. Dialling up via a computer also requires a 'box', approved by the telephone company, known as an ACU (Automatic Call Unit).

Word/text processing

The Teletex terminal includes editing and text-handling functions fully comparable with present-day word/text processing systems. Editing and altering can be done on all levels of text, from individual characters to whole items or sections.

File handling and database access

The system's internal database allows processing and storage at the record or file level. Sorting and searching will be possible in the future.

Connection of computers and private networks

The Teletex network is designed to allow terminal traffic with public and private databases. These are thereby given traditional subscription to the Teletex network. The database computers, as mentioned earlier, contain hardware and software for interfacing with the network's standards. Private networks will be able to be connected to the Teletex network via special interface units provided by the Telecom administration. These carry out the required conversions regarding codes, format and communications procedures.

Further developments

In its first design, the terminals will be individually connected to the Teletex network. There are plans, however, to bring out a Teletex exchange to be placed between terminals and the network. Intermediate storage and concentrating of the traffic will take place within this exchange.

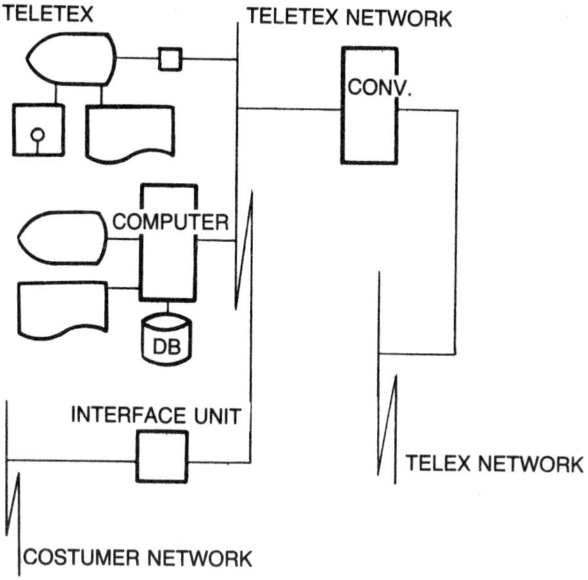

Figure 4.14 Teletex network

4.6 ECHO mode

Used mainly in asynchronous transmission over long distances to check the transmission without having to use special control characters.

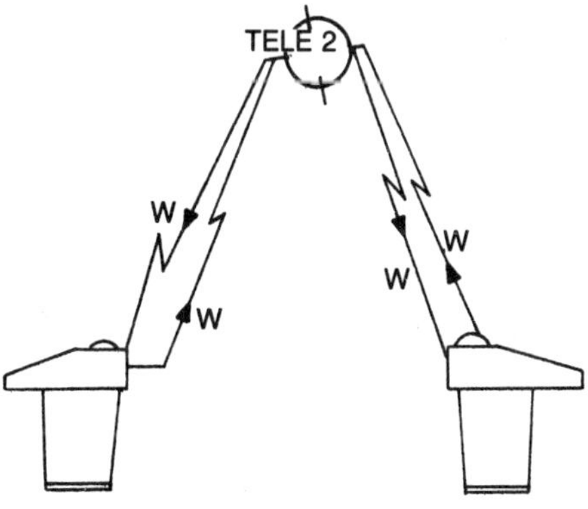

Figure 4.15

4.7 FDM (Frequency Division Multiplexer)

Multiplexing is a method of transmitting more than one data flow on a single channel at the same time. Where a channel is divided up into a number of subsidiary channels by using different frequencies, the technique is known as FDM.

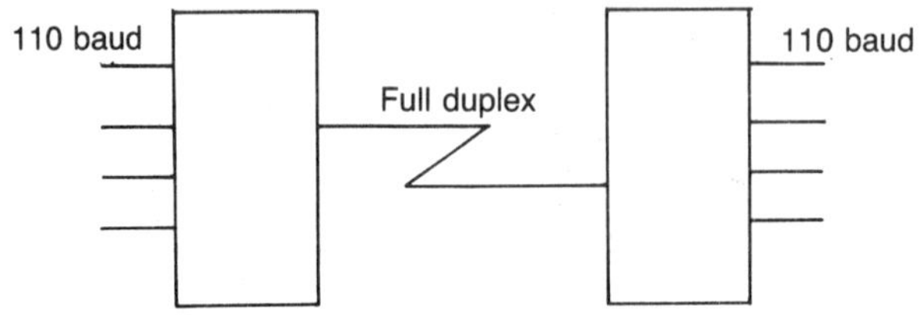

Figure 4.16

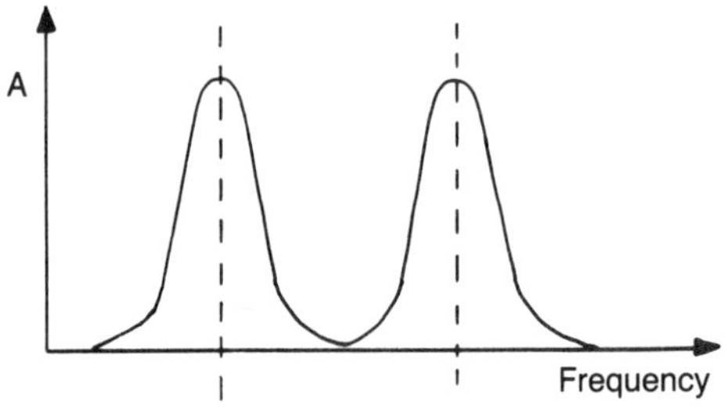

Figure 4.17

FDM allows several of the slower types of terminal to be driven on one line. While these multiplexers themselves give each of the different channels a frequency range, they act at the same time as a modem, which is in the province of the telephone company. Special approval is therefore required. At the receiving end, the different carriers can be separated because they are of different frequencies, and therefore of different wavelengths.

4.8 TDM (Time Division Multiplexer)

Where several subscribers can share the available information capacity in such a way that each one is apportioned a certain recurring time 'window', the technique is known as time multiplexing (TDM).

The principle is that all subscribers in turn send one word of their message.

When the last subscriber has sent his first word, the first subscriber can send his second word, then the second one his word, etc. See Figure 4.18.

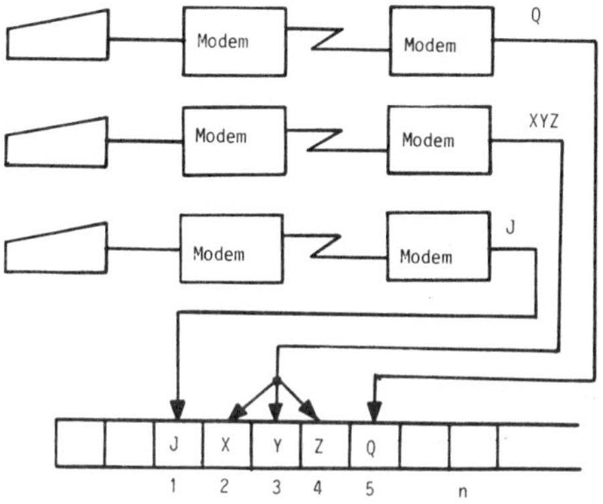

Figure 4.18

4.9 Concentrators

To start with, let's see a comparison between multiplexers and concentrators:

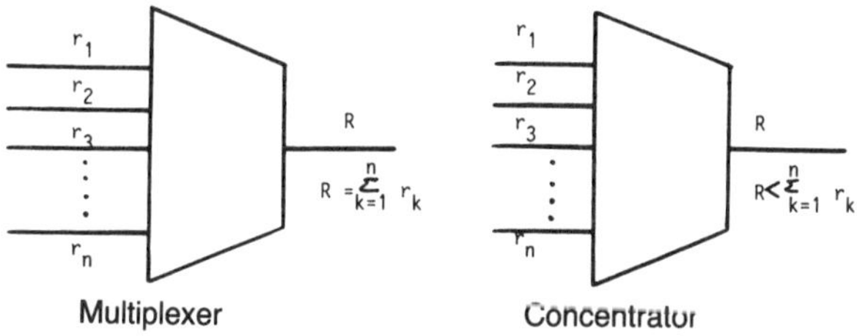

Figure 4.19

A *Multiplexer* combines ("multiplexes") data coming in on several lines with constant traffic into outgoing data on a single line, so that the sum of the data speeds is the data speed of the outgoing line. Multiplexers do no processing of the data.

A *Concentrator* combines ("Concentrates") data coming in on several lines with more or less sporadic traffic into outgoing data on an outgoing line whose transmission speed is less than that of the sum of the speeds of the data on the incoming lines. Concentrators can carry out processing of the data.

Concentrators are used for the following reasons:

- reduce line costs in large networks,
- contain software for
  - line procedures for terminals
  - line procedures for the master computer system (Node)
- queue handling
- error checking
- facility for "data compression". Two methods are commonly used. On the central side, the concentrator replaces consecutive repetitions of the same character with one of them together with a number symbol. The second method involves recoding of the information to be transmitted using the Huffman coding system, where shorter code words (i e fewer bits) are used for the most frequent characters, and longer ones for the less frequent characters
- automatic code and speed detection of user equipment
- traffic statistics.

5 Protocols and line procedures

5.1 Introduction

The use of data communication has increased much during recent years. It is therefore important for the relevant international standards to be adhered to, both by the user and the supplier of equipment.

Even in the simplest data communication system – transferring data from a transmitter to a receiver – certain rules must be observed. It is necessary for the receiver to understand what the transmitter is saying. This implies both that the information must have a certain structure which the receiver can recognise, and that each piece of information is represented by a code which is understood by both transmitter and receiver. In addition, there must be rules for what the receiver is to do when an error is detected. If the communication system is enlarged to encompass several transmitters and receivers, there will be requirements for addressing, prioritising, etc.

The all-embracing name for such rules is *protocol.* The protocol defines in detail the electrical data to be used at each connection point, what functions there will be and how these will be used, and how the users will organise their data flow to the communications equipment.

There now follows a short review of some of the rules on which the members of the standards organisations have managed to agree during their innumerable meetings. The problem has been structured into layers, and a classification has been produced which determines the rules for each layer. The rules are far from complete; at the time of writing only the first three of the seven layers have been complete. However, progress has been made on Layer 4 recently, with the publication of a workable draft proposal.

5.2 Protocol layers

In order to create a suitable structure for the protocols, they have been classified hierarchically into different layers.

Each layer must describe certain well-defined functions in communication and be functionally independent of other layers.

Figure 5.1 shows the seven different layers of protocols which have been defined. The lowest three layers, 1–3, concern communication over a single link in the system. The overall connection between sender and receiver may consist of several such links.

Layers 4–7, on the other hand, are independent of type of network, and concern control of the communication from one end to the other.

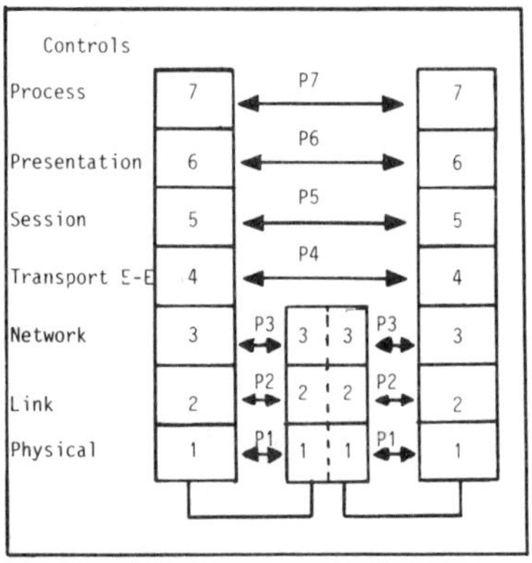

ISO Reference Model in seven layers.
P1, P2, P3: Protocol for a single link.
P4, P5, P6, P7: End-to-end protocol.

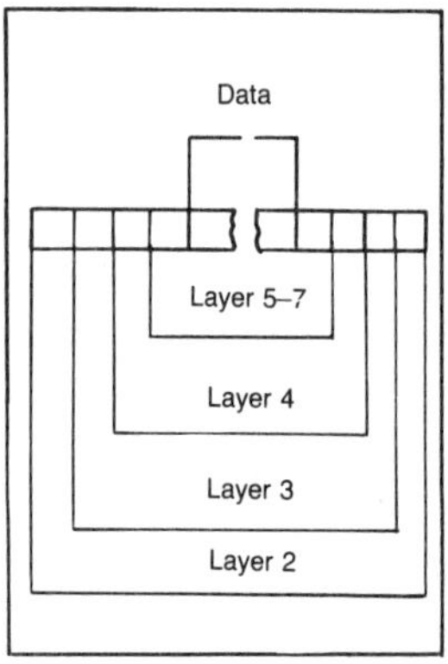

Datapacket with seven layer information.

Figure 5.1 Protocol layers

Layer 1. Physical control

Definition: Mechanical, electrical and functional interface for the establishment, retention and breaking of the physical connection between the user's terminal equipment and the connecting unit of the network.

There are standards for layer 1 which define the physical interface between the user's terminal (DTE) and the network's connection unit (DCE). On the telephone network, the DCE consists of modem equipment, while on a data network the DCE also contains certain additional logical functions.

The standard must cover both the electrical characteristics for the respective signal leads in the interface, and also which control signals are to be exchanged over the interface during the different phases of data transfer. A special standard is therefore needed for, among other things, how connection and disconnection are to be carried out in a network in which connection functions exist (telephone network, general data network).

Standard V.28 (for further information on V.28, V.24, X.26 etc see Chapter 4) defines the electrical characteristics for the interface circuits, while the functions of the individual lines are given in V.24.

V.24 defines some 50 interface signals. Connection of a particular modem involves using a selection of these lines, the actual ones depending on the relevant V recommendation for the actual modem (e g V.21 for 200 bits/s, V.26 for 2400 bits/s). Automatic dialling on the telephone network is specified in recommendation V.25.

Recommendation V.28 limits the cable lengths to 15 m, depending partly on the data speed. Two alternative recommendations, V.10 and V.11, for the electrical characteristics of the interface, have been produced recently. Both of these permit a considerably longer length, of the order of 1200 m. However, these interfaces have been used relatively little so far.

Interfaces of the V.24/V.25 type contain a large number of lines. In the production of new interfaces for the public data networks, one aim has been to reduce the number of these lines, while at the same time making a simple procedure for passing signals over the interface possible.

Interfaces for data networks are specified in CCITT's X series of recommendations. Electrical characteristics are defined in X.26 and X.27 (identical with recommendations V.10 and V.11 respectively). The line functions are defined in X.24. The connection and disconnection procedures are defined in X.20 and X.21, among others.

The most important difference between the X and V interfaces are that in the X interfaces the ordinary data lines are also used for the transfer of certain control information onto the network (e g subscriber's number), while in the V interfaces all control information is transferred over separate lines.

Layer 2. Link control

Definition: Functions for achieving secure and reliable data transfer over a simple communications link between two points, or nodes, in a network.

The protocol for layer 2 is sometimes called the line procedure.

The protocol for layer 2 – line procedure – must make possible an effective and reliable transfer of data over a particular data line. Three main tasks can be noted:

- Synchronisation, i e detection of certain control information, and recognition of the beginning and end of the user's data flow.
- Traffic flow control, i e distribution of the traffic flow to the different receivers, and distribution of the time available for which a line can be used between the different users.
- Error detection/correction, i e offering methods for detecting transmission errors and correcting them.

The functions in the protocol are partly dependent on network configuration. The data link may be of a point-to-point type over leased or dialled lines, or leased multi-point lines. Furthermore, the communication can be symmetrical (balanced) or unsymmetrical (unbalanced). In the former case, symmetrical communication, the communication occurs between two stations with identical responsibility for line control, while in asymmetrical communication one station takes total responsibility for line control.

If the receiver is to be able to detect the control information correctly, determining the correct data requires the data flow to follow a set pattern. The protocols usually work, therefore, using some form of division of the data into blocks. This pattern for dividing the data up into blocks is called formatting (see Figure 5.2).

A typical data block starts with a 'header' with the various types of control information, a 'text field' containing the user's data, and a 'trailer', which signifies the end of the block and also contains certain check bits for error detection.

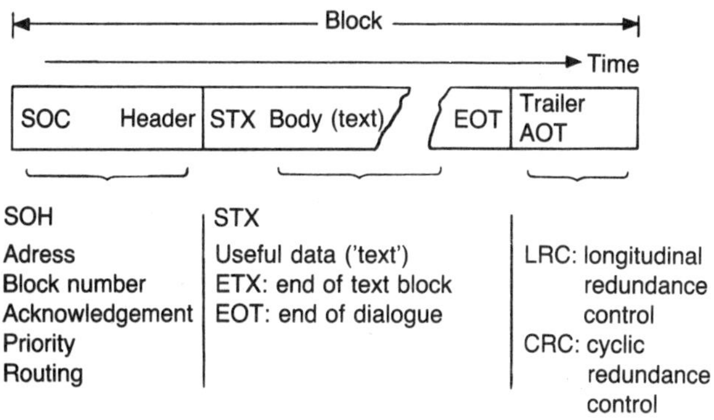

Figure 5.2 General block format

Transmission error is detected

The protocols include error detection, e g a parity bit for each character, or the addition of a number of check bits at the end of each data block. These check bits are calculated according to specific rules (VRC = 'Vertical Redundancy Check', or CRC = 'Cyclic Redundancy Check') by both transmitter and receiver. If a difference is found, the block is rejected as bad and a repetition is requested.

The protocol may work with immediate acknowledgement, positive or negative, after every block, or with delayed acknowledgement where several blocks are sent in succession without receiving an acknowledgement. Delayed acknowledgement requires some form of block numbering.

Character or bit orientation?

The text section in the format contains user data which must not be altered during transmission over the network. Neither should a protocol impose any constraints on this data, either on its format or content, but should be completely transparent.

Protocols are either character or bit orientated.

A character orientated protocol requires the text to consist of a number of complete characters of a specific length, usually 8 bits. The end of the text is defined with a certain character, which can therefore not be allowed in the body of the text. The protocol is thus not completely code-transparent.

Full code transparency can however be created using a particular trick. The protocol can for example contain a function which marks out disallowed control characters within the text section by the inclusion of an extra special character. This character is then ignored after being received.

Bit-orientated protocols mark the start and end of the text section using a certain bit sequence, a 'flag', e g 01111110. In order to give full code transparency, the protocol then inserts an extra zero whenever five ones in succession occur in the text section. The extra zero is removed after reception.

The advantages of bit-oriented protocols over character-orientated ones include the fact that they are simpler to implement both in software and hardware.

Protocol ISO 1745

ISO have produced a standardised protocol under the number ISO 1745. This is a relatively old standard, and new systems are using this standard less and less. See also Section 5.3.

ISO 1745 is a character-orientated protocol which uses the control characters as given in the CCITT alphabet No.5 (ISO 7-bit code). This uses a block format where the text section must contain a whole number of characters. Error detection is by parity bits on each character, and by an 8-bit control character per block. Immediate acknowledgement is given after each block.

ISO 1745 can be used on both point-to-point and multi-point lines. It can only be used in half-duplex mode. More can be found on point-to-point and multi-point systems in Chapter 6.

Many manufacturers use procedures similar to ISO 1745 for line control in their communication systems. However, the ISO standard was produced so late in the day that there were already many systems in use whose line procedures differed somewhat from ISO 1745. Also, ISO 1745 is so formulated as to give a certain latitude in its application. The consequence has been that the manufacturers often have their own procedures which are similar to ISO 1745, but are not identical and therefore cannot work with it.

Protocol of the ISO 1745 type have until now been very common. A common variant of ISO 1745 is IBM's BSC procedure, which has also been implemented in equipment from several manufacturers other than IBM.

ISO HDLC line procedure

A more recent standard than ISO 1745 is ISO HDLC (High Level Data Link Control). Several ISO documents on HDLC's structure and function have also been published. The most important of these are the following

• ISO 3309	HDLC–Frame structure
• ISO/IS 4335	HDLC–Elements of procedures
• ISO/IS 6159	HDLC–Unbalanced classes of procedures
• ISO/IS 6256	HDLC–Balanced class of procedures

HDLC corresponds to a large degree with the American ADCCP (Advanced Data Communication Control Procedure) standard, but there are certain minor differences.

In the same way as for ISO 1745, there are manufacturer-specific variants of HDLC, such as Burroughs BDLC, IBM SDLC and Sperry UDLC. Of these, SDLC is the oldest, and therefore differs most from the ISO HDLC standard.

HDLC is a bit-orientated standard with a text section, i e an information field, which can contain an arbitrary number of bits. The flag is 01111110, which is used to separate the blocks or frames.

The format includes certain fixed fields before the information field, which contain address information, block number, etc. Errors are detected with the aid of 16 control bits per block, CRC, and correction is by repetition. Delayed acknowledgement (or no acknowledgement) of the block is valid for up to 7 blocks. However, one option allows the first acknowledgement to occur after 127 blocks. The protocol thus allows full duplex, i e simultaneous data transmission in both directions over the data link.

HDLC contains functions for both balanced and unbalanced communication and can be used on both point-to-point and multi-point lines.

Standards for layer 2

• ISO 1745	Basic Mode
• ISO 3309	HDLC Frame
• ISO 4335	HDLC Procedure elements
• ISO 6159	HDLC Unbalanced classification
• ISO 6256	HDLC Balanced classification
• CCITT X.25	Packet switched networks

Layer 3. Network Control

Definition: Functions for sharing out the transmission capacity of a communications link into several logical channels and the transmission of data on these.

Layer 3 is currently used on, among others, packet-switching data networks, and contains rules for the format of the data 'packet'.

In addition, this layer offers the ability to establish, maintain and break network connections. It allows transport units to be independent of choice of route and network connection conditions which are tied up with the establishment and running of a network connection.

Standards for the network layer

- CCITT X.25 and X.75 Packet-switching networks
- CCITT T.70 For Teletex.

Layer 4. Transport end-to-end control

Definition: Network-independent interface at the ends of the line to communications functions.

This layer contains protocols for transfer of data between the two ends (users). The layer is designed always to present a unique interface to layer 5 regardless of the interface of the lower layer. The differences in the lower levels are resolved in layer 4.

The aim of the transport layer is to give the session layer (data flow control) services for the transparent transfer of data between session elements. The transport user is thereby freed from concern over the details (economic and of reliability) of the way in which data transfer is carried out.

The transport service offered by layer 4 covers all the relevant functions associated with use of the most suitable aids and with the quality of service from the underlying layers. The transport layer must optimise the use of the available communications resources in order for them to meet the needs of every transport user. Account must thus be taken of the limitations which depend on the needs of all the simultaneous users of the transport and on the relevant limitations of the resources. The transport layer's protocol is of the end-to-end type, where the endpoints are defined as the respective transport elements.

Standard for the transport layer

- CCITT T.70 For Teletex

Layer 5. Session control

Definition: User functions for maintenance of dialogue between the current processes (programs) at the end points, block division and buffering.

The session layer (data flow control), which comes just under the presentation layer in the reference model, has the aim of supporting data exchange between the coordinating elements in this layer. This is done by the establishment of logical communication routes called sessions. Two applications which have to work together are connected together via elements at the presentation layer into a session. This allows them to exchange data as though they were connected by physical circuits. The lower layers of the model are used to bring this about. Having established a session by connection of elements at the presentation layer, and thereby of the applications, the session layer maintains this session during the data transfer stage and ends it afterwards.

An example of a session is where a terminal operator wants to update interactively a geographically distant database.

- CCITT T.62 For Teletex

Layer 6. Presentation control

Definition: User functions for data transformations, such as code or format conversion, encryption and data compression.

The aim of the presentation layer is to present data to the respective applications elements, when required, for conversion of character codes, representation of data elements and message structure (syntax) without distortion so that the data can be processed.

Handling of presentation is a dialogue between units in the presentation layer on the request of units in the applications layer. This is in order to decide upon representation of data in the OSI environment.

Standard for the presentation layer

- CCITT T.62 For Teletex

Layer 7. Application control

Definition: Functions on the applications layer for control of the user's processes and system resources.

As the uppermost layer in the reference model, the applications layer provides services to the user. It forms a window between users through which occur all exchanges of data which are meaningful for the users.

A user is represented in the applications layer as a functional element which corresponds to the functional elements in other systems.

The services to the user may include, but are not limited to, the following:

- Identifying the proposed communicating parties (end user), via name and address, or by a specified or generic description,
- Determining whether the parties are available for communication,
- Confirming that the parties are authorised to communicate,
- Agreeing procedures to be used for integrity protection,
- Confirming the identities of the communicating parties and their right to communicate,
- Determining the method of cost-sharing,
- Determining availability of the resources required,
- Determining the quality required of the transfer service (response time, error tolerance, cost etc),
- Synchronising applications which are working together,
- Selecting rules for the dialogue, including introduction and ending,
- Deciding who has responsibility for error correction,
- Determining the data protection procedure,
- Determining character codes, data element catalogues and message structure,
- Transferring the user's data.

The applications layer contains all the functions included in communication between open systems and those which are operated by people or programs, and which are not carried out in the underlying levels.

Elements which are included in an application can be divided up internally into groups of functions. Usage of one such group may depend on the use of other functions and the active functions may vary during the time of connection.

The control functions for the system and the application fall into the applications level, which also contains functions which affect its own control such as activation and error control.

Because the applications layer has to cope with a large number of different applications, there must also be a large number of protocols to support them. These have been divided into five groups:

(1) *System control protocols*
These are the protocols which are required for the functions which control and monitor the open system. They include, for example, protocols for controlling the opening and closing of interconnected tasks, monitoring of their work and error checking.

(2) *Applications control protocols*
These are for the functions which control and monitor the current applications. Typical functions for these protocols are checking that only authorised users or applications use the filing, control point functions and accessing.

(3) *System protocols*
These protocols cover functions for data processing, such as access to files, remote feeding-in of jobs, and process initiation.

(4) *Special applications protocols for companies or industries*
Where the applications in question are specific to a particular industry, such as banks or airlines, certain protocols can be identified which are applicable to all the organisations in the same line of business. Some such protocols already exist in this group, e g the higher level in the SITA system for airline seat bookings.

(5) *Company-specific applications protocols*
The protocols in this group are specific to a particular company, and include applications such as order processing systems.

Higher order protocols

Protocols for layers 3 and higher have not yet been standardised to the same extent as those for layers 1 and 2.

Important work is in progress on a protocol for network control in networks with "packet-switching". This work comes under the CCITT, and the protocol is known as X.25 and covers layers 1–3. "Packet-switching" means transmitting of standardised "message sections" through the network (see Chapter 6.9).

X.25 is structured in layers 1, 2 and 3. For level 1 V.24 is the primary recommendation, and for layer 2 an application of HDLC is used.

Layer 3 in X.25 specifies how a succession of data packets from the sender can constitute a logical channel, and how several such logical channels can be combined on one and the same physical data link.

IBM's SNA, Sperry's DCA and Digital Equipment's DECNET are examples of this system philosophy which are founded on layer classification according to the principles described earlier.

The advantages of a common standard for data communication at the higher layers are, however, considered to be very important. In the longer term, therefore, one may expect that these layers will also be covered by international standards.

Addresses and identities in data communication according to OSI (Open Systems Interconnection)

Introduction

Terminal addresses and identities are needed for the user program to be able to identify the terminal or operator from which it received a message, and also so that many terminals can be connected to the same line. Sending and receiving of messages are then controlled with the aid of terminal addresses. This has led to different types of terminal identifiers and different ways of transferring these to the computer.

The ways in which address and identity information is handled in different types of conventional data communication between terminals and computer are discussed below. The addressing methods differ depending on the type of application. There are certain common practices, but it is difficult to structure the addressing problem generally.

The OSI model is built up systematically in seven levels. Several different protocols, depending on application, is developed and used for the OSI model's layers. These protocols may differ in format (structure) and the appearance and positioning of the address information. The standardisation work includes attempts to create unity in this too.

Examples of protocols for the different layers, together with comments on format and codes for the address field, etc, are given in the section "Format and codes for address information".

Older types of terminals

The types of terminals covered in this document use synchronous line procedures in accordance with ISO 1745 (or similar), or asynchronous stop-start transmission. No major differentiation has been made for those parts of the addresses used for line procedures or for message identification.

Point-to-point-connected terminals

RJE terminals and TTY-compatible terminals are normally connected to the computer via their own point-to-point lines. These connections may be leased telephone lines or dialled connections. RJE terminals are used for data entry, and are often provided with console, card-reader, printer, tape decks, cassette drives or floppy disc units. TTY-compatible terminals are use for transaction-orientated transmission for e g time sharing or information-seeking transactions, but they can also be used for data entry. The TTY terminal is a slow printer or VDU screen.

These types of terminal have no addresses attached to them. In order to identify the user, one or more ID codes are sent in to the computer. (log on, sign on, remote no., password). These ID codes are generally fed in from the keyboard, but they can also be stored on floppy disc or other medium and fed in automatically.

Terminals connected to multi-point networks

Terminals connected to multi-point networks generally consist of one or more VDU screens and one or more printers connected to a common control unit (CLUSTER). They are used for transaction-orientated transmission in information-seeking traffic, updating transactions and time-sharing.

There is often an address in these terminals which is linked to the data station's control unit, and which is entered manually or fed in by the program which controls the data transmission.

In addition, every VDU or printer has its own address character whose code is dependent upon how it is connected to the control unit.

The address characters are used for identifying the terminal which sent or is to receive the messages, and also to identify the messages themselves and for controlling the line in general. Addresses are normally sent as part of every message.

For the types of system which require some form of identification of the operator, some ID characters are sent after the addresses in the information part of the message. These characters may have been read in from a magnetic or optical card, or similar, or have been fed in via the keyboard.

New types of system and the OSI model

Most suppliers have produced new types of terminals recently. The terminals (data stations) have now become more flexible and various types of data transfer, such as data entry, file transfer and updating and information-seeking transactions, can be carried out at the same terminal.

Along with producing new types of data terminals, some suppliers have introduced new communications procedures into their computer systems, and taken the OSI model into account in the design of the terminals and associated new software.

According to the OSI model, all control information which is of concern in any particular layer is placed in a header reserved for that layer. This means that the various types of addresses and ID codes have to be put into different headers and used within the particular layer.

Layer 2

In layer 2 a protocol in accordance with HDLC is allowed. In the header, as defined by HDLC, there is an address character of 8 bits. (By special agreement, the address character can be increased to several 8-bit characters.) This address character identifies a secondary station (on a multi-point line with one or more secondary stations and one primary station) or one of the two combined stations (on a point-to-pint line).

Normally, only one address character is required for this layer.

The address character identifies the data station on the line to which perhaps several printers and VDU's are connected.

If only one terminal unit can be connected to the data station, it can be identified definitively by the station address (link address). For more than one terminal unit, further identification is required at higher layers.

On point-to-point lines no address character is used to select the receiver, as there only is one. Only one address character is needed for a connection between a secondary and a primary station. The same character can always be used as the address. Two address characters are needed between two combined stations, which can be the same for dialled or fixed lines. Compare the packet-switching network where only two different addresses are defined, one for DTE and one for DCE.

HDLC also allows the transmitting of a special message when making the connection, which identifies the type of station, and which can also contain various parameters and information on the terminal type.

Layer 3

In layer 3, the choice and identification of a route through the network (e g the general data network) occur at the connecting-up stage. This means that when a connection is made, the required subscriber number is sent so the telephone or data network which connects to the correct subscriber called. In a circuit-switching network, addresses in layer 3 can in certain circumstances be dropped, because the subscribers have their own line connected between them. In the packet-switching network the number of a logical channel is used to identify the current connection.

In the general data network, an identification (the respective subscribers' numbers) may be obtained either from the caller or the receiver after connection. During the data transfer phase on a fixed or dialled network with several network nodes, the network address is used to find the correct way through the network.

Layers 4 and 5

In layer 4 the user, which could for example be a VDU, a printer or a program, can be identified. In a more complex system, such as an advanced teletex terminal, sub-systems can be selected by means of an address in layer 4 (the transport address). Identification of the current session or dialogue takes place in layer 5 by means of a session address. One of these identification codings can be used to identify conclusively the current receiver and sender if there are more than one user of a station address in layer 2.

Layer 6

The header in layer 6 generally needs no address when a particular session normally gives the same presentation unit.

Layer 7

In order to achieve the correct user process (starting point and comprehensiveness of the applications program), a transaction code, job name or similar is used. This can be treated as an address in layer 7.

If the current application is of such a kind that a special operator's ID code needs to be checked in order that the transaction can be carried out, the ID code should be checked by the application in layer 7. The ID code can be fed in from an ID card or from the keyboard. The ID code should be included every time a new transaction (request, updating, alteration) is initiated. In some cases where secret data is concerned, the ID code should also be kept secret, and not, for example, be displayed on a screen. In applications where open information is processed, the ID code can identify on the screen a person who requests information.

The ID code used in the establishment of a session also belongs to layer 7.

Formats and codes for address information

For *layer 2*, the current bit-orientated line procedures are unified and agree with HDLC.

The commonest example of *layer 3* is the CCITT X.25 recommendation on packet protocols. On connection, both transmitter's and receiver's addresses (network address = subscriber number) can be sent. The address lengths are given in binary code in fixed 4-bit indicator fields, and the address format is in binary-coded decimal form (four bits) for the purely numerical characters. It must however be noted in this connection that X.25 is a specific application (packet-switched data networks). The type of network determines the type of protocol used, and this in turn, of course, controls the address format.

There are proposals for a generally useable protocol for *layer 4* (transport protocol), namely ECMA-72 and CCITT recommendation S.70 for teletex. The ECMA standard does not lay down how the address field should be coded. In Teletex, characters according to CCITT character code No.5 are used for address coding.

The Teletex protocol will also serve here as an example for *layer 5*. Layer 5 follows to a large extent what has been said about layer 4.

Layer 7 contains identity information which is wholly application-specific, and which can be specified as a norm for a specific application.

Summary

When new systems are being developed, the guidelines shown in the OSI model and the section "new types of system" should be used. This means that the different types of addresses and ID codes, where there is a need for the respective address, should be organised in the respective layers as follows:

- Layer 2 Link address – data station address
- Layer 3 Network address
- Layer 4 Transport address
- Layer 5 Session address
- Layer 7 Transaction code and operator ID.

5.3 Terminal types and their line protocols

Line protocols only control the use of the line. The characteristics of the individual terminals, such as formula processing on the VDU screen, are then superimposed on these. The fact that several terminals may be stated to be equipped with a particular line procedure is no guarantee that the characteristics of the terminals are the same.

Example:

IBM3270, Alfascop 3270, ITT3280

All use the same line protocol, but their characteristics are different. The Alfascope has more function keys, etc.

Some of the common line procedures will now be reviewed.

ISO 1745

ISO 1745 is a character-orientated protocol. It is used in transferring between data structures, using 7-bit character coded (+parity bit) and longitudinal parity checking.

The protocol describes the course of events during three of the five phases usually defined for data communication.

These phases are

1 Connection of the physical link
2 Establishment of the data link
3 Information transfer
4 Termination
5 Disconnection of the physical link

The events under phases 1 and 5 are only concerned with the physical connection and are not dealt with in the standard. The other three phases, 2, 3 and 4, are covered in detail in ISO 1745. Phase 2, establishment of the data link, means that part of the process which prepares transmitter and receiver (may be more than one) for the transfer of useful information. According to the standard, Phase 2 can be done in three different ways, namely:

- switching
- polling
- selecting

Switching has so far not been covered by the standard. Polling is a method whereby each terminal is interrogated in turn by the computer to determine whether it is ready to receive or transmit data, and 'selection' prepares the receiving terminal to receive data.

Phase 3, information transmission, is that part of the transaction where useful data is transmitted. The transmitting terminal is then known as the master, and the receiving terminal is thc slave. Phase 4, termination, is that part of the transaction when the transmission of useful information stops (temporarily or finally). Figure 5.3 shows the different phases, and summarises the events and the tasks of the equipment involved during each phase. Note that with polling, one of the terminals must control the sequence of events; this terminal is known as the control, and the terminal polled is the 'tributary'. If the tributary has information to send, it does so immediately after polling, whereupon it then 'governs' the data link and takes upon itself the task of 'master'; the original master terminal has to act as slave while information is being transferred. When the useful information has been transmitted, it is terminated by EOT (end of transmission), and control of the data link reverts to the master terminal.

Phase		Function: Action	Function: Reaction	Station's name: Responsible	Station's name: Responsive	Transmission control characters used in basic mode: Forward	Transmission control characters used in basic mode: Backword	Notes
1 Establishment of connection over general network	a) Switching b) Identification							CCITT Responsibility
2 Establishment of data link	a) Switching	Call	Answer	Calling	Called			Not covered at present
	b) Polling	Poll	Replay	Control	Tributary	(EOT), ENQ	(EOT)	
	c) Selecting	Select	Replay	Master	Slave	(EOT), ENQ	ACK, NAK	
3 Information transfer		Transfer	Supervision	Master	Slave	SOH, STX ETB, ETX, (EOT)		ACK, NAK, (EOT) for Supervision
4 Termination	a) Return to neutral state	Terminate Interrupt		Master	Slave	EOT	EOT	
	b) Return to control station	Terminate Interrupt		Master	Slave	EOT	EOT	
	c) Disconnect	Disconnect Disconnect		Master	Slave	DLE, EOT	DLE, EOT	
5 Clearing of connection								CCITT Responsibility

Figure 5.3 Data communication, phases

3270 BSC procedure

One message format for data communication which was introduced by IBM in 1968, and which is used by most other suppliers, is shown in Figure 5.4. This protocol, known as BSC (Binary Synchronous Communication), also includes rules for control and monitoring.

The line protocol is commonly known as "the 3270 procedure".

Alfaskop, ITT 3280 and IBM 3270 are VDU terminals which work in EBCDIC under the BSC poll/select protocol.

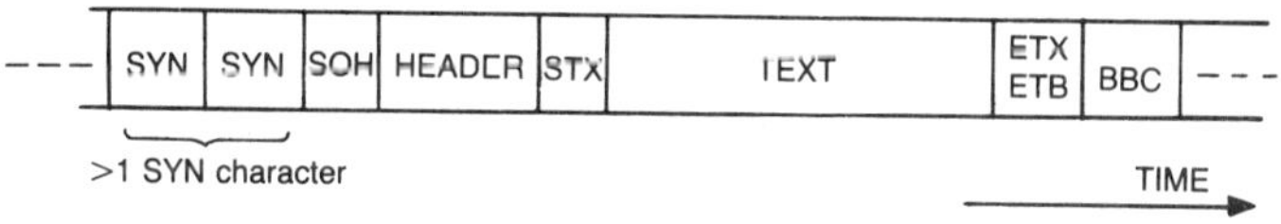

SYN =synchronisation word
SOH =Start of header
STX =Start of text
ETX =End of text
ETB =End of block
BCC =Block contol character

Figure 5.4 BSC format

UTS

UTS is the line protocol used for communication between UNISCOP terminals and Sperry computers.

It is a synchronous standard procedure, 7 bits (+parity bit) modified ASCII code, Poll/Select. See Section 11.5.

2780/3780 protocol (EBCDIC)

This BSC protocol is an IBM procedure offered by most manufacturers. Communication is between 'remote batch' terminals and host computers, but the protocol can also be used in computer-computer communication.

Dialogue is of the 'contention', type, i e a passive form of line control where the terminal or computer requests access to the line (line bid), and then sends its text block.

Differences between 2780/3780

- Both send fixed-length blocks of 512 characters, but 3780 has as a standard function the ability of 'space compression', i e the compressing of space characters.
- Every record in a text block from 2780 is terminated by a 'US unit separator' control character followed by CRC, whereas the 3780 only carries out the CRC check at the end of block.

NTR and REM1

These protocols are used in 'remote batch' communication between the central equipment and the locally-situated remote batch equipment (which can be a minicomputer).

NTR

NTR is a program which was designed for running in RBT equipment connected to Sperry computers by full- or half-duplex communication lines.

The message format consists of 8-bit characters.

Figure 5.5

A message is always preceded by four SYN characters, then starts with an SOH character and ends with an ETX.

There are four different types of message (MSG):

- the *sign on* message is the first one sent from the RBT equipment, and comprises 6 characters
- the *control* message, which carries information on the characteristics of the equipment
- *data* is the third variation of message, and the most common. Length of data blocks depend on the equipment in use
- the fourth type is *ACK* or *NAK*, which are control words for the communication.

REM1

The message format in REM1 communication is given below:

Figure 5.6

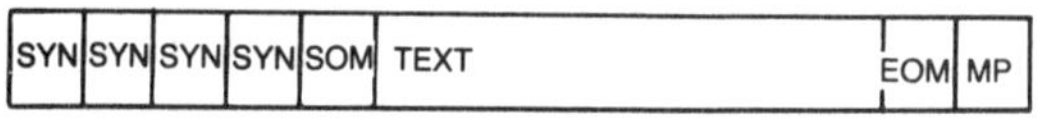

Each message consists of a number of 7-bit characters (6 bits+parity bit) of XS-3 code positioned between two groups of special transmission codes.

The messages can be of two types:

- Functional messages
- Data messages

SYN	=synchronisation character	Even parity
SOM	=start of message	Even parity
TEXT	=data message or functional message	(max 330 characters) odd parity (max 6 characters) odd parity
EOM	=end of message	even parity
MP	=message parity	used for additional error checking of the data message.

TTY procedure

TTY-compatible terminals, such as the Silent 700, TermiNet 1200 or Tandberg TDV 2215, use asynchronous transmission in communication with the host computer, i e transmission occurs character by character. In this case the only condition is that the interface is RS-232-C, which is the general standard TTY interface. One advantage of TTY terminals is that they can be connected to almost any computer.

HDLC (High level Data Link Control)

This standard is new, and different parts of it are at different stages of standardisation, from fixed standards to working papers. Many new systems today use suppliers' versions of HDLC, which more-or-less follow the ANSI (the American National Standards Institute) version, ADCCP (Advanced Data Communication Control Procedures). The basic classifications of HDLC, UNC (unbalanced normal), UAC (unbalanced asynchronous) and BAC (balanced asynchronous) are all to be found in ADCCP. Test and response commands are not included, but otherwise the repertoire of commands and responses is the same. As mentioned earlier, the HDLC procedure allows code-transparent transfer of data via connections working with synchronous transmission. It can be used in point-to-point and multipoint connections, both in fixed or dialled networks. During transmission the information is divided up into blocks (frames), which are acknowledged on the reverse line.

FLAG	ADR	CONT	INFO	RCS	FLAG
8	8	8	n	16	8

FLAG =011111110
ADR =address field
CONT =control field, containing control information
INFO =information field
FCS =checksum, which includes ARD, CONT and INFO

Figure 5.7

Each information block is given an order number, and acknowledgement is generally not requested before module No. M-1 (M=8, or optionally 128) is reached, which gives a higher effective data speed.

Code transparency is achieved by "bit-stuffing" in the ADR-, CONT-, INFO- and FCS- fields. (A zero is inserted between the 5th and 6th '1' where these occur in succession.)

Data: ....0010011111110....
Stuffed: ....00100111110110...

HDLC. The international standardisation work within ISO

The work of standardising with HDLC is divided into three phases. The first phase was that of standardising the 'frame', and this produced a result in ISO 3309 "Frame Structure", produced in 1976. This was updated in 1979. The second phase was standardisation of commands and responses. These are reviewed in ISO standard 4335, "HDLC Elements of Procedures", 1979, and "Draft Addendum ISO 4335/DAD 2". These three documents are also brought together in the working paper numbered ISO/TC 97/SC 6 N2100.

The third phase of the standardisation covers which commands and responses from ISO 4335 are to be used for which connections. There are standards for point-to-point and multi-point connections, ISO 6159:1980 "HDLC unbalanced classes of procedures", and a proposed standard for point-to-point connections, ISO/DIS 6256 "HDLC balanced class of procedures". These two documents are also published together in working paper No. ISO/TC 97/SC 6 N2009.

ISO 3309, "Frame Structure"

This description follows mainly ISO 3309 published in 1979.

In HDLC, both control and other information are sent in a frame. The format of the frame is specified in Figure 5.8. Transmission is between two or more stations/terminals.

Flag F 01111110	Adress A 8 bits	Check C 8 bits	Information I	FCS 16 bits	Flag F 01111110

Figure 5.8

The flag is used for synchronisation and as the first and last character in a frame. The flag consists of six ones surrounded by a zero in front and behind.

In order to obtain code transparency, and so that no combination of bits will produce a false flag, a zero is placed after 5 ones in a row in other parts of the frame. These zeroes are removed by the receiver.

The address in the command always identifies the station to which the command is directed. The address in the response always identifies the station which sent the response. The address field can be enlarged by further 8-bit fields.

The control field (C) is used to transfer a command to the target station to tell it to carry out a special operation, and to transmit a response to such a command. The response is transmitted from the station addressed. C also includes the sequence number for information sent and received. C can be optionally enlarged.

The information field is completely bit-transparent, and its length is limited. It may also be omitted.

FCS (Frame Checking Sequence) is a 16-bit check character obtained by (among other things) division modulo 2 using a particular polynomial.

In ISO 3309 Annex B, which is not part of the standard, it is stated that an address of 8 ones is reserved as a "global" address, for example to poll an unknown terminal on a dialled-through line, and that an address of 8 zeroes should never be assigned to a station but used instead for testing. Several stations can be given a common group address, but not 8 ones or 8 zeroes.

Procedure element ISO 4335, "Elements of Procedures", with expansion

This description largely follows ISO/TC 97/SC 6 N2100

The HDLC procedure is designed to allow synchronous data communication regardless of the particular succession of bits in the I field. Under the HDLC procedure, frames containing information are normally transferred from a data source to a data receiver. The frames are acknowledged by a frame with or without information in it in the other direction, by transmitting the next expected sequence number. Control of traffic between source and receiver uses cyclic numbering of frames. Each combination of data source and receiver on the data link uses sequence numbering independently of any others.

The HDLC procedure is used for both balanced and unbalanced data links between stations. An unbalanced data link consists of a 'primary' data station and one or more 'secondary' data stations. A primary data station controls the data flow and is responsible for error recovery. A balanced data link comprises two data stations combined, which each have the same responsbility for the data flow and error recovery.

The frames sent by the primary station are known as commands, and those sent by the secondary station as responses. A combined data station can send both commands and responses. ISO 4335 defines particularly what is to be done when secondary or a combined data station receives a command.

The data link can either be in the 'active' or the passive ('idle') state.

The link is active when a frame, an 'abort sequence' or a fill-in character (inter-frame time-fill) is sent. The abort sequence can be put in anywhere. This consists of 7 to 14 ones, and is used to tell the receiver to ignore the frame which ends with the ones. Fill-in characters comprise flags which can be sent between frames; there is no facility to send them within a frame.

The link switches to the passive or idle state when 15 ones are sent, which means that transmission has ceased on the line. This can for example be used in half-duplex in order to change the direction of transmission.

The standard defines operational and non-operational modes.

Three different operational modes are defined, two for unbalanced link (normal response mode, NRM, and asynchronous response mode, ARM), and one for balanced links (asynchronous balanced mode, ABM).

In NRM, a secondary station may only start sending under direct orders from a primary data station. This occurs with a special poll bit (P) in the control field from the primary station. A secondary station may send several frames one after the other, and the last one is marked with a 'final' bit (F) in C.

In ARM, a secondary data station may send without direct orders from a primary station.

In ABM, the two combined data stations can send commands and responses on their own initiative.

Three different non-operational modes are defined, two for 'disconnected' modes (normal disconnected mode, NDM, and asynchronous disconnected mode, ADM), and one 'initialisation' mode (IM).

'Disconnected' mode differs from the operational modes in that information and acknowledgements cannot be transmitted. This gives a well-defined basic condition in which the system finds itself, e g before an exchange of information. The difference between 'normal' and 'asynchronous' is the same as in the operational modes.

'Initialisation' mode (IM) is used where a secondary/combined data station needs to update the program or for the transmission of parameters for link control.

Control field

There are three different formats for the control field. These are defined in the following table, extracted from ISO 4335:

CONTROL FIELD FOR	CONTROL FIELD BITS							
	1	2	3	4	5	6	7	8
Information transfer command/responce (I frame)	0		N(S)		P/F		N(R)	
Supervisory commands/ responses (S frame)	1	0	S		P/F		N(R)	
Unnumbered commands/ responses (U frame)	1	1	M		P/F		m	

N(S)= Transmitting send sequence number (bit2=low-order-bit)
N(R)=Transmitting receive sequence number (bit6=low-order-bit)
S= Supervisory function bits
M= Modifier function bits
P/F= Poll bit – primary or combined command fram transmission
Final bit – secondary or combined responce frame transmissions (1=Poll/Final)

Procedure classes ISO 6159, "HDLC unbalanced classes of procedures" and ISO/DIS 6256, "HDLC balanced class of procedures"

This description largely follows ISO/TC 97/SC 6 N2099. The nomenclature for the classes and options has also been taken from this document.

ISO 6159 and ISO/DIS 6256 describe the HDLC unbalanced procedure classes and the HDLC balanced procedure class. In the unbalanced classes, the data link consists of one primary data station and one or more secondary data stations, and works either in 'normal response mode' (NRM), when the class is known as UNC, or in 'asynchronous response mode' (ARM), when the class is called UAC, on a multi-point or point-to-point connection. Only one secondary station can work in ARM at a time. In the balanced class, the data link consists of two combined data stations which work in 'asynchronous balanced mode' (ABM) on a point-to-point connection, and the class is known as BAC. The balanced class is intended for use where the same control of transmission is required at both ends of the data link. All three classes can work either in alternating or simultaneous two-way (TWA or TWS) transmission.

Each class contains certain commands and responses which are included in their basic repertoire. There are a number of additional options which extend or reduce the number of commands and responses allowed. The address and control fields can also be extended.

UDLC (Universal Data Link Control)

UDLC is a more recently developed protocol. It is UNISYS variation of HDLC.

UDLC is a bit-orientated protocol which allows arbitrary bit combinations in the text section of the message, and which is therefore *information transparent*. It allows transmission of any type of code: ASCII, EBCDIC, pure binary code, etc.

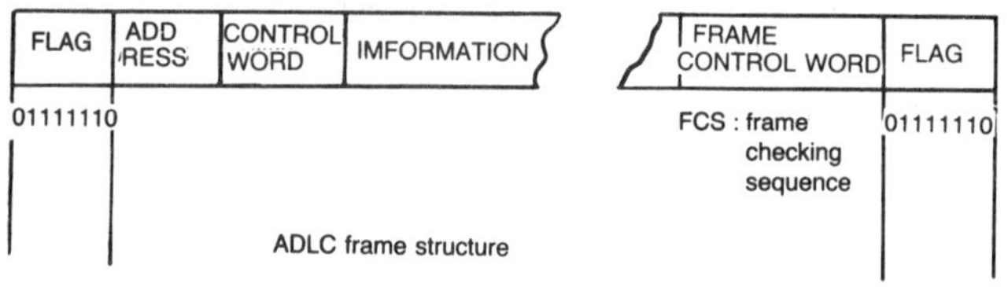

Figure 5.9

The information section can be as long as desired – the number of bits does not need to be a multiple of 8 – followed by a 16-bit control word. In order to avoid any part of the arbitrary bit sequence being interpreted as a flag, the transmitter inserts a zero as soon as it detects five ones in a row. This applies only to the part which lies between the flags. At the receiver's end, the bit stream is monitored continuously, and when five ones in a row are encountered, special note is taken of the bit following them. If it is a zero, it is removed from the message. If on the other hand it is a one (followed by a zero), his means that a flag has been received. In this way, any type of information can be transmitted in the message without any part of it being interpreted as control information.

IBM SDLC

These details of SDLC are based on the IBM document 'IBM Synchronous Data Link Control, General information' (GA 27-3093-2). This document also includes specifications for 'loop link applications'; this is an extension which falls outside the scope of the international standard.

SDLC is one of the HDLC classes, 'unbalanced normal', UNC, as far as 'basic repertoire' and also a number of options are concerned (see under classes). No other classes are included.

Configuration

The configurations for SDLC include unbalanced links, point-to-point or multipoint.

Modes

A secondary data station can be ordered to take one of three different modes: 'normal response mode', NRM, 'normal disconnected mode', NDM, and 'initialisation mode', IM. The first two are defined in SDLC in overall agreement with HDLC. However, for specification of IM procedures, the SDLC document refers the user to the actual product description.

Format

The format agrees completely with HDLC. Format extensions, which are options under HDLC referring to the address field (option 7) and the control field (option 10) are not found in SDLC.

'Channel states'

The two conditions, 'idle channel state' and 'active channel state' are defined similarly in SDLC and HDLC.

In SDLC, a further 'transient state' is defined, where neither the conditions for 'idle' or active' are fulfilled. This condition is included in the physical connection, and with the switching over of a half-duplex line.

Classes

SDLC fits into one of the HDLC classes, namely the 'Unbalanced operation, Normal response mode' class, UNC.

Adding the available options, SDLC can be specified using the HDLC description in the following way:

Class UNC, 1, 2, 4, 5, 12, 13.

Note that this is only a classification by the descriptions given of commands and responses. No proper classes are given. As examples, the application for the 3270 VDU terminal corresponds to class UNC 1, 12 or UNC 1, 5, 12 depending on model.

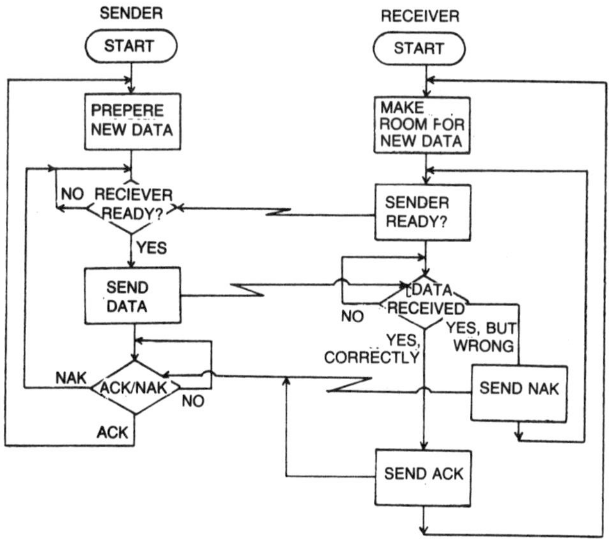

Figure 5.10

6 Private and public data networks

6.1 Introduction

For many years there has been a need to connect together users who made use of data communication in larger and larger systems. This has meant the introduction of 'data networks'. A data network is characterised by all subscribers being able to reach all the others with the aid of data communication. (In some cases, a certain group of subscribers only has access to a limited number of others). All subscribers have followed a particular protocol, which in most cases has been unique to each data network. If two data networks are to be joined up into a larger network, problems may occur if the protocols are different in each network. Because the large computer manufacturers have each developed their own methods, one tends to be bound to the supplier used in the building up of the data network.

Telecommunications administrations in different countries did not keep up with the rapid developments at the beginning, and therefore could not offer the services which were widely required. The users had to look after themselves as far as data communications were concerned, and buy the equipment they needed. Now, we have reached the stage where pure data communications services can be offered. The term data network now means a communications network with means of connection and end-equipment (i e terminals) which are designed solely for data communication.

We shall now look at some component parts of data communication networks in detail.

6.2 Transmission directions

The direction of transmission in a data network can either be one-way or two-way.

Simplex

Unidirectional transmission which takes place in the same direction the whole time.

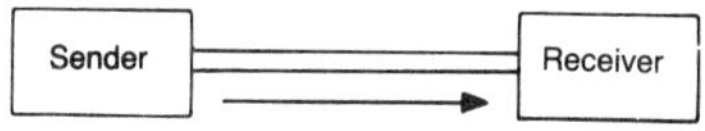

Figure 6.1 Simplex

Half duplex

Transmission may be in either direction, but not simultaneously.

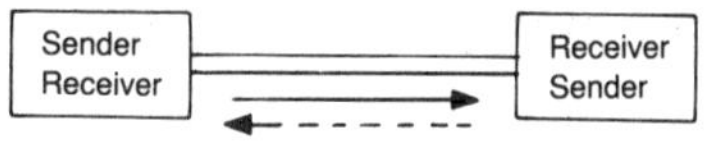

Figure 6.2 Half duplex

Waiting time with half duplex

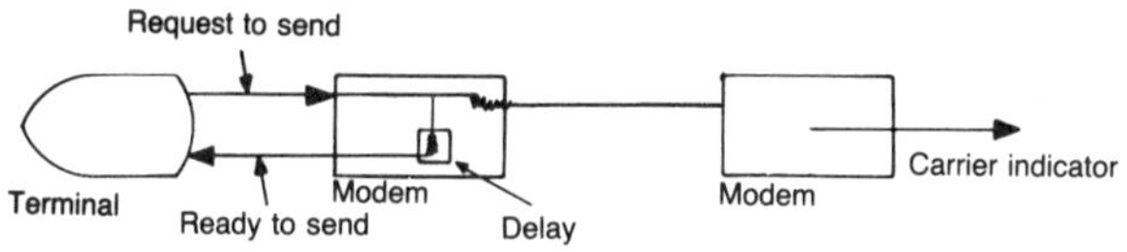

Figure 6.3 Waiting time in data transfer

Waiting time is always involved in half duplex. This is one reason for investing in full duplex, even if the line protocol only uses half duplex.

Typical waiting times:

- dialled connection 250 ms
- fixed connection 40 ms

Full duplex

Transmission can take place in both directions at the same time.

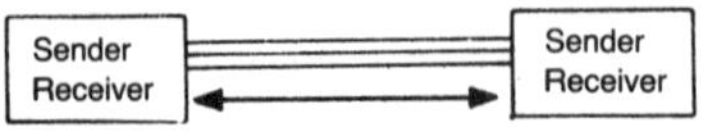

Figure 6.4 Full duplex

6.3 Centralised data communication and data processing functions

Point-to-point connection

This system forms a question/answer application in real time, with a relatively high requirement for short response times. There is only one user per line. Both ends of each line are equipped with data transmission equipment. The requests go from terminal to computer and responses in the opposite direction. There is no traffic between terminals.

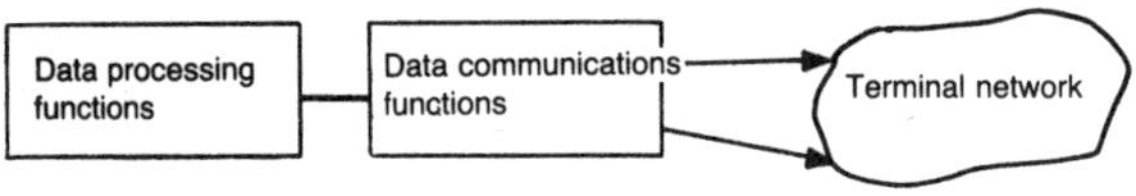

Figure 6.5

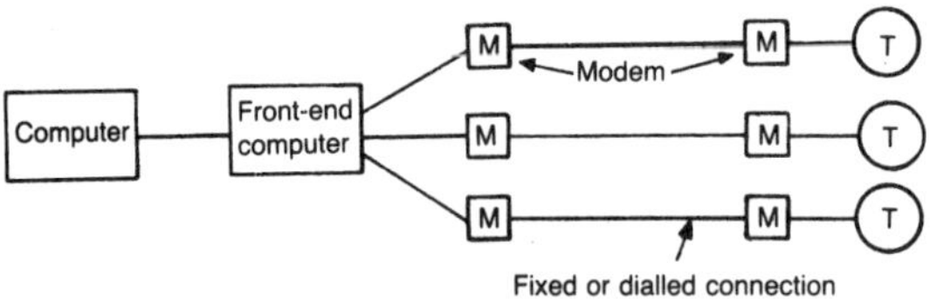

Figure 6.6 Point-to-point

One fixed connection per terminal is a very costly exercise, with poor use of lines.

Dialled lines are unsuitable in a data network because of the long connection times.

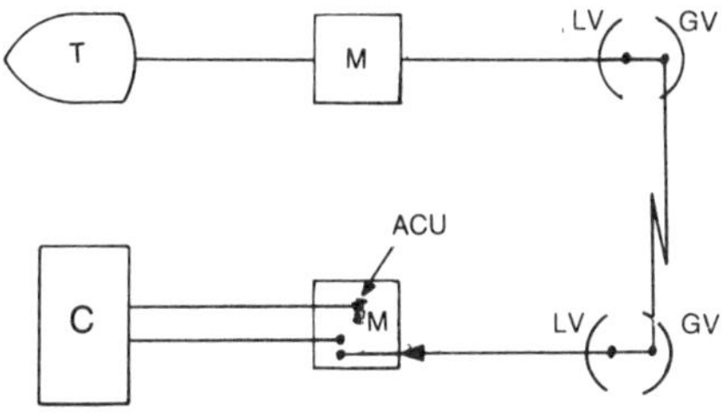

C=Computer
T=Terminal
M=Modem
LV-GV=Selector, public exchange

Figure 6.7

Multi-point configuration

Better use of a fixed line can be obtained by connecting several subscribers to a common line under the control of a computer. The computer controls the use of the line with the aid of a data communications procedure. The subscribers' transmissions are controlled by polling. The polled terminal sends its block, prepared beforehand, and receives acknowledgement from the computer. If a transmission fault is detected during the block check, a negative acknowledgement is received and the terminal sends it again. If the terminal has nothing to transmit, it sends a special control character. The computer then passes on immediately to the next terminal or control unit. The method requires the computer to poll every control unit or terminal individually. The transmission of data to the terminals is done by 'addressing'. Two methods are used for this. 'Fast select', where the address is sent in the same block as the message, and 'normal select', where the terminal is first asked whether it is ready to receive.

By choosing the right number of drop points on the line, a balance may be struck between good traffic usage and short response time. The method requires a high polling frequency on the part of the computer, as the waiting time between successive pollings is added directly to the response time.

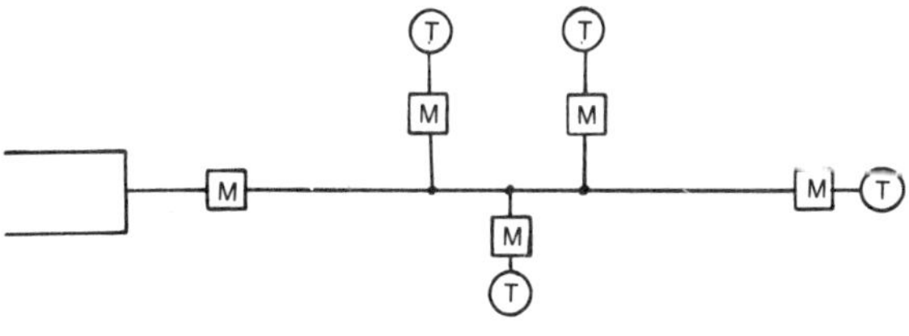

Figure 6.8

Loop configuration

The frequent polling in multipoint configurations means that the probability of a 'nothing to send' response is high. The polling also causes a load on the computer's CPU. This led in many earlier computer systems to the choice of another network configuration with a lower number of polls and a lower proportion of fruitless ones. This network design is usually known as a loop.

A loop network consists of subscribers and a computer which controls the transmissions. All traffic goes clockwise around the loop (see Figure 6.9). In a loop system, each subscriber's equipment passes on what it received round the loop from the previous terminal, with the possible addition of its own information. The computer controls the subscribers' traffic by polling.

The computer first sends out a 'general poll'. In response, those terminals which have something to send add their own address, and send the poll and the address further round the loop. Terminals which have nothing to send just pass on the poll and earlier addresses without adding their own. At the other end of the loop the computer receives the poll, together with the identities of the relevant terminals. Thereafter, the computer polls these terminals in turn. The terminals send their information on round the loop when they are polled.

Acknowledgements are sent by the computer in the same transmission direction and they are repeated round the loop. The computer regards a correctly received positive acknowledgement as showing that the terminal in question has also received it correctly. The terminal exchanges a negative acknowledgement for a re-transmission of the same information.

Traffic to the terminals is addressed via a select command. Transmission also occurs clockwise in this case. In order that removal of a terminal does not cause failure of the whole loop to function, there is an automatic through connection if a terminal becomes inoperative.

Multipoint configurations are considerably more common than loop models in modern networks. This is partly because these systems include powerful front-end computers (communications computers). The front-end computer does all the polling and selecting, and thereby relieves the central computer from this work.

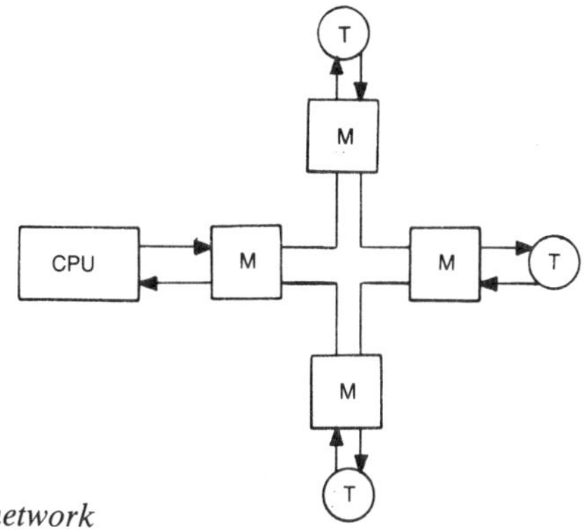

Figure 6.9 Loop network

6.4 Distributed communications functions

Star configuration

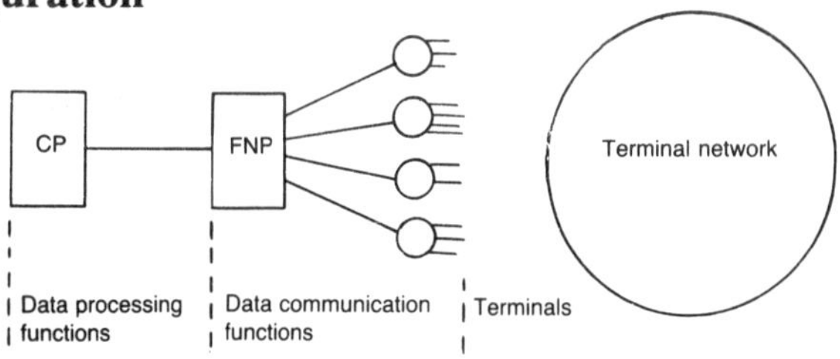

Figure 6.10

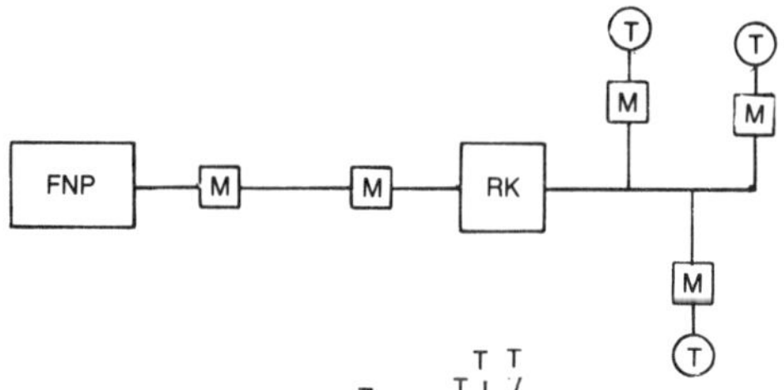

Figure 6.11

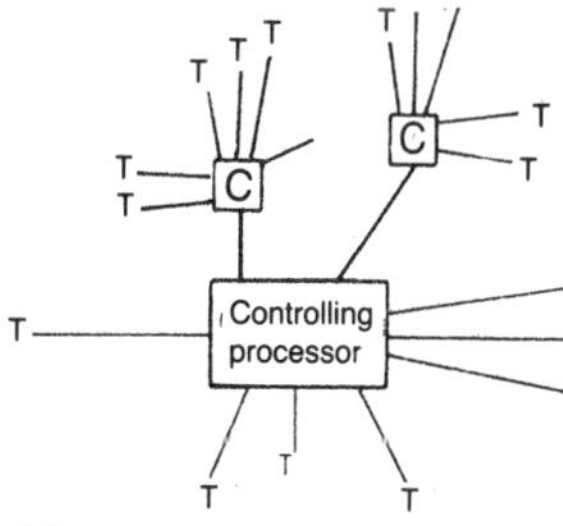

Figure 6.12 Star network with concentrators

As in previous examples, it is the computer (usually a communications computer) which controls the whole configuration. In the system illustrated in Figure 6.12, a number of terminals have been connected to a concentrator (thus forming a star in the network). In this way, the number of incoming lines to the central computer can be reduced. Line costs can thus be kept down, and better use made of the lines in use.

Polling is reduced, as the communications computer only has to poll the concentrators, so reducing somewhat the central load.

The concentrators are 'intelligent', so that apart from polling terminals, they can also carry out some processing on the incoming data. This is an additional help in reducing the load on the central processing unit.

Star configurations are the most common types today.

6.5 Distributed data processing functions

Mesh configuration

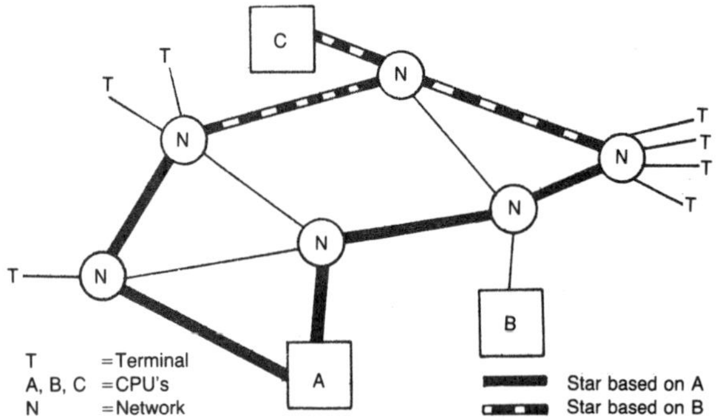

Figure 6.13

In a distributed system, traffic must be able to be exchanged between a number of terminals and computers in any combination; terminal-terminal, terminal-computer and computer-computer. The connections must be able to use different data speeds for different users. The traffic is characterised by varying demands on transfer time for different types of traffic.

The network is built up of a number of intermediate nodes, which are connected together by fixed two-way lines. Each section of line works with a full duplex data communication protocol. Terminals or computers are connected to the nodes in the network.

The traffic routes are selected adaptively at each node. The transmitter specifies the receiving node and address in the message (block) header. The route which the node chooses is that which will give the shortest transfer time to the receiver node on each occasion. As a basis for such decisions, each node contains a table which gives the expected transfer time via the respective lines to all other nodes in the network. The table is updated periodically by information exchange with neighbouring nodes. The times vary according to the current traffic loading and any interference on the lines between the nodes and in the nodes themselves.

The network can be designed so that the choice of route is adaptive even for different blocks in the same message. The ordering of the blocks may be changed, as an earlier block in a message may happen to be sent on a route which turns out to be longer that than for a later block in the same message.

In such a network, it rests with the receiver node to store the blocks temporarily, and to sort them into number order before sending them on to the receiving terminal. In order to avoid this, other types of networks fix the route after it has been chosen, so that the blocks following on always take the same route as the first one.

Every computer in a distributed system is a ‘central computer’ in its local part of the network.

6.6 Separated communications and data processing functions

General data network

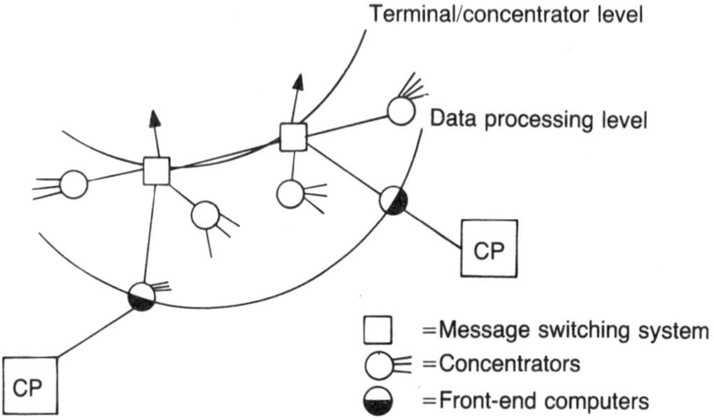

Figure 6.14

A general data network may be thought of in broad terms as similar to the above diagram. It is optimised from the very beginning for data communication, and is given features required for that purpose.

The traditional telephone network allows very little in the way of error checking of, for example, the modem; the service level is therefore low. There are failures from the point of view of data security. The transmission characteristics of the telephone network are optimised for speech communication.

The limitations of the telephone network have contributed to the development of a data network for general use, the 'public data network', which in its turn can be either 'general' or 'private'.

Large private networks which have been in use some years are ARPANET (USA), SWIFT (banks in Europe and North America) and SITA (the network for e g seat reservations between airline companies). A typical feature of these 'large' data networks is that they consist of an interconnection of many 'small' data networks.

Three types of switching in data networks may be categorised

- CIRCUIT switching
- MESSAGE switching
- PACKET switching

6.7 Circuit switching

Definition (from Swedish Standards Organisation, SIS):

- A process which on demand connects two or more data terminals, and which allows exclusive use of data lines until they are disconnected.

Some other characteristics

- Dialling
  - one transmission channel is reserved
- Transmission
- direct acknowledgement that the message has arrived
- no intermediate storage
- same transmission speed at both ends
- synchronous or asynchronous

Circuit switching is in all essential aspects similar to conventional connections in a telephone network. Here, a line is connected between sender and receiver. The line remains connected until data transmission is over and disconnection is requested.

The Scandinavian data network is based on the connection principle. For further information on DATEX see section 6.10.

6.8 Message switching

SIS definition:

- A process for the transmission of messages by receiving, storing and re-transmitting complete messages within a data network.

Some other characteristics

- Transmission
  - intermediate storage in the transmission system
  - storage can cause problems of security
  - transmitting and receiving terminals can have different speeds
  - asynchronous
- Not real-time
- Saves lines

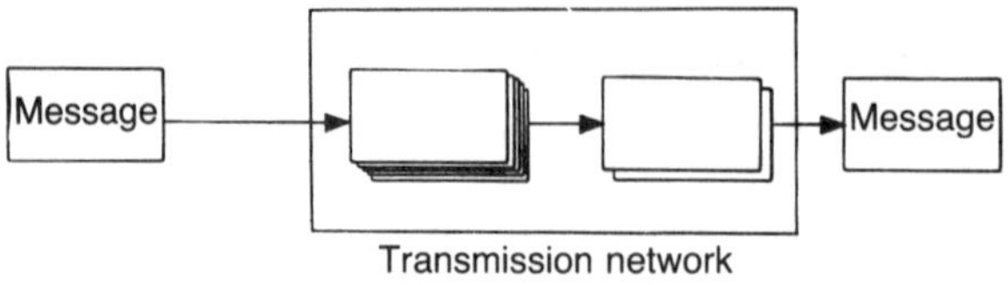

Figure 6.15

Message switching works on the following principles. Messages from different transmitters to the same addressee are collected up in the nodes of the network and then sent on, perhaps through several nodes. This only occurs when enough messages have been collected to make a long-distance connection economic.

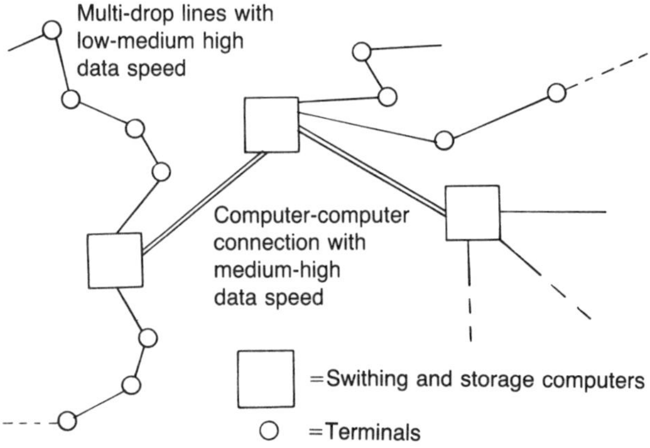

Figure 6.16 Network configuration for message system

Figures 6.16 and 6.17 show the design of a message switching network. The nodes, which can be regarded as equivalent to concentrators with considerably extended functions, consist of a computer with large storage capacity. The computer collects messages from, and distributes messages to, the local terminals. Messages to a distant suscriber are collected in the node's disc memory. When a suitable number of messages which are to be sent to addressees at the same node have been collected, they are sent on their way. At the next node they may perhaps be split up and stored (for a further short time). Together with other messages, they reach their destination. Message switching is used where a certain amount of delay in the network can be tolerated. It is particularly suitable where the demand on transmission time depends on the type of message, and where every message can be assigned a certain priority.

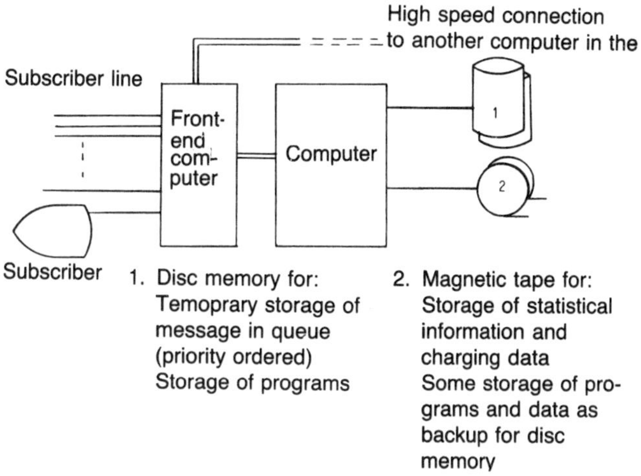

Figure 6.17 Node in a message switching network

6.9 Packet switching

SIS definition

- A process for the sending of data as addressed packets, whereby the line in question is responsible only for the transfer of the data packet, and is then freed for other transmissions.

Some other characteristics

- Transmission
  - synchronous
  - transmitting and receiving can be done at different speeds
  - the message can be sent by many different routes, giving greater security.
- Saves lines
- Lines are used more effectively
- Faster than message switching

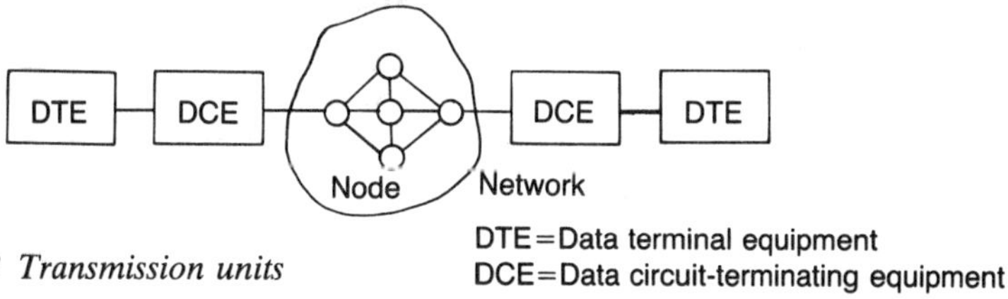

Figure 6.18 Transmission units

Subscribers are connected to 'nodes', and the nodes are connected by links. Certain nodes sometimes only have switching capabilities. There is a computer at every node which switches incoming packets to the right link, 'routing', or out of the network to the addresse. In the nodes to which subscribers are connected, there is also a PAD (packet assembler/disassembler), which is a device for forming packets and the combination of packets into messages. The interface between the data network and the subscribers may be said to be the PAD.

For the user, transmission through the network behaves like circuit switching, but with practically no connection time. The user gives the message to the network via the PAD and receives complete messages from the network, wholly unaware of the highways and byways which the parts of the message (=packets) have been through in the network before they reach the addressee. In the network, meanwhile, a rather complicated process has been in progress. The packets are rapidly sent by PAD on their way out into the network. The first packet has already gone before the message, if it is a long one, has been delivered to PAD. As in most traffic systems, the task of the network is to get rid of the traffic. If the traffic is high, each node must make sure that it delivers the packets which are already there before any new ones are let into the node from PAD. Road traffic is a useful comparison. At a roundabout, those cars which are already on the roundabout are usually allowed to proceed before those who want to come onto it. If, on the continent, one kept strictly to the principle of giving way to traffic on the right, it would soon fill up in heavy traffic and cause a jam.

At each node, the packets from the incoming links are sorted out into transit packets if they are to go further over the network, and into outgoing packets if the addressee is connected to that node. The transit packets are stored in the buffer ready to be sent by certain lines to the correct node. Every packet sent off is held in the buffer until ACK has been received from the node at the other end of the line.

The task of the node is to get rid of the incoming packets as quickly as possible. (One descriptive nickname which has been applied to the data packet system is the 'hot potato system'!). If the shortest route to the addressee node is busy, so that the next node on the route cannot receive more packets because its buffer is full, the node can choose another, longer, route, if this is forthcoming. The main reason is that the node tries to avoid filling its buffer up. However, it must be aware that some packets have a higher priority than others. Queues may then occur, when the buffers fill up even more. This happens when the incoming traffic is greater than the outgoing. (Traffic is measured in numbers of packets per unit time). If a node fills up its buffers, then no other node can get rid of those packets which have to go to the full node. The buffers fill up in more and more nodes, and the system soon snarls up.

In order to avoid a total stoppage in the packet switching system, a network control computer often has to be used to change the existing priority rules so that the whole thing will work. The control computer, which is normally an expanded node computer, needs information on the traffic situation at every node for this job. This status information is sent over the same lines on which the packets are transmitted. This status information is given the highest priority of all, so that it will be transmitted even when the system is filling up or becoming blocked. Each buffer has a reserved space which can only be used for status messages (status information contains considerably fewer bits than data packets).

The job of choosing links at a node is clearly no easy job, assuming that the system has not been over-sized so that blockages could only occur in exceptional circumstances. There are several methods for choice of link, and these are four of the common ones

- *Pre-determined routing*
  The route through the network is decided upon before the packet is sent off. Either the user or the network control computer can decide the route.

- *Calculated routing*
  Each node from the sender to the receiver calculates the route to be used from a simple algorithm.

- *Table routing, static*
  Each node has a 'table', which specifies which link is to be used for packets with a certain address. The table can be altered by the control computer.

- *Table routing, dynamic*
  This is the most sophisticated method. The node computer modifies the table according to the traffic situation, so that the best link is chosen.

One may now ask what advantages a data packet switching system, which to say the least looks complicated, has over a circuit switching system, which appears simple and straightforward. The answer is that a well-dimensioned data packet system gives a very efficient use of the lines, but at the cost of more complicated switching equipment. For data communication with many users spread out over a large geographical area, and where there are proportionately few lines installed, data packet switching can sometimes be the only economically feasible alternative. In Sweden and the other Scandinavian countries there is a very well-developed telephone network, where lines can be 'leased' for data communication without noticeably affecting other telephone traffic. This is why the simpler circuit switching system has been able to be used instead of data packet switching in the Scandinavian data network.

Most of the large networks are of the packet-switching type. An interface is therefore required between the Scandinavian network, which is based on X.21, and the other large networks based on X.25, if any form of communication between subscribers to the respective networks is required.

Finally, there follows a general overview showing how two X.25 terminals communicate.

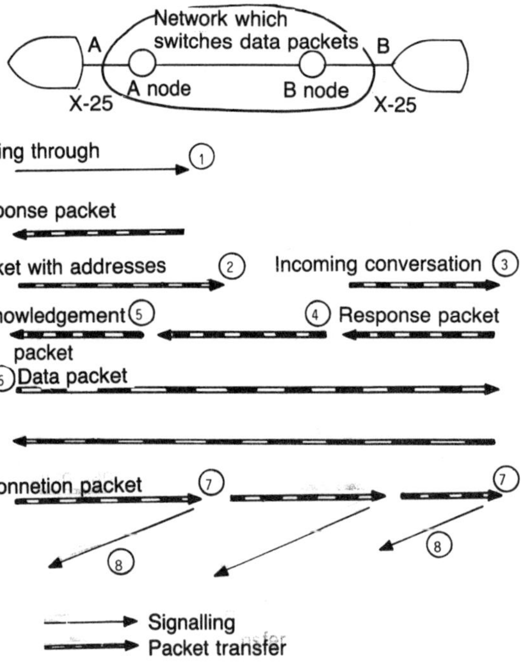

Figure 6.19

When a subscriber wants to establish a connection with node A, he activates the node via the connection ①. When he has received the response signal, the subscriber can begin to send a control packet with both his own and the receiver's addresses ②. If the network is not at fault or overloaded, a packet is sent which indicates to the receiver's node (node B) that an incoming message is on the way ③. If there is a fault in the node or if the network is overloaded, a response packet is sent explaining why the packet sent out cannot be received. When the target subscriber has received a positive response, node B sends an acknowledgement packet to this effect to node A ④. Later, node A sends an acknowledgement packet to the A subscriber to say that the data connection has been established ⑤. The A subscriber can then start to send his data to the target subscriber ⑥. The line is disconnected by sending a special control packet ⑦, and finally, disconnection ⑧.

6.10 The Scandinavian data network DATEX

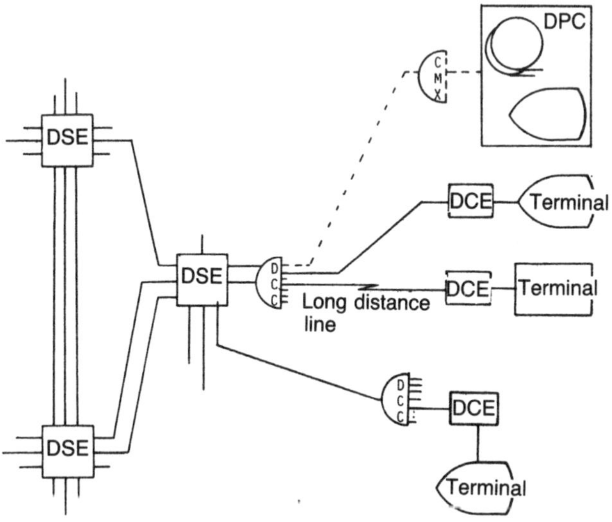

Figure 6.20 DATEX network design

DSE Data switching exchange
DCC Data circuit concentrator
DTE Data terminal equipment
CMX Customer multiplexor
DPC Data processing center
DCE Data circuit terminating equipment

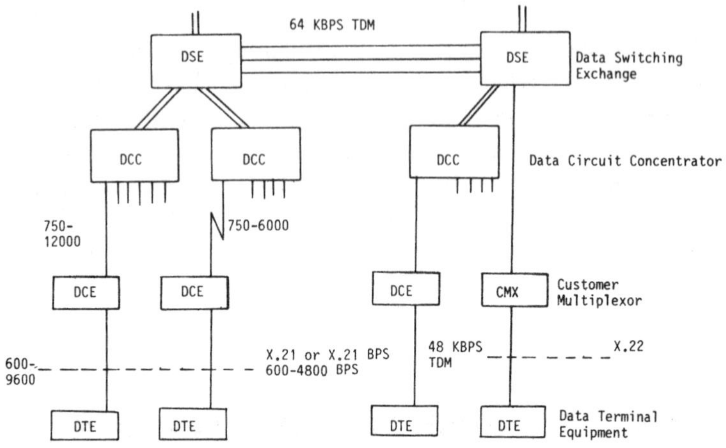

Figure 6.21 DATEX structure

Basic characteristics

- wholly synchronously-connected network
- time division multiplexing technique (TDM)
- data exchanges controlled by program memory (SPC)
- functional and capacitative modularity
- advanced running and maintenance system
- follows the applicable CCITT recommendations
- suited to today's and tomorrow's terminals
- uses formatted transmission in the network (format 8+2).

Structure of the network

The Datex network is a coordinated network covering Denmark, Finland, Norway and Sweden.

The network is structured according to the existing relevant international recommendations. This means that computer equipment with an internationally approved interface can be connected to the network.

Technically, the network is of the circuit switching type. This means that a fixed connection is set up through the network during the whole data transfer period.

All transmission is synchronous, i e data transfer follows the speed given by the network. It is however possible to connect asynchronous low-speed terminals via an interface in the network's connection equipment.

Internally within the network, transmission uses the format 8+2 bits. The extra two bits are added into the bit sequence and taken out by the network itself. They are used for synchronisation and to distinguish customer data and signalling information from each other. This means that the network works internally at a speed 25% higher than that used by the subscriber.

The components of the Datex network are connected up as shown in Figure 6.20.

DSE is the electronic Datex exchange which controls the connection and disconnection of data calls and monitors the functions and connections in the network. The DSE contains running and maintenance functions, and it also copes with the charging and collects statistics. There are at present about 20,000 possible connections, and 100 dialogues per exchange can be connected each second. See Figure 6.22.

The concentrators DCC are connected to the DSE via time-multiplexed high speed lines with a speed of 64 kbits/s. The concentrator collects traffic from a number of different subscriber lines, and it is controlled and monitored from the data exchange.

The outermost part of Datex is the Datex connection unit DCE, and this is placed with the subscriber (see also Chapter 14). Its task is to provide the standardised interface with the network. The network contains a completely automatic monitoring and fault localisation system, and the DCE is also included in this.

There are four types of DCE, depending on the type of connection

- if the computer equipment is suited to general data networks using the circuit switching technique, the DCE is of the DCE-X type. With this DCE it is possible to use all the subscriber services on the network.
- If the data equipment is actually designed for connection to the telephone network, the DCE is of type DCE-V, DCE-VP or DCE-VPC. Some of these (DCE-VP, DCE-VPC) are provided with a numeric keypad through which information on choices can be entered into the network. If the data equipment is asynchronous, a DCE is used which converts the data to a synchronous character stream (DCE-VPC); see the table on DCE's below.

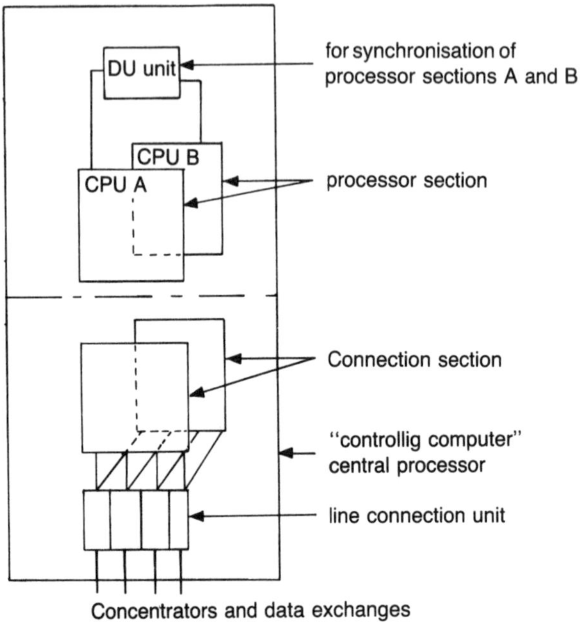

Figure 6.22 Main parts of a data exchange

The DCE has indicators on it which tell whether the synchronisation on the network is working, and whether the DCE is being tested. Depending on the type of connection, suitable modem equipment may be built on or connected separately to the DCE.

The Datex network transmits data in four different speed classes, 600, 2400, 4800 or 9600 bits/s. Datex can thus be looked on as being four different networks by the user, one for each speed class. The lowest speed class can also be used for data equipment designed for lower transmission speeds, e g 300 bits/s.

Table of DCE

- DCE-X DCE with X.21 interface
- DCE-V DCE with V.24 interface
- DCE-VP DCE with V.24 interface and panel for manual signalling
- DCE-VPC DCE with V.24 interface and panel for manual signalling and asynchronous/synchronous conversion.

Subscriber services

There are two groups of services in Datex

- Basic services (network parameters or basic characteristics)
- Additional services which the user can subscribe to as required

Basic services

Connections

The data equipment is connected to the network via standardised data interfaces (X.21) or a modem-like interface (X.21 bis/X.20 bis, corresponding to V.24). Connection is made via a Datex connection unit (DCE) which the Swedish Telephone company issues. Connection using X.21 gives the user flexible access to all the basic functions of the network and the possibility of using all the additional facilities.

Full duplex

Full duplex means that data can be transferred at the same speed at the same time in both directions. (When the call is connected through, all bit combinations can be transmitted, so that the user is free to choose his own code, format and transmission procedure).

Synchronisation

All synchronous data equipment connected up is synchronised by the network, which gives a pulse for each data bit (bit synchronisation). In addition, a separate pulse can be given every 8th bit if required (byte synchronisation). The speed is the same for both the sending and the receiving equipment.

Transmission speeds

The user can subscribe to the 600, 2400, 4800 or 9600 bits/s synchronous transmission speeds. However, 9600 bits/s can only be used by subscribers with short connection to the network. With the aid of special data network connecting apparatus, asynchronous terminals at up to 2400 bits/s can also be connected. In this case the network timing pulses are ignored by the DCE, and the terminal understands the transmission to be asynchronous. Seen from the network, however, the transmission is synchronous.

Subscriber numbers

Each connection to Datex is normally given a six-digit number. The number series covers the whole country, so that town or county codes are not required. The first part of the number gives the accounting area and is used for determining traffic costs. If a subscriber moves within his area, he can keep the same number.

Calling

Calling can either be done manually from data equipment or the Datex connection unit, or automatically from a terminal, depending on the type of interface. A subscriber can call up any other within the same speed class. A dialogue is begun by the transfer of the desired number to the network. Data transmission can occur any time after this, as soon as the network has said that the connection is made.

Automatic answering

DATEX is designed so that a response is given automatically from all lines called. Manual answering is not possible.

Connection time

The time taken from when the desired number is sent to the Datex network until the network informs the subscriber that data transmission can begin is specified as follows

<100 ms for 90% of calls (country-wide traffic)
<500 ms for 99% of calls
<2 seconds for 100% of calls

Disconnection time

The time taken between the subscriber giving the finish signal and the network closing down the connection is specified as follows

< 50 ms for 90% of calls
<200 ms for 100% of calls

Status signals

All calls from data equipment are answered automatically by the network. If the dialogue cannot be established immediately, Datex gives information on the status of the call. If, for example, the subscriber tries to call a unit which is in 'local' mode, he will be informed by Datex why the connection cannot be made. The various status signals are given below.

DATEX status signals

02 Transferred call. The subscriber called can't receive data (e g due to malfunction). The call is transferred to another subscriber. Wait for connection.

03 Wait in queue. The subscriber called is engaged. The call is stacked in a queue. Wait for your turn.

20 Try again.

21 Engaged. Try again later.

22 Procedure error. Calling procedure has not been followed.

23 Transmission fault. An error has occurred on the call signal on its way to the central control.

41 Lack of authorisation, e g because the subscriber called is not part of the same closed user group.

42 Number changed.

43 Number unobtainable. The subscriber called is no longer connected.

44 Seek information. The subscriber called is temporarily out of order.

45 Local mode. The subscriber called is working in local mode.

46 DTE failure on called subscriber. The subscriber called is out of the traffic.

47 Power failure at called DCE.

48 Disallowed service. Attempt made to use a disallowed service.

49 Fault on subscriber's line. The fault lies with the subscriber called.

51 Contact the telephone company.

52 Wrong speed. The subscriber called is using another speed class. The line cannot therefore be connected for technical reasons.

61 Network blockage. Temporary network problem.

69 Keyboard is functioning. Proved by test of own DCE.

96 Test OK. Proved by test of own DCE.

Additional services

If the user wants more services from Datex than those that come with the subscription, he can subscribe to one or more additional services. These allow limitation of the calls made to or from a terminal (for data security), simplified connection methods, different debiting methods, etc.

The subscription is ordered either for continued or time-limited use. The services are accessible according to three principles

- automatically for every dialogue
- automatically for every call during a period defined by the subscriber
- only where the service is requested when the call is made.

The access to the services depends on the type of service and how it is arranged in the data network.

These are some examples of additional services

- Direct calling can be used when one terminal is always to be connected to one and the same connection. An example of this may be a terminal which always calls the same service bureau. This service at the same time prevents unauthorised use of the terminal.
- Blocks on outgoing or incoming calls are two services which can also be used to restrict traffic to the terminal or computer.
- The choice of short numbers means that frequently-called numbers can be given a short code, which shortens calling time. A subscriber can have up to 99 short numbers.
- A closed user group means that a number of connections form a sort of own network group. Calling to or from terminals outside the group is prevented by the network. This service can be used from the data security point of view, for example a company's computer system with distant terminals.
- Group numbers are used when several connections, e g to a service bureau computer, are equivalent. All connections get the same subscriber number and traffic is spread over the ingoing lines. This service can, for example, simplify the calling of a central computer from terminals.
- Queuing space for incoming calls allows incoming calls to wait if the line is engaged. The caller gets a status signal which indicates waiting. It is possible to subscribe to a service 'not allowing waiting' to avoid paying for time spent waiting.

- It is possible to obtain identification both of the number called and the one calling from the network. This can be used to raise the level of data security. This service is only available for subscribers with DCE-X.
- Payment for incoming calls means that the subscriber called is debited for the cost of the dialogue. This can simplify accounting in a data collection system with widespread terminals.
- Charging information can be obtained from the network for all calls or only those requested. Costs can be followed continuously using this service. The service is only available to subscribers using DCE-X.

Subscribers' DCE data equipment

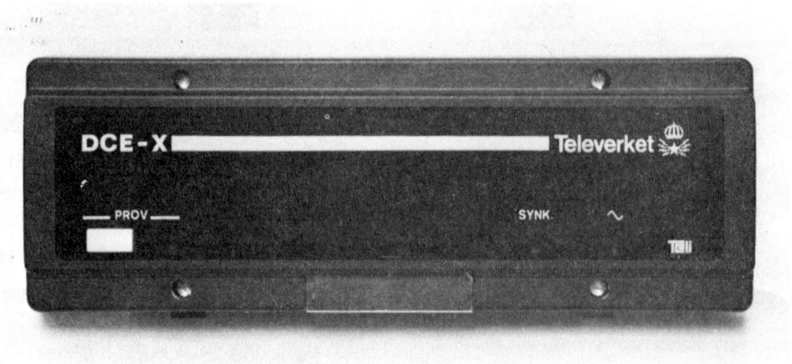

Figure 6.23 DCE-X

DCE-X is used when the data equipment is designed for connection to synchronous circuit-switched data networks, i e the data equipment is suitable for using the Datex network to its full, including all the additional services.

There are three lamps and 1 button (the test button) on the front panel.

~	The lamp lights when the power is connected.
TEST	The lamp lights when the button is pressed in, indicating testing of the terminal or the network. The lamp flashes if the test is satisfactory. If the lamp stays on, the test was not successful.
SYN	The lamp lights as long as the DCE is format-synchronised to the network.

Interface

Connection of the subscriber's equipment, DTE, is via a 15-pin plug, complying with international standard ISO DIS 4903, on the back of the DCE.

The interface, whose functioning is described in CCITT recommendation X.21, contains the following interface circuits:

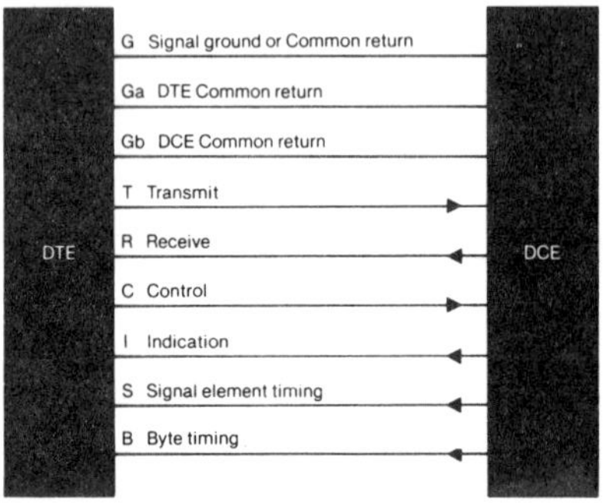

Figure 6.24 Interface circuits

The DCE-V series (types DCE-V, DCE-VP, DCE-VPC) are used when the data equipment is actually designed for connection via a modem to the telephone network.

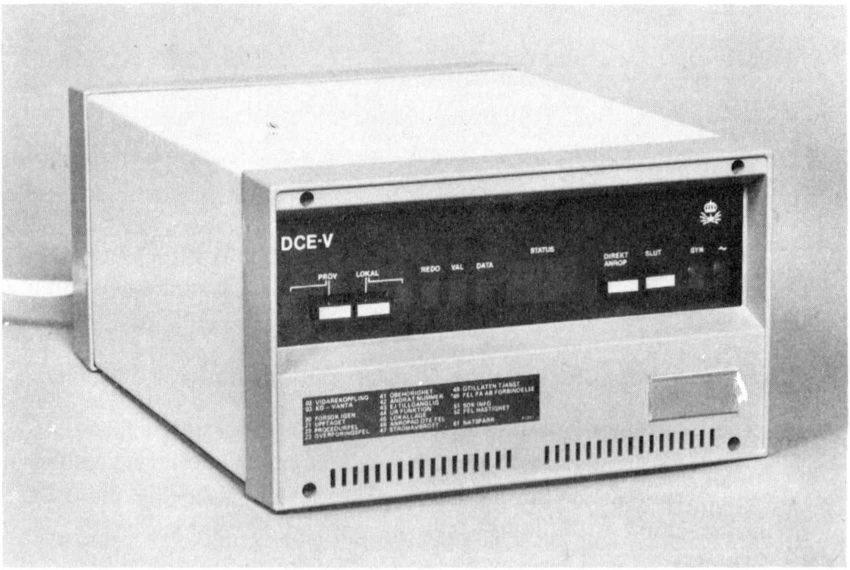

Figure 6.25 DCE-V

Using DCE-V types imply a limitation to the network's facilities which can be used. The three types are functionally different:

V = suited for connection of data equipment via the V interface
C = supplied with asynchronous/synchronous converter for the connection of asynchronous data equipment
P = fitted with a numeric keypad for numerical input.

DCE-V used with synchronous data equipment which is not used for outgoing calls, or is only used for direct calling in conjunction with the additional services. Direct calling can take place either from data equipment or DCE.

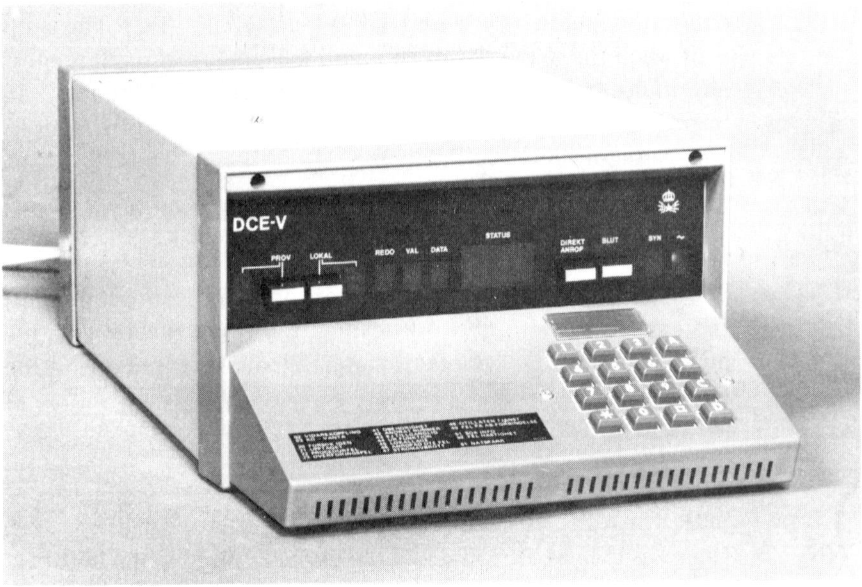

Figure 6.26 DCE-VP and DCE-VPC

DCE-VP used with synchronous data equipment where numerical input, direct calling or selectable direct call is to be carried out from the DCE. Direct calling can also be done from the DTE providing that other ways of calling are not to be used.

DCE-VPC is used with asynchronous data equipment where the factors for calling are the same as for DCE-VP.

Lamps and buttons on the front panel have the following functions:

~	Lights when mains power is applied.
TEST	The lamp lights when the button is pressed in (e g in fault localisation), or when tests are carried out from the network.
LOCAL	This button is used to switch the DCE to local mode, e g for a local test of the data equipment. When the DCE is in this condition, the subscriber can neither call or respond to calls. The lamp lights when the button is pressed.
READY	The lamp lights to indicate that calls can be made or received.
CHOOSE	(Only applies to DCE-V). The lamp is lit to indicate that the network has received the subscriber's call request and is in the connection phase. (Only for DCE-VP and DCE-VPC). The lamp is lit when the network has accepted the subscriber's call request and indicates at the same time that the choice of number can begin. With direct calling, it indicates that the network is in its connecting-up phase.
DATA	The lamp lights as long as the line is connected to the called subscriber.
STATUS	Shows the status signals from the network when connection fails. In connections with network testing, the result is shown on the number indicator. A table of status signals is supplied with the DCE.
DIRECT CALL	Used for connecting the line in 'direct call'.
END	Used when the line is disconnected.
SYN	Lights as long as the DCE is format synchronised to the network.

On DCE-VP and DCE-VPC there are also the following buttons on the panel, for use when connecting up

	numbers 0–9
*	=call
#	=end of numerical choice
A	=prefix to short number choice
B	=distinguishing characters on the choice of several services (not valid in the first stage of the network)
C	=End of services selection
D	=End (disconnection)

Interface

Connection of the subscriber's equipment is via a 25-pin plug on the back of the DCE.

The plug follows the international standard ISO/DIS 2110.2. Where the data equipment is supplied with a 37-pin socket (in accordance with ISO/DIS 4902), connection to the DCE is via an adapter.

The interface, whose function is as described in CCITT recommendation X.21 bis for synchronous and X.20 bis for asynchronous data equipment, contains the following interface circuits:

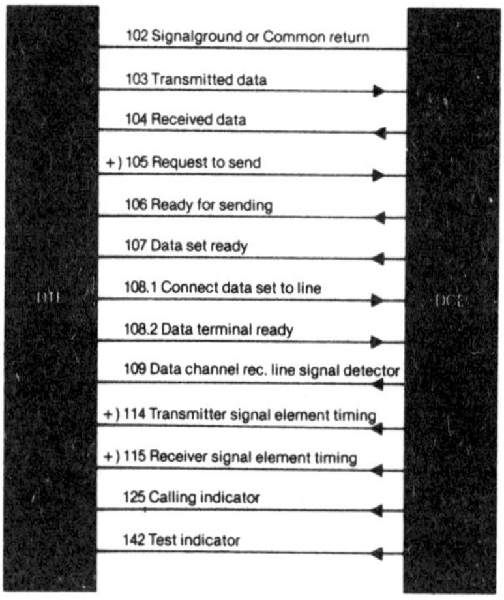

Figure 6.27 Interface circuits

Further developments

In 1981, the Datex network had the capacity for about 5,000 subscriber connections. The present expansion plans stretch to 1988 when the capacity is estimated to be 50,000 lines. Thereafter, the network will be expanded in line with demand.

Several data networks in other countries are designed using packet switching (Datapak). In order to be able to offer subscribers the ability to exchange data with these networks, the packet switching service Datapak was introduced 1981.

This means that Datex connections via Datapak can talk to packet-switching networks in other countries.

For subscribers with large volumes of traffic, it can often be practical to concentrate the traffic at the periphery of the network. This is possible through the development of a special subscriber CMX multiplexer. This replaces a number of DCE's and is installed at the subscriber's terminal.

General data networks in Europe

Country	Type	Name	Running in 1982	Capacity in 1982
West Germany	CS	Datex-L	Yes	6000
	PS	Datex-P	Yes	1000 C 71 P
Denmark	CS	Datex	Yes	3600
Spain	PS	IBERPAC	Yes	15.600 C 395 P
Finland	CS	Datex	Yes	1500
France	PS	Transpac	Yes	2700 C 6300 P
Italy	CS		On trial	
Norway	CS	Datex	Yes	2200
	PS	Norpak	Yes	
Holland	PS	Datenet 1	Yes	1800 P
Great Britain	PS	PSS/ISS	Yes	2500 C 1200 P
Sweden	CS	Datex	Yes	8000
	PS	Telepak	Yes	128 C 60 P
Switzerland	PS	Telepac	Yes	200 C 200 P

CS =circuit switched
PS =packet switched
C =character mode ports
P =packet mode ports

Information for Datex subscribers

Charging principles

The following charges apply generally to Datex subscribers

- one-off charge for main subscription
- subscription charges for main subscription
- traffic charges
- charges for additional services

One-off and subscription charges are fixed and independent of traffic. One-off charges vary with transmission speed.

The subscription charges vary partly with transmission speed and partly with distance code and the number of call units begun. In addition, charges are made for all calls, whether they are successful or not. However, no charge is made for calls not leading to dialogue because of faults or blockages on the telephone company's equipment.

Traffic charges

Sweden is divided into 24 geographical Datex charging areas (DCA's). The first two numbers in the subscriber's number give the DCA of the subscriber. Call charges are dependent on distance, and are divided into three distance classes. Connections to other Scandinavian countries and West Germany are debited by special charges.

7 Distributed data networks

7.1 Introduction

Most of the larger computer suppliers use the term "network architecture" to describe the system philosophy which is based on division into levels. This is descibed in Chapter 5. Manufacturers love abbreviations. Here are some examples:

- IBM SNA Systems Network Architecture
- UNISYS DCA Distributed Communication Architecture
- Honeywell Bull DSA Distributed System Architecture

This philosophy must become reality before distributed data processing and all its possibilities can fully benefit its users. We are already part of the way there today by the moving of data processing resources closer to the user.

The architecture is based on the production of rules which describe the design, construction and running of communications systems in a standardised way. The large computer manufacturers have their own well-developed concepts, which allow cooperation between systems of their own make, but which do not allow communication between different makes. Is this a familiar story?

7.2 SNA (Systems Network Architecture)

The IBM network architecture – SNA, which is the best known, was produced in order to satisfy the need for flexibility and to allow the building up of an effective network at a reasonable cost. The logical interface within the system – between control units, lines and terminals – is standardised. By this means it is possible to build up a network in which everyone has access to most of the applications to be found in the central system.

SNA defines the units in a communications system (CS), their functions and the links between them. The junctions in the network are known as nodes, i e physical units. These take a central role, as there is there a certain degree of 'intelligence'.

There are the following types of nodes

- Host Node (HN)
- Communications Controller Node (CUCN)
- Cluster Controller Node (CCN)
- Terminal Node (TN)

The Host Node is comparable with the central system (CPU) with operating system, file handling system, databases and applications programs (Figure 7.1).

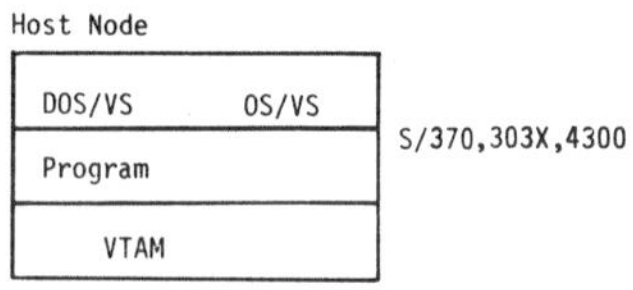

Figure 7.1 Host Node

The Communications Controller Nodes are programmable units, and may be regarded as 'slaves' to the Host Node. The main task of the CUCN is to control that part of the network to which it is connected. Some of its functions are to handle the communications lines, remove and insert control characters, activate and deactivate lines, translate character codes, etc. The aim of the node is to control that part of the network which lies outside the Host Node (Figure 7.2).

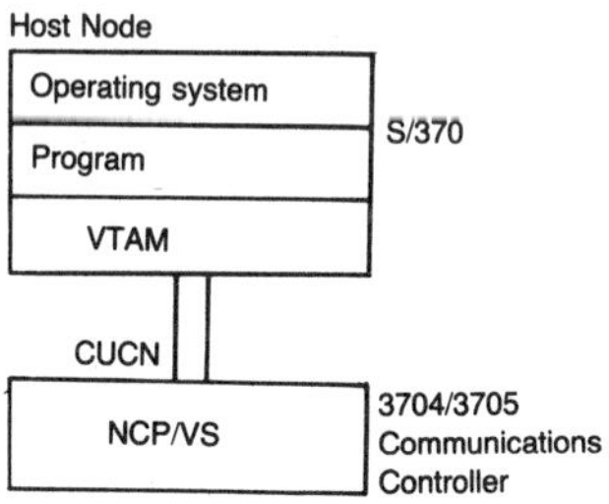

Figure 7.2 Communications Controller Node

The Cluster Controller Node is a control unit which makes it possible for an 'end user' (i e terminal operator) to get information out of the database in the central system. A large number of terminals and printers of various types can be connected to this control unit. It appears as a terminal to the communications system (CS), but it can also carry out data processing, and it is in itself a 'small' computer (e g 8100). There are also types of CCN which cannot carry out data processing (3276). This node could therefore be regarded as a distributed data processing system within the SNA system (Figure 7.3).

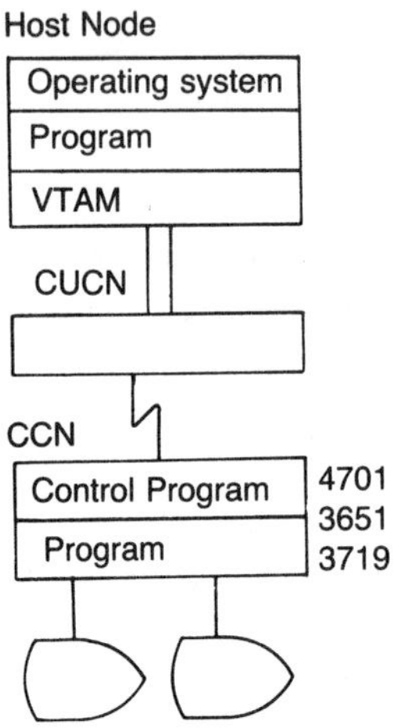

Figure 7.3 Cluster Controller Node

The Terminal Node, which is not programmable, is used for fetching in and sending data from and to the Host Node. Examples of TN's are IBM 3277, 3767, 3614 and 3624. Figure 7.4 shows all four types of terminal and the IBM description of the respective units.

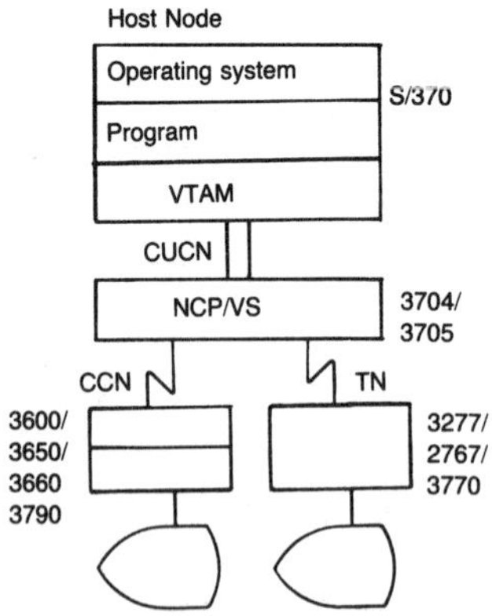

Figure 7.4 Four types of nodes including TN's

And now for some more definitions of terminology from the three SNA layers:

End user – to be found at the ends of the communications system (CS).

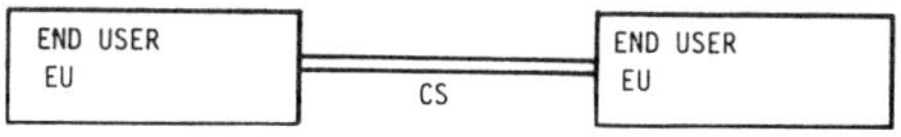

Figure 7.5

An end user is

- Transmitter/receiver of data
- Applications program in Host Node and CCN
- Terminal user (TN)
- Control program for the network

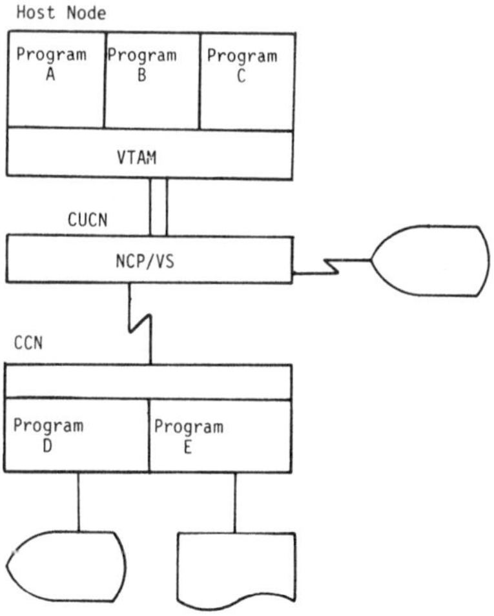

Figure 7.6

A Logical Unit is the port through which the end users gain access to the communications system and can exchange information. This means that every LU has a network address.

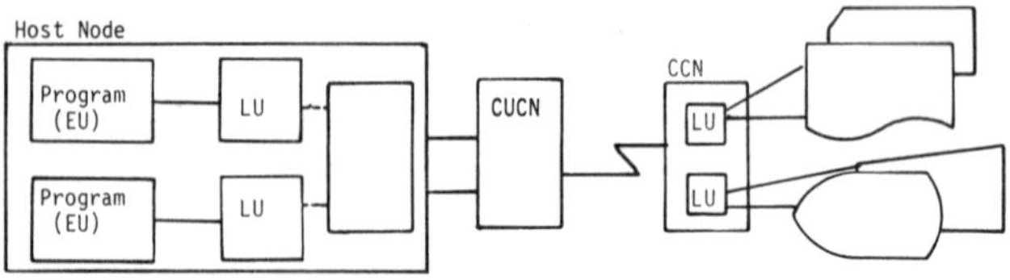

Figure 7.7

The Physical Unit (PU) has, in common with the LU, a network address. Every node in a SNA network contains a PU which is programmable, and programmed to take care of certain functions, such as

- to control the physical configuration
- to control the resources contained in the node
- to collect statistics for preventative reasons.

In principle, the PU is activated as soon as the SNA system is started up, when the control program for the network established contact with all configured PU's on start-up.

SSCP – System Services Control Point; to be found in the Host Node which owns and activates the whole or part of the network. The SSCP holds a catalogue of all addressable elements in the whole of the communications system. It is via the SSCP that an end user and LU can establish connection with another end user. When this contact is ready, the SSCP is temporarily disconnected, so that for example the information exchange itself between two LU's does not go via the SSCP. Figure 7.8 shows how the SSCP is positioned in the communications system.

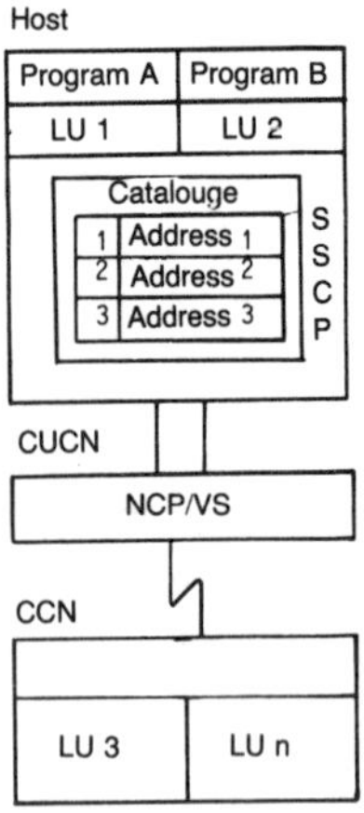

Figure 7.8 Systems Services Control Point

The whole of the CS is controlled by a network monitor with the help of commands, determining which parts of the network are to be activated, disconnected, etc. The three units involved (LU, PU and SSCP) are together called NAU's, Network Addressable Units.

As mentioned previously, a connection between two LU's must be established before the end users can exchange information. Such a channel between two LU's is called a session.

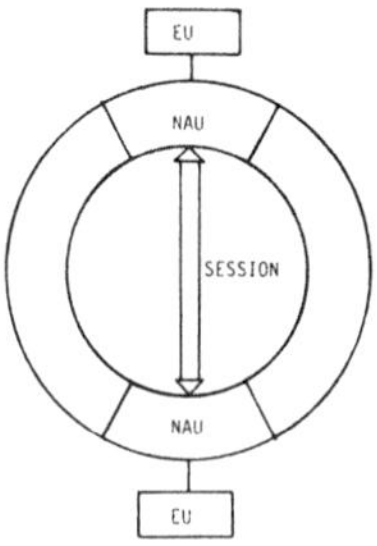

Figure 7.9 Session

Sessions must be established between the SSCP and every active LU or PU.

SNA defines the general data format for all types of data transmission according to Figure 7.10.

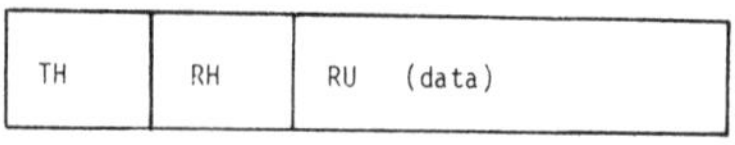

Figure 7.10 PIU, Path Information Unit (SNA data format)

The first part is known as the Transmission Header, the second as Request/Response Header, and finally the third as the Request/Response Unit. The last part contains the data which is sent between two LU's in the form of SNA commands or list information, etc.

SNA communications functions have been divided into seven layers

- Applications layer
- Presentation/Function Management layer
- Data Flow Control layer
- Transmission Control layer
- Path Control layer
- Data Link Control layer.

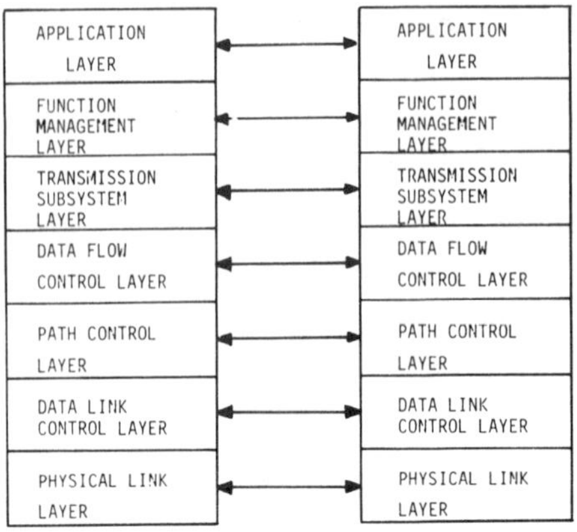

Figure 7.11 SNA layers

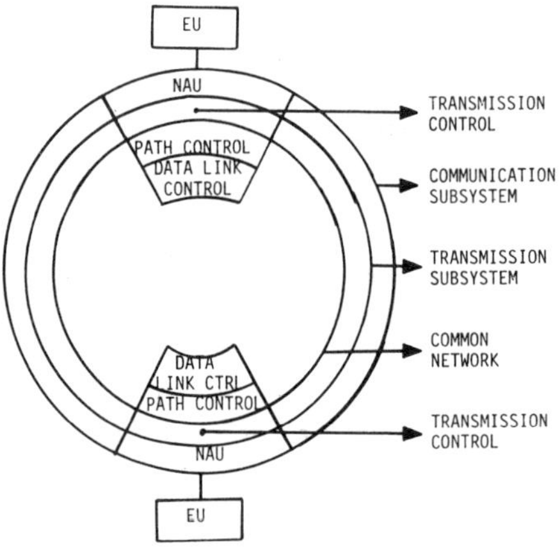

Figure 7.12 SNA structure

We shall review very briefly below the elements which are mentioned in the Figure. For further study, the handbooks issued by IBM are recommended. The sources for the material given here include 'G 276-3548-0 Field Engineering Handbook – Systems Network Architecture', GC 30-3072-0 and GC 30-3073-0.

Application layer

This layer is the 'window' between the communicating users, through which occurs all exchange of meaningful information.

Contact with CS goes via the Function Management (FM) layer.

Function Management layer

This layer is concerned with the transmission of data from one application or end user to another. The following functions are carried out

- initiate connection between the LU's wishing to communicate
- fetch data from the Application layer and transfer it to the Transmission subsystem for transmission
- fetch data from the Application layer and transfer data to the Application layer
- control the flow of data between LU's
- add and remove control information required for the transmission.

This layer is shown diagrammatically in Figure 7.13.

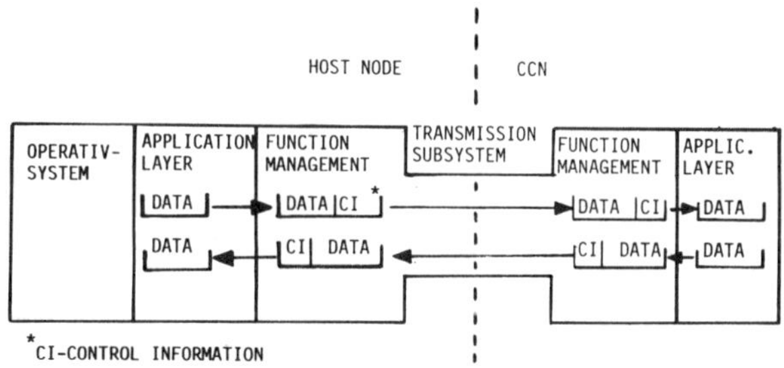

Figure 7.13

Transmission Subsystem layer

This level contains functions for controlling data between NAU's. These functions are to be found in HN, CUCN and CCN in the form of the subsidiary levels Connection Point Manager (CP), Path Control (PC) and Data Link Control (DLC)

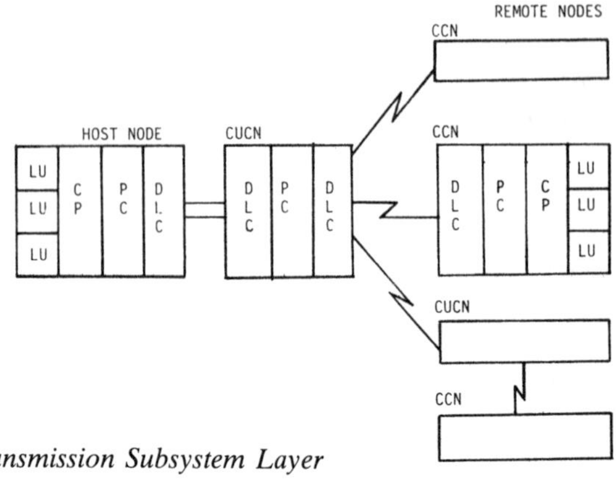

Figure 7.14 Transmission Subsystem Layer

The Connection Point Manager controls the transmission of data, the issuing of sequence numbers to messages and the checking of these. CP is one of the three components comprising Transmission Control (TC). The other two are Session Control (SC) and Network Control (NC), whose job is also to monitor data transfer.

Path Control directs the data via the lines in the network to the correct receiver.

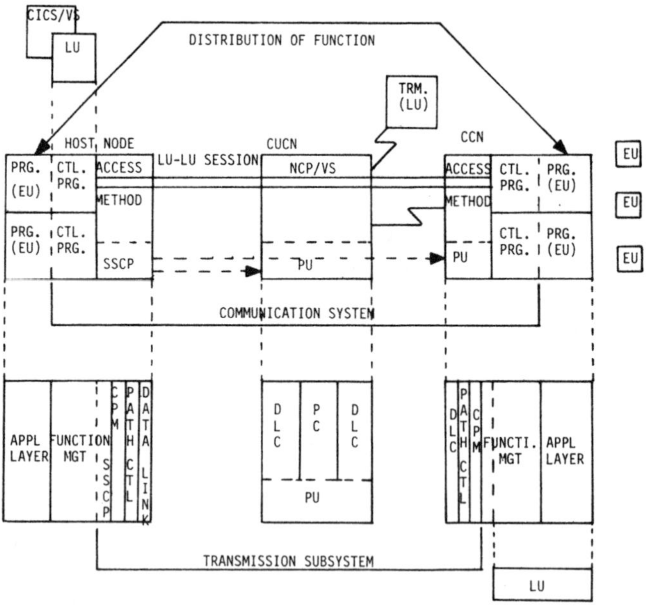

Figure 7.15 SNA units and layers

Data Link Control looks after an individual link between two nodes. DLC adds in the control information needed for transmission and removes it again when it has reached the correct receiver.

To round off this section, Figure 7.15 gives an overview of the components and layers comprising SNA.

7.3 DCA (Distributed Communication Architecture)

UNISYS have called their system DCA.

What is DCA?

Well, it describes

- design
- construction
- running

of communications systems in a standardised way.

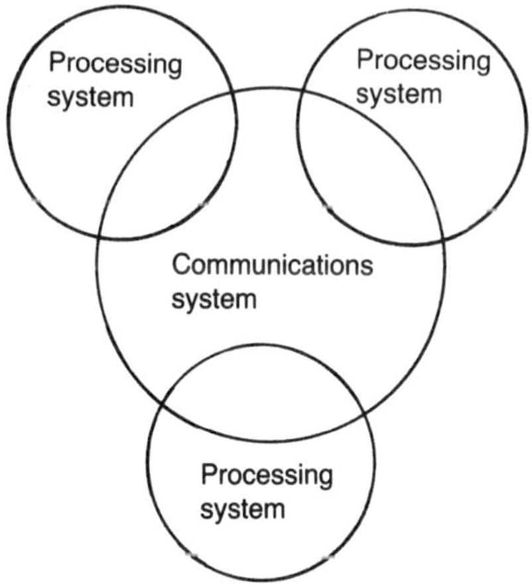

Figure 7.16 The DCA philosophy

With this philosophy (remember the 7 layers) DCA can offer

- a transparent communications system
- free choice of network
- control and monitoring in the network
- use of general data networks
- savings in CPU time and memory
- reduced number of communication lines
- possibility of connecting other makes of computers and terminals

Figure 7.17 expands Figure 7.16 and shows the logical parts in a DCA network.

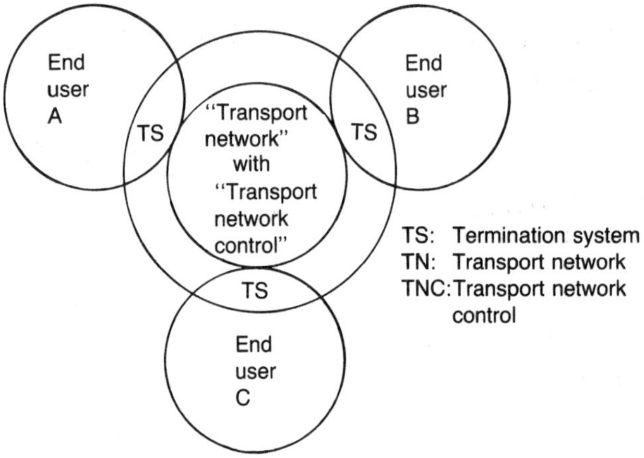

Figure 7.17 Logical parts of DCA network

Now follows a very brief description of the logical parts.

Suppose that communication occurs between two end users.

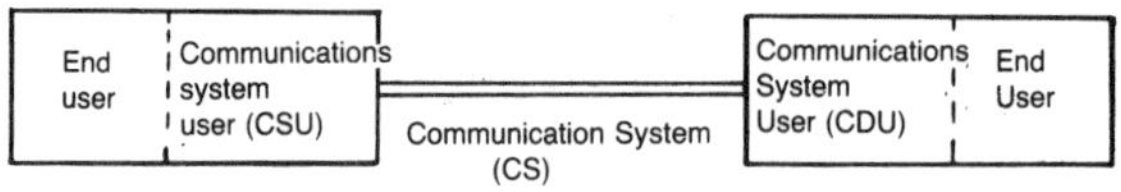

Figure 7.18

An end user is

- transmitter/receiver of data
- application program in computer or terminal
- terminal user
- network control program

The Communication System (CS) consists of

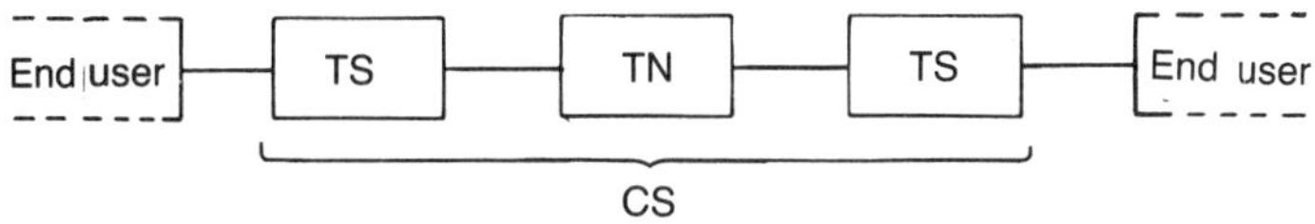

Figure 17.19

The Terminal System (TS) forms the Communication System's interface with the end user.

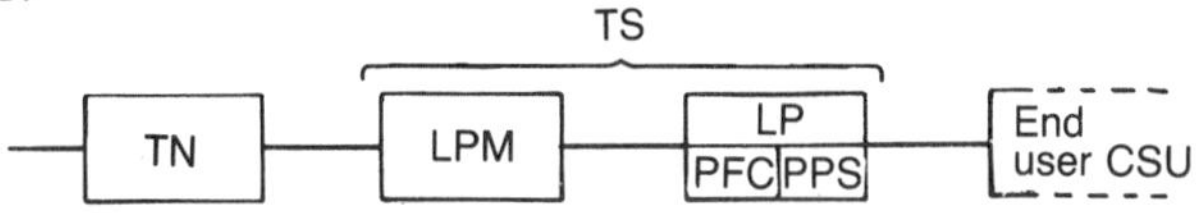

Figure 7.20

LP *logical port*

- transforms data to a form suitable for the CSU
- regulates the data flow

LPM *logical port multiplexer*

- directs data to the correct LP
- is responsible for sending data to TN

TN *transport network*

- transmits units of information between connected LP's along the communications line CS
- consists of one or more TNC's (control units)

TNC in its turn consists of

- DUC Data Unit Control
- RTC Route Control
- TC Trunk Control

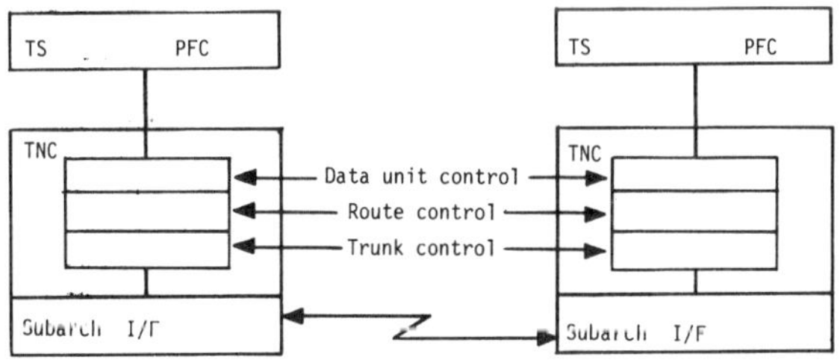

Figure 7.21 TN (Transport network) structure

Logical functions of TNC

- DUC
  - interface between TS/TN
  - 'ENTRY' and 'EXIT' points for data to the network.
- RTC
  - determines the route through the network
- TC
  - determines the flow of data between TNC's.

Figure 7.22 is a diagrammatic summary of DCA, and also shows the 7 layers and their interconnections. For each layer, the functions concerned with the communication have been standardised.

Figure 7.23 gives an example of what a DCA network can look like.

For further study, material is available through UNISYS.

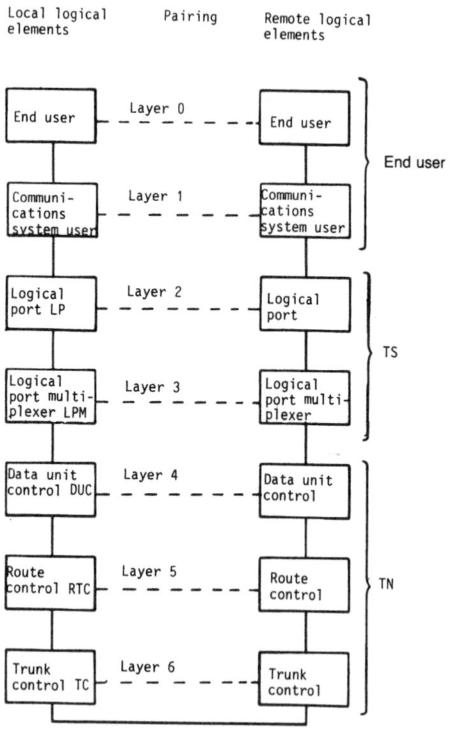

Figure 7.22 DCA layer

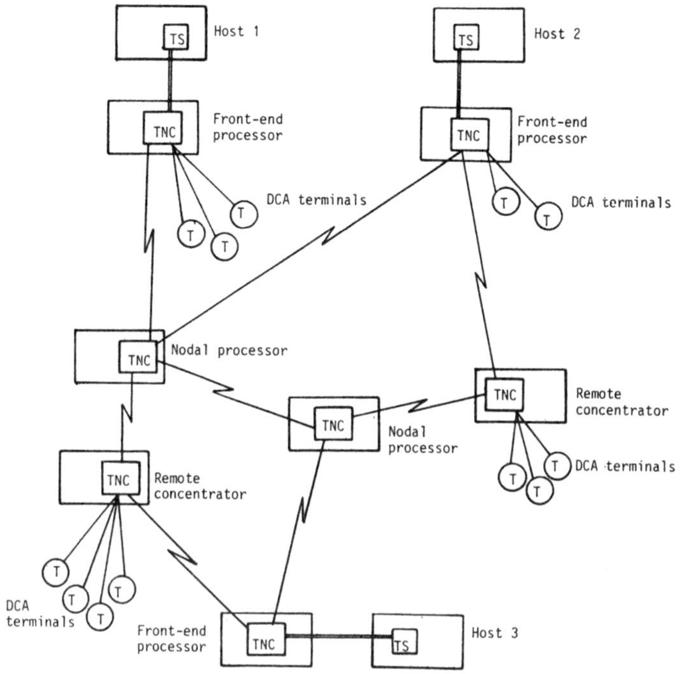

Figure 7.23 DCA Network

7.4 DSA (Distributed Systems Architecture)

Like other manufacturers, Honeywell Bull as well has a solution for how a distributed system based on HB's products and hardware should function. DSA follows largely the model and conventions recommended by ISO. The model specifies the rules by which different activities (programs, terminal operators) should exchange information.

As with all other architectures, HB's model for distributed data processing is also built round a number of layers.

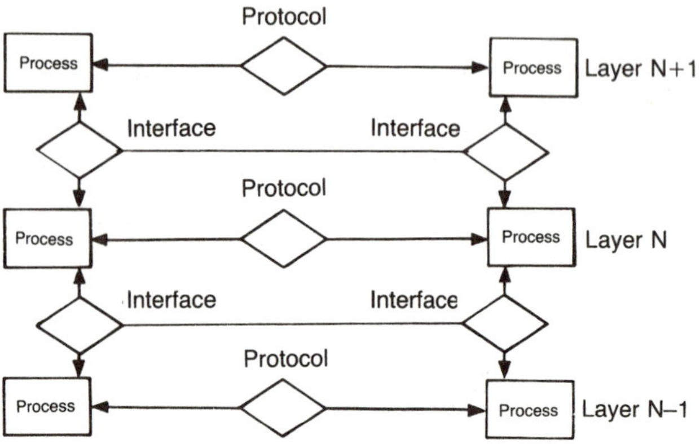

Figure 7.24 Layers, interfaces and protocols

The rules for how information and data are to be exchanged between the end points are formed into a hierarchical structure. The exchange of data between two end points passes one or more layers. Every layer contains functions which make the data exchange easier, such as

- a layer offers 'service' to the next highest layer
- this service reaches through the interface to the next highest layer
- functions on one layer work with functions on the same layer according to a protocol which specifies how these layers shall work together.

Another way of looking at the above is to take the example of the handling of mail.

Layer N+3 You write a letter to someone and give it to your secretary.

Layer N+2 The secretary puts it in an envelope, writes the name and address on it (and your name and address on the back), sticks a stamp on it and puts it in the post.

Layer N+1 The postman collects the letters and delivers them to the post office. Sorting now takes place, so that all mail is distributed to the correct post office out in the country.

Layer N The main post office distributes all the mail to the receiving offices.

Layer N+1 The receiving office checks that mail has been correctly delivered, and then sorts all the mail to a certain pattern in order to arrive finally with the postman who will deliver your letter.

Layer N+2 The secretary of the person to whom you wrote the letter keeps only that post whose address is correct, and then hands over your letter to her boss.

Layer N+3 Her boss takes the letter and slings it in the bin. No, joking apart, he reads your letter and is very glad to be able to play golf with you next weekend.

This example shows how control information (address) is added to the data (the letter), and how this control information is used by the next layer. Finally it reaches the right destination (the equipment) and the right person (end point) who understands what you have written (protocol).

Now it's time to learn more manufacturer-specific terminology. Some of the foundation stones of DSA are

- end point
- logical connections
- site
- path

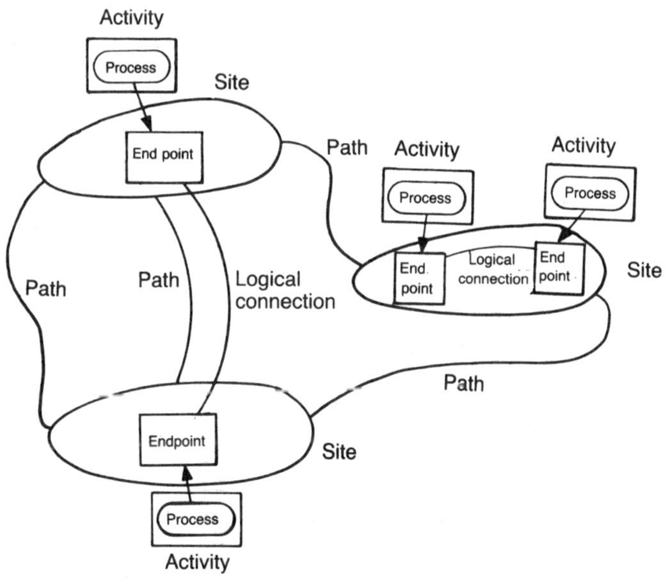

Figure 7.25 Foundations of DSA

An end point is the interface between an activity and the network. It has a unique address which makes it possible for activities to exchange information.

A logical connection may be seen as a line between two end points, through which messages are passed. This connection only exists as long as the data exchange between two end points is going on.

A site is a number of end points, all of which represent activities which use the same hardware and software resources, e g host computer, secondary network with communications computers or concentrators. The connection between two sites is via lines. Between each pair of sites there are as many logical connections as there are pairs of end points.

A path is the route through the network followed by the logical connection between two end points in different sites.

The architecture in an HB system is based in two principles

1 Definition of the rules which will apply to the exchange of data between two end points.

2 To try to use the communications sections in the best way during information exchange between two end points situated in different sites.

The layers for DSA have been divided into two parts, each of which covers points one and two above, namely Message Management and Communications Management.

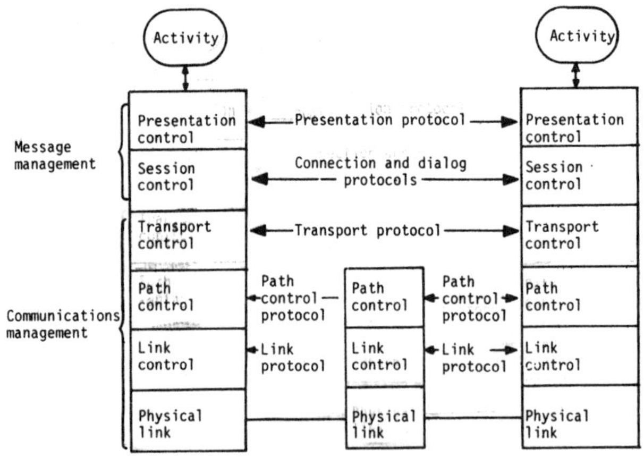

Figure 7.26 Details of layers in DSA

Message management

In order for two processes to work together, two functions are required – one to coordinate the data exchange and one to guarantee that every process interprets the information (data) and the control information which is sent.

These two functions are controlled by the layers

- Presentation Control
- Session Control

Presentation Control

The representation of the data which is handled by a program/process depends on the hardware and software which is installed. It is therefore necessary, when data is sent between two processes, that the pattern in which the data is built up is specified, in order to allow its eventual transformation. The layer allows the transformation of data, and has the following protocol

- Standard device Protocol
- Transparent Protocol
- Data Description Protocol

Code conversion, packing/unpacking of data, encryption, etc, also occur under this level.

Session control

This layer uses two protocols. Connection protocol connects and disconnects a logical connection. This protocol also contains the rules covering data transfer. Dialog Protocol monitors the data exchange in a logical connection and synchronisation and reconstruction. This protocol also has the following functions

- specifying who has the right to send data
- allowing one communication process to break off another
- adding in control points to make reconstruction easier if the logical connection should be broken.

Communications Management

Where communication is between two end points in different systems, the transmission is controlled in this layer. There are resources for handling several types of transmission such as

- microwave connections
- telephone connections
- general and private data networks which use circuit- or packet-switching techniques.

The level offers two types of multiplexing, where for economic reasons it is not possible to have as many connections (lines) as there are 'end-to-end' communications.

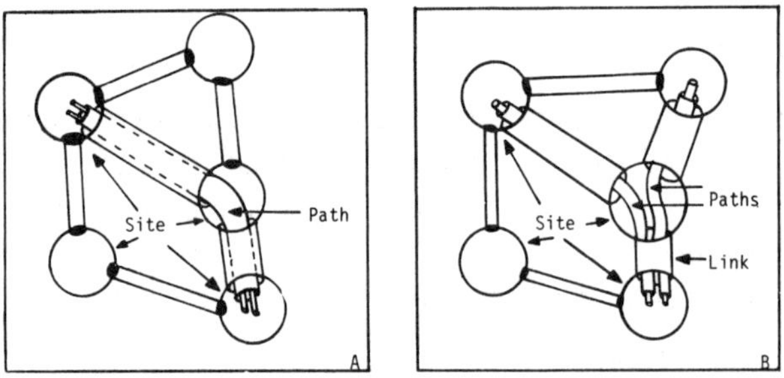

Figure 7.27 DSA multiplexing techniques

The first allows logical connections between two sites to exist on the same path. The other allows a number of paths to use the same line.

And now for the levels within Communications Management.

Transport layer

This layer has two main functions

- to multiplex all logical connections which use the same path (see Figure 7.27 A).
- to try to achieve error-free transmission in both directions for each of these logical connections, and to give warning messages if transmission is interrupted.

Depending on the communications medium, the following options may be implemented

- fragmentation
- flow control
- error control
- reconstruction

Network layer (Path Control layer)

This layer is used for controlling data between the 'transport layer' in two different sites (see Figure 7.27 B). The way in which this layer is implemented depends on the type of network, general or private. There are four methods

- datagram packet switching
- virtual circuit packet-switching
- circuit-switching
- dedicated lines

The first three are covered in Chapter 6. The fourth implies that there is only one connection between two sites, and this layer is then not required.

Link Control layer (Data Link layer)

This layer deals with the transmission of data between two nodes over a physical line. The protocol used in the transmission is HDLC (see Chapter 5).

Physical Link layer

This layer specifies characteristics of the connection between two nodes, or properly the modem interface.

In order to administer a network built up around DSA, Honeywell Bull have produced several documents which make it easier for the user to control the whole communication system. These functions will not be covered here.

8 Local data networks

8.1 Introduction

We find ourselves at the beginning of an information age, where data technology is developing rapidly and the users are more and more demanding. The need for information in society is rising. Decentralisation and influence are among the reasons for the spread of information which is going on. Technical developments have led to smaller and cheaper computers, even down to lap-held personal computers. The computers can be sited where the need is greatest, near the data source or near the place where the data is used. As a user, one will always wish to be able to use the system which is installed, regardless of where it is situated in the organisation. More and more office employees have access to data terminals in order to carry out their jobs. Such efficiency is thus obtained only after coordination of the total data communication of the organisation.

As far as design is concerned, there is a range of alternatives. The choice of a solution must be controlled by the functional requirements of the application, but must at the same time allow cross-fertilisation with the constant developments in the data processing area.

In earlier chapters we have looked at public and private data networks. Now it's the turn of local data communication or Local Area Networks.

8.2 Background

Recent developments have led to the introduction of aids and systems which make it easier to store and retrieve information. Just think of all the fat computer listings which are produced, and how difficult it can sometimes be to get any meaningful information out of these. Overall, the largest amount of information is internal. There has previously been no coordination of different information media. Various aids have been used for information processing. In each department or function, people have solved their information problems themselves. An American survey in 1980 (Yankee Group) showed that 60% of a company's information flow was of a local nature (see Figure 8.1).

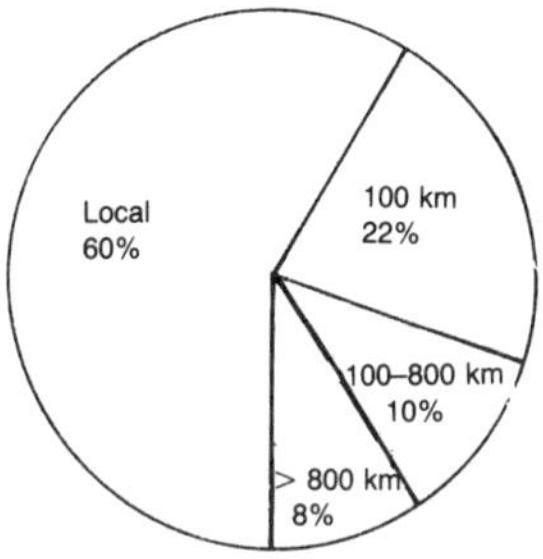

Figure 8.1 Geographical distribution of companies' information flow in the USA

Looking at the Swedish situation, the split is probably 80–20%; i e 80% of all information is of a local nature.

One way of coordinating this mass of information is to try to combine together the equipment used for information retrieval and distribution. In the market place, methods, solutions, equipment and systems exist for building up local networks. As the technique still is new to the users, most are perhaps a bit unsure of what they can offer and what possibilities the current developments within the area will result in. There are problem areas and trends, but more of that later. Firstly, something about the equipment which can be connected to local data networks, types of application and different network types.

Equipment

Look round your workplace, and you will discover that the information routes are many, as are the ways or media by which information is disseminated.

There are local computers and memories for storage and processing of data which the user can make use of, in the form of information on a terminal or data listing.

There are printers connected to terminals which allow copies to be made of what is on the screen.

There are communications computers for keeping track of all the terminal users, and which direct the data information to the right operator.

Word and text processing equipment, telefax equipment, etc, are another group of advanced equipment which is used to distribute the information.

Copying machines and telephones are other media which we use when we which to exchange information.

The following is often true where the above equipment is to be found at the workplace

- Copies and letters are distributed via the internal post or by postmen.
- A cable goes from every terminal to a main connection point (control unit, computer). If a terminal is to be used with two different computers, there are often double cables.
- Telephone wires are everywhere.
- The same lead cannot to used to connect together the different types of information equipment.

For some years now, it has been possible to use one and the same line for distributing information by building up local area networks. The principle for going about these has long been known. It is based on cable TV technology. But what applications are suitable for coordinating and for using on local area networks? Here are some examples.

Applications

Telefax

A telefax system consists of a sender and a receiver with one connection, a telephone line. In the system sold by the Swedish telephone company, transmitter and receiver are in the same apparatus (NEFAX 3500).

Telefax can be used for sending or receiving e.g. letters, drawings, sketches, contracts, invoices, maps, handwritten messages, etc. The format is A4.

Firstly, the document is placed in the telefax machine. Then, one rings up the receiver, waits for the telefax tone and then presses the start button.

The operator at the receiving end does not need to hang around by the apparatus; it all happens automatically when the sender presses the start button. The receiver can also start the sending apparatus, providing that this has been loaded up in advance.

Up to 30 documents can be put in on every call. These are fed in automtically. A photocell in the apparatus reads off the text and the copy ends up at the receiver as an endless pile of paper.

The telefax apparatus can also be used as a copying machine, as it is a combined sender and receiver. One can thus send to oneself.

Figure 8.2 shows what a telefax system may look like.

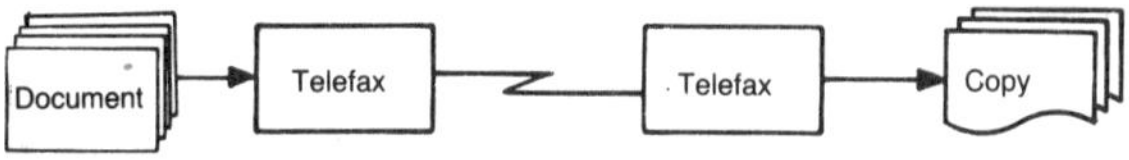

Figure 8.2 Telefax

Datapak

Datapak is the name for the Swedish telephone company's packet-switching service. It is primarily designed for international data communication, where the larger communications networks are of the packet-switching type (see Chapter 6).

In packet switching, the information is divided up into data packets and given an address and sequence number. By means of these markings, many users' information can be transported through the network simultaneously. Data transfer is in both directions at once (full duplex) at speeds of between 300–9600 bits per second.

As far as equipment is concerned, there are in the main two forms of connection. For asynchronous connections, an asynchronous terminal (start-stop) is used for speeds of 200/300 or 1200 bits/s full duplex. For synchronous transmissions, equipment with the X.25 interface is used at speeds of 2400–9600 bits/s.

Using Datapak, assuming one is authorised, one can 'go into' other data bases and fetch out information – information retrieval. This is a quick and easy way of getting information, in research work, for example.

Datapak can be used for sending messages to distant offices or round the world, so-called 'electronic mail'. Message transmission works by writing a message at a simple typewriter-terminal, connected to Datapak, and this is

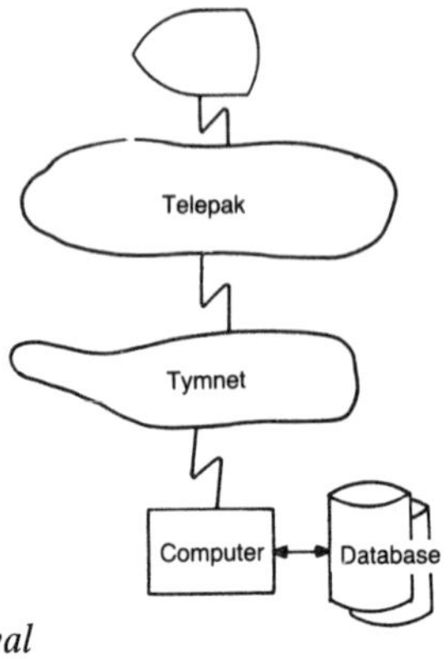

Figure 8.3 Information retrieval

then sent off to what is known as an 'electronic mailbox'. The receiver opens the mailbox by going in, using a terminal, and asking whether there are any messages for him. This is one way of reaching the branch offices, etc.

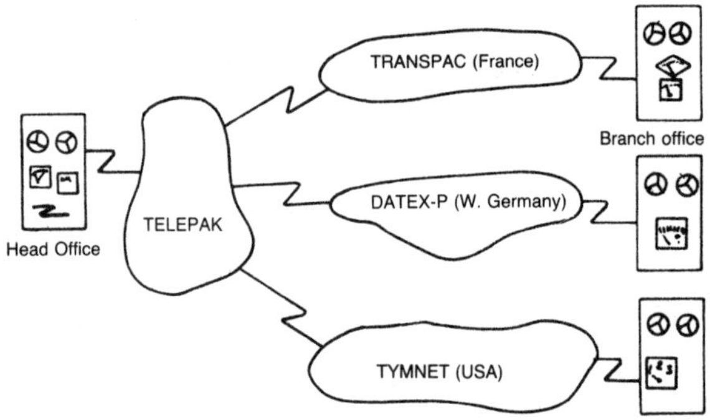

Figure 8.4 Electronic mail

In the same way as information retrieval, the various networks may be used to connect oneself up to any computer in the world and to use their programs for solving or analysing complex problems.

Datapak can be used in companies which have branches around the world for sending and receiving information.

Word and text processing

Connection of word or text processing equipment allows text and data to be distributed to other places within a company.

This type of equipment is becoming more and more common at our workplaces. It is therefore important to choose unified equipment which makes it possible to use information stored over the whole line, i e within all departments in the organisation.

8.3 What is a local area network?

A local network is a step in the right direction in the building up of the integrated office system. It is a question of building up a network to which nearly any type of equipment can be connected, which displays, stores and shows text and data. Data communication systems are constructed with the following characteristics

- limited
- high transmission speed and capacity
- high transmission quality
- flexible connection capabilities
- independent of the telephone company
- different types of equipment can be connected.

Certain conditions must of course be fulfilled before equipment can be connected to the network, and standardisation work is also going on in this area. It will take time before the organisations working on these questions will be united on what these norms will look like. There are many interests to be reconciled.

"One more step towards the realisation of general networks for office automation – i e, so that equipment can be connected up regardless of make – was taken when the international standards organisation ISO decided on a standard."

Figure 8.5 is an example of the components of which a local area network may consist, and Figure 8.6 shows a broad-band coaxial system with equipment connected.

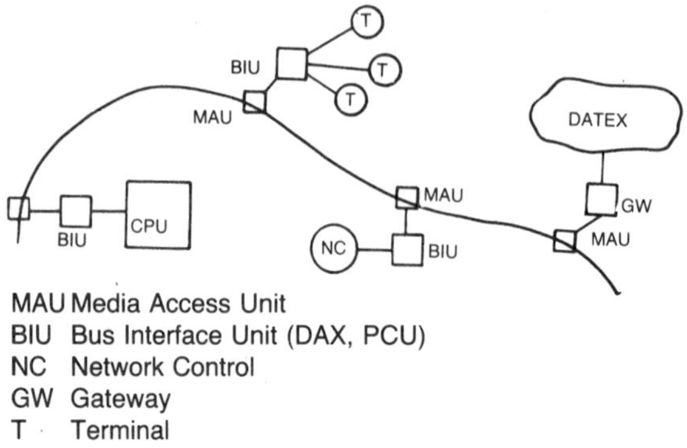

Figure 8.5 Components in a local area network

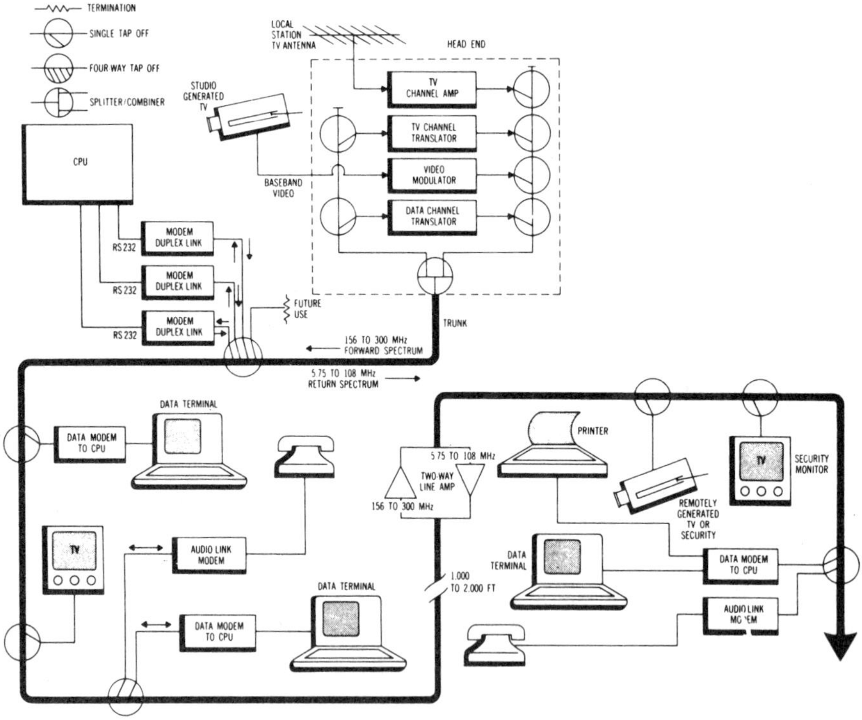

Figure 8.6 Broad-band system with its components and connected equipment in the form of CPU, terminals, TV, monitoring equipment, video, telephone etc

Transmission media

There are many different types of cables and techniques used in the design of local area networks. The structure below shows what is on offer – it's just a question of choice.

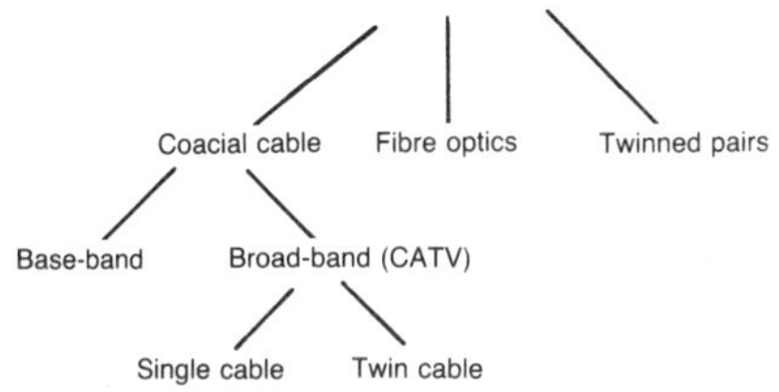

Figure 8.7 Transmission media

8.4 Types of network

As far as types of network for local area communication are concerned, there are three types which also occur in conjunction with other types of network.

Star network

The format of a star network is shown in Figure 8.8.

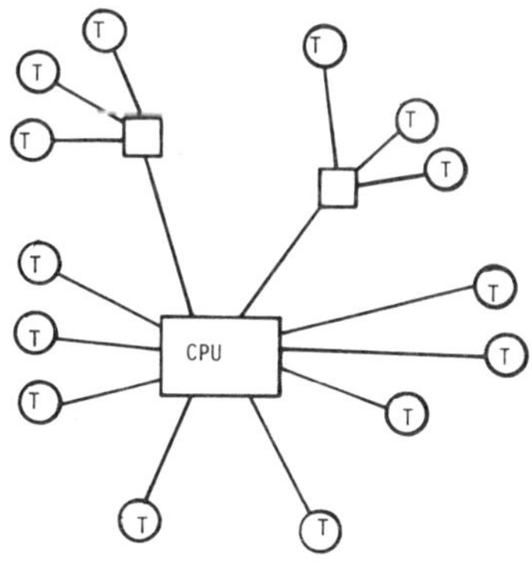

Figure 8.8 Star configuration

PABX – Private automatic branch exchange

This type of network uses as its connection units a hybrid type of subscriber exchange for both telephone and data use. It is based completely on digital technology and distributed exchanges in the network. Contacts with the world of computers is via a modem pool.

Data transfer speeds are relatively low, 9.6–128 kbits/s, and are by two-lead cables.

The advantage of the star configuration network is that it is simple to install, and that their cost is justifiable even if the network is only used for telephony. Extra computer power is required if the network is to be used for electronic mail, and the mailbox equipment is connected to the network via the modem pool. It also requires extra equipment to use the network for data communication.

PABX cannot be used for video.

A 345 – telephony and data communication in the same system

The Swedish telephone company has a system called A 345. This is a computer-controlled telephone system which gives users new opportunities for improving their telecommunications. The system has an inbuilt flexibility which allows the company to re-program the system according to its needs.

The following functions are available as a telephone system

- Three-way conferences – two internal connections and one external can talk on the same line at the same time
- re-dialling function
- choice of short numbers
- common group numbers, e g for a department
- re-direction of calls

A 345 offers both telephony and data communication in the same system. One and the same cable is used for both purposes. This is just what is needed when building up local area networks, i e no extra cables. There is a special terminal extension, DCE-T, for the telephone apparatus which allows terminals with standard interfaces to be connected. In the central control equipment of the system there is a memory and software to control the data flow both locally to the host computer and over distances via modem and phone lines.

DCE-T is a microprocessor which controls the communication between terminals and other units in the system.

A 345 central equipment functions as a data exchange (PABX) in communication between terminal-terminal and terminal-host computer. It functions as a communications computer via centrally-situated modems for communication between terminals-distant systems.

Having telephony and data communication in the same system means that the functions of the telephone system can be used for terminal work.

Re-dialling – if a line or host computer are fully loaded at that instant, the system rings up the terminal when transmission or retrieving of information can begin.

Redirection of calls – the ability to direct information and quantities of data to another terminal in the system.

The A 345 system is shown in Figure 8.9.

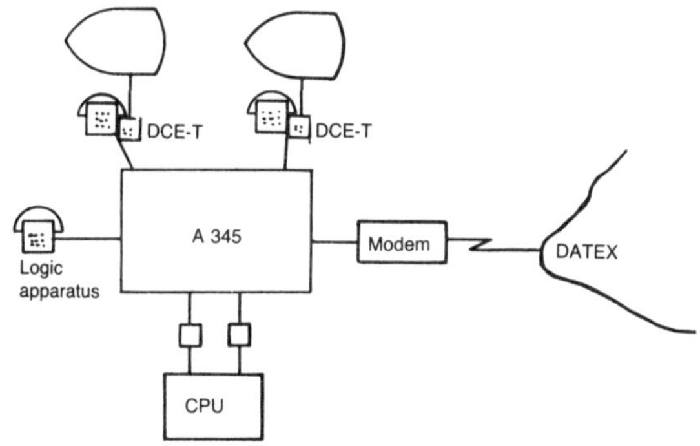

Figure 8.9 A 345. Telephone and data communication in the same system

MD 110 – a digital subscriber exchange

MD 110, a subscriber exchange for 100–10,000 lines. It is a digital, program memory-controlled exchange which allows integrated speech and data communication. MD 110 was developed by ELLEMTEL for Ericsson and the Swedish telephone company. MD 110 is a microprocessor-controlled subscriber exchange which comprises line connection units, LIM. Figure 8.10 shows the design of LIM.

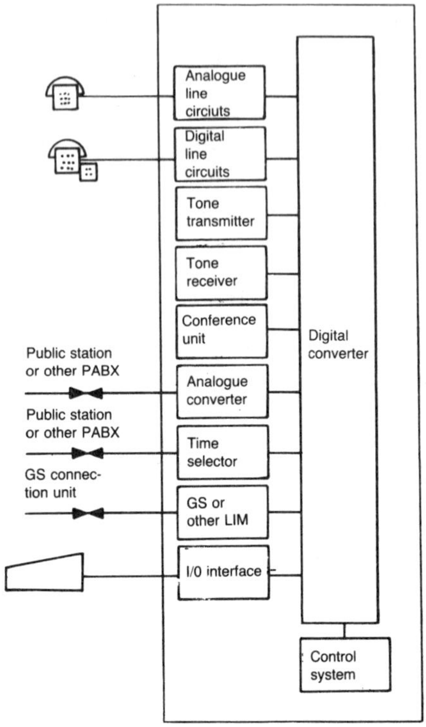

Figure 8.10 Block diagram of LIM

The line selector has 512 inputs for speech and data, each of which has the capacity for 64 kbits/s. Every LIM, which has a capacity of about 200 lines, is configured to the customer's wishes with a free choice of combinations of terminal units for analogue and digital apparatus, telephonists' equipment, data terminals and lines to the public networks.

In larger installations, each LIM is connected to a central group selector, GS (Figure 8.11), which can be expanded for up to 248 PCM links each of 2.048 Kbits/s. The group selector, which is a digital selector, has the task of transmitting PCM-coded speech, data and control signals between different LIM's. The GS itself has no control equipment, but is controlled wholly by the connected LIM's.

If a company has many geographically isolated units, MD 110 can be adapted for this. The different LIM's in the exchange can be situated together or spread out to nearby or distant units. System lines with speeds of 2 Mbits/s are used when the distance between LIM and GS exceeds 500 metres.

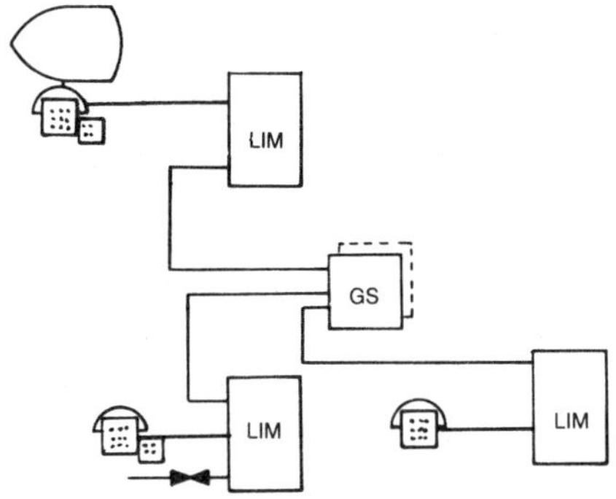

Figure 8.11 Design of the MD 110

The connection lines are two-wire. Digital equipment has a 96 kbits/s duplex connection to the exchange implemented with time-multiplexed with burst signalling. The bursts are sent at speeds of 256 kbits/s and consist of 12 bits, as shown in Figure 8.12.

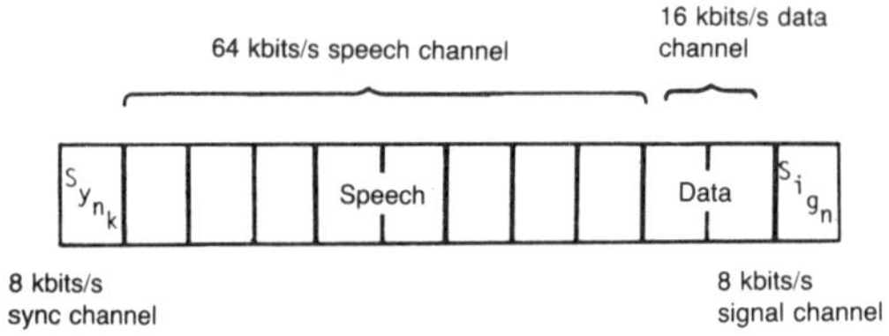

Figure 8.12 Channel allocation in a digital data stream

The bit streams are divided into four channels. One channel at 8 kbits/s is used to synchronise the burst signal. The PCM-coded speech or high speed data is transmitted at 64 kbits/s. The third channel at 16 kbits/s is used for data transfer, and the last at 8 kbits/s for control signalling between digital equipment and LIM.

The data channel shown in Figure 8.13 makes it possible to transmit both synchronous and asynchronous data transparently. The MO bit is used for telling whether the data field is user data or signalling.

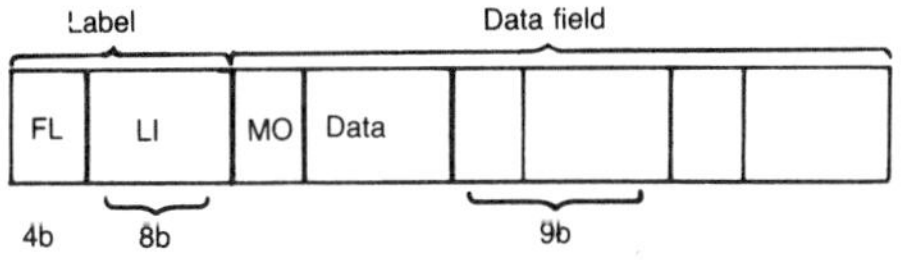

Figure 8.13 Data channel format

Terminal and modem connection

DCE-T is a special terminal attachment which is connected directly to the telephone apparatus. Data terminals can be plugged into it using a standard interface.

External fixed data connections are connected via modem to special line units known as MGE (Modern Gateway Equipment). With low quantities of terminal traffic not requiring fixed lines, a suitable number of modems can be connected up as an independent modem pool.

The data communication service in MD110 covers both synchronous and asynchronous data terminals.

Services and areas of use

Apart from just making the connections and telephonist services, there are several system-orientated services on the telephony side. None of these services will be dealt with here (although some are taken up in the section on A345). This book is concerned more with data communication.

- Connection without dialling
  To this end there is in most terminal-DCE interfaces a calling function which in MD110 automatically initiates connection to a given address.
- Moving of computer applications
  In order to satisfy the computer centre's need to be able to move individual systems from one computer to another, the address can be modified, and the user does not need to be informed of the move. This is possible because MD110 allows a unique address for every system.
- Choice of name
  The same group of computer ports can be called with several choices of adress, corresponding to the program applications to be found in the computer.
- Switching between speech and data
  An established speech connection can be changed to a computer connection by pressing a function key.
- Short numbers
- Manual dialling
- Automatic calling

- Automatic answering
- Group searching etc.

The transparent data communication in MD110 can be extended when conversions are added. It is possible to emulate the 3270 protocol for connection to IBM's communications computers. Cheap character-orientated synchronous or asynchronous terminals can be connected. Figure 8.14 gives an overview MD110 applications.

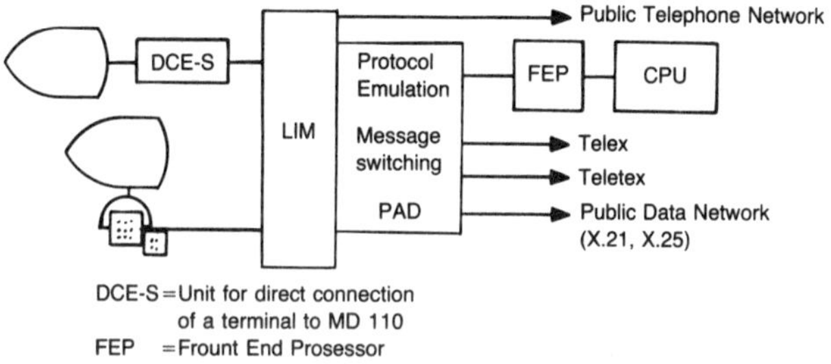

Figure 8.14 MD110 applications

Electronic message switching is one of the areas for which MD110 can be used. Terminal users can send and receive messages in the text-switching system over connected lines.

Large companies with geographically widespread units can install LIM units in the various sites and maintain unified and efficient communication.

It is also possible to use packet-switching by using a PAD unit in MD110.

Over and above all this, there are functions for simplifying running and maintenance.

Ring networks

Each message sent goes onto the ring in sequence and goes once round from device to device. The receiving device copies the message and acknowledges it. The sending device removes it after one revolution. There are different types of access methods or rules on how messages can be sent.

Two examples: Slotted ring, token-passing.

Slotted ring, as used in POLYNET, works as above, and where the receiving device is able to carry out the following with a message

- accept it
- reject it on the grounds that
  - the receiving device is still working on the previously received message,
  - the sending device is not known, i e is not in the directory of sending devices.

Token-passing means that the device which has the token can send, and after sending, the token is passed on to the next device on the ring.

Both these access methods have a fixed delay at each device, independent of load. This type of network allows a high proportion of usage of the transmission medium, which is normally a two-wire cable. It is cheap and easy to install.

Polynet

Polynet, from Logica VTS Ltd. in England, is based on the 'slotted ring' principle developed at Cambridge University. Figure 8.15 shows an example of a ring network configuration. The diagram is taken from a presentation brochure from Logica VTS.

Polynet consists of a number of network nodes connected up to a closed ring. In addition, there is a monitoring device and a sufficient number of PSU's (Power Supply Units) to guarantee that data signals and messages will still pass round the loop if one of the units connected to a node should fail. The distance between nodes can be up to 100 m in a maximal configuration of just over 200 nodes. Each node has a unique address between 1–254. A computer is connected into the ring via an interface unit (IU). There are two types of IU, one (DMA) giving a transmission speed of 1 Mbits/s between nodes on a point-to-point connection, and the other (PI) having a speed varying between 100–300 kbits/s.

The principles on which the 'slot' concept works have been described earlier. It is based on an empty slot circulating continously in the ring. After this, every node is responsible for filling and emptying this slot. Every slot is 38 or 40 bits, and the amount of data per slot is 2 bytes.

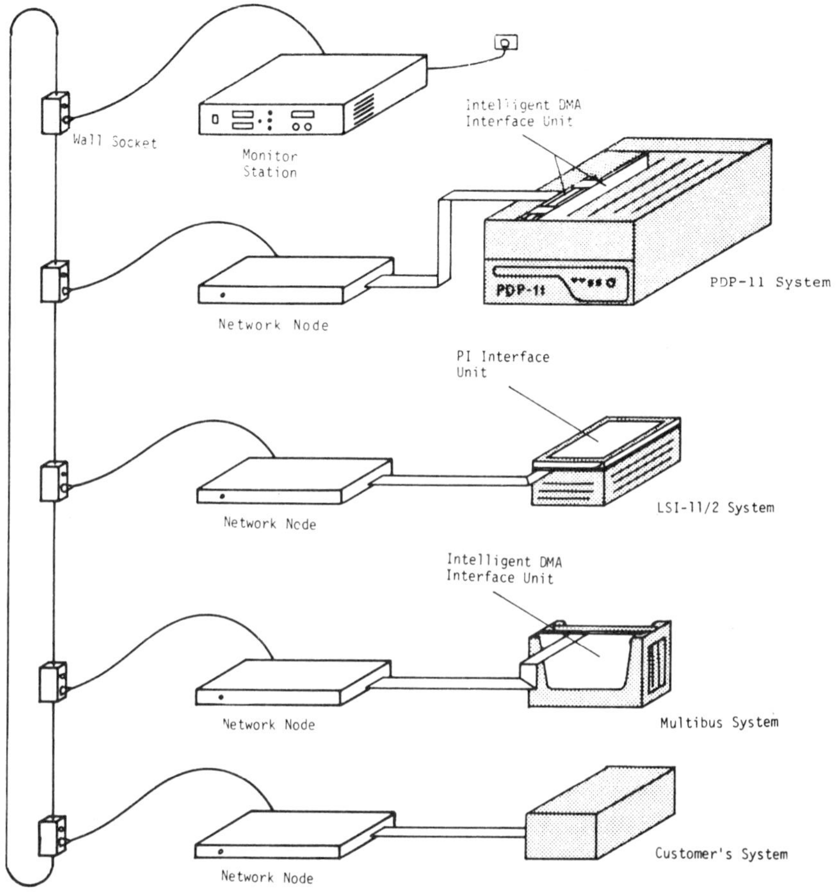

Figure 8.15 Ring network – Polynet

Components

The network node is a box which is directly connected to the ring, and via a ribbon cable to the device to be connected. The connection to the ring itself consists of a wall plug which is similar to a telephone jack. A node can be connected to and disconnected from Polynet while it is active.

The monitor station is included to set up the slot structure when the system is powered up. It contains reserve power sufficient for 8 nodes, and it also logs any errors which may occur. Each new group of 8 nodes requires a PSU.

In addition, a number of IU's have various interfaces in order to be able to connect up different types of equipment.

Bus network

Two techniques are used in the design of bus networks, baseband and broadband. Coaxial cable is used in both cases as the transmission medium. Figure 8.16 shows an example of an expanded broadband bus network.

Baseband has long been used for data transmission, particularly in local area networks. Now in the 1980's it is beginning to have competition from broadband. The technology applied in broadband transmission has long been known; it is based on transmission technology from cable TV.

On the physical level, there is not much to distinguish baseband from broadband. The cable used for baseband has a sheath of copper, while that for broadband is of aluminium. The transmission technology used for broadband is RF (radio frequency), which means that a single broadband cable can manage a speed of 150 Mbits/s. The capacity of a broadband system is about 50 times higher for broadband than baseband.

This capacity can be used, if so wished, solely for data communication, and then one can understand its possibilities. The fact that this technology has not been used earlier for data communication is seen by many to be because developments on the computer side and those on cable TV have continued on their own paths, without anyone taking a 'sideways view' at the other.

This broadband technique has been tested/used primarily in the USA, in the spheres of business, industry and research along with the development of local area networks. These installations have high demands for transmission speed and the ability to connect different types of device for information processing and dissemination.

The transmission techniques which are usually used for transferring several data streams at once in the same cable are:

- Packet-switching, which allows several terminal devices (BIU, PCU or DAX are some of the names chosen by different manufacturers for these interface units) to coexist on the same cable, takes up bandwidth only during sending of data.
- CSMA/CD is a 'listen while talk' collision detection technique which allows several devices or nodes to share one frequency channel.
- FDM (Frequency Division Multiplexing) allows several frequencies on the same cable.

Baseband

Figure 8.16 shows how a network of this type may look schematically. Examples of such are ARC from Datapoint and ETHERNET from Xerox, DEC and Intel.

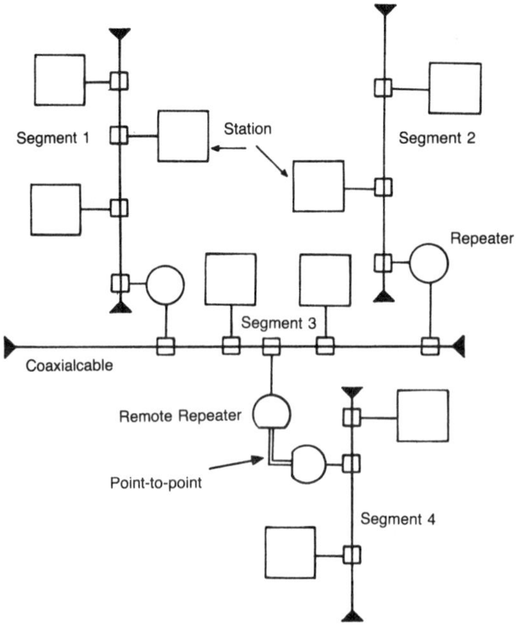

Figure 8.16

The CSMA/CD communications protocol has the following positive and negative characterstics:

+ will be the IEEE standard
+ simple
+ allows a large number of stations
+ little delay during low level of channel usage
– limited channel usage
– limited physical distance of network.

Other characteristics of baseband are the following:

The maximum length of each segment (see Figure 8.16) is 500 metres, and there may only be two repeaters/amplifiers between two stations, which means that the maximum distance between two MAU's is 1500 metres. The distance between two MAU's must be at least 2.5 metres. The maximum number of

MAU's is 100 per segment. 1000 metres is the longest point-to-point distance for any one link. This leads to a limited physical size of network if the installation is not to become too complicated and costly.

The transmission speed can be as high as 20 Mbits/s. It is expected that the price of baseband will fall faster than for example that of broadband.

Broadband

Broadband networks are extremely flexible and can be used in the design of all traditional types of network. Figures 8.17 and 8.18 are examples of some of these:

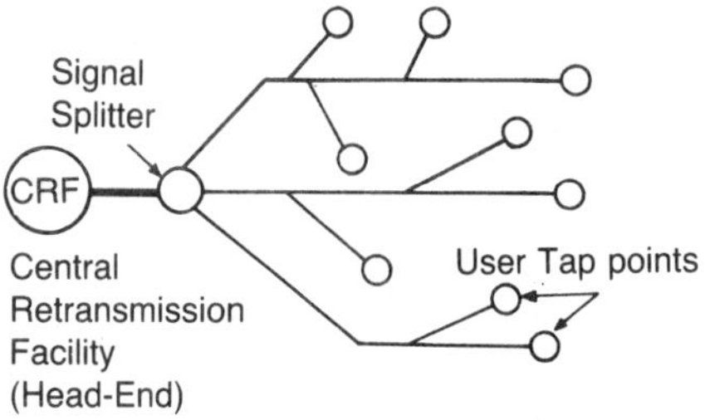

Figure 8.17

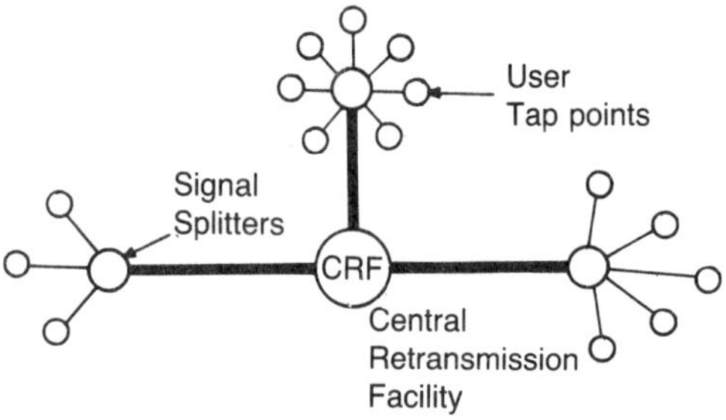

Figure 8.18

The network is completely protocol-transparent. It is relatively simple to connect new stations (devices) to the network, just by changing the configuration of the number of stations, and connecting in the RF modem. New branches in the network are formed by attaching a new coax cable. When the traffic load starts to reach the maximum the cable can take, the network can be reconfigured into a hierarchy with a sub-network. Standard components for a broadband system are amplifiers/repeaters and branches. This allows the network to extend to 50–60km, and it can easily be expanded and have branches added. The way in which broadband, which operates at over 300 MHz, can be used is illustrated in Figure 8.19. It is divided into TV channels of 6 MHz.

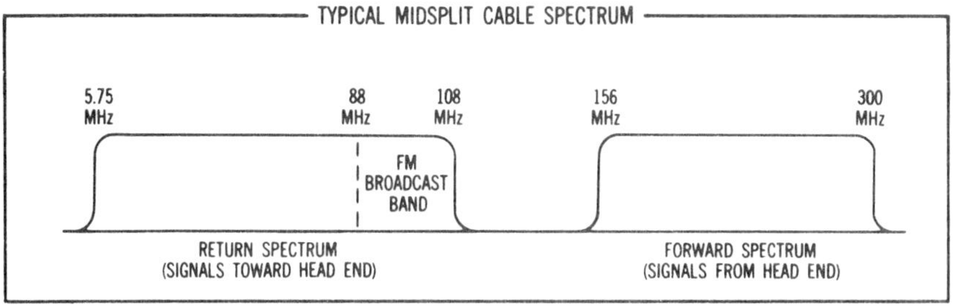

Figure 8.19 RF spectrum – broadband

The function (CRF) of the head-end equipment, which plays a central role, is shown in Figure 8.20. It is a translator which filters and regenerates signals. At the head end, i e at one end of the network, sits the equipment for amplifying, checking and adjusting signals. When the signals are returned from the head end, they are sent out a higher frequency. The DAX translator used as head-end in AMDAX uses 156.26 MHz.

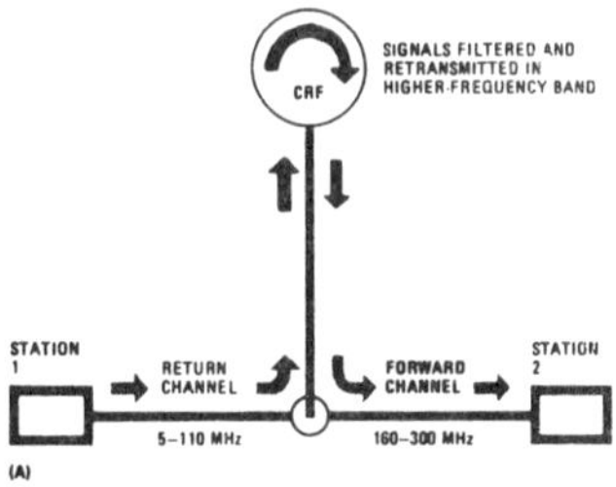

Figure 8.20 Central Retransmission Facility (Amdax)

The coaxial cable may either be single or twin. In single cable, the frequencies up to 156 MHz are sent in one direction and higher frequencies in the other (Figure 8.18). In the twin cable system, the whole capacity is available on each cable in its respective direction.

Using the FDM technique, the broadband can be divided up into a number of sub-channels with different transmission speeds, ranging from 9.6 kbits/s to 14 Mbits/s. It is theoretically possible to get 10,500 channels at 9.6 kbits/s in one system. Data channels, video and speech (point-to-point) can be mixed. Table 8.1 shows the capacity of a single (coax) cable in a broadband network.

Table 8.1 (From AMDAX information material)

Transmission speed	Type of connection	Usable bandwidth	Bandwidth required per link	Number of connections*
9.6 Kbit/s	FDX, S, A	105 MHz	10 KHz	10500
19.2 Kbit/s	FDX, S, A	105 MHz	20 KHz	5200
56 Kbit/s	FDX, S	105 MHz	60 KHz	1750
230.4 Kbit/s	FDX, S	105 MHz	240.4 KHz	437
512 Kbit/s	FDX, S	105 MHz	520 KHz	200
1.544 Mbit/s	SX, S	105 MHz	1600 KHz	65
3.088 Mbit/s	SX, S	105 MHz	3200 KHz	32

S=Synchronous, A=Asynchronous
* Divide by two for full duplex

Broadband has the following positive and negative characteristics

+ large bandwidth (15 ETHERNETs on the same cable)
+ very low error rate
+ 'open-ended', i e can mix data, video and speech (Figure 8.6)
+ simple to expand
+ long distance – 'unlimited'
+ protocol-transparent
– head-end equipment is sensitive – doubling-up is necessary
– high cost for RF modems

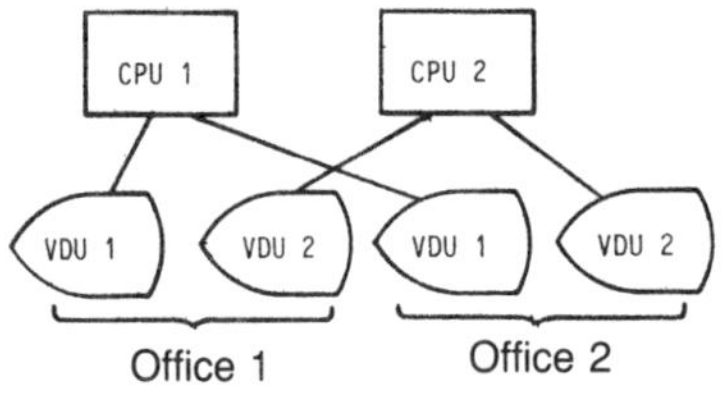

Figure 8.21 Twin-cable

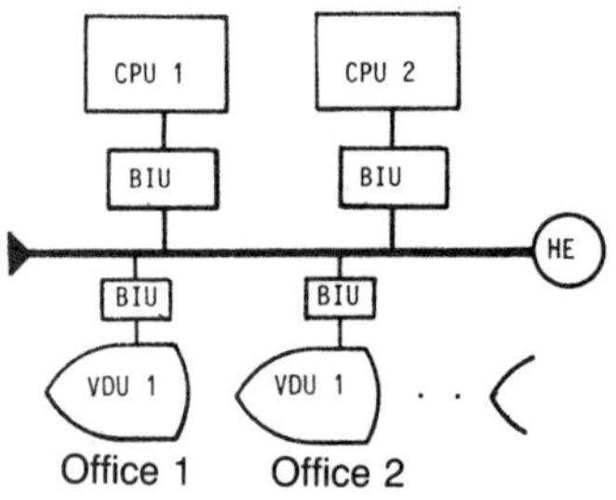

Figure 8.22 Broadband

Figures 8.21 and 8.22 show the differences between common twin-cable connection and a broadband network with head-end and RF modems.

Figure 8.23 shows how a local area network can branch out into the world via satellite links, microwave links and fibre optics. The configuration is possible in a broadband network without extra interface units or different sorts of cable.

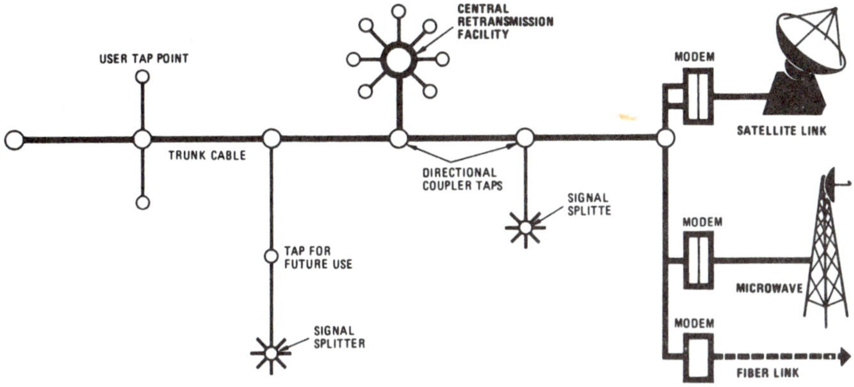

Figure 8.23 A branched local area network (AMDAX)

Finally, some pictures of broadband equipment from AMDAX.

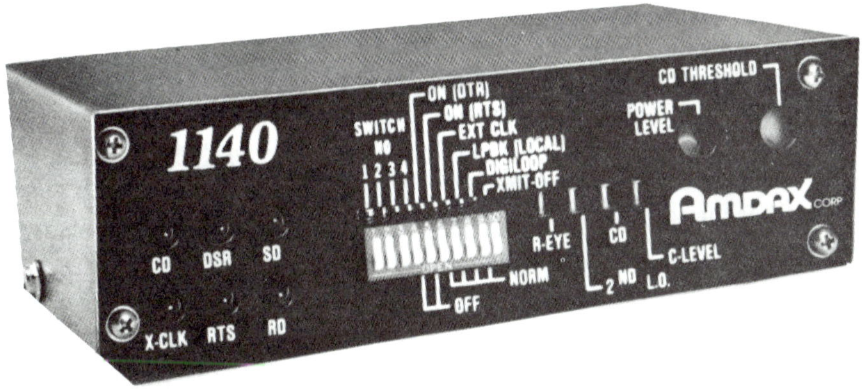

Figure 8.24 DAX 1140 (a high-speed RF modem, 50–56 kbits/s) for point-to-point or multi-point connection

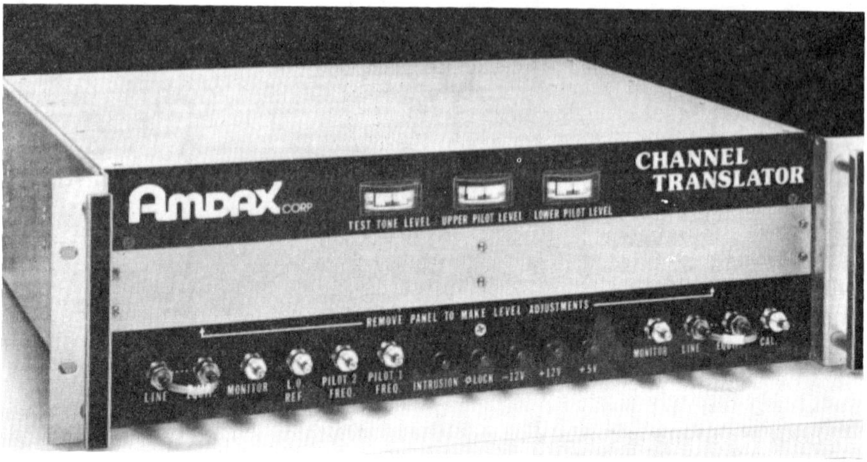

Figure 8.25 DAX 1009 W wideband translator. A head-end device with 54 MHz bandwidth

8.5 Problem areas

Local area networks are still relatively new for the users. They are therefore unsure of their needs and what possibilities the technology can actually offer them. Many have already invested money and built up their own networks, laid a mass of cables to terminals, etc. What way the developments will take is another question which is difficult to answer.

The range on offer from the manufacturers is still limited. Even if they promise much in their brochures, the number of installations possible on certain types of network is not so great. The users are still doubtful.

Standardisation is another factor to be reckoned with. What will happen in this area? In which direction will it go? Which manufacturers will follow the standards? Interesting questions.

Last, but not least, what will IBM offer? Many manufacturers are keeping a low profile until IBM has presented its solution. Just a guess – they will go their own way.

8.6 Trends

Broadband networks, with their almost unlimited possibilities, are of increasing interest.

Only the larger companies are setting up pilot networks to test them.

They are trying to understand the possibilities they can offer. What will this mean in terms of cost?

The systems which have been installed so far are primarily in university environments.

The range of products on offer increases when components of these systems are considered (head-ends, RF modems, repeaters, etc).

Only when IBM have lifted the lid and presented their solution will development and the range of products take off. It is clear that local area data networks have a very important function to fulfil. Varying types of equipment can be connected to the cables which are laid. It is only a question of 'plugging in' those units which are to be used in order to ease office work and improve the spread of information. There are good grounds for hoping that the apparatus needed for building local area networks falls in price and that standardisation work in the area will proceed. Then there will probably be network installations too.

8.7 Conclusions

Looking at the installations exiting today, not just in Sweden but around the world, the total system solution will not come from just one supplier. There are varying demands, e g MBL in Sweden, which make it difficult for a single manufacturer to be able to offer a complete system solution. Another reason is of course that not all suppliers have a full range of product types. Mixing of systems and equipment from several suppliers presupposes that a standard is used for functions and interfaces. Work is continuing within national and international standardisation organisations on the determination of norms for general communications networks for the connection of different equipment, apparatus and systems. It is important, therefore, for all manufacturers to follow this work so that the products they sell can be suitable for the development and changing of the standards. It is also important that the decision makers' choice of system solution, and primarily communication solution, has guarantees that the system which is invested in will also be usable in several years' time. This also refers to local area networks, in spite of the fact that several of them offer very flexible solutions.

9 Transaction systems, queues and queueing theory

9.1 Transaction systems

Introduction

In today's society it is often necessary to have direct contact beteen user and computer. This involves access to terminals of some sort (printers, VDU screens) and connection with a computer. In addition, there must be a system for storage of data in the secondary memory of the computer, a database system. This direct contact is known as on-line processing, transaction system or real-time processing. The various computer manufacturers have their own terminology and definitions for these.

Direct contact with a computer in a real-time environment means that a user has up-to date information on what the various elements in a database contain the whole time. Information is fed into the computer at the same instant that it happens. A somewhat cryptic definition of a real-time system is: "A system which controls its environment by receiving data, processing data, and taking actions or transmitting results fast enough to affect certain events in the environment in question at that point in time".

Examples of this type of computer application are bank terminals, seat reservations at airlines or travel agents, and large stock control systems for spare parts withdrawals.

Figure 9.1 Direct contact with a computer in a transaction system

Another area for real-time applications is process control, where a computer is fed with information in real-time about how the process is working, e g in paper and pulp production. The computer takes any necessary actions and controls the process continuously.

The opposite of real-time processing is, of course, batch processing, where information is collected over a certain time (e g a day) in order to be fed into the computer for processing at a predetermined time.

The characteristic of a real-time system is that time-critical information must be processed sufficiently rapidly by the computer. For this reason, such information, i e transaction, is processed by the computer in a real-time environment with very high priority. The data processing which a transaction initiates must be handled immediately, and finished, i e it must not be interrupted by lower priority jobs or stopped. In addition, the computer must be able to be affected by, and to affect, several ongoing jobs simultaneously. For this reason the response time demands are an important factor in real-time applications.

A real-time system is often combined with batch processing. This can be started up on particular occasions such as back-up of files or during complex calculations.

A transaction in a real-time system can be defined as the result of an event which demands immediate processing by the computer.

9.2 System components

A real-time system consists of the following components

- terminals
- data network
- computer
- files or database
- transaction program or real-time program

Terminals

Terminals are the user's interface with the system. A suitable type of terminal for a real-time system is the polled VDU for synchronous transmission. This type of VDU is supplied by all the large manufacturers in a number of versions. Printers can also be used as real-time terminals. One advantage of the polled terminal is that the computer can detect immediately whether there are difficulties in communication during data transmission. For more about terminals, see Chapter 11.

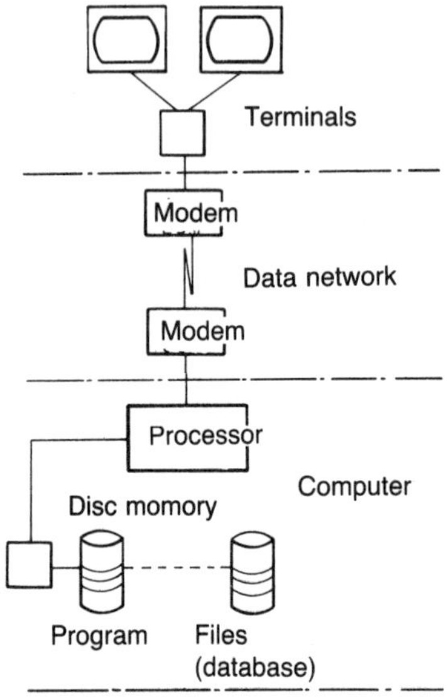

Figure 9.2 Real-time system components

Data networks for real-time systems

Data is transferred between terminals and computer via private data networks or over the general DATEX network. Dialled up terminals on the general telephone network can also be used.

Private networks can be of the point-to-point type, multipoint connections or in a ring format. After the advent of the DATEX network, more and more users have started using these facilities. In the future, private networks will become of great importance in real-time applications. A data network for real-time systems includes modems, multiplexers, concentrators, drop points and connections.

Computers for real-time applications

A computer for real-time processing comprises processor, arithmetic unit, input and output units, primary and secondary memories, together with communications multiplexers or special communications computers.

Files for real-time applications (databases)

Files for real-time applications are stored on secondary memories, usually disc types. There are several methods for storing the amount of information required in the system. There are three methods for random access to files:

- direct addressing
- look-up tables
- calculated addressing

Real-time programs (Transaction programs)

A common language used for writing programs is COBOL. There are certain aids available for program development on the host computer. Programs can be classified into three types

- Self-destructive programs (not re-usable)
  A new copy of the program must be loaded in for each execution

- Re-usable programs (self initiating)
  The same copy of the program can be re-used without having to be reloaded. The program itself initialises the working areas in an initialisation phase.

- Re-entrant programs (re usable, parallel)
  The same copy of a program can be run by several users simultaneously.

A real-time program in COBOL is divided into two parts, an instruction part and a data part (I bank and D bank), which consist of the program's PROCEDURE DIVISION and DATA DIVISION.

For the first two types of program mentioned above, both the program and the data parts are unique for every transaction. In re-entrant programs, several transactions already started use the same instruction part of the program simultaneously. However, the data part of every program must be unique for every transaction.

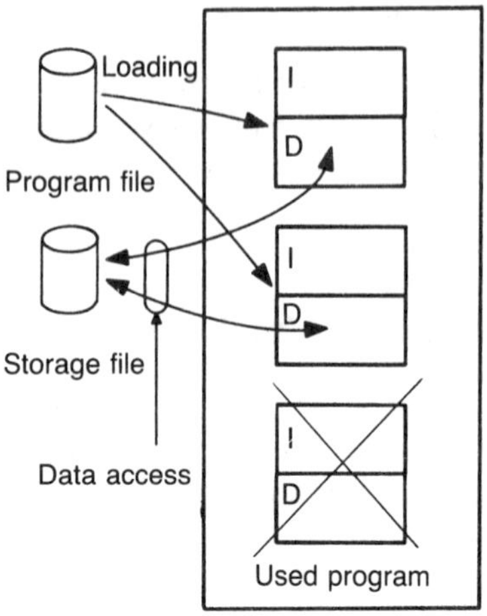

Figure 9.3 Self-destructive programs

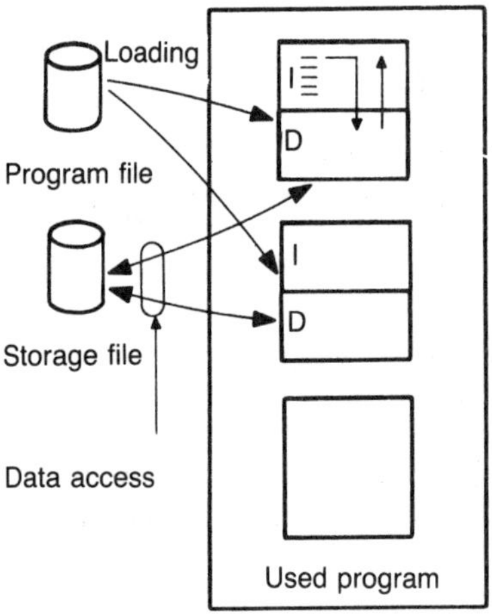

Figure 9.4 Self-initialising program

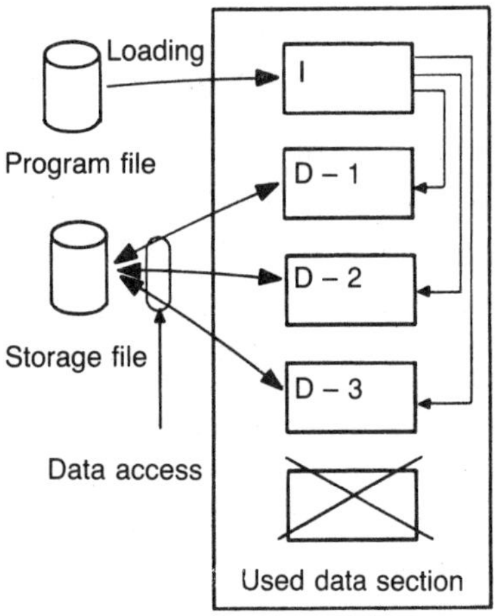

Figure 9.5 Re-entrant program

Formula processing

'Forms' are stored in the host computer, either in the 'picture library' or linked into the program. Forms (e g menu 'pages') are sent to the terminal when called up. They consist of field control characters with or without accompanying text. The field control characters define, among other things, the protected field and the input field. Protected fields cannot be changed by the operator, who can only write into the input fields. When a field is full, automatic tabulation is carried out to the first position in the next unprotected field. Tabulation can also be done from the keyboard or ordered by the computer.

```
821020 17.10
ARENDE: LBVAL                                48
BILD  : VALUTAKURSER
VALUTADATUM: 008241                          VALUTA                           OMRAKN     VALUTA
         VALUTAKOD   VALUTAKURS              KOD     BENAMNING                FAKTOR     KURS
           GBP                 ;             GBP     PUND STERLING             1.000      12.5400
           USD                 ;             USD     US $                      1.000       7.3175
           DEM                 ;             DEM     VASTTYSKA DM              0.010     291.9500
           FRF                 ;             FRF     FRANSKA FRANCS            0.010     103.2500
           BEC                 ;             BEC     BELG. FRANCS              0.010      15.0500
           CHF                 ;             CHF     SCHW. FRANCS              0.010     342.2000
           NLG                 ;             NLG     HOLL. FLORINER            0.010     267.1500
           DKK                 ;             DKK     DANSKA KR                 0.010      82.1000
           NOK                 ;             NOK     NORSKA KR                 0.010     101.3500
           FIM                 ;             FIM     FINSKA MARK               0.010     134.5000
           ITL                 ;             ITL     ITAL. LIRE                0.010       0.5150
           ATS                 ;             ATS     oST. SCHILLING            0.010      41.5500
           CAD                 ;             CAD     CAN. $                    1.000       5.9700
           YEN                 ;             YEN     JAPANSKA YEN              1.000       2.7600
                               ;

                             P1=VAL AV DATUM
                             P2=NYA VALUTAKURSER
S-P1=AVSLUTA/NYTT ARENDE
```

Figure 9.6 Example of a form. (Swedish State Power Board delivery monitoring system, currency file)

Protected or unprotected fields are produced by a sequence of field control characters which give certain characteristics to the field. Certain fields can for example be in low or high intensity or flashing text. One can also allow just a single number or letter to be put into a field. The field control characters themselves do not appear on the screen.

9.3 Queues and queueing theory

Introduction

The more advanced a real-time system is, the more important it is to coordinate the various activities, events and resources. Increased demands are made on quality, quantity, space and time. By over-dimensioning the quality, quantity and time, the difficulties of the work of coordination can be reduced.

However, overdimensioning of quality and quantity are often costly, so what remains is to lengthen the times. In many situations this is the only way in which an activity can proceed. And this is the way waiting is caused and queues are formed. Raised costs or queue problems – the optimal solution has to be found, as far as possible. It is natural to try to reduce waiting time, as this gives rise to irritation and stress.

These problems have created the need for methods of coping with such situations. Methods which mean on the one hand avoiding any queues arising due to accessible factors being incorrectly utilised, and which on the other hand can weigh up the sacrifices of waiting in the queue against those for overdimensioning of quantity or quality.

One very common requirement when dimensioning a transaction system is that a certain response time should be maintained. This is usually expressed in such terms as 95% of cases for a defined transaction having to be less than a certain value. By response time is meant that time between the terminal operator sending a transaction and when the first character in the response appears on the screen.

Mathematical formulae can be used in the dimensioning work, simulations can be carried out, and the results of studies and calculations/dimensioning carried out previously can also be used.

Simulation is reckoned to be the best aid, but the building of a complex simulation model is very demanding on time. Queueing theory, with its formulae and models, is much more easily handled and gives fully satisfactory results.

Mathematical model

When dealing with queuing problems, there are four factors which determine how the system will function

- the queueing situation
- the arrival process
- the service process
- queue discipline

Queueing situation

There are four basic types of queueing situation

- one queue and one service point
- one queue and several service points
- one queue and series-coupled service points
- one queue and several series-coupled service points.

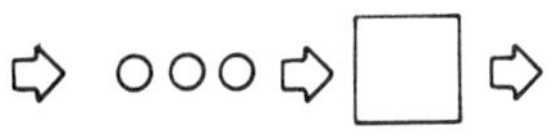

Figure 9.7 One queue, one service point

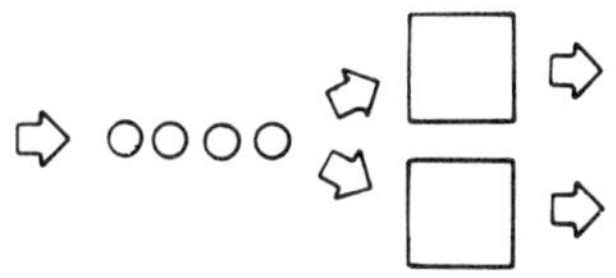

Figure 9.8 One queue, several service points

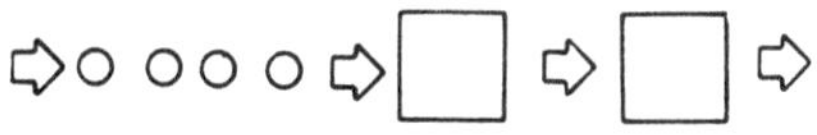

Figure 9.9 One queue, series-coupled service points

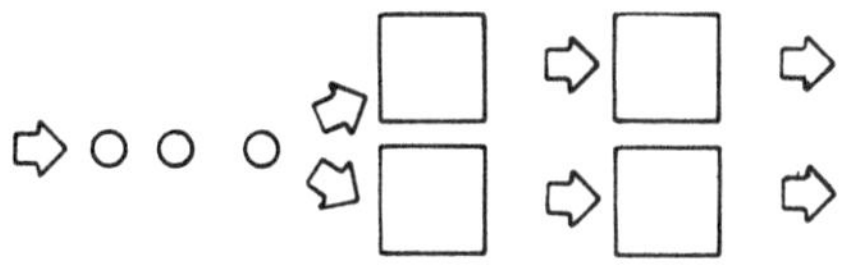

Figure 9.10 One queue, several series-coupled service points

Arrival process

This process means the times when an event or a transaction comes to some point in the queueing system where it will be serviced. This process can either be controlled or completely independent of other processes. As far as transaction systems are concerned, the arrivals are purely random. The intervals between transaction arrivals have a Poisson distribution. The probability that a transaction will arrive during the time interval will thus be

$$P(t, t+dt)\lambda dt$$

where λ=arrival density.

The time interval between arrival has an exponential distribution, and the probability $P_n(t)$ for n transactions arriving during time interval t is

$$P_n(t)=\frac{(\lambda \cdot t)^n}{n!} \cdot e^{-\lambda t}$$

$$n=1, 2, 3 \ldots$$

It has been found in practice that the arrival process is Poisson distributed and is not controlled.

Servicing process

In a similar way to the arrival interval, the servicing time also varies according to what needs doing. The probability B(t) of the servicing time being longer than t, for a random variation in servicing times, is

$$B(t)=e^{-\mu t}$$

where μ is the average servicing density.

Queue discipline

If there is no queue, processing occurs immediately. It is most common, however, that the last event/transaction ends up last in the queue. One way of getting round this is to give certain events/transactions priority, which means that they go to the front of the queue.

Servicing factor

Finally, the servicing factor ϱ has also been defined as

$$\varrho=\frac{\lambda}{S \cdot \mu}$$

This is equal to the degree of utilisation of the servicing point (see Figure 9.11).

λ=arrival density
S=number of parallel servicing points
μ=servicing density

In order for the queueing system to function, $\varrho<1$. If $\varrho \geq 1$, the queue will be infinite.

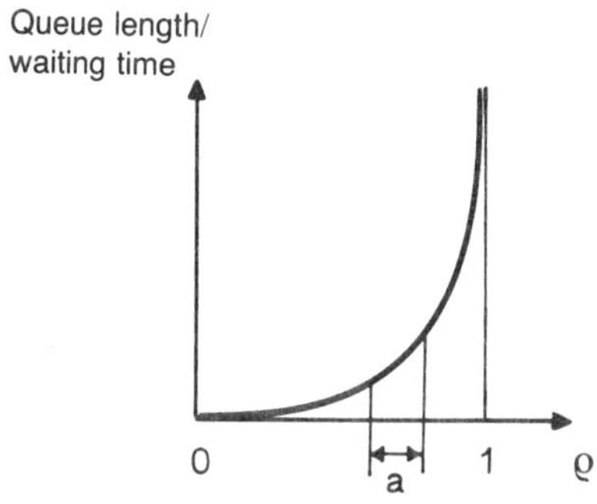

Figure 9.11 Queue length and waiting time as a function of degree of utilisation ϱ

As mentioned earlier, response time is of special interest in the dimensioning of transaction systems. The waiting time must be kept down, and no queue must be allowed to grow out of control. Problems of this type can be solved mathematically where the practical assumption is made that arrivals to the system occur according to the Poisson distribution. The time between two successive arrivals is exponentially distributed. By using the Khintchine-Polloczek formula for systems with exponentially distributed arrival intervals, expressions for queue length and waiting time in the queue can be derived

$$E(\omega)=\frac{\varrho^2}{2(1-\varrho)}\left\{1+\left[\frac{\sigma t_s}{E(t_s)}\right]^2\right\}$$

$E(\omega)$ =average queue length
$E(t_s)$ =average servicing time
ϱ =degree of utilisation
σ =spread of servicing times

The section of the curve in Figure 9.11 which is interesting lies in the interval a. Within this interval, small changes in σ give relatively large changes in queue length and waiting time. We shall not go too deeply in this book into all the calculation methods used in queueing theory. Advanced systems make the queueing theory formulae required for the calculations difficult to handle. Sufficient accuracy can be obtained by reading the required result from graphs produced by these methods. The graphs shown in Figures 9.12–9.18 are taken from James Martin's book "Systems Analysis for Data Transmission". Chapter 31 in Martin's book gives an exhaustive review of how these graphs can be understood and used. Similar information is also to be found in his book "Design of Real-Time Computer Systems".

When dimensioning terminals (servicing points) and lines (communication networks) for a system, one should start with the terminals. The number of terminals can be determined from the formula

$$M=\frac{E(n)\times E(s)}{\varrho}$$

where

M =number of terminals
E(n) =average number of transactions arriving at the system per second
E(s) =Average servicing time for a transaction
ϱ =servicing factor

The servicing factor is given a suitable arbitrary value.

With the aid of Martin's graphs, it can now be checked that the actual number of terminals gives a waiting time in a queue and a queue length which lie within the limits of the predetermined requirements. By varying the degree of usage (ϱ) by the terminal operator of the servicing points, the calculations can be repeated until a tolerable queue length is obtained.

When the number of terminals per department or terminal site is fixed, it is time to dimension the lines. The number of lines needed depends on several factors, such as

- the comprehensiveness of the system
- transmission speed
- how many terminals can be connected to each line
- type of connections
- response time requirements.

To this end, there are ready-made 'crib-sheets' which are used by those responsible within the communications area for dimensioning of communications networks.

As a rule of thumb, for high loads on a fixed 9600 bps multi-point line, a maximum of 10 terminals can be connected. A lower loading allows a larger number of terminals, but not more than 16.

Graphs

The graphs which follow are taken from James Martin's book "Systems Analysis for Data Transmission". Seven graphs have been copied altogether. This is only a part of material to be found in his book.

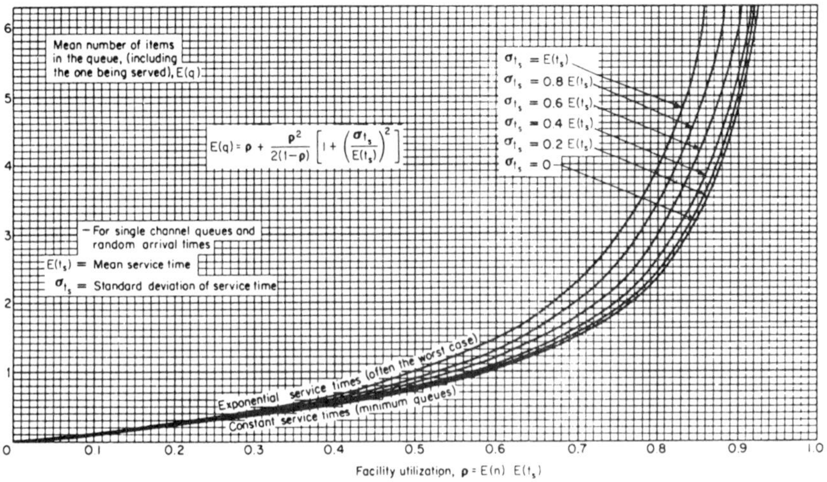

Figure 9.12 Average queue length including those being serviced at the time, where one customer is being serviced at a time

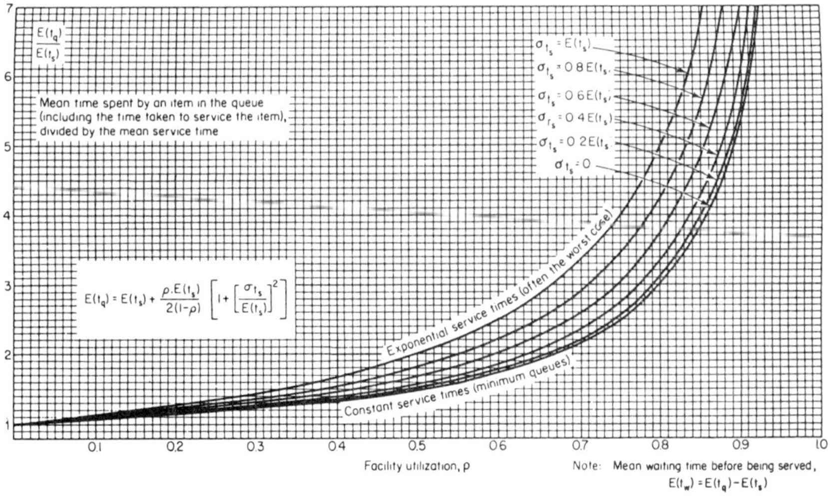

Figure 9.13 Average queue length including service time, where one customer is being serviced at a time.

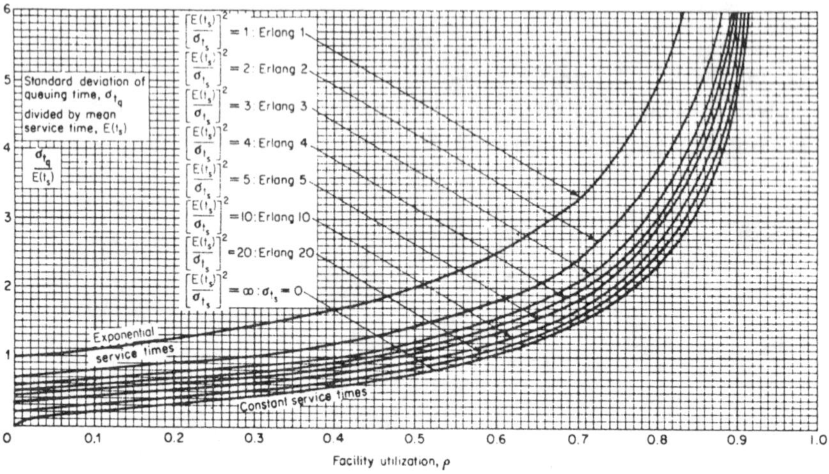

Figure 9.14 Standard deviation of queueing time including servicing time where one customer is serviced at the time

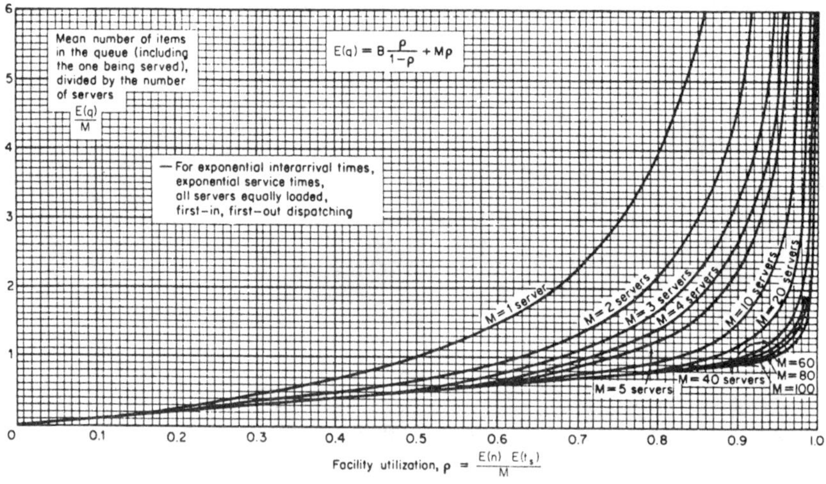

Figure 9.15 Average queue length including those being serviced at the time, where several customers can be serviced at one time

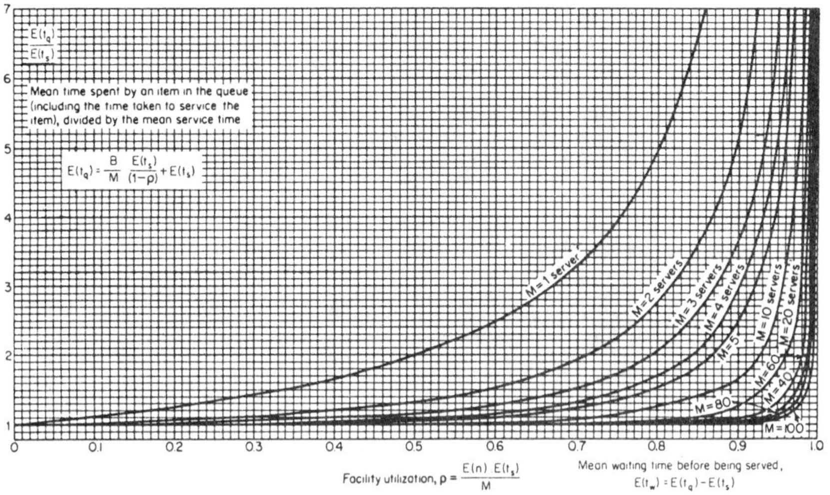

Figure 9.16 Average queue length including service time, where several customers can be serviced at one time

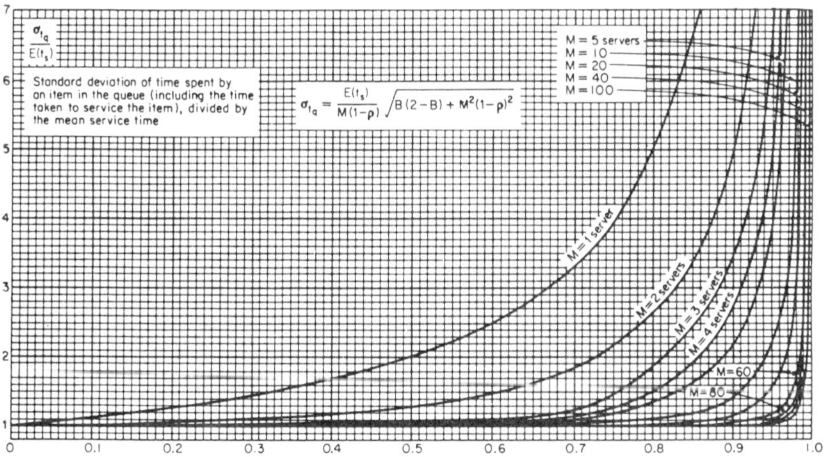

Figure 9.17 Standard deviation of queueing time including servicing time where several customers can be serviced at one time

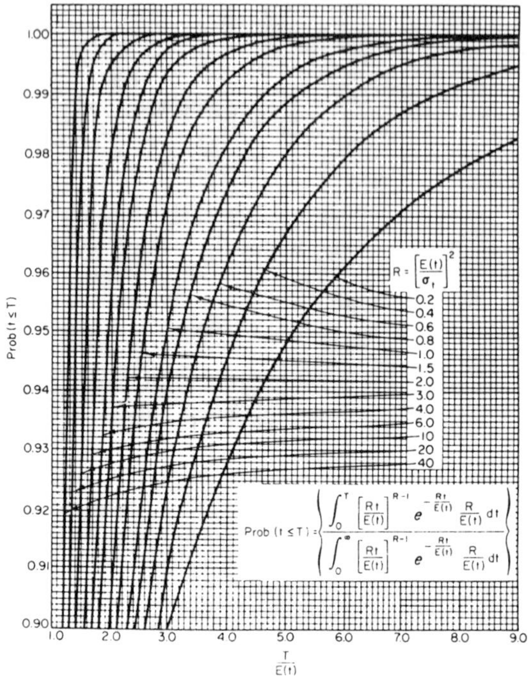

Figure 9.18 The gamma function

10 Data and telephone connections

10.1 Introduction

There are two basic types of data line provided by the Swedish telephone company

- temporarily connected lines through the telephone network and exchanges
- permanently-connected long-term leased lines.

The lines in both cases can consist of leads for physical traffic, coaxial cables and radio links.

Dialled-up connections are the more flexible, as connections can be made to different receivers. If individual lines become damaged, the dialled network can often find alternative routes around the damaged area. Disadvantages include limited transmission quality, more recently compensated for by automatic equalisers in the modems; and also, from the data viewpoint, the long connection time (often over 10 seconds).

Fixed lines are notable for simplicity in use and rapid access. The line is ready for immediate use without connecting up. It also usually means a higher transmission speed than a dialled-up connection, as it can be equalised in advance. The line can be monitored continuously so that any break or other fault is immediately detected. Among the disadvantages of fixed lines is their lack of flexibility. Transmission can only be between two fixed end-points. The efficiency is therefore low in many applications where the data flow is not sufficient for the capacity of the line.

10.2 Two-wire connections

In a two-wire line, a single pair of leads is used for transmission in both directions. Subscriber telephone lines are always two-wire.

Figure 10.1 Two-wire connection

In order to minimise the risk of 'crossed lines' or transfer between pairs of wires in the same cable, the signal level in a line must not be too low, because a nearby line could then affect it. For this reason, the lines must be fitted with amplifiers or repeaters.

Line amplifiers, whose principle is shown in Figure 10.2, unite two wires which are connected to the two-terminal pair A and B. The amplifiers, which amplify in the direction A–B and B–A respectively, are connected to the wires via the terminating set consisting of the differential transformers Ta and Tb and the line-balancing impedances Ba and Bb. Each line balancing impedance comprises a passive linear two-terminal-pair network, dimensioned so that the impedance is as similar as possible to the incoming line's characteristic, which is in practice equal to the line's input impedance. The differential transformers then form a 1:1 relationship in a balanced bridge, with the line and the balancing impedance as arms of the bridge, and the input of one amplifier and the output of the other as the diagonals of the bridge. In this way feedback, which could cause oscillations in the system, is prevented.

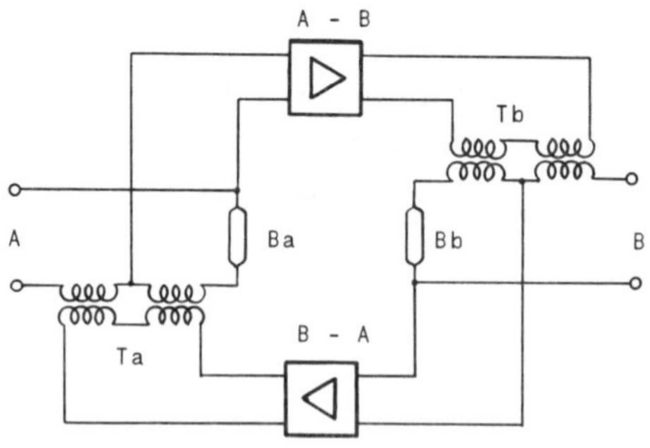

Figure 10.2 Principles of the two-wire amplifier

Figure 10.3 shows a two-wire connection between end-stations A and B with three amplifiers on the line, and the transmission level diagram for directions A–B and B–A respectively. These diagrams show the transmission level on the line as a function of the distance S from station A taken along the line. The distance between amplifiers is of the order of 100 km.

The transmission level lies within certain determined limits.

Cable type	**Max level**	**Min level**	**Max amplification**
Plain wires	0	−1.5	1.5 neper
Cable lines	0.5	−1.8	2.3 neper

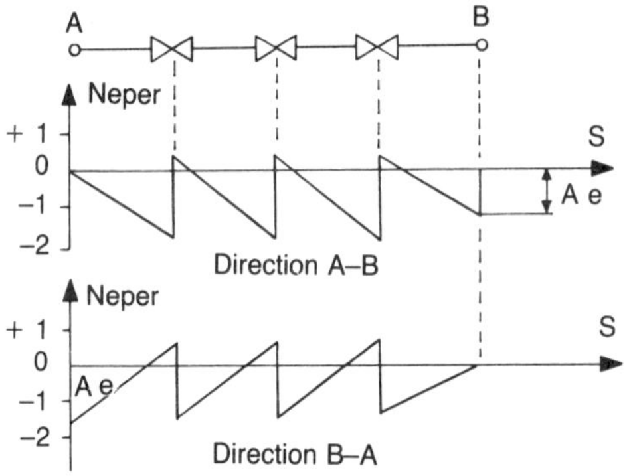

Figure 10.3 Transmission diagram for two-wire lines

10.3 Four-wire connections

In a four-wire connection one pair of wires is used for transmission in one direction and one pair for the other direction. The connections between distant stations on the Domestic network are always four-wire.

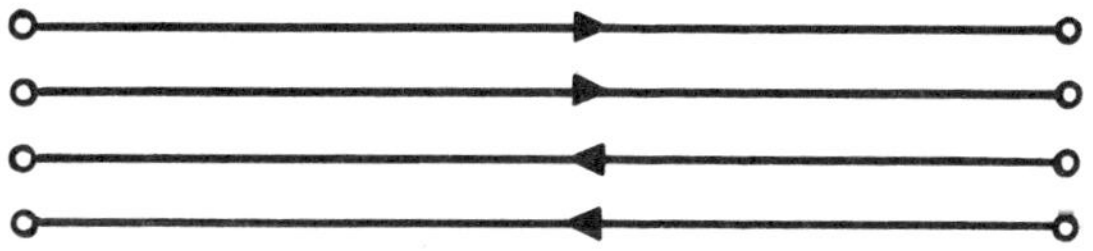

Figure 10.4 Four-wire connections

Four-wire connections use two double cables, La-b and Lb-a for transmission in directions A–B and B–A respectively. In this way line balancing and instability in the four-way line amplifiers $A_1 \ldots A_2 \ldots A_n$. are avoided. On the other hand, terminating set must be used for the four-way connections at the end-points of the line.

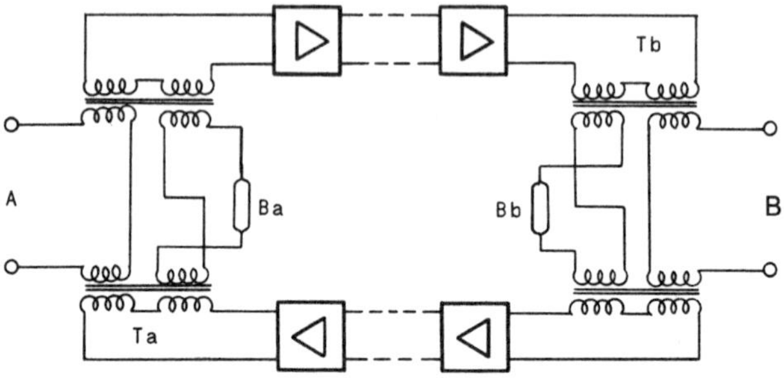

Figure 10.5 Principles of four-way lines

The greater amplification used on four-way lines as compared with two-way also of course gives greater differences in transmission levels. CCITT gives the following limits for transmission levels in four-wire connections:

Max level	Min level	Max amplification
1.1	−3.0	4.1 neper

Figure 10.6 shows examples of two transmission level diagrams for a four-wire connection, one for each direction of transmission.

As will be seen, there is less drop in level at the endpoints of the lines.

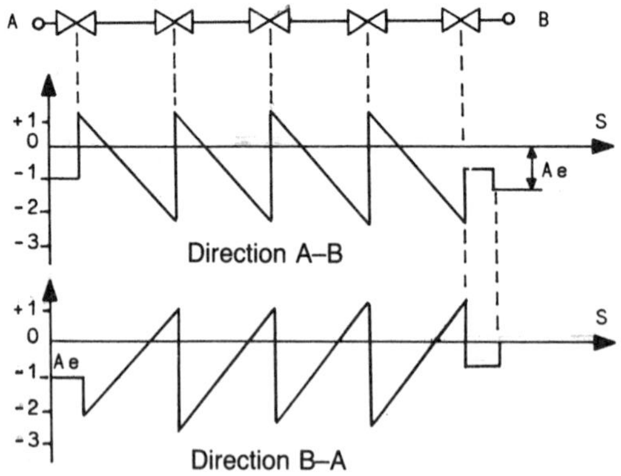

Figure 10.6 Transmission diagram for four-wire connections

10.4 Connection methods

Phantomising

Two pairs of wires form a quad line. If the two double lines in such a four-way line are connected to a line transformer with a centre tapping, this gives three possible ways of connecting up. Apart from the main 'trunk' lines, there is a third lead, the so-called phantom lead. One of its branches consists of the parallel-connected wires in trunk 1, and its other branch of the wires in trunk 2. The current directions in the phantom lead are shown in Figure 10.7. If the trunk transformer's midpoint is well-balanced and the branches of the trunk leads are equal, the current divides equally into both half windings and there is no resultant field in the iron core of the transformer, so that no voltage is induced into the trunk circuits. The same thing is true in the opposite direction, where the currents in the trunk circuits do not have any effect on the phantom circuit either.

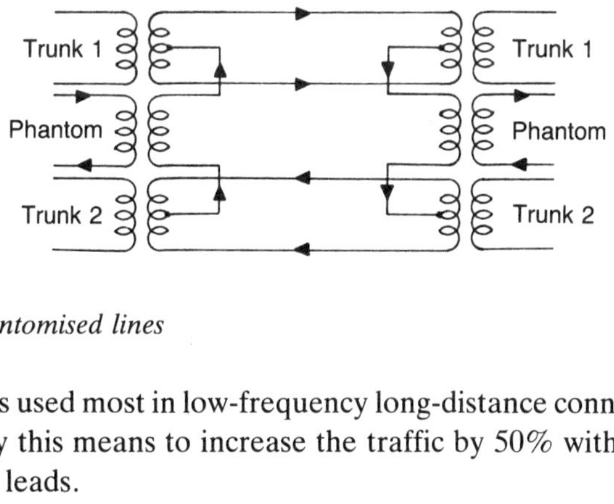

Figure 10.7 Phantomised lines

Phantomising is used most in low-frequency long-distance connections, where it is possible by this means to increase the traffic by 50% without increasing the number of leads.

Pupinising

Pupinising involves increasing the self-induction of a line by connecting coils in at equal intervals, if the distance between the coils is small compared with the frequency of the wavelength of the transmitted speech frequencies.

The American Michael Pupin, who researched the question of distances, found that what is now known as the Pupin distance must not exceed one seventh of the smallest wavelength occurring along the line without inductance coils.

The inductance coils for this purpose are called Pupin coils and commonly consist of a toroidal iron core with windings in a similar layout to the surrounding circuitry.

The connection of Pupin coils into a line is known as pupinisation, and is carried out almost exlusively in cable lines. The pupinisation of a quad line at each Pupin point, the principle of which is shown in Figure 10.8, involves a Pupin coil T in each trunk line and a Pupin coil Ph in the phantom line. The windings are divided up and spaced out on the iron core in order to achieve the greatest possible symmetry with respect to earth. The three coils are mounted in a sheet-steel box filled with moisture-repellent compound, and called three-coil units.

A larger number of three-coil units would be collected together in a steel container called a Pupin box, which would also be filled with a moisture-resistant compound. Pupin boxes are often buried in the ground, where they sit on a concrete base and are provided with a concrete cover.

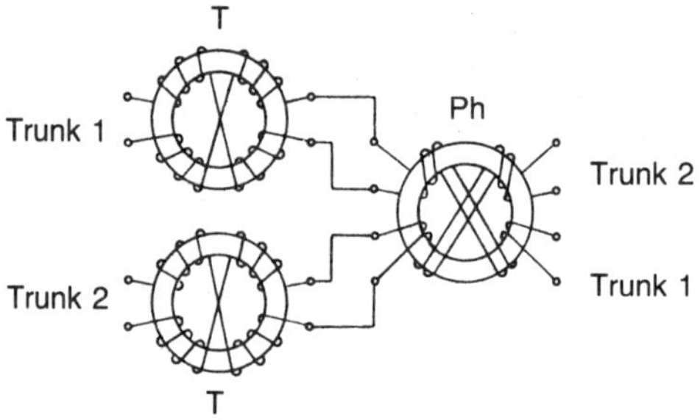

Figure 10.8 Pupinisation of quad lines

10.5 Carrier Frequency (CF) connections

Introduction

Using the carrier frequency system, hereafter referred to as the CF system, the number of existing physical lines can be multiplied many-fold.

The cost of the apparatus required for a CF system means that it only becomes economic to use it over greater than a certain minimum distance.

However, developments seem to indicate that this distance will shrink, due to the fact that the relative cost of laying physical connections or lines is tending to rise.

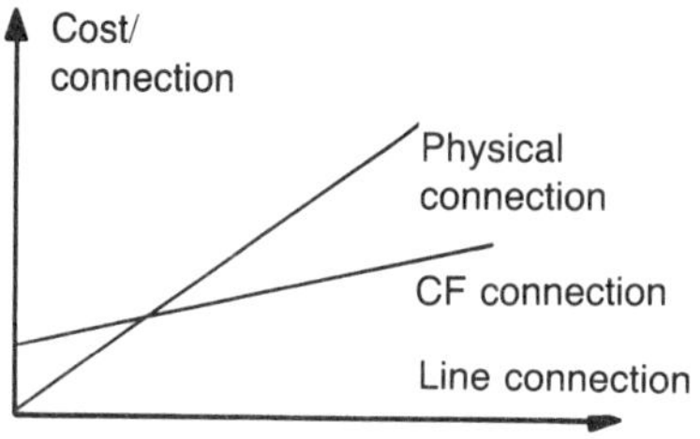

Figure 10.9 Cost as a function of line distance

The transmission quality on CF lines is always better over long distances than on physical lines. A CF line works in principle the same as a four-wire line – even though it only uses two wires – and therefore has the stability characteristics associated with a four-wire system. On overhead lines, CF transmission gives less distortion and shorter delay time on cables, and thereby less time distortion than on physical lines.

CF system categories

The CF system can be categorised by the number of carrier frequencies it allows. One can speak of a 12-channel system, for example, and mean by this a system which gives 12 carrier-frequency lines. The term channel refers properly to a transmission route in one direction.

CF systems can either use the same cable pair for both transmission directions, or have different cable pairs for each direction. This therefore gives high-frequency two-wire or high-frequency four-wire systems.

CF systems may also be categorised on whether they use both sidebands, one for each transmission direction, and those which only use a single sideband.

CF connection on two- and four-wire cables

Low frequency, long distance telephony uses mainly pupinised cables. For heavy pupinisation, i e where the Pupin coils in the line have large inductance values, the damping is relatively low, but at the same time the limiting frequency is low and the delay time longer. Lighter pupinisation causes lower line damping and the limiting frequency is higher, thereby giving a greater transmission range. In addition, the delay time is shorter.

Where multi-channel systems are to be used on cables, the frequency band must be increased still further. In order to obtain any worthwhile damping gain at high limiting frequencies, the Pupin coils need to be situated very close together, which becomes very costly. It has therefore been shown to be advantageous to transmit multi-channel systems over unpupinised cables, despite the fact that the distance between amplifiers then has to be relatively short. The determining factors for line damping for the stretches between amplifiers are partly the transmitted level and partly the lowest receiving level. The transmission level is determined with reference to distortion in the amplifiers. For an 8-channel system, for example, this is standardised at 0.5 nepers. The lowest receiving level (at the highest frequency) is determined by the thermal noise on the line and noise in the amplifiers, together with the number of amplifier stations on the stretch.

On the high-frequency side, CF connections on cables can either be sent over two-wire or four-wire systems. On solid cables it is always two-wire, and in this case there must be different frequency bands for each transmission. Where different lines within cables can be used for different transmission directions, and obtain sufficiently low levels of cross-talk, four-wire transmission may be used with the same frequency band in both directions. Figures 10.10–10.12 show examples of some of the different methods.

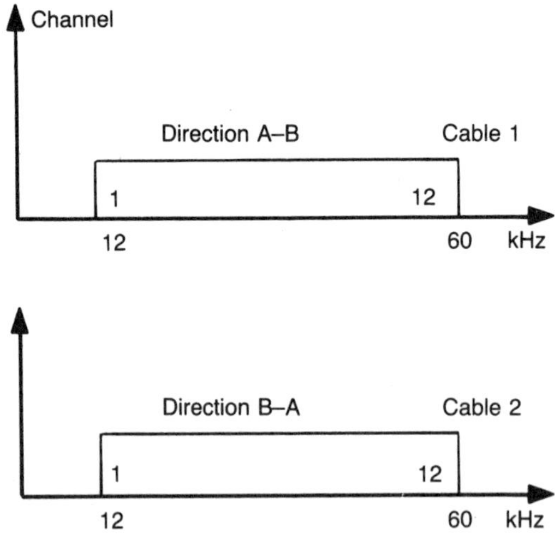

Figure 10.10 Frequency spectrum for 12-channel systems in four-wire mode. One cable for each direction of transmission

Figure 10.11 Frequency spectrum for an 8-channel system running on the same cable pair (two-wire system)

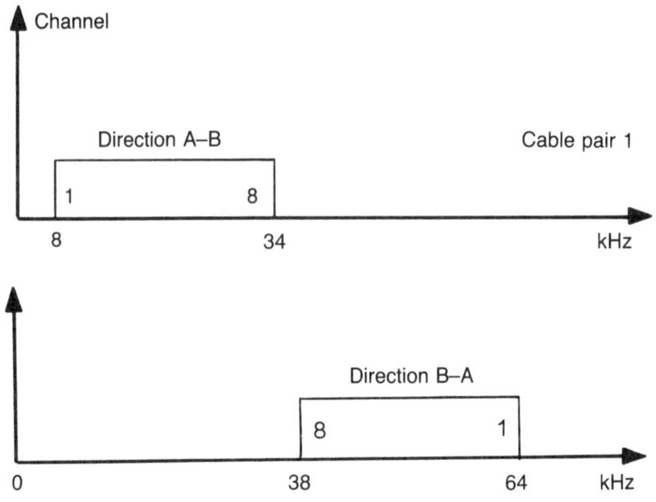

Figure 10.12 Frequency spectrum for an 8-channel system with four-wire running and different frequency bands for each direction of transmission

Broadband system for coaxial cables

Where it is desired to increase the number of lines, one must have a wide frequency band and also make use of the higher frequencies. The most suitable type of cable is the coaxial cable. A coaxial cable has the characteristic that the outer lead itself forms a shielded cover, and the shield frequency is higher the higher the frequency is. One can therefore lay two or more tubes beside one another without cross-talk, even between transmissions in different directions, being troublesome.

10.6 Pulse Code Modulation (PCM)

Basic principles of PCM

More than 40 years ago, A.H. Reeves sought a patent for a new method of speech transmission using the time-multiplexing principle. Instead of transmitting, according to the principle of Pulse Amplitude Modulation (PAM) in the time slot, a pulse whose amplitude was directly proportional to the momentary value of the speech voltage, he chose to code this value so that it resulted in a series of pulses, i e a kind of telegraphy character. The coding was binary, i e each pulse could be one of two values, either a one or a zero. The larger the number of pulse positions per character, the greater the accuracy with which the speech voltage level could be reproduced. In today's technology this number is 7 or 8 per value sent (sample), thereby representing 128 or 256 different voltage levels. The original continual amplitude scale is thus divided up into a finite number of intervals or quantisation steps – the direct analogue representation is replaced by digital representation. The method is called pulse code modulation (PCM). Material in Section 10.6 is from LM Ericsson's "Digital Telephony".

The conversion of an analogue signal to a digital one is based on three main principles: sampling, quantisation and coding, as shown in Figure 10.13.

Information theory shows that for transmission of information in a signal, it is not necessary to transmit the whole signal. It is sufficient to send 'test sections', or samples, of the signal which are taken at a frequency at least twice the signal frequency. This condition is usually known as the sampling theorem.

Samples taken from a signal within the speech frequency range represent a succession of amplitudes which, within certain limits, can take any value they like. The next stage in the analogue/digital conversion is to divide up the amplitudes into a limited number of size classes. All samples whose amplitude falls within the interval for a particular size class are given the same value. This is still called quantisation. The inevitable distortion this process causes is known as quantisation distortion.

The quantised sample is then coded into a suitable code. Figure 10.13 shows coding into a normal binary code. The signal can now be transmitted as a pulse train using binary pulses.

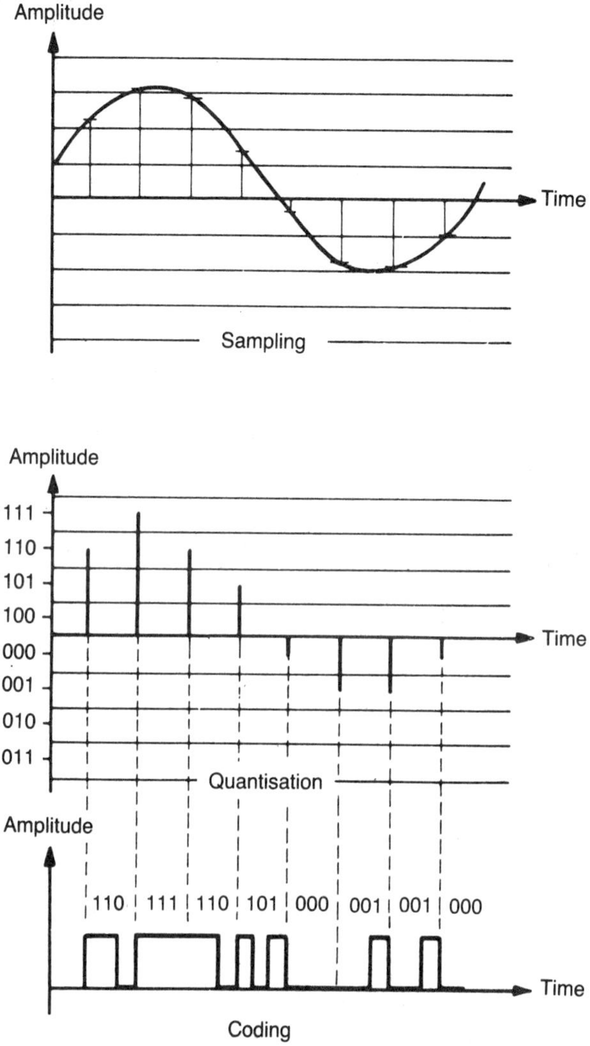

Figure 10.13 The principles of pulse code modulation

This is the principle on which the PCM transmission system is based. The main components in such a system comprise a sender and a receiver connected by a transmission line (see Figure 10.14).

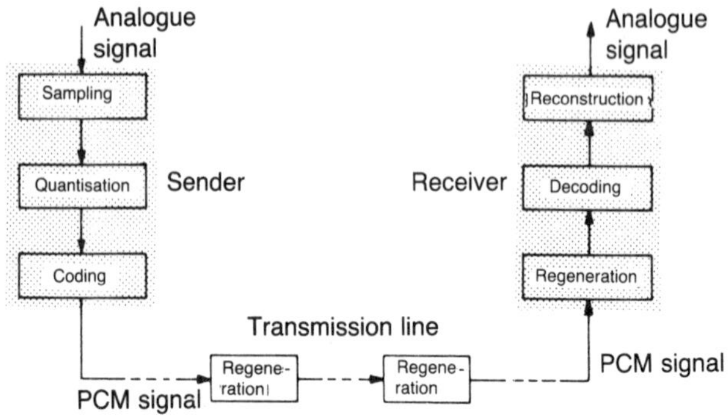

Figure 10.14 Pulse code modulation. Functional block

The PCM system is designed to use time multiplexing (TDM) in order to increase its transmission capacity.

As the code generated for each sample can be sent very rapidly, it is possible to allow samples from other sources to share in a common transmission route by using different time points. Each sample is allocted a separate "time slot", forming what is known as a first-order PCM system.

In an analogy with the frequency multiplexing system, combining a number of first-order PCM systems produces a second-order PCM system, and so on. This builds up what is known as a multiplex hierarchy.

Reasons for PCM

The following are some of the motives for using PCM technology

- *Transmission quality* is almost independent of distance. The characteristic of a digital signal is its insensitivity to interference. Digital signals can be regenerated at intervals along the line without losing any quality. This is not the case with analogue signals, where not only the signal but also the interference is amplified in the intervening amplifier stages. In the case of digital signals, the amplifier only needs to decide whether an incoming pulse is a 'one' or a 'zero'. When a pulse has been identified, the amplifier sends out a fresh pulse. There is a high probability that a number of the incoming pulses will be so disorted that they cannot be identified correctly, but equally well this error count can be made so low as to be acceptable. It should however be observed that the PCM systems used in practice and specified by CCITT are no better from the point of view of transmission than the FDM system specified by CCITT.

- *Time division multiplexing*. The TDM principle allows an increase of capacity on cable pairs which were originally used for individual telephone channels. Instead of laying new cables, PCM can be introduced on existing cables.
- *Economy for certain connection links*. In certain applications, especially in the wire lead network, the PCM technique has shown itself able to compete with every other transmission method. The length of the transmission link should keep within the range where ordinary voice lines tend to be too long and FDM links too short. The optimal distance interval is highly dependent on local factors such as subscriber density, land topography, etc, and can therefore vary widely.
- *Economy in combination with digital connection*. A large proportion of the costs of a PCM system can be due to the terminals. The introduction of digital connections reduces these costs considerably, as in this case one can take the digital bit stream directly without needing to use costly analogue/digital conversion. The combination of digital connections and transmission thus provides the opportunity to reduce the overall costs.
- *IC technology*. Technological developments of integrated circuits indicate that one can expect an advantageous price level and high reliability.
- *Integration of services*. In its role as a digital transmission medium, a PCM link can transfer not just speech, but also data, telex, coded pictorial information, etc. A PCM link has a capacity of 64,000 bits/s, which makes it a very powerful data channel.
- *New transmission media*. Future broadband transmission media, such as waveguides and optical fibres, are more suitable for digital than for analogue transmission.

Sampling

In the world of electricity, sampling means making regular instantaneous measurements of the amplitude of an analogue signal (see Figure 10.15).

The sampled signal forms a train of pulses whose envelope is made up by the original signal. But how many samples per second should one take, i e what sampling frequency should one choose? The answer to this is given by the sampling theorem, which also gives information on whether the sampled signal contains all the information from the original signal, on condition that:

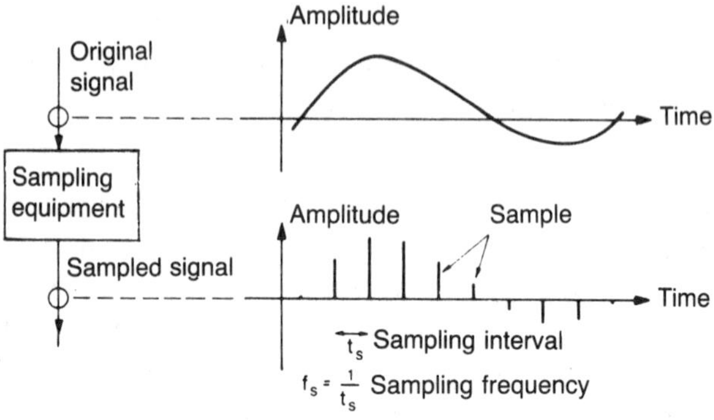

Figure 10.15 The sampling process

- the original signal has a limited bandwidth, i e that in its spectrum there are no frequency components over a determined frequency B,
- that the samping frequency is equal to or greater than twice B, i e $f_s \geqslant 2B$.

The sampling theorem is illustrated in Figure 10.16. The sampled signal obviously contains the original signal's frequency spectrum, which means that no information has been lost.

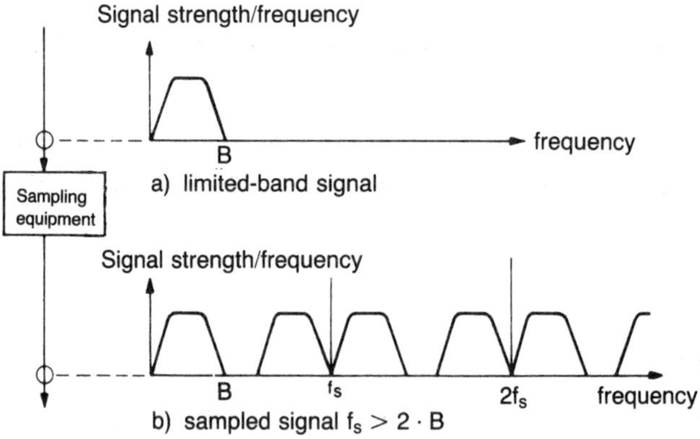

Figure 10.16 Spectrum of a) limited band signal, b) sampled signal

In telephony, that part of the spectrum lying between 300 and 3400 Hz is used. The human voice spectrum goes from a couple of hundred Hz up to very high frequencies. The telephone apparatus reduces this frequency range, but not sufficiently at higher frequencies. In order to come under the 3400 Hz level, the speech signal must go through a low-pass filter before sampling.

The PCM system uses a sampling frequency of 8000 Hz. This frequency results from the difficulty in getting a low-pass filter with a sharp enough cut-off. The frequency is more than twice as high as that used in telephony.

The sampled signal is often said to be pulse amplitude modulated, because it consists of pulses whose amplitudes have been modulated from the original signal. Pulse amplitude modulation (PAM) is an analogue pulse modulation method, because the amplitude of the pulses varies in accordance with the original signal variations.

The relatively simple design of the PAM system makes it attractive for certain telephony applications. However, the PAM system is unsuitable for transmission over long distances, because of the difficulty of regenerating the pulses with sufficient accuracy; this is important, because the information resides in the height of the pulse in the PAM system.

Quantisation

The quantisation process involves breaking down the pulse amplitude range successively to give a limited number of amplitude values. The amplitude range is divided into intervals, and all samples whose amplitudes fall within a certain quantisation interval are rounded to the same value (see Figure 10.17). The rounding process introduces an error into the signal which cannot be corrected; this is known as quantisation distortion.

This consciously introduced source of errors, whose effect can be made sufficiently small by making the number of amplitude levels sufficiently large, can be accepted, because it is possible to make the transmission error-free by only having a discrete number of allowable amplitude levels.

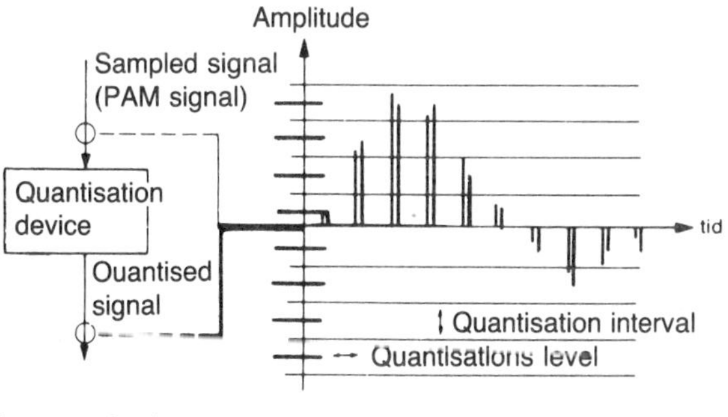

Figure 10.17 The quantisation process

The extent of the quantisation distortion, as seen in Figure 10.17, is independent of sample amplitude. This means that the listener hears an equal amount of distortion whether the speaker is speaking loudly or softly. In comparison, the low speech level generates much greater distortion than the high level. In addition, statistical analysis shows that an individual subscriber's speech is more likely to have small amplitudes than large ones.

In order to obtain an acceptable level of quantisation distortion over the whole of the dynamic range, the quantisation interval must be dimensioned with reference to low speech levels, which means that the quantisation intervals must be very small. In this way, the quantisation distortion at high speech levels will be much lower than necessary. This, however, is obtained at the cost of a large number of quantisation intervals.

It becomes clear that the quantisation error doesn't need to be independent of sample amplitude, but instead can be related to amplitude in some way, so that small amplitudes should give small quantisation errors and large amplitudes can give larger ones. The aim of this is to bring about an optimal compromise between transmission quality and the number of quantisation intervals.

This can be done in two ways, either by compression of the dynamic range of the signal before quantisation with subsequent expansion at the receiving end, or by the use of a quantisation interval which grows with amplitude. This process is usually known as companding (compression and expanding). Modern PCM systems use this sort of companding. If the size of the quantisation interval grows approximately according to a logarithmic scale, it is possible to achieve a roughly constant signal/distortion ratio over a broad dynamic range, and at the same time it is possible to use fewer levels than would be necessary with unitary quantisation intervals. CCITT have recommended two formulae in the use of PCM for telephony, which are generally known as the A law and the μ law. The A law is shown in Figure 10.18. These laws are also called coding laws, as in practice the quantisation process takes place in the coder.

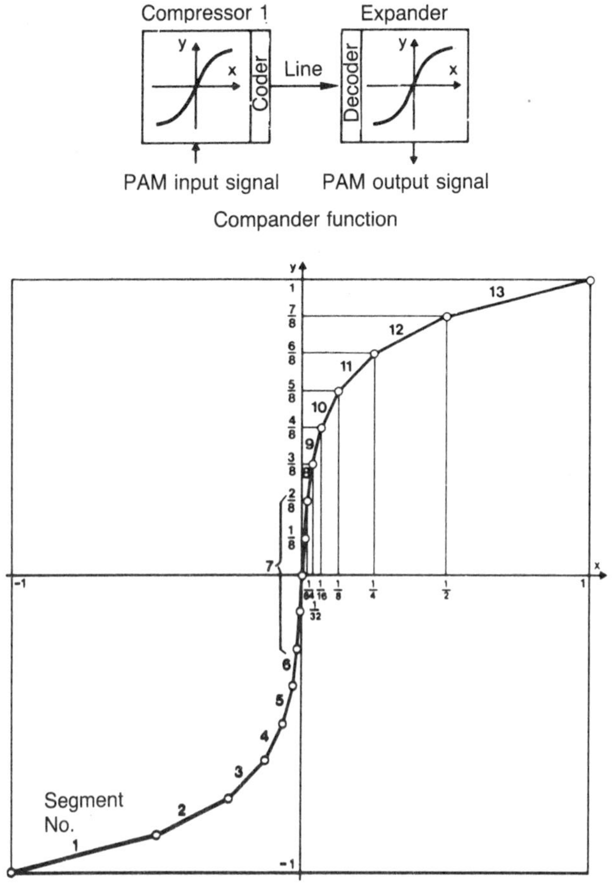

Figure 10.18 The A law. The μ law has a similar appearance, but has 15 segments

Coding

The quantised samples themselves are suitable for transmission over lines, because it would be difficult to build regeneration circuits which could differentiate between the large number of sample amplitudes, commonly 256, which are required for speech signals.

However, there is great latitude available in the coding of these amplitudes into a form suitable for transmission. As a rule, a quantised sample can be coded into two or more pulses with fewer amplitude levels per pulse. A group of n pulses, each with b possible different amplitude levels, can represent b^n quantised amplitude levels (see Table 10.1).

As mentioned, pulses with two levels, i e binary pulses, are suitable for transmission because they are easy to regenerate along the line. It is not difficult to design regenerating circuits which only have to distinguish between the presence or absence of a pulse.

The PCM systems on the market use binary coding of the quantised samples. As there are 256 quantisation levels in telephony applications, each sample is coded into a group, or PCM word, consisting of 8 binary pulses (8 bits).

The sampling frequency used is up to 8000 samples per second, so a pulse-modulated speech signal will generate a 64 kbits/s digital signal.

Table 10.1 Table of coding alternatives for quantised samples with 256 amplitude levels

Number of amplitude levels b^n	Number of pulses n	Number of levels per pulse b
256	1	256
256	2	16
256	4	4
256	8	2

Transmission

Digital signals within the terminal are commonly sent in the form of a unipolar pulse train on the "non-return-to-zero" (NRZ) method (see Figure 10.19). This signal method is not suitable for transmission over long distances. A better method is to use bipolar "return-to-zero" signals. The advantage of such signals is:

- The lower part of the signal's spectrum is low in energy, i e there is no DC component, because of the changing polarity of the pulses
- The return-to-zero method also reduces interference between close-lying pulses.

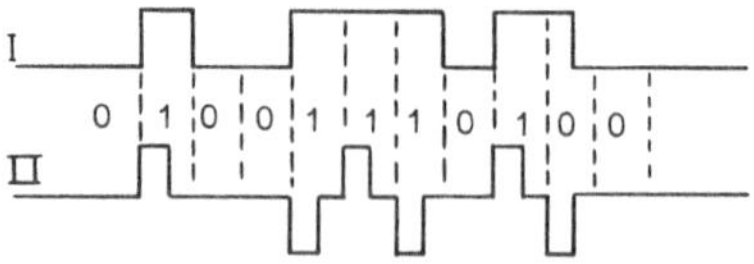

Figure 10.19 Binary information represented by: I. a unipolar non-return-to-zero (NRZ) pulse train, and II. a biopolar return-to-zero (RZ) pulse train

Naturally, even these signals will be damped and disorted, and noise will be added.

At some point along the transmission line, the shape of the signal must be reinstated. This is done by a device which firstly examines the disorted pulse train to see which pulses are to be interpreted as "ones" and which as "zeroes". Based on the results of this, new pulses are generated and sent on out over the line. This unit (see Figure 10.20) is known as a regenerator.

While the pulses are being recreated, the noise which is added during transmission is eliminated. This is true for each case where the interference signal's amplitude is not so great as to cause the code signal received to end up on the wrong side of the decision level during regeneration.

Normally the regenerated code signal is identical with the code signal originally transmitted. Even after a large number of regenerations, the coded signal is practically identical with the original. This is the reason for the high transmission quality which can be obtained with the PCM transmission system.

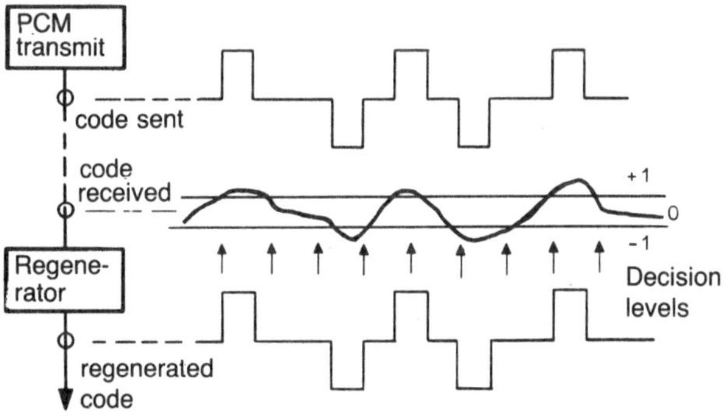

Figure 10.20 Pulse shapes on a transmission line

Demodulation, PCM

For converting the incoming PCM signal to an analogue signal in the receiver, the following processes are used: regeneration, decoding and reconstruction.

The regeneration process has the same aims and is done in the same way as in the regenerators along the transmission line, i e the distorted pulses are replaced by new square-wave pulses (see Figure 10.20). Before the pulses are fed into the decoder, the bipolar pulses are reconverted to unipolar ones.

During the decoding process, the code words generate pulse amplitudes whose size is the same as in the quantised sample which originally generated the code words. This means that on the output side of the decoder we have once again got back to the original train of quantised samples (see Figure 10.21).

The analogue signal is reconstructed in a low-pass filter (Figure 10.22), and the way this functions is shown in Figure 10.23. As seen already in Figure 10.16, the frequency spectrum of the sampled signal also contains the spectrum of the original signal. Using a low-pass filter with a limiting frequency of B Hz, all components above B Hz are removed, thus only leaving the spectrum of the desired analogue signal.

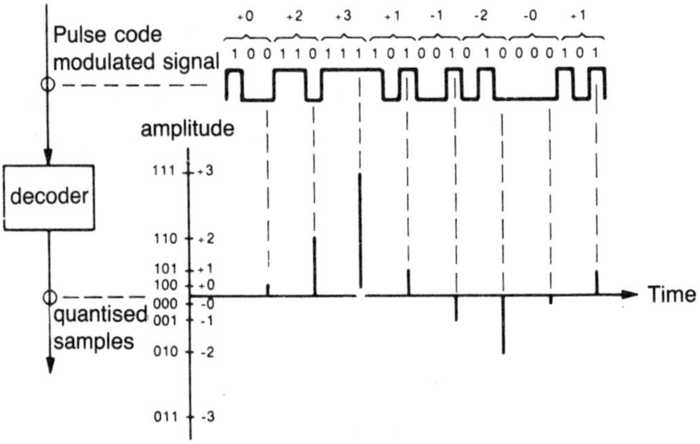

Figure 10.21 *Decoding of coded amplitude levels*

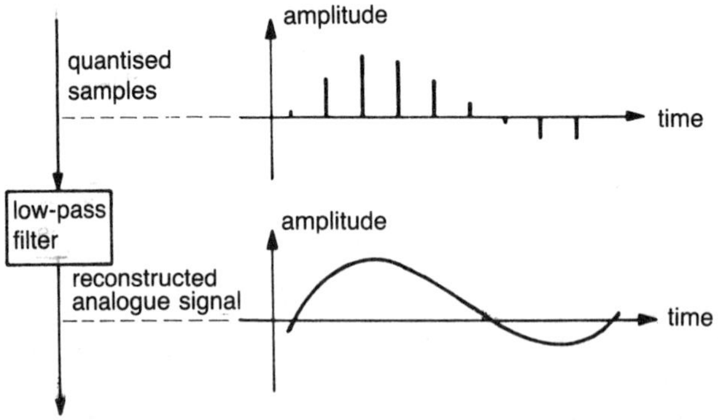

Figure 10.22 *Reconstruction of the analogue signal*

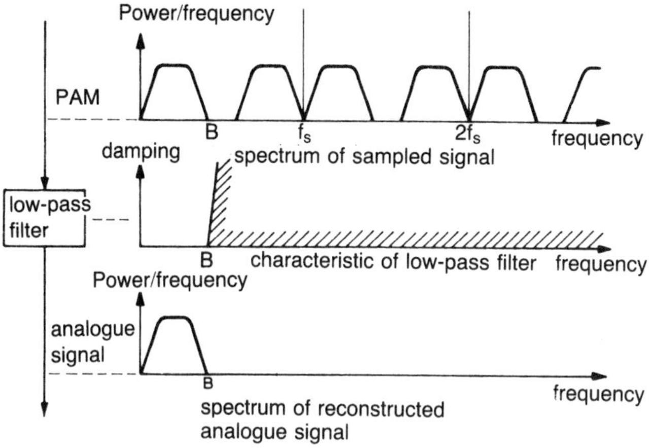

Figure 10.23 Reconstruction of the analogue signal shown in spectrum diagrams

10.7 Summary

In this chapter we have shown some of the older line and connection methods which exist very widely, and today's modern PCM system. A large amount of capital has been invested in network and telephony stations in many countries, which means that the old and the new technologies will have to live side by side for a long time to come. In Sweden, the older autmatic telephone exchanges (Ericsson's 500-selector type) are gradually being changed to AXE program memory controlled stations. The solid core wires out in the country are also being changed for cable or radio links.

By arranging for suitable data communication connections, our data can thus use both the older and the more modern technologies.

It may seem a backward step to transfer digital data between two points by first transforming it to analogue form, and then reconverting it to digital form at the receiving end. It would be more logical if the whole link between the two points were digital. The technology for digital networks already exists today. However, it is a slow process to install digital networks with the existing analogue ones. In most countries, therefore, analogue equipment will dominate the telephone networks for the rest of this century. On the other hand, new network installations will to a great extent be of digital types.

11 Terminals

11.1 Introduction

Various types of terminal equipment are used in communication between man and computer. Terminals can be positioned close to the computer, ie at a distance which can be bridged without special communication equipment being needed. Terminals can also be connected at great distances, for example in networks which are geographically widespread. Terminals can be classified according to how data is fed into or presented on them. The choice of terminal is usually a question of cost, but is also dependent on application. Other important factors are response time and ergonomics.

Data terminals are mainly of two types:

- data printer or printing terminal
- data monitors (VDU's)

Data printers are similar to the common typewriter. They are connected to the computer either directly or over the telephone network. VDU's (Visual Display Units) are provided with a typewriter-like keyboard and a TV-like presentation screen. Text fed in from the computer or from the keyboard is presented on the screen.

The VDU screen is the most attractive piece of terminal equipment, partly because of its simplicity in use and its flexibility.

One disadvantage is that applications developed for a certain type of terminal may be difficult to use on another type, due to the different characteristics of the terminals. During system development, it often happens that some of the terminal's features, such as the characteristics of the function keys, forms handling, etc, are built into the system so that they can be used by the users at various stages in the production system.

There are various systems solutions for various types of VDU. These are some examples

- Automatic monitors provided with suitable communications logic and their own memory buffer. These are often connected via a multiplexer which is transparent to signals between computer and terminal.
- VDU's connected to a common, relatively complex control unit. The memory buffer for the units connected and all the logic for the data communication are placed centrally in the control unit. There are also VDU's with their own memory buffer which are connected to the control unit.
- VDU's connected to a terminal computer. The memory buffer can either be placed in the unit or in the memory of the terminal computer. The terminal computer takes care of data communication.
- As far as the monitor itself is concerned, the so-called CRT screen is the one most commonly used at present, but graphics monitors are beginning to be used more. The latter are considerably more complicated and thus more expensive. Colour monitors are also becoming more common on the market, mainly because their price has been dropping.

Figure 11.1 Visual Display Terminal (VDT)

Figure 11.2 Printer

11.2 Printers

Alphanumeric printers

It is often the volume of print-out which determines the most suitable choice of printer. The differences in printing speed are very great, from slow character printers to fast line printers.

Character printers or serial printers have a very variable printing speed. This depends partly on transmission speed, and also whether they print in both directions. The effective speed is also dependent on the length of the line and the number of characters per line.

A distinction is usually made between dot-matrix printers and other types of serial printers. The dot-matrix printer normally has 7 or 9 pins as its printing mechanism. The printing speed can be over 200 characters per second. Printers have a buffer to even out the speed at which characters are printed. The printing head and the line feed mechanism move slowly compared with the time taken to transmit a character. This means that a character could be lost if there was no buffer room. There are two methods of ensuring that the buffer in its turn doesn't overflow.

The first method is known as XON/XOFF, where the terminal sends a message via its software to the computer when the buffer has reached a certain degree of fulness, and another character when it has been emptied below this point. The codes used are DC1–DC4 (see Figures 11.17–18).

The second method is for the terminal to control lead 108 in the interface.

Printers have a paper contact which gives a signal to the computer when the paper runs out in the feed mechanism. The contact controls the terminal in the same way as filling the buffer.

Drum printers and line printers, as the names suggest, print a whole line at a time, and the length of the line has little if any effect on printing time. This type of printer comes into its own when print-out volumes are large.

When small amounts of information are to be printed out in a short time, the electrostatic printer is an alternative. Printing is done on paper sensitive to static electricity. The paper costs are higher than for ordinary line-printing paper, and no extra copies can be made from the printer.

Terminals which are 'teletype-compatible' work on the basis of character-by-character transmission, i e asynchronous sending-receiving. Apart from the 8 data bits (7 information bits+1 parity bit), there is a start bit and one or two stop bits. An asynchronous character is at least 10 bits long.

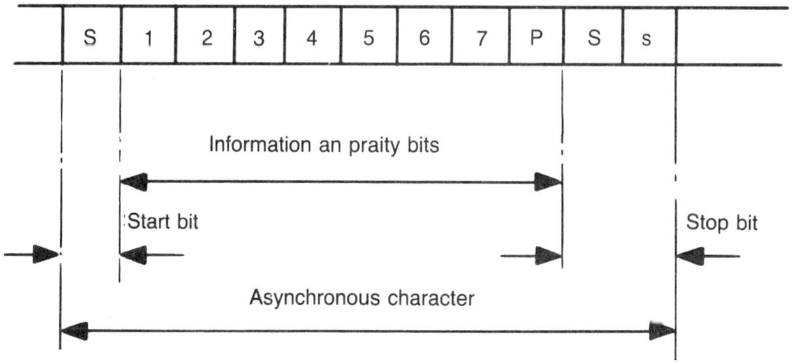

Figure 11.3 Asynchronous character

Developments in printers are rapidly advancing. More and more intelligence is being given to them, giving more functions. There are asynchronous printers which can be switched between synchronous and asynchronous protocols. There are also asynchronous VDU's with inbuilt memories which allow certain editing functions. Different types of script can also be obtained from modern printers.

```
This was printed on the
               LA120 DECwriter III.

It has eight font sizes so you can
select BIG LETTERS
for report headings or
little ones if you want 132 columns on an 8 1/2 inch wide sheet
or ANY mix that you want on one line.

LA120 font sizes include:

$%&*0123?@ABCD                                     5 CPI
$%&*0123?@ABCD[^`                                  6 CPI
$%&*0123?@ABCD[^`a                               6.6 CPI
$%&*0123?@ABCD[^`abcd{|                         8.25 CPI
$%&*0123?@ABCD[^`abcd{|}~$%&                      10 CPI
$%&*0123?@ABCD[^`abcd{|}~$%&*0123                 12 CPI
$%&*0123?@ABCD[^`abcd{|}~$%&*0123?@A            13.2 CPI
$%&*0123?@ABCD[^`abcd{|}~$%&*0123?@ABCD[^`abc   16.5 CPI
```

Figure 11.4 An example of different typefaces available on the DECWRITER LA120 printer

Dot matrix printers

An example of the type

The PHILIPS PER 3100 dot matrix printer is an example of an asynchronous printer. It is a widely-used bank and post office terminal over the whole of Sweden. The 'bank' version has a special keyboard. The terminal is also used for program development in contact with the host computer. It can also be used as a 'hard copy' unit for a VDU monitor, and in this case doesn't need its own keyboard. The printer is supplied with different types of interface board depending on the functions it is to perform.

Figure 11.5 PHILIPS PER 3100 dot matrix printer

Print head

The print head is mounted on a carriage which slides on a track. The speed of the carriage is determined by clock pulses from an oscillator. The print head has 8 pins, which are controlled by electromagnets via a flexible cable which goes along with the carriage.

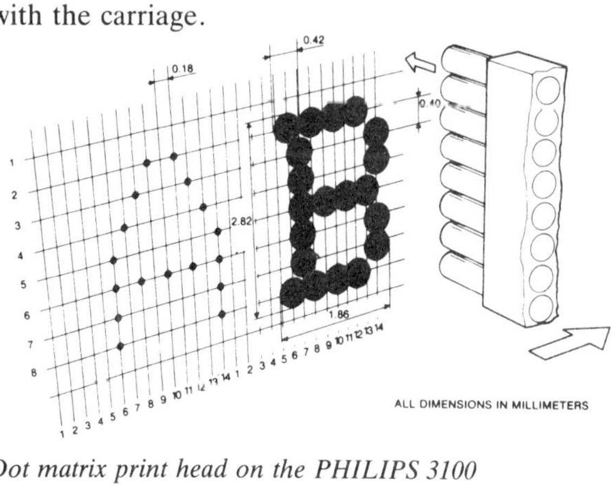

Figure 11.6 Dot matrix print head on the PHILIPS 3100

The print mechanism can produce up to 50 characters per second, and a maximum of 3 copies of normal line-printer paper can be obtained.

Signal lines to the print mechanism

Transfer of data to the printer mechanism is by parallel transmission on 7 leads, together with 6 control lines.

Keyboard

The keyboard can be connected directly to the printer or via a cable. The keyboard has what is known as an 'N-key rollover' function. The keyboard layout is shown in Figure 11.7.

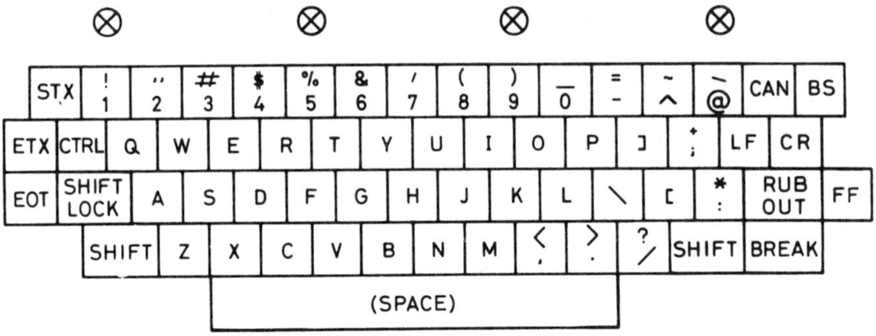

Figure 11.7 Keyboard layout for PHILIPS PER 3100

The codes generated via the keyboard are shown in Table 11.1.

Tabell 11.1. Hexadecimal keyboard codes for the PHILIPS PER 3100

Key	NORM	SHIFT	CTRL	CTRL/ SHIFT	Key	NORM	SHIFT	CTRL	CTRL/ SHIFT
A	61/41	41	01	00	STX	02	02	02	00
B	62/42	42	02	00	ETX	03	03	03	00
C	63/43	43	03	00	EOT	04	04	04	00
D	64/44	44	04	00	BS	08	08	08	00
E	65/45	45	05	00	LF	0A	0A	0A	00
F	66/46	46	06	00	FF	0C	0C	0C	00
G	67/47	47	07	00	CR	0D	0D	0D	00
H	68/48	48	08	00	CAN	18	18	18	00
I	69/49	49	09	00	< ,	2C	3C	00	00
J	6A/4A	4A	0A	00	= –	2D	3D	00	00
K	6B/4B	4B	0B	1B	> ·	2E	3E	00	00
L	6C/4C	4C	0C	1C	? /	2F	3F	00	00
M	6D/4D	4D	0D	1D	_ 0	30	5F	1F	00
N	6E/4E	4E	0E	1E	! 1	31	21	00	00
O	6F/4F	4F	0F	1F	" 2	32	22	00	00
P	70/50	50	10	00	# 3	33	23	00	00
Q	71/51	51	11	00	$ 4	34	24	00	00
R	72/52	52	12	00	% 5	35	25	00	00
S	73/53	53	13	00	& 6	36	26	00	00
T	74/54	54	14	00	' 7	37	27	00	00
U	75/55	55	15	00	(8	38	28	00	00
V	76/56	56	16	00	) 9	39	29	00	00
W	77/57	57	17	00	* :	3A	2A	00	00
X	78/58	58	18	00	+ ;	3B	2B	00	00
Y	79/59	59	19	00	` @	40	60	00	00
Z	7A/5A	5A	1A	00	~ ∧	5E	7E	1E	00
[	7B/5B	5B	1B	00	SPACE	20	20	20	00
	7C/5C	5C	1C	00	RUB				
]	7D/5D	5D	00	00	OUT	7F	7F	7F	00

The ordinary typewriter has a shift position for capital letters and special characters, whereas the PER 3100 has three shift positions. Apart from Shift there is CONTROL and the combination CONTROL/SHIFT. The keys A–Z used in conjunction with the CONTROL key are the control characters for communication (see section 11.5).

Three different character generators can be fitted in the printer

- ASCII standard 64 characters (CCITT No 5)
- 57 characters (basic ISO)
- programmable ROM with 7 characters (used together with the 57 character set-up).

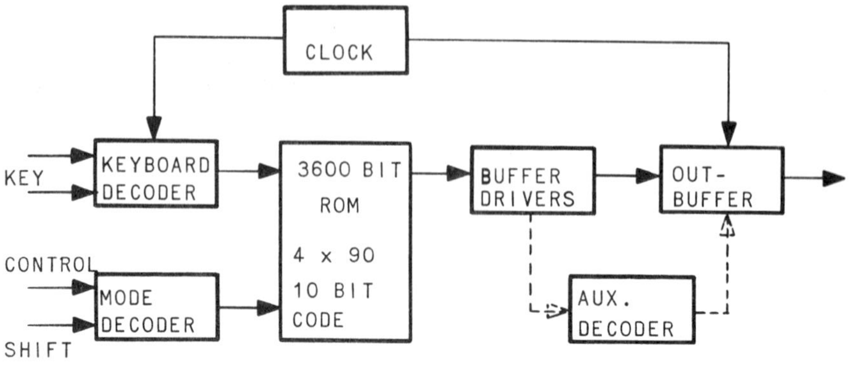

Figure 11.8 Keyboard logic for the PER 3100; block diagram

Modem interface

As mentioned in the introduction, the printer can be fitted with various circuit boards according to the functions required. The V.24/V.21 interface communicates with modems on the following lines

Data received	104
Data sent	103
Request to send	105
Channel clear	106
Modem ready	107
Terminal ready	108
Carrier present	109

The modem interface features the following

- selectable speeds from 110–600 bits/s
- 64 character buffer
- parity checking
- half- or full-duplex transmission
- 'direct' printing from the keyboard
- indication of PRINT SUPPRESS, BREAK and DATA SET READY
- 'off-line' can be set from the keyboard
- priority for data received via the line over that from the keyboard without information being lost from either.

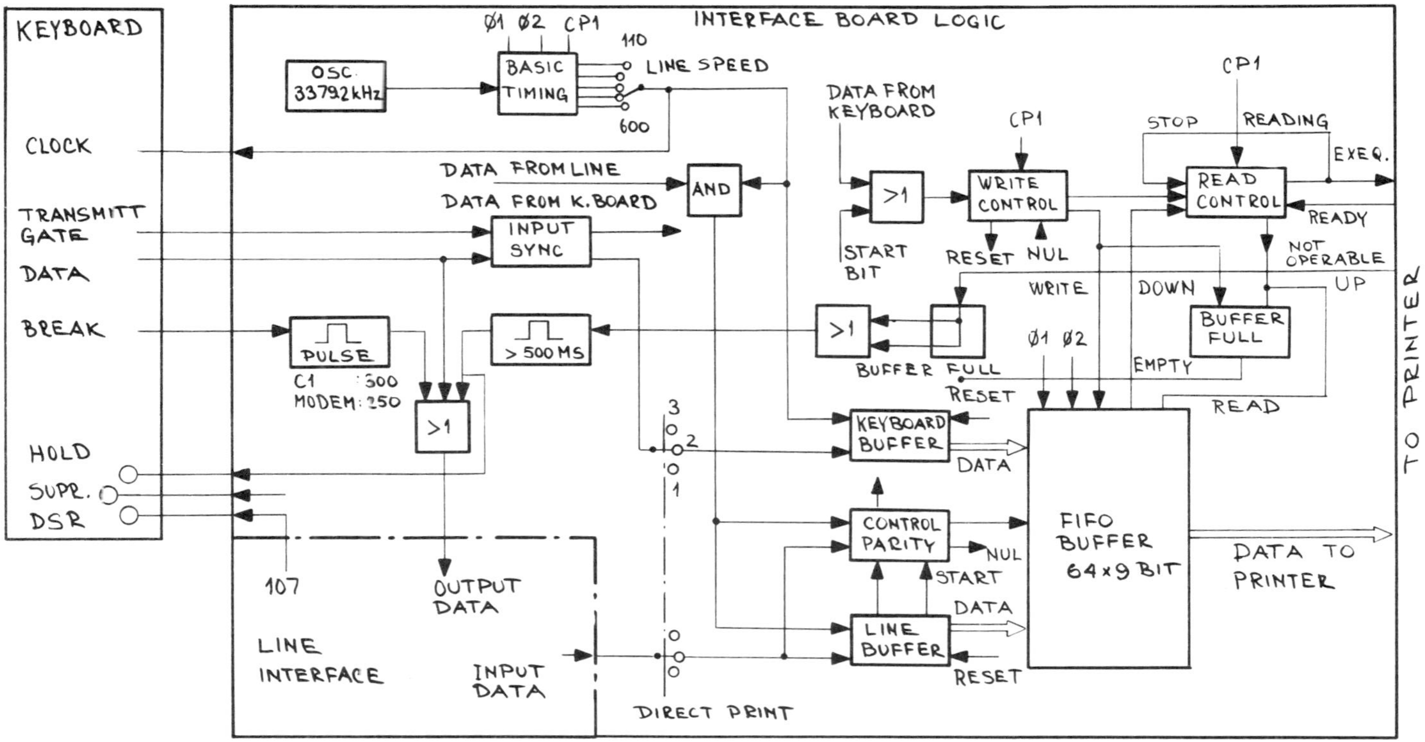

Figure 11.9 Block diagram of PHILIPS PER 3100

How it works

The circuit board logic accepts the following selectable speeds: 110, 150, 200, 300 and 600 bits/s. The data format is 8-bit together with a start and one stop bit. The correct speed is set by means of switches.

An oscillator running at 3379.2 kHz is used for clock pulses to the keyboard and for scanning of the incoming data from the line via the modem. Incoming data characters come via lead 104 into a 10-bit buffer, which is actually a shift register. The keyboard characters are transferred on DIRECT PRINT into an 8-bit buffer, where start and stop bits are shifted out.

Data coming from the line and from the keyboard is transferred in parallel form to the 64×9 bit FIFO (first in, first out) buffer. Where parity is to be checked, this is done before the data is moved over to the FIFO buffer.

The WRITE signal for writing to the FIFO comes from WRITE CONTROL circuits, which are triggered either by data from the keyboard or by a start bit from data on the line. The FIFO buffer can take up to 64 characters.

The EMPTY signal to the READ CONTROL shows that there are characters in the FIFO for transferring to the printer in parallel form, whereupon the EXECUTE signal is sent to the printer and data is transferred over the DATA lines.

FIFO has a BUFFER FULL COUNTER which holds 64 characters. When 57 characters remain in the FIFO which have not been written, the BUFFER FULL signal is sent. This lights the HOLD lamp on the keyboard. BUFFER FULL is counted up by READ signals and down by WRITE signals.

11.3 Visual Display Units (VDU's)

VDU components

There are numerous different marks and types of VDU monitors. We shall look briefly at the workings of a monitor.

The only visible components at a VDU workplace are the keyboard and the monitor. If the VDU is broken down into functional blocks, the following parts may be found

- screen
- memory
- keyboard and decoding logic
- character generator
- modem interface
- microprocessor

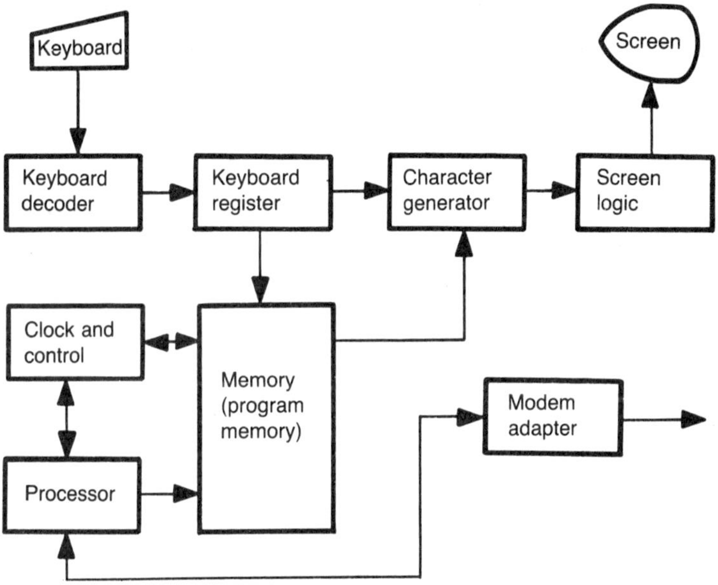

Figure 11.10 Block diagram for VDU terminal

Screen

The screen used in VDU's is very similar to that used in the common television set, and is known as a CRT (cathode ray tube). The screen is an output device which displays directly the data sent from the computer to the terminal, or the data fed in from the keyboard. The data transmitted in binary form is translated into alphanumeric visual characters. The screen consists of

- glass tube
- electron-beam source
- beam control system (electrostatic plates)
- a layer of oxide on the inside surface of the screen.

The cathode ray 'tube' has a rectangular screen at the front and the air is evacuated from it. Its rear end is a thin glass cylinder with contact pins at the back.

The cathode ray tube works on the following principles: the cathode of the tube, which is usually indirectly heated, emits electrons, and these are accelerated by a high positive voltage on the anode. The electrons are concentrated in a beam. If the electron beam is sufficiently intense, the screen will light up at the spot where the beam hits it. This spot can be scanned over the surface of the screen, either electrostatically or magnetically.

Memory

There are different types of memory in a VDU for different purposes. RAM (random access memory), which can be both read from and written to, and ROM (read-only memory) which can only be read from.

Screen memory ('refresh' memory)	• storage of characters fed in
Program memory	• storage of the terminal's program and line procedures
Keyboard memory	• storage of ASCII or EBCDIC characters.

Cursor and cursor memory

The cursor is a special symbol on the screen. It functions as a pointer to the current position, and it has a register which always contains information on the current cursor position. This has a row and position part. Using this register, the position is updated in x–y coordinate form. It is usual to have two 6–8 bit registers for this job. If the space bar is pressed, for example, the x register is increased by one and the cursor is moved one position to the right on the screen. If the cursor control keys are used to move the position down one line, one is added to the y register, while the x register is unaffected and the cursor is moved one line down.

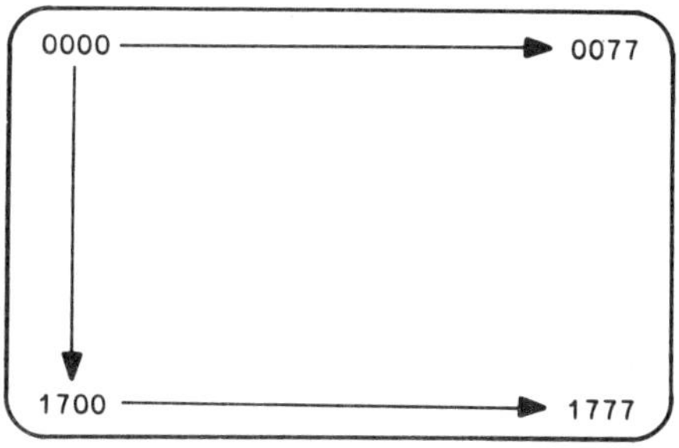

Figure 11.11 Screen positioning

Character generation and the character generator

The character generator is a hardware part of the screen logic, and it fetches the binary information from the 'refresh' memory and translates these characters into a visual form on the screen.

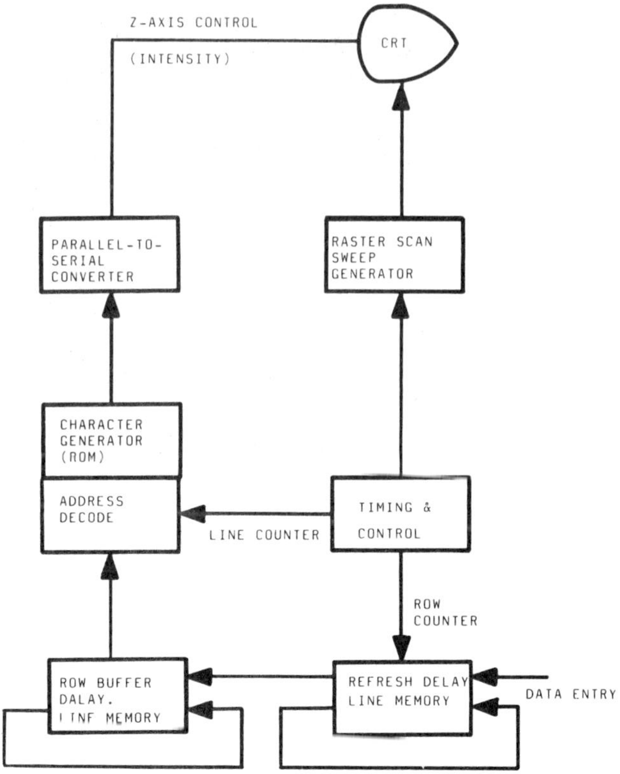

Figure 11.12 Character generator

There are a number of methods for character generation, of which the most common is known as a point matrix. Every character is built up of a series of points in a matrix. The more points there are, the clearer becomes the character displayed. There are matrices with 9×7 points, but even larger ones are common.

Refresh memory

The duration of the visible spot which is produced when the electron beam hits the fluorescent screen is short. The light rapidly disappears after the beam has left a point. The beam therefore has to come back repeatedly to all those points which are to be illuminated at a certain regular frequency in order to get a flicker-free picture. By lighting all these points continually at a frequency of 50–60 times per second, such a picture may be obtained.

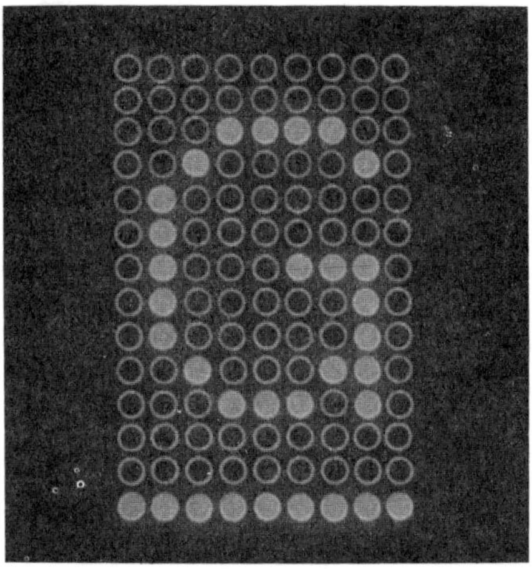

Figure 11.13 Point matrix with 9×14 points

The screen therefore has a memory where every position in the x and y direction is stored, and 'updates' the oxide-covered screen surface. Each row on the screen is in its turn divided into a number of lines determined by the size of the matrix in the y direction. Let's look at a screen whose matrix consists of 5×7 points. In the example in Figure 11.14, there are for the sake of simplicity only two characters stored. On row 1 position 1 is the character 'A', and in the next position a 'Z'. These two characters will be built up with points. The code 00100 is fetched from the refresh memory for line 1, which lights the top point of the 'A', and for the 'Z' the code is 11111. As there are no more characters to be displayed on the line, we go on to row 1 line 2. The next part of the 'A' consists of 01010, and the 'Z' of 00001. Line 3 gives us the code 10001 for 'A' and 00010 for 'Z'. Line 4 gives 11111 for 'A' and 00100 for 'Z. When all the points for row 1 have been lit in this way, the 'refresh' continues for row 2 line 2. This process continues until all the points over the whole screen have been lit, whereupon it starts again from the beginning.

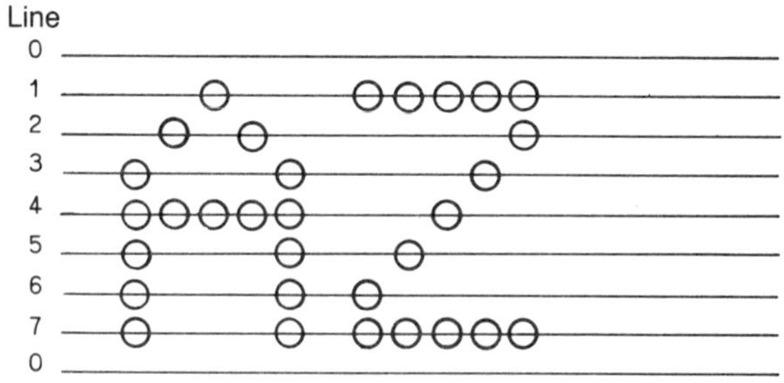

Figure 11.14 "Refresh" of a point-matrix

Microprocessor

Every VDU contains a microprocessor. This can be anything from a microprocessor to an advanced minicomputer in a distributed system. When the screeen exchanges traffic with a host computer, it is in reality the two processors which are communicating.

The processor controls and checks the line procedure with the host computer. The processor has contact with the terminal's memory and input and output channels via a bus system. The processor is controlled by interrupt logic for the processing of input and output data.

Keyboard

The keyboard is the operator's interface between the terminal and the computer. The operator can feed data into the memory of the terminal from the keyboard, and request data from the host computer. Each key operates a switch, which is sensed by a decoder which generates a unique code for every key.

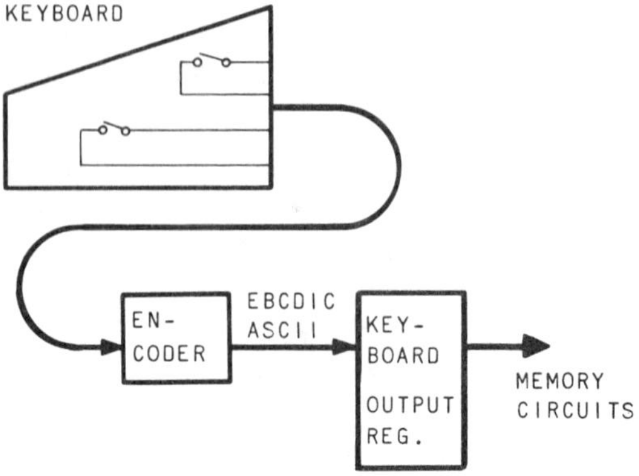

Figure 11.15 Keyboard, block diagram

The code passes via a register to the screen memory for decoding. There is logic in the decoder which determines whether it is a function key or a character key which has been pressed. In the first case the data is sent to the host computer at the next poll, and in the second case the character is to be transferred to the screen and the cursor moved to the next position.

A typical keyboard is shown in Figure 11.16. It is reminiscent of an electric typewriter keyboard. Apart from the alphanumeric keys, there are a number of keys which may be divided into different groups.

Figure 11.16 Keyboard for a UNISYS terminal in the UTS-4000 series

Message keys

Key	Key function
START OF ENTRY	This key puts a 'Start of entry' on the screen, which shows the start address of the message to be sent and stretches from the last SOE character up to the cursor
TRANSMIT	Causes all the data on the screen, apart from that in protected fields, to be sent.
PRINT	Sends all data on the screen from (and including) the last SOE character up to the cursor to the output unit which is connected to the terminal.
MESSAGE WAITING	Sends a special message to the computer on the next poll to indicate that the unspecified awaited message can be received.

Editing keys

Key	Key function
INSERT IN DISPLAY	When this key is pressed, all the data on the screen to the right of the cursor in moved one character to the right, and a blank character is put where the cursor is positioned.
INSERT IN LINE	As above, but only a single line is affected.
DELETE IN DISPLAY	Causes all data after the cursor to be shifted one step to the left, with blanks filling out the end positions of the last line.
DELETE IN LINE	Causes all characters on the same line as the cursor to be shifted one step to the left, and blanks to fill in the last position. The character where the cursor stood disappears.
CYCLE	Repeats the character or function for as long as the key is pressed.
ERASE CHARACTER	Put a blank at the cursor position.
ERASE TO END OF LINE	Blanks out the whole line on which the cursor stood (not protected fields).
ERASE TO END OF DISPLAY	Blanks out the whole of the screen from the cursor onwards (not protected fields).

Protected format keys

Key	Key function
ERASE UNPROT DISPL	Blanks out all unprotected fields from the cursor position to the end of the screen.
TRANSMIT UNPROT DISPL	Only the information in unprotected fields is sent. No protected data can be sent except SOE (▷ character). Only the information between the last SOE character and the cursor is sent.
ERASE FIELD	Blanks out the unprotected field from the cursor onwards. Only the unprotected field in which the cursor is positioned is blanked out.
TRANSMIT DISPL	Causes sending of everything on the screen.

Cursor control keys

Key	Key function
	The space bar moves the cursor one step to the right at each depression. The cursor does not stop over protected fields.
/UP/DOWN/ /LEFT/RIGHT/	Each key moves the cursor one position in the direction of the arrow, and repeats this for as long as the key is pressed.
TAB	Moves the cursor to the next tabulator stop position. The cursor stops in the first non-protected field after the TAB stop. If there are no TAB stops, it goes to the HOME position.
TAB SET	Sets the tabulator position, which is stored in the terminal's memory. Moves the cursor to the first non-protected field every time the key is pressed.
CURSOR TO	Puts the cursor in the top left-hand position on the screen.
RETURN	Corresponds to Carriage Return on a printer terminal. The cursor goes to position 1 on the next line.

Function keys

Key	Key function
F1–Fn	When these keys are pressed, they produce a special code which is sent to the computer at the next poll. The function of the keys depends on how these codes are handled in the respective programs.

Character keys

Key	Key function
ALPHANUMERIC	Represents the current character set. Certain keys represent two characters. The layout of the keys follows the typewriter standard.
SHIFT	When the SHIFT key is pressed, the keyboard changes to upper case characters, i e the key symbols produced are shown on the upper section of the respective keys.

11.4 Communication routines

General

In order to administer the traffic flow on the communications lines between computer and a number of terminals, a certain methodical procedure is required. One common method for controlling is known as the poll-select system. In systems like this, the computer controls all the traffic to the terminals by polling them in turn and choosing a certain terminal for an output message. Messages into the computer are sent by the operator pressing a send-key when a complete message has been fed into the terminal and onto its screen. The keyboard is now locked until the computer has sent a reply (acknowledgement) to the message sent. The terminal sends the message on the next poll from the computer. After the message has been checked, an acknowledgement is sent to the terminal, whereupon the terminal is unlocked again.

At the start of data communications, the manufacturers made up their own line procedures which only suited their own products, in order, of course, to exclude the competition. However, terminal manufacturers rapidly came to simulate (or emulate) a particular terminal procedure and in this way allow connection of their products to other makes of computer. Many terminal manufacturers today have procedures for connection to IBM, Unisys, Honeywell-Bull and other computers.

We have chosen two different line procedures to examine more closely below, Unisys UTS procedure and IBM's 3270 procedure.

11.5 UTS procedure

International alphabet No 5 (CCITT rec V.3)

The UTS procedure uses alphabet No 5 (CCITT rec V.3). The differences between this and the various national standards are primarily in the different language characters, e g å, ä and ö. The control characters for communication are the same.

ASC II STANDARD

Binärt						b7	0	0	0	0	1	1	1	1
						b6	0	0	1	1	0	0	1	1
						b5	0	1	0	1	0	1	0	1
					Hexa-		0	1	2	3	4	5	6	7
b4	b3	b2	b1	dec	okt		00	02	04	06	10	12	14	16
0	0	0	0	0	0		NUL	DLE	SP	0	É / @	P	é / `	p
0	0	0	1	1	1		SOH	DC1	!	1	A	Q	a	q
0	0	1	0	2	2		STX	DC2	"	2	B	R	b	r
0	0	1	1	3	3		ETX	DC3	#	3	C	S	c	s
0	1	0	0	4	4		EOT	DC4	¤ / $	4	D	T	d	t
0	1	0	1	5	5		ENQ	NAK	%	5	E	U	e	u
0	1	1	0	6	6		ACK	SYN	&	6	F	V	f	v
0	1	1	1	7	7		BEL	ETB	'	7	G	W	g	w
					okt		01	03	05	07	11	13	15	17
1	0	0	0	8	0		BS	CAN	(	8	H	X	h	x
1	0	0	1	9	1		HT	EM	)	9	I	Y	i	y
1	0	1	0	A10	2		LF	SUB	*	:	J	Z	j	z
1	0	1	1	B11	3		VT	ESC	+	;	K	Ä / [	k	ä / {
1	1	0	0	C12	4		FF	FS	,	<	L	Ö / \	l	ö / ¦
1	1	0	1	D13	5		CR	GS	–	=	M	Å /]	m	å / }
1	1	1	0	E14	6		SO	RS	.	>	N	Ü / ^	n	ü / ~
1	1	1	1	F15	7		SI	US	/	?	O	_	o	DEL

Figure 11.17 ASCII standard character set (CCITT rec V.3)

VERSION 2 SWEDISH STANDARD SEN 85 02 00

				b7	0	0	0	0	1	1	1	1
				b6	0	0	1	1	0	0	1	1
				b5	0	1	0	1	0	1	0	1
b4	b3	b2	b1	Column / Row	0	1	2	3	4	5	6	7
0	0	0	0	0	NUL	DLE	SP	0	É	P	é	p
0	0	0	1	1	SOH	DC1	!	1	A	Q	a	q
0	0	1	0	2	STX	DC2	"	2	B	R	b	r
0	0	1	1	3	ETX	DC3	#	3	C	S	c	s
0	1	0	0	4	EOT	DC4	¤	4	D	T	d	t
0	1	0	1	5	ENQ	NAK	%	5	E	U	e	u
0	1	1	0	6	ACK	SYN	&	6	F	V	f	v
0	1	1	1	7	BEL	ETB	'	7	G	W	g	w
1	0	0	0	8	BS	CAN	(	8	H	X	h	x
1	0	0	1	9	HT	EM	)	9	I	Y	i	y
1	0	1	0	10	LF	SUB	*	:	J	Z	j	z
1	0	1	1	11	VT	ESC	+	;	K	Ä	k	ä
1	1	0	0	12	FF	FS	,	<	L	Ö	l	ö
1	1	0	1	13	CR	GS	–	=	M	Å	m	å
1	1	1	0	14	SO	RS	.	>	N	Ü	n	ü
1	1	1	1	15	SI	US	/	?	O	_	o	DEL

Figure 11.18 Swedish standard SEN 85 02 00

Control characters

The control characters are unique to communication, and must not be used in the message itself. They consist of the codes $(00–1F)_{16}$. Control characters are of four types:

Communication control

Characters which are only used for control of traffic between computer and terminal.

Form effector

Characters used for positioning and layout (formatting) for printer and screen.

Device control

Characters used for control of equipment.

Information separators

The use of information separators varies with procedure and application. Information separators are used hierarchically.

Control characters

NUL $\mathbf{(00)_{16}}$	Null	Null is a fill-in character which can be used anywhere in a text except between ETX and BCC. The character is not shown on the screen.
SOH $\mathbf{(01)_{16}}$	Start of Header	SOH is the first character in the header section of message.
STX $\mathbf{(02)_{16}}$	Start of text	STX is the first character in the text section of a message.
ETX $\mathbf{(03)_{16}}$	End of text	ETX is the first character in the TRAILER section of a message.
EOT $\mathbf{(04)_{16}}$	End of transmission	EOT is used as a two-character sequence EOT EOT together with ETX and BCC to indicate when there is no message to send (in response to poll).
ENQ $\mathbf{(05)_{16}}$	Enquiry	ENQ is used in the header part of a message from the computer to the terminal when a request to send is received.
ACK $\mathbf{(06)_{16}}$	Acknowledge	Sent in response to a correctly-received data transmission (however, not in the UTS 4000 procedure).

BEL **$(07)_{16}$**	Bell	The BEL character is used by both computer and terminal. If the character is included in a message to the terminal, it denotes that there is a message to the terminal. If the character is in the message to the computer, the operator is ready to receive the message.
BS **$(08)_{16}$**	Backspace	Moves the print head or the cursor on the screen one space backwards.
HT **$(09)_{16}$**	Horizontal Tabulation	Moves the printer or screen cursor to the next predetermined horizontal position (tabulation or 'tab').
LF **$(0A)_{16}$**	Line feed	Moves the printer or cursor position one line on, maintaining horizontal position.
VT **$(0B)_{16}$**	Vertical tabulation	Moves printer or cursor one line on, maintaining horizontal position (VT is often followed by x- and y-coordinates for positioning).
FF **$(0C)_{16}$**	Form feed	Moves the printer position to the next predetermined position (page feed).
CR **$(0D)_{16}$**	Carriage Return	Moves the print head or cursor back to the first position on the same line.
SO **$(0E)_{16}$**	Shift Out	Used to indicate that the character which follows SO is to be interpreted from outside the ordinary code table (used to extend the character repertoire).
SI **$(0F)_{16}$**	Shift In	Used together with SO and ESC to indicate that normal interpretation is to be resumed according to the coding table.
DLE **$(10)_{16}$**	Data Link Escape	The DLE character is used in the HEADER part of a message, and has different meanings depending on the character immediately following DLE.
DLE 0	Response	Response to poll.
DLE 1	Acknowledge	Response to good transmission.
DLE ?	Busy	Printer busy.

DLE;	Through	Printer ready.
DLE >	Ready	Printer connected.
DLE <	Not ready	Printer not connected (out of paper or switched off).
DLE :	Parity error	Parity error in data to printer.
DLE ENQ	Reply request	Demand for identification ('are you there?').
DLE NAC	Retransmit request	Request for data to be transmitted again.
DC 1–4 **(11–14)**$_{16}$	Device control	These characters are used to control connected printers, etc, in the communication system.
NAC **(15)**$_{16}$	Negative acknowledge	Request for retransmission of a message. NAC is used in combination with DLE.
SYN **(16)**$_{16}$	Synchronous Idle	Used as the first part of a message to synchronise the receiving equipment with the transmitter.
ETB **(17)**$_{16}$	End of Transmission block	Indicates the end of a data block.
CAN **(18)**$_{16}$	Cancel	CAN is the first character in a sequence where the following characters are in error.
EM **(19)**$_{16}$	End of medium	EM signifies the physical end of medium (e g tape end), and is used differently depending on system and application.
SUB **(1A)**$_{16}$	Substitute	Used as a replacement character if a character in a message is destroyed or wrong.
ESC **(1B)**$_{16}$	Escape	Used to indicate that the character immediately following is to be interpreted from outside the ordinary code table (extends the character repertoire. See also SI and SO).
FS **(1C)**$_{16}$	File separator	Information separator
GS **(1D)**$_{16}$	Group separator	Information separator

RS Record separator Information separator
(1E)$_{16}$

US Unit separator Information separator
(1C)$_{16}$

Message format

Synchronisation part

In UTS, the message always starts with a synchronisation part. This consists of at least four SYN $(16)_{16}$ synchronisation characters. The SYN characters are there so that the sending and receiving apparatus will be in phase at the start of transmission. This synchronisation must not be confused with what the modem carries out before the message can be sent. At least two SYN characters in succession must have been received correctly before synchronisation can be said to have taken place.

HEADER section

The HEADER part is included in all types of message apart from a NO TRAFFIC response from the terminal. The HEADER always begins with SOH followed by the address sequence, which in turn consists of three characters. The HEADER part includes the SUPERVISORY part which contains control characters preceding the actual message. The SUPERVISORY characters may be from zero to a maximum of four in number, and their meaning is, among other things,

- Acknowledgement for good transmission
- Status poll and information
- "Message wait" function
- Request to send
- Program choice and program function keys.

Synchronization Section				**Header Section**					**Text Section**		**Trailer Section**	
S Y N	S Y N	S Y N	S Y N	S O H	R I D	S I D	D I D	Communication Control Characters	S T X	Text	E T X	B C C

|← Address Sequence →|← Supervisory Sequence →|

Figure 11.19 Message format for Unisys UTS

TEXT section

The TEXT part of the message always begins with STX $(02)_{16}$, followed immediately by the message. The maximum length of the message varies in different applications.

TRAILER section

The message conclues with a TRAILER part, which begins with ETX $(03)_{16}$ followed by the BCC character. The BCC character may be any value between $(00\text{–}FF)_{16}$. Calculation of the BCC character starts from SOH and ends with ETX (both included).

Addressing

All messages except NO TRAFFIC from the terminal always contain an address part within the HEADER section. The address comprises three characters and follows directly after SOH. The three characters are called RID, SID and DID.

RID (remote identifier)

RID is the first address level and addresses all terminals on one control unit or multiplexer. RID may be any character from $(20\text{–}4F)_{16}$ in the ASCII table. The first character $(20)_{16}$ is called GID and has a special function. If GID is the first character in the address sequence, all units in a multipoint configuration are addressed.

SID (station identifier)

SID is the second address level and addresses modules within the control unit or multiplexer. SID can be any character from $(50\text{–}58)_{16}$ and from $(60\text{–}68)_{16}$ in the ASCII table. The first character $(50)_{16}$ is GID (general identifier) and has a special significance. For each poll of the terminals, GID is used in the SID position to poll all terminals on the same control unit simultaneously.

DID (device identifier)

DID is the third address level and picks out a particular apparatus within the module on a control unit. DID selects screen, printer or tape unit. DID can be any character from $(70\text{–}73)_{16}$ in the ASCII table. The first character $(70)_{16}$ always addresses a screen.

BIT NO	7 6 5	0 0 0	0 0 1	0 1 0	0 1 1	1 0 0	1 0 1	1 1 0	1 1 1
4 3 2 1	R \ C	0	1	2	3	4	5	6	7
0 0 0 0	0			*GID*			*GID*		*GID*
0 0 0 1	1								*TERMI-NATION*
0 0 1 0	2								*NOT USED*
0 0 1 1	3								
0 1 0 0	4								
0 1 0 1	5								
0 1 1 0	6								
0 1 1 1	7								
1 0 0 0	8								
1 0 0 1	9								
1 0 1 0	10								
1 0 1 1	11								
1 1 0 0	12								
1 1 0 1	13								
1 1 1 0	14								
1 1 1 1	15								*PRINT*

Bit No. 7 is the most significant. ← *RID* → ← *SID* → ← *DID* →

Figure 11.20 Addresses for RID, SID and DID in the Unisys UTS procedure

Addressing – examples

The first example of addressing is a simple connection with just a screen and a printer. See Figure 11.21.

The printer is addressed with $(32\ 51\ 73)_{16}$, and the screen is addressed with $(32\ 51\ 70)_{16}$. When polling, the computer sends $(32\ 50\ 70)_{16}$.

The next example is more complicated. The configuration comprises two branches (drops) with one control unit on each. The first branch has three VDU's and a common printer. The second drop has four VDU's, where the first has a printer attached, the next two share the same printer, and the fourth is just the single screen.

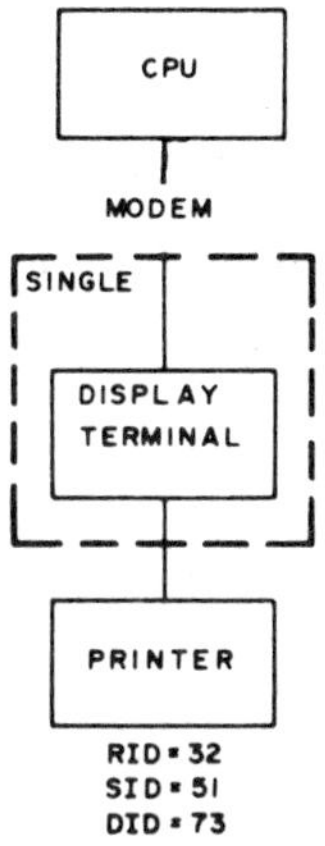

Figure 11.21 Example of addressing VDU and printer under the UTS procedure

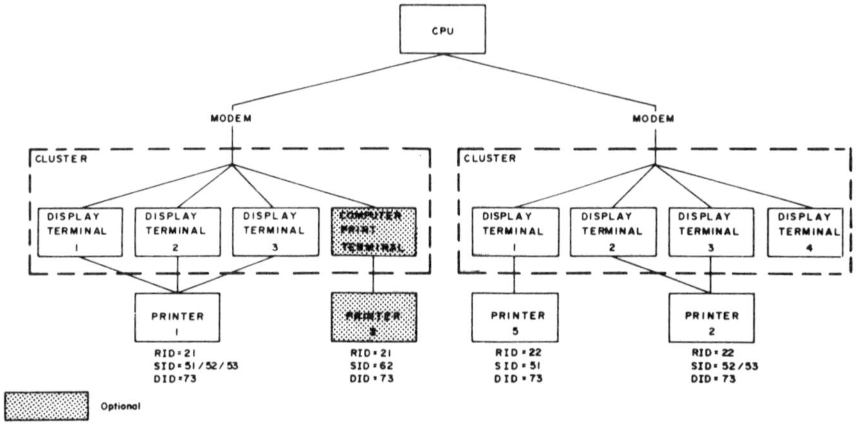

Figure 11.22 Example of addressing in a multipoint network under the UTS procedure

The addresses of the VDU's in the first drop are: $(21\ 51\ 70)_{16}$, $(21\ 52\ 70)_{16}$ and $(21\ 53\ 70)_{16}$. The VDU's on the second drop are addressed using $(22\ 51\ 70)_{16}$, $(22\ 52\ 70)_{16}$, $(22\ 53\ 70)_{16}$ and $(22\ 54\ 70)_{16}$.

Polls

There are two types of poll, TRAFFIC and STATUS polls. The STATUS poll merely asks whether the terminal has a message to send. On succeeding TRAFFIC polls, the terminal sends the message. Both TRAFFIC and

STATUS polls can be sent with or without ACKNOWLEDGEMENT of messages sent earlier. In this way the line procedure is speeded up, as two statuses are sent in the same message.

On a GENERAL TRAFFIC poll, all terminals on the same control unit are asked whether they have any message to send.

Parity bits and block checking

Every character in a message has a parity bit, and the UTS procedure uses odd parity. Each message also has a BCC character (Block Character Check). Calculation of the BCC for a message begins immediately after SOH or, for the NO TRAFFIC message, immediately after the second EOT. All succeeding characters except SYN and NUL characters are included in the calculation. The last character to be included in the BCC calculation is ETX. The BCC character can thus be any value between $(00\text{–}FF)_{16}$. Computer and terminal calculate the BCC value synchronously for every character using a logical operation (XOR). After each message the calculated and received BCC's are compared. If these values are different, there has been an error in the transmission and a request for retransmission is sent (DLE NAC).

BIT	8 7 6 5 4 3 2 1		
XOR ⇨	1 0 0 0 0 1 1 0	character	1
	0 1 1 1 0 1 0 1		2
	1 1 1 1 0 0 1 1	BCC	

Figure 11.23 Calculation of the BCC character in the UTS procedure

Line procedure

The UTS line procedure works on the poll-select principle. The computer polls the terminals (control units) in a certain order, and chooses a certain terminal for its output message. The computer continuously administers the traffic flow on all configured lines, which may be connected up to a single terminal or a very complicated multipoint network with many VDU's and printers. As soon as the computer has sent a message on a line, no other message may be sent on the same line until a response has come from the selected terminal or printer, otherwise there would be a collision of messages on the line. If there is no answer within a suitable time, it may be taken that the message has gone missing or has not been understood by the receiving equipment. This event is known as TIME OUT, and the computer can repeat the message or transmission again. If a response is received this time, the line procedure can continue its endless loop. If there is no response to the repeated message, the apparatus addressed is assumed to be out of order, and the drop, line or terminal is taken out of the system as being no longer logically addressable. The operators at the central console or special network console are then informed about this error situation.

In the descriptions of the message formats, the following are included;

	R		R		G
where	/	means	I	or	I
	G		D		D
	S		S		G
where	/	means	I	or	I
	G		D		D
	D		D		G
where	/	means	I	or	I
	G		D		D

Message format from computer to terminal

Message	Format	Explanation
TRAFFIC poll without acknowledgement of previously-sent message	S R S D E B O / / / T C H G G G X C	Message request for terminal or control unit.
TRAFFIC poll with acknowledgement	S R S D D E B O / / / L 1 T C H G G G E X C	Message request for terminal or control unit and acknowledgement of earlier message.
STATUS poll without acknowledgement	S R S D E E B O / / / N T C H G G G Q X C	Message request for terminal or control unit without answer to previously-sent message.
STATUS poll with acknowledgement	S R S D E D E B O / / / N L 1 T C H G G G Q E X C	Message request for terminal or control unit with response to earlier message.
Text	S R S D S E B O I I I T ← Text → T C H D D D X X C	Text to terminal.
Message waiting	S R S D B S E B O I I I E T T C H D D D L X X C	Message to terminal. A message to the terminal in question is waiting.
Retransmission request	S R S D D N E B O I I I L A T C H D D D E K X C	Request for retransmission of the last message sent by the terminal.

Message format from terminal to computer

Message	Format	Explanation
No message to send	E E E B O O T C T T X C	Indicates that the terminal or control unit polled had no message to send.
No message	S R G G E B O I I I T C H D D D X C	Indicates that the terminal or control unit polled had no message to send.
No message to send	S R S D D E B O I I I L 1 T C H D D D E X C	Acknowledgement of earlier message, and that there is nothing new.
Printer engaged	S R S D D E B O I I I L ? T C H D D D E X C	Response from printer that it is already printing.
Text	S R S D S E B O I I I T ← Text → T C H D D D X X C	Text from terminal (response to TRAFFIC poll).
Text with acknowledgement	S R S D D S E B O I I I L 1 T ← Text → T C H D D D E X X C	Text from terminal and response to earlier acknowledged transmission from the terminal.
Response to STATUS poll	S R S D D E B O I I I L 0 T C H D D D E X C	Indicates that the terminal polled has a message to send.
Response to TRAFFIC poll with acknowledgement	S R S D D D E B O I I I L 1 L 0 T C H D D D E E X C	Acknowledgement of earlier message, and that the new message is ready to send.
Send waiting message	S R S D B E B O I I I E T C H D D D L X C	Indicates that the operator is ready to receive a message waiting in the computer.
Send waiting message, and acknowledgement of earlier message	S R S D D B E B O I I I L 1 E T C H D D D E L X C	Indicates that the terminal (operator) is ready to receive a message waiting in the computer, and acknowledgement of earlier message.
Printer ready	S R S D D E B O I I I L ; T C H D D D E X C	Indicates that the printer has finished printing out, or has returned to the ready state.
Printer ready and acknowledgement of earlier message	S R S D D D E B O I I I L 1 L ; T C H D D D E E X C	Indicates that the printer has finished printing out, or has returned to the ready state, and acknowledgement of previously-sent message.

Message	Format	Explanation
Retransmission request	S R S D D E E B O I I I L N T C H D D D E Q X C	Request retransmission of acknowledgement for last message sent.
Printer status	S R S D D E B O I I I L > T C H D D D E X C	Response from printer (ready to print).
Printer status with acknowledgement for last message sent	S R S D D D E B O I I I L 1 L > T C H D D D E E X C	Response from printer (ready to print), and acknowledgement of earlier message.

The UTS-4000 terminal system

System design

The free-standing UTS 4020 terminal processor can contain up to 256 Kb of memory. The 4020 can be connected to up to 12 workstations (UTS 20 W), which can be occupied on different tasks simultaneously. In addition to these, 16 peripheral units can also be connected. The peripherals can be connected up at any point. Apart from the peripherals connected centrally, each workstation can be supplied with a printer and an ID card reader. See Figure 11.24.

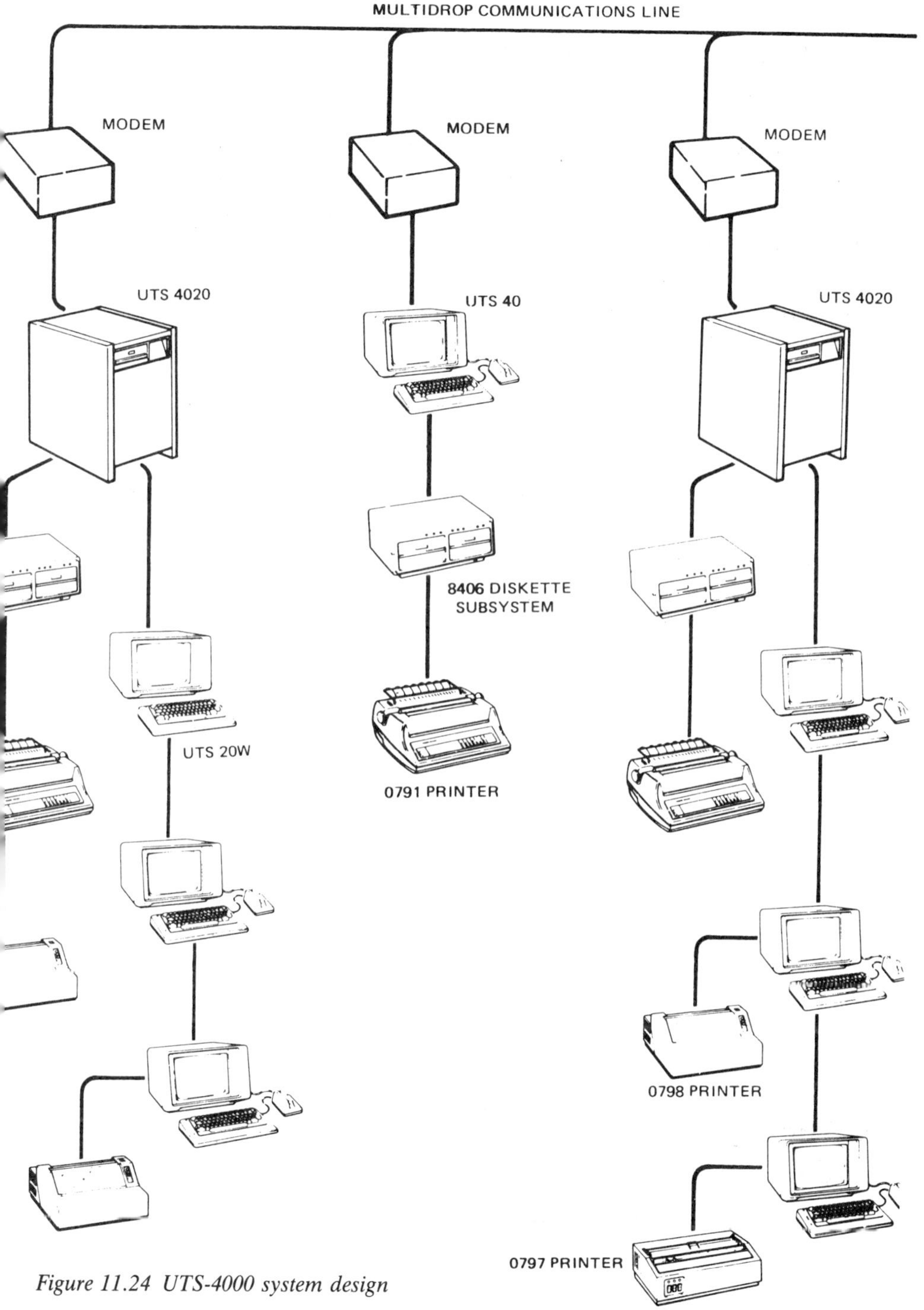

Figure 11.24 UTS-4000 system design

11.6 3270 procedures

Introduction

The 3270 procedures are used to connect terminals to the IBM 360/370 in two different ways, either locally or via distant connections. For local connection, the communication control units are coupled directly to the computer via BYTE MULTIPLEXER or BLOCK MULTIPLEXER channels. The way in which locally-connected units function differs from that for distant ones. We shall only deal here with remote terminals and their procedures. Such terminals are usually connected via modems using CCITT V.24.

Remote connection

Remotely-connected control units can use transmission speeds of 1200–9600 bits/s, two- or four-wire. The control units can be connected either individually or as multidrop connections.

EBCDIC code

Terminals working on the 3270 procedure use the EBCDIC code, which is an 8-bit code used by all IBM computers.

	Bits[1] 7,6 →	00				01				10				11			
	Bits 5,4 →	00	01	10	11	00	01	10	11	00	01	10	11	00	01	10	11
Bits 3210	Hex 1 / Hex 2	0	1	2	3	4	5	6	7	8	9	A	B	C	D	E	F
0000	0	NUL	DLE			SP	&	–									0
0001	1	SOH	SBA					/		a	j			A	J		1
0010	2	STX	ERA		SYN					b	k	s		B	K	S	2
0011	3	ETX	CP							c	l	t		C	L	T	3
0100	4									d	m	u		D	M	U	4
0101	5	HT	NL[2]							e	n	v		E	N	V	5
0110	6			ETB						f	o	w		F	O	W	6
0111	7			ESC	EOT					g	p	x		G	P	X	7
1000	8					#	¤	"	!	h	q	y		H	Q	Y	8
1001	9		EM[3]			é	É	ü	Ü	i	r	z		I	R	Z	9
1010	A					ö	å		:								
1011	B					.	Å	,	Ä								
1100	C		DUP[4]		REP	<	*	%	Ö								
1101	D		FSO		NAK	(	)	_	'								
1110	E		FM[5]			+	;	>	=								
1111	F		ITB	USM	SUB	|	¬	?	ä								

Figure 11.25 EBCDIC code table

Notes:
1) Bit 7 is the most significant bit in the code
2) NL is shown as '=' on the screen but is 'printed' as a space.
3) EM is shown as S on the screen but is 'printed' as a space.
*4) DUP is displayed and printed as **
5) FM is displayed and printed as ;

Codes $(00–3F)_{16}$ are used as control codes for the communications procedures. These control codes must not be used in a message. Characters in Figure 11.25 lying outside the shaded area are undefined as part of the text and are not displayed on the screen or printed out. Communication control characters are the following:

PAD PAD "PAD" is a fill-in character which can be sent
$(FF)_{16}$ by computer or terminal in cases where a message has to contain a certain number of characters.

SYN **$(32)_{16}$**	Synchronous idle	Used in the first part of a message to synchronise sending and receiving equipment.
DLE **$(10)_{16}$**	Data link escape	The DLE character goes into the HEADER section of a message, and has different meanings depending on the character which immediately follows it.
ACK 0 **$(10\ 70)_{16}$**	Even acknowledgement	ACK 0 is a two-character sequence which the terminal sends to the computer in response to acknowledged addressing, whereby the terminal indicates that it is ready to receive the message. ACK 0 is sent from the computer when an even-numbered block has been received and checked as accurate.
ACK 1 **$(10\ 61)_{16}$**	Odd acknowledgement	ACK 1 is a two-character equivalent to ACK 0 but for odd-numbered blocks.
NAK **$(3D)_{16}$**	Negative acknowledgement	The terminal sends NAK when: • the transmission is followed by ENC • the transmission contains a faulty BCC • the text contains TTD (temporary text delay), i e the computer cannot send a message immediately.
ENQ **$(2D)_{16}$**	Enquiry	The terminal sends ENQ: • as a transmission request to the computer after 'time out'. • a retransmission request of the last message from the computer. • when WACK has been received from the computer. When the terminal gets ENQ in response to a transmission, the message is repeated.
WACK **$(10\ 6B)_{16}$**	WAit before transmit. Positive ACknowledgement	WACK is a two-character sequence sent by the terminal to denote that it is not immediately ready to send text. WACK is used in exchanges with the printer. If a WACK is sent from the computer, the terminal must respond with ENQ.

RVI **$(10\ 7C)_{16}$**	Reverse input	RVI is a two-character sequence which a 'slave' terminal uses when a job already started is to be interupted by a higher priority message from a 'master' terminal.
STX **$(02)_{16}$**	Start of text	STX is the first character in the 'text' part of the message.
SOH **$(01)_{16}$**	Start of header	SOH is the first of three characters in the HEADER section of a message.
ETB **$(26)_{16}$**	End of block	ETB character indicates the end of a text string which began with SOH or STX. The BCC character follows immediately after ETB. The ETB character is processed in the same way as ETX. The BCC check is carried out and ACK 0, ACK 1, WACK or NAK is sent in reply.
ETX **$(03)_{16}$**	End of text	ETX ends a message which began with STX or SOH. The BCC character follows immediately after the BCC character.
EOT **$(37)_{16}$**	End of transmission	The EOT character indicates to a 'slave' terminal that the message is complete and that transmission has ended.
ITB **$(1F)_{16}$**	End of intermediate transmission block	A message may be subdivided inteo a number of sub-messages using the ITB character, whereupon a BCC check is done for each subsection of the message.
ESC **$(27)_{16}$**	Escape	The ESC character precedes messages of the READ, WRITE and CONTROL types.
TTD **$(02\ 2D)_{16}$**	Temporary text delay	TTD is a two-character sequence sent by the computer when it wants to maintain contact with the terminal, if the message to the terminal is not immediately ready to send. Terminals cannot send TTD characters.

3270 message format

The message format for the 3270 is the same as for UTS. It consists of four parts

- Synchronisation part
- HEADER part
- TEXT part
- TRAILER part.

BCC checking is done on the same principles as in UTS.

A terminal will always be in one of three conditions:

CONTROL MODE

The terminal always goes into CONTROL MODE when it is sending or has received a terminated transmission (EOT). When the terminal is in the CONTROL mode it investigates the traffic coming to the control unit to see whether:

- a poll or text is coming to the terminal
- a text sequence which contains DLE STX is coming, which puts the terminal into TRANSPARENT MONITOR MODE.

TEXT MODE

In TEXT MODE a terminal works either as slave or master. The terminal is known as a slave when it is receiving text, and a master when it is sending text. When a transmission is completed it returns to CONTROL MODE.

TRANSPARENT MONITOR MODE

A terminal cannot send in TRANSPARENT MONITOR MODE, but on a line common to other terminals it can put out messages. A terminal which is not in TRANSPARENT MONITOR MODE must switch to this mode when text/DLE STX arrives. In this mode, the terminal selected must ignore all characters except:

- TRANSPARENT SYN (DLE SYN)
- transparent text termination (DLE ITB, DLE ETB or DLE ENQ).

The terminal has to go back to CONTROL MODE if a TRANSPARENT SYN sequence is not received within a certain time (TIME OUT), or if a termination of TRANSPARENT MODE is received.

Polling and addressing

There are two types of poll. The SPECIFIC poll addresses a specific terminal on a control unit.

On a GENERAL poll it is really the control unit which is addressed, and this in its turn investigates whether any terminal has anything to send. The control unit has two different addresses for poll and SELECTION respectively. On a poll, the first control units is addressed by $(04)_{16}$, and on SELECTION the same control unit is addressed by $(06)_{16}$.

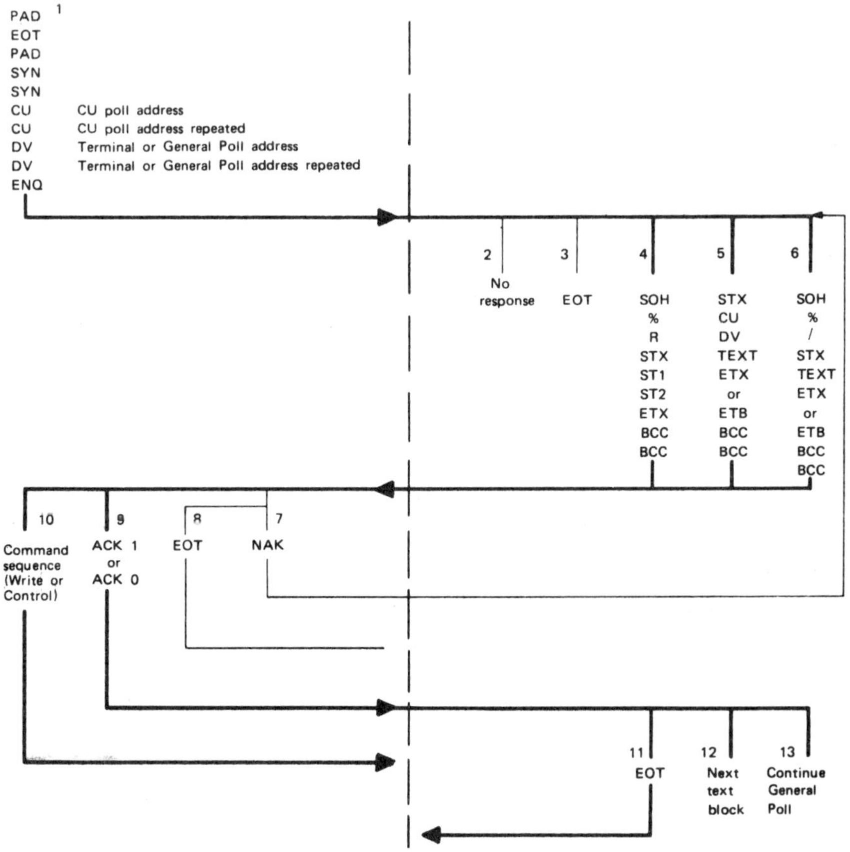

Figure 11.26 Examples of polls and addressing in the 3270 procedure

Comments on Figure 11.26.

1) *The computer sends GENERAL or SPECIFIC poll.*
2) *Terminal does not respond due to transmission error or it is switched off.*
3) *Terminal answers with EOT = nothing to send.*
4) *A status message is sent in response to poll.*
5) *Normal message.*
6) *Test message is initiated if the operator presses the TEST key.*

In acknowledgement of messages 2–6, the computer can now send:

7) *Response to a negatively-acknowledged message, where the BCC character does not agree.*
8) *If after repeated attempts the terminal has not been able to transmit the message correctly, the computer stops further attempts by sending EOT.*
9) *The computer has received and acknowledged a message. ACK 1 is sent after the first block and after all succeeding odd blocks. ACK 0 is sent after each even-numbered block.*
10) *This message must be a WRITE or CONTROL type, and is sent to the terminal which sent the last message in response to a GENERAL poll.*

In response to computer messages 7–10, the terminal sends:

11) *EOT, normal ending to GENERAL or SPECIFIC poll.*
12) *The next block in the message.*
13) *The control unit sends text from the next terminal on the polled control unit.*

A further difference of the addressing in the 3270 procedure compared with the UTS procedure is that the 3270 terminal addresses are on two levels, whereas in UTS they are on three levels. On 3270 each address character is repeated once, so that control units and terminals are described by four characters in the address part.

SELECTION ADDRESS SEQUENCE

When a message is to be sent to a certain terminal, it must be preceded by a SELECTION ADDRESS SEQUENCE in order to determine whether the chosen terminal can receive the message.

The addressing sequence is the same for the poll, except that the address for the first control unit on the line has the address $(60)_{16}$.

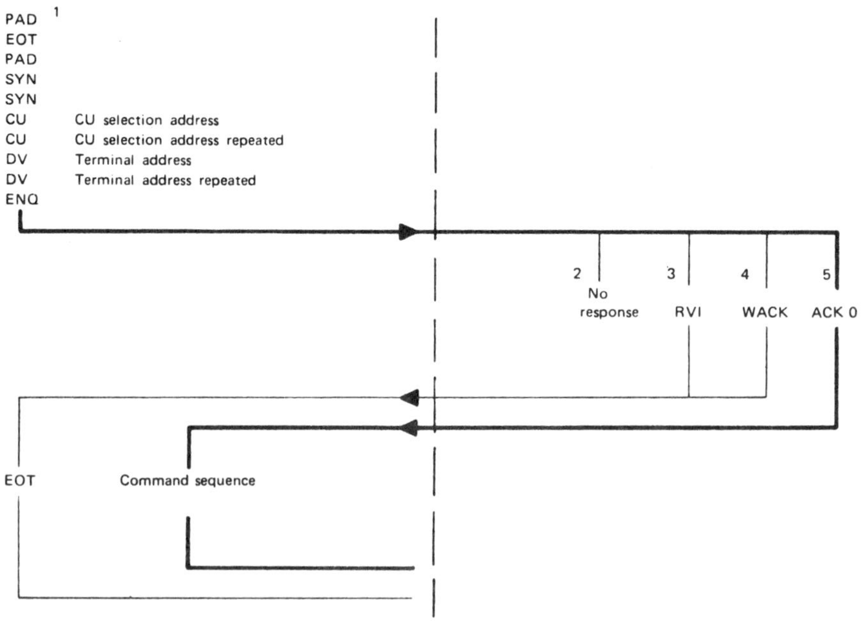

Figure 11.27 Selection address sequence under the 3270 procedure

Comments to Figure 11.27:
1) The computer sends SELECTION address sequence.
2) The terminal does not respond if there is a transmission error.
3) By sending RVI, the terminal states that the SELECTION messages has been understood but that its actual message must be 'retrieved' via a poll. The computer responds with EOT.
4) The terminal responds with WACK to indicate that it is busy with work started earlier. The computer answers EOT to break off.
5) A correct address (SELECTION) has been received. Hereafter the computer can send WRITE-type or READ-type commands.

Commands and orders

Commands are sent from the computer to order a certain type of processing such as printing, reading or removing data from a certain terminal. There are four main types of command:

- READ TYPE — Send data (text) and status information to the computer.
- WRITE TYPE — Send orders from computer to terminal.

- CONTROL COMMANDS — Used for producing printout on printer or screen.
- SENSE COMMANDS — Only used in local (directly connected) configurations (not dealt with here).

READ TYPE (read and print messages)

The READ command implies an operation where the computer first selects a terminal with a special command, and then reads the acknowledgement (response) to this command. There are the following commands:

- READ BUFFER $(F2)_{16}$
- READ MODIFIED $(F6)_{16}$

The first is used for diagnostic purposes. The second type is dependent on actions carried out previously by the terminal operator.

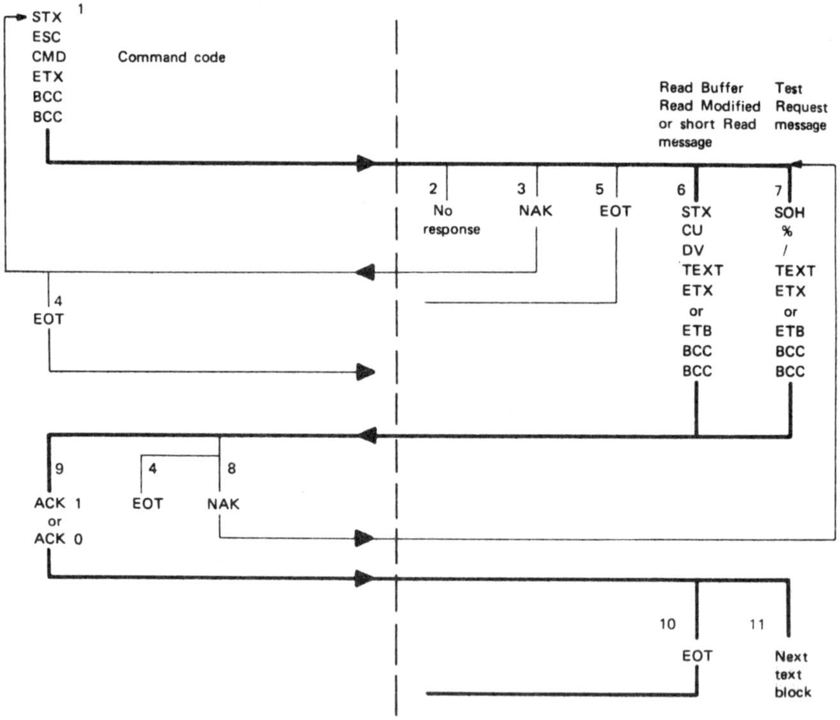

Figure 11.28 READ type commands, traffic flow diagram

Comments on Figure 11.28:

1) *The command sequence must have been preceded by a poll or SELECTION.*
2) *The command sequence has not been understood or has been received wrongly.*

3) The terminal has received a command where the BCC is wrong.
4) In spite of repeated attempts, the terminal has not understood the command correctly. The computer breaks off further sending attempts by sending EOT.
5) The terminal cannot carry out the required command because it is busy or there is a fault on the unit selected.
6) Normal response to READ BUFFER or READ MODIFIED command if text is available for sending.
7) Response to READ MODIFIED generated by the program when the operator has pressed the TEXT key.
8) Computer has detected an error while transmitting.
9) Computer has received and acknowledged a text string. (ACK 0 or ACK 1 depending on block).
10) Normal end to whole message. Last block has been sent to the computer.
11) Next block in the sequence for sending.

WRITE TYPE (write message)

WRITE commands can be sent immediately after SELECTION. There are the following WRITE types:

- WRITE $(F1)_{16}$
- ERASE WRITE $(F5)_{16}$
- COPY $(F7)_{16}$
- ERASE ALL UNPROTECTED $(F6)_{16}$

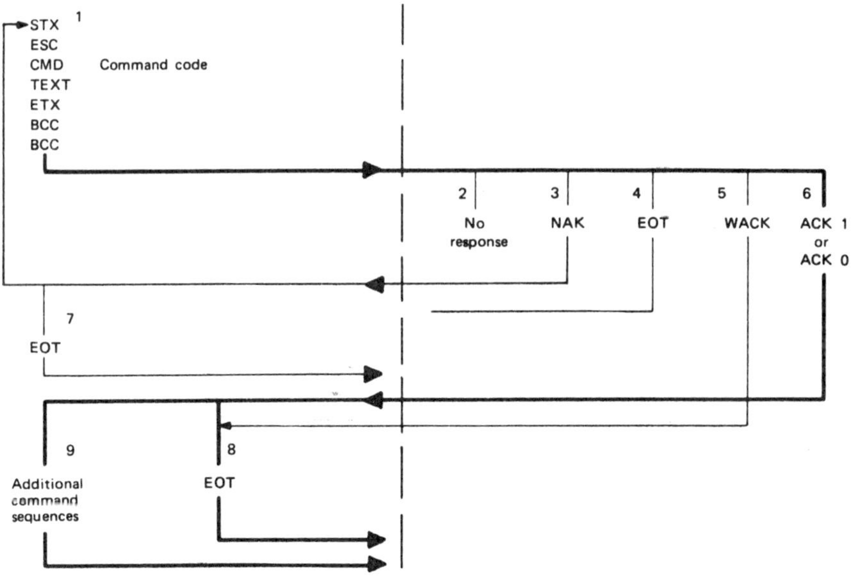

Figure 11.29 WRITE type commands; traffic flow diagram for 3270 procedure

Comments to Figure 11.29:

1) *The command sequence must have been preceded by poll or SELECTION, the terminal must have been selected. If the command is "erase all unprotected fields", there is no other text in the message.*
2) *The command sequence has not been received correctly.*
3) *The terminal has received a sequence where the BCC character is wrong.*
4) *The terminal cannot carry out the required command because it is busy or there is a fault on the unit selected.*
5) *WACK shows that the message has been received correctly and that it is busy with printout.*
6) *The terminal has received and carried out the command ordered. ACK 1 is sent in response to the first and succeeding odd blocks. ACK 0 is sent to all even-numbered blocks.*
7) *Despite repeated attempts to send, the computer cannot transmit the command to the terminal. The computer breaks off the attempts to send with EOT.*
8) *Normal end to command.*
9) *Next command.*

CONTROL COMMANDS

These are a type of transmission which the computer orders the terminal to carry out. The commands are not true messages. There are the following CONTROL COMMANDS:

• COPY	Remote terminal
• ERASE ALL UNPROTECTED	
• SELECT	Local terminal
• NO OPERATION	Local terminal.

Only the first two of the above commands are used for remote terminals. The copy command is used to transfer data between terminals connected to the same control unit. The format is as follows:

• STX	Start of text
• ESC	Escape
• CMD	Command code
• OP	Operation code
• FDV	Transmitting terminal
• ETX	End of text.

The ALFASCOP System 41

System design

The ALFASCOP System 41 contains two types of communications processors. One is dedicated to local terminal systems, and is connected to the data channel in the IBM System 360/370/303X or 4300 Series. The second is designed for remote connection to the host computer via modems and telephone lines or data networks. In its basic configuration, the communications processors contain eight connections for VDU's and/or floppy disc units. Extension modules can be added, in multiples of eight, to give up to 32 terminal workplaces connected to one communications processor. The total memory capacity in a communications processor can be extended to 64 Kb. See Figure 11.30.

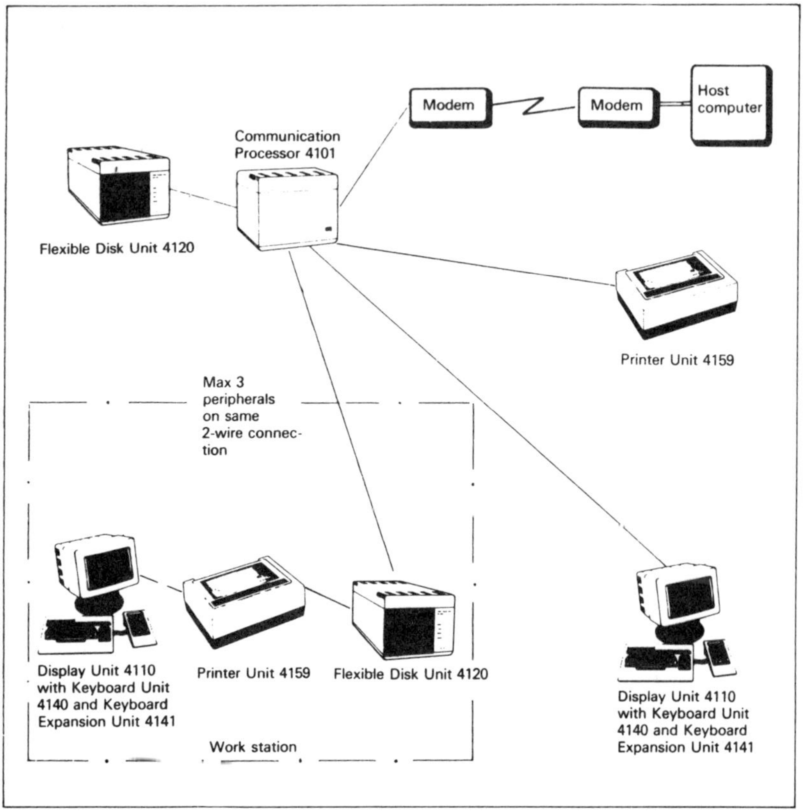

Figure 11.30 ALFASCOP System 41: system design

11.7 Summary

There is a large range of terminals on the market nowadays. Terminals are continually being changed and updated, and provided with new facilities. The person responsible for the building up of a terminal-based system finds it no easy task to choose the most suitable terminal. There are three basic requirements which must be demanded from a terminal and its supplier:

- The terminal must function in the way described in the specifications, and work with the host computer. This may appear to be self-evident, but it is not always so in reality. The terms of reference must be studied in order to determine the most suitable choice before purchase.
- The terminal supplier must be able to guarantee continuity. It is another self-evident requirement that a supplier's products must survive the next year, and that future products are compatible with the older ones.
- The supplier must be able to offer service facilities for both hardware and software. If terminals from one supplier are connected to a computer from another, one must be fully convinced that qualified service can be obtained from both suppliers. Otherwise, one can soon run into difficulties. On the asynchronous side it is easier to connect different makes of terminal to a host computer than for synchronous ones. One should if possible avoid the latter case.

The procedure descriptions for UTS and 3270 are taken from UNISYS and IBM manuals respectively, and they describe the most important principles. The comprehensive amount of local processing which can be done by the product examples given has hardly been touched upon. The full story is given in the respective suppliers' manuals. However, it is not certain that a line procedure will always be fully documented. When working with procedures and emulators, one quickly discovers that none of the exceptions or the rules for how the procedure works are documented.

It can often be difficult to understand the description of a procedure. There are different interpretations as to how it should work. Continual updates are also going on, and perhaps not all of the changes are documented. It is rather like a language which is continally changing without the grammar being able to keep up. There is, in other words, room for surprises when working with a procedure.

One trend for procedures working on the poll-select principle is that they will be replaced by bit-procedures. IBM call their system SDLC, and UNISYS is UDLC.

12 Communication computers

12.1 Introduction

The trend away from batch-processing systems and towards real-time systems (transaction-processing systems) and distributed systems has meant an enormous increase in the volume of data processing and data communication. The terminal has become the means for the user to access these systems, and programmers/systems analysts use terminals to develop them. The demands of data communication are central. A large proportion of new tasks to be processed by the computers depends on these demands. Tasks such as putting characters together into messages, programmed controls, terminal identification, etc, are simple examples, while the functions and levels built into network architecture are among the more complex.

All these tasks can of course be carried out in the central computer, but there are several decisive reasons for placing them in a box by themselves. The following are usually given

- to offload the central computer and look after the first control level
- economic reasons
- security reasons
- concentrators for terminals
- network computer in large complex communication networks
- are often the hub of a network.

This 'box' is usually a programmable computer, and is known as a communications computer or FEP (Front End Processor). We shall now look at the design of an FEP and its positioning and functions in a data processing system.

As far as the hardware is concerned, and the ways in which the various functions are carried out by communications computers, it is clear that there are many differences between manufacturers. The goal they are aiming for, however, is the same.

12.2 Hardware

General

There are many makes of communications computers. Their design is modular, so as to suit the majority of customers who have the type of data processing where an FEP is needed to offload the central processor. It is important for this to be adaptable, in order to be able to keep up with the growing data processing demands. On day one a new system is installed; on day two, x terminals of make 'y' have to be added on.

Several of the manufacturers have chosen to base their computers around a 'Megabus' or 'Bank'. This has a number of inputs to which a range of units are connected. Figure 12.1 shows which units can be connected to the Megabus on Honeywell Bull's DN 7100.

The Megabus is the actual heart of the DN 7100, round which everything else revolves. All units are connected to it, and all data transmission between units goes through it. To avoid blocking of the various units, all those connected to the Bus have a priority depending on where they are connected (see Figure 12.1).

Units are connected in such a way as to allow the fastest possible data throughput. When two or more units want to access the Bus simultaneously, the one with the highest priority gets a 'Bus cycle', i e a certain unit of time. Information exchange between units is on a master-slave basis.

Transmission speed is up to 6 million bytes/second.

Components

Processor

The DN 7100 processor works with a 16-bit word and a 20-bit address field, which is a relatively common length for this type of computer.

Other characteristics

- microprogrammed
- single or double word access to memory
- 64 interrupt levels fully independent of the priority given by the Bus
- direct addressing for ordinary I/O (DMA)
- queues and stacks organised by the hardware.

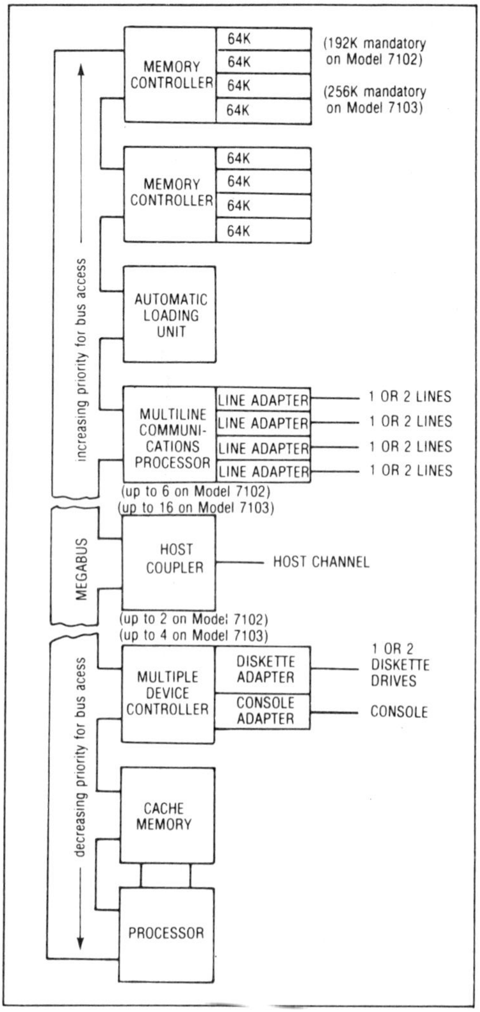

Figure 12.1 Datanet 7100

Memory

The DN 7100 has MOS memory based on 16 Kbit chips. The cycle time is 550 nanoseconds per 2 words. In addition, each word contains a 6-bit 'EDAC' code for detecting and correcting any errors which may occur in the memory (EDAC=Error Detection and Automatic Correction). The minimum and maximum memory size limits are 192 K words to 512 K words, which are also the usual memory limits.

Cache memory

This is a high-speed memory or buffer memory (access time 110 nanoseconds per word). It is used to speed up the memory operations. Refined algorithms ensure that the data required most often is stored in the cache memory. This type of memory is only in the largest models of communications computer, among them the DN 7103, as shown in Figure 12.2.

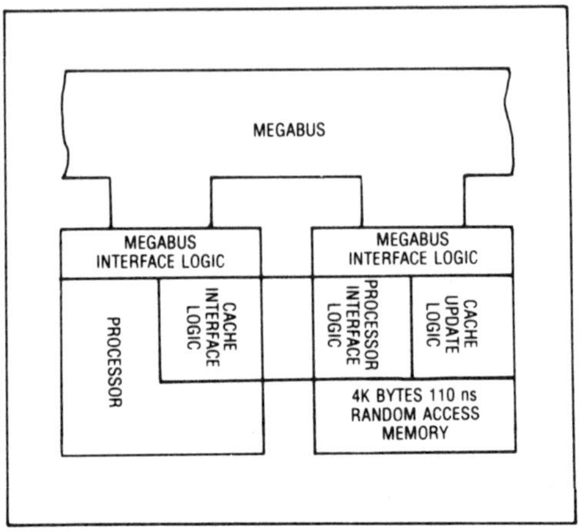

Figure 12.2 Cache memory on the DN 7103

Device controller

This unit is for monitoring other units which can be connected to the communications computer, such as console and floppy disc drives. The unit itself is a microprocessor, containing data buffers for speeding up data transfer between external units and the memory.

Automatic Loading Unit

This unit consists of a 4 Kword ROM (Read-Only Memory) which makes it possible to load and start up the DN 7100 via a connection over the primary network or via a channel from the host computer.

Multiline Communications Processor (MLCP)

This processor administers the lines comprising the 'primary' and 'secondary' network. Line adaptors look after adaptation to the type of transmission (See Table 12.1).

NUMBER OF LINES	LINE TYPE	MAXIMUM SPEED (BPS)	MODEM INTERFACE
2	HALF OR FULL DUPLEX ASYNCHRONOUS	9 600	V24
2	HALF OR FULL DUPLEX ASYNCHRONOUS	9 600	V24
1	HALF DUPLEX ASYNCHRONOUS	72 000	V35
1	HALF OR FULL DUPLEX HDLC	9 600	V24
1	HALF OR FULL DUPLEX HDLC	56 000	V35
1	HALF OR FULL DUPLEX HDLC	9 600	X21

Table 12.1

Figure 12.3 shows the architecture of the MLCP. The ROM contains the microprogram needed to drive the MLCP. RAM (Random Access Memory) is the buffer for input and output data, and also contains programs for the line protocols which are implemented. Each MLCP can handle up to 8 lines.

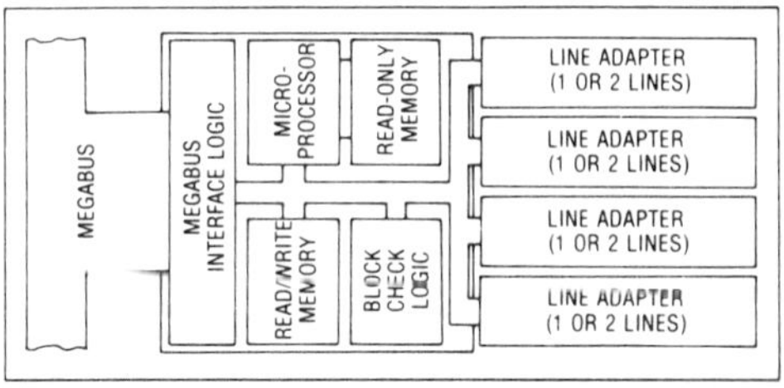

Figure 12.3 MLCP

Other manufacturers' communications computers have their own special design. UNISYS DCP/40 is shown in Figure 12.4.

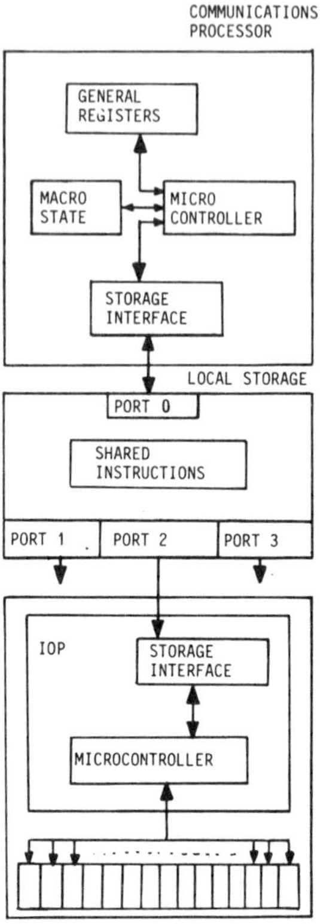

Figure 12.4

12.3 Software

All communications computers are programmable. The software usually consists of a number of modules. The supplier will help in putting these together into a functioning package, corresponding to the functions which the communications computer is designed to carry out. The program modules are responsible for:

- interface/communication with the central system
- dealing with the protocols and types of terminal in the network
- interface/communication with other computers
- interface with primary and secondary networks (see section 12.4)
- administrative routines, statistics, etc
- buffer processing, code transformation, checking, etc
- the supplier's network architecture (layers) – see Figure 12.14.

Where the software is built round a number of modules in reentrant code, only those modules required for the particular functions need to be implemented. This method means that the memory can be used better. In many cases it is only those modules which are active (e g modules for 3270 terminals) which reside in memory. All others are on disc, and are read in when needed. In order to avoid too much swapping of modules in and out, one can declare which ones one wants resident in memory. The manufacturers try to get as clear a distinction as possible between the modules (standardisation within the area of communications leads to this) in order to simplify program maintenance. Figure 12.5 shows the DNS software and its modules and relationships. DNS (Distributed Network Supervisor) is the operating system for Honeywell Bull's DN 7100.

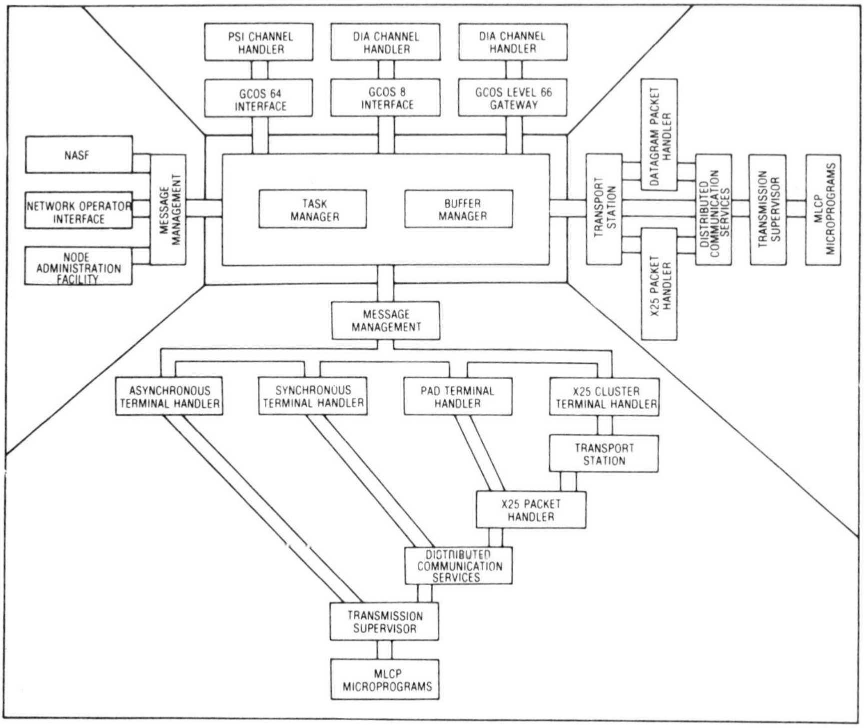

Figure 12.5 DNS

Operating system generation

All the software required for installation of a communications computer is supplied on magnetic tape. The manufacturer's specialists now take over and create a program library on a disc memory file with all the modules in it. Creating (or 'generating') a functional operating system from this position involves selecting the modules needed, 'linking' them, and building up system tables and control structures which make them work with the hardware of the front-end computer. With the aid of these modules, one can specify for the FEP what the network looks like, what protocols are used, terminal types, memory sizes, types of line, buffer sizes, etc.

The host computer must also be made aware of the communications computer, and this is usually done by adding extra parameter cards in the program module which specifies how the host computer is configured, i e what units are connected to it.

When all the necessary modules have been installed and the necessary changes made, it is time to initialise the communications computer and to get started with the communication and terminal traffic. Generation and configuration errors are often met with at first, but they can usually be sorted out. One of the great advantages of communications computers is that the network can be changed by changing the configuration, and initialising or regenerating the communications computer system again without having to shut the central sytem down. If the customer has more than one FEP, certain parts of the terminal network or all terminal traffic (depending on how the computers are configured) will still work even when one of the communications computers has to be reinitialised.

Figure 12.6 shows the principles of system generation in a DNS.

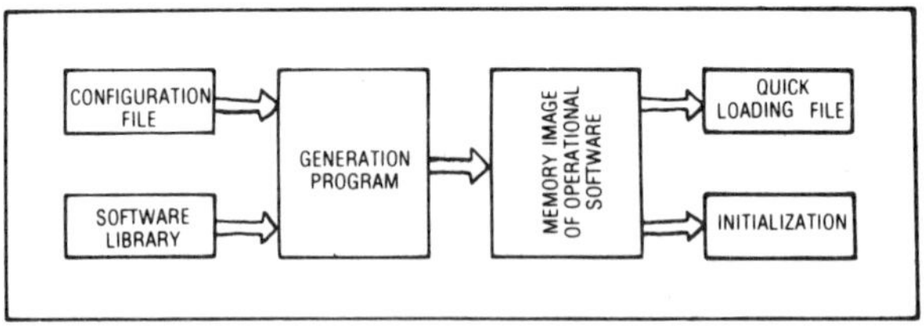

Figure 12.6 System generation in a DNS

In today's systems it is even possible to change the configuration from some other point (node) in the network. There will be a copy locally of the configuration to be found centrally. When the necessary changes have been made, the new configuration is sent through the network ('down line load'), and a new sysem generation or initialisation can be started. This is described in Figure 12.7.

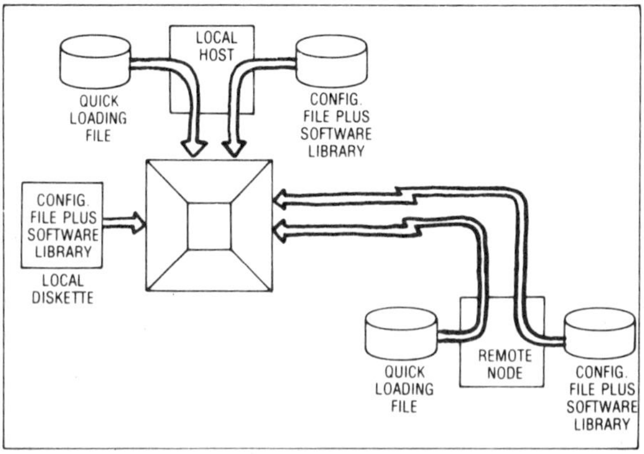

Figure 12.7

When the configuration, system generation and initialisation phases have been completed and all tests carried out, the communications computer can be started up and the new functions used.

12.4 Functions

Communication computers and their software are designed to follow the manufacturer's architecture for the distributed system. This implies an individual solution to the communication between user and system for each manufacturer. The DN 7100, for example, can be a front-end computer, concentrator or switch, depending on its positioning in the network, and programmed accordingly. Figure 12.8 shows the role of the communications computer, and Figure 12.9 gives other elements with which it communicates.

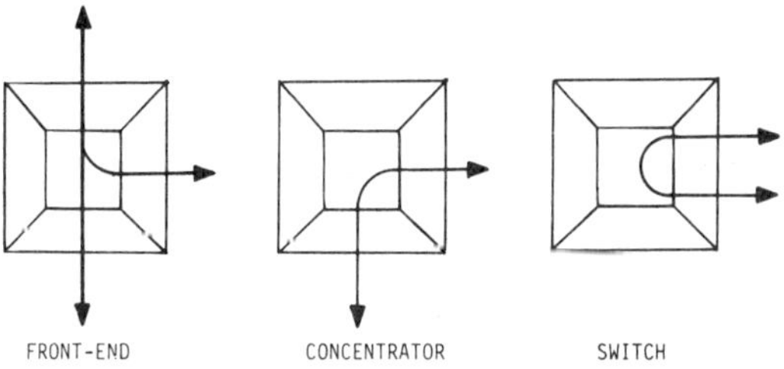

Figure 12.8

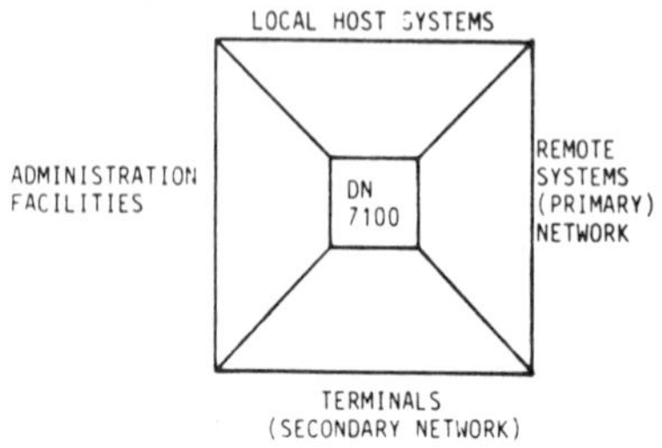

Figure 12.9

As front-end computer, it forms the interface between one or more host computers and the primary/secondary network.

The concentrator function means that the computer is the interface between the primary and the secondary network, i e between the user and the central system. In the old days, concentrators were used only for blocking and forwarding incoming messages from the terminals to the host computer. Today's programmable node computers are 'intelligent', and can be used in a completely different way. Examples of this are input data checking, authority checking, formula processing, etc.

When working as a switch, it just controls/forwards messages in the primary network.

Front end

The front-end computer is connected to the host computer via a normal data channel if the computers are sited in the same computer room, or via what is known as a "hyper-channel" if the distance is too far for normal signal cables. As a front-end computer, it off-loads all the communications traffic from the host computer and administers it itself. It forms the interface between the host computer and the rest of the network.

Concentrator

Figure 12.10 shows the concentrator function in a network structure consisting of a primary and a secondary network. The Swedish National Insurance current network is an example of such a network. It consists of a hierarchical concentrator network comprising fixed, leased, four-wire lines. The concentrators are connected to the central system via the primary network, which consists of point-to-point connections. The secondary network (between terminal and concentrator) consists of multipoint connections.

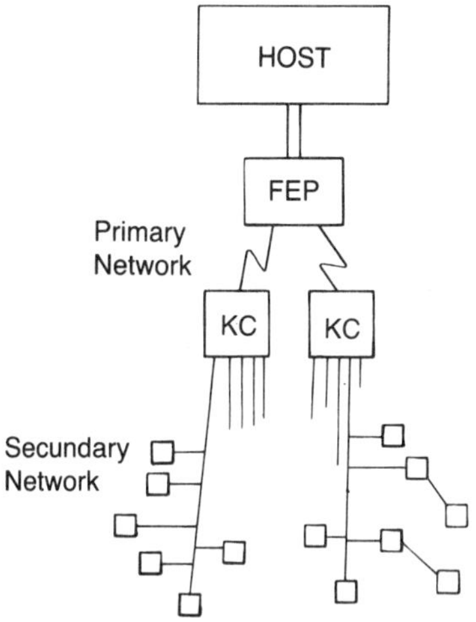

Figure 12.10 Concentrator functions in a primary and secondary network

Primary networks

When it comes to the primary network and the DN 7100, Figure 12.11 shows which DNS modules and DSA (Distributed Systems Architecture) levels are involved.

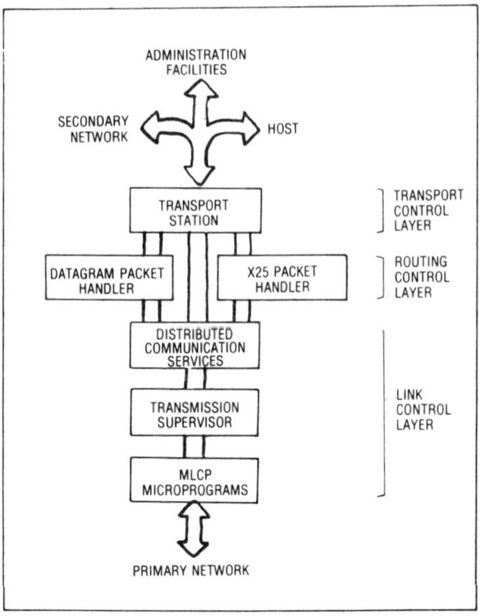

Figure 12.11 Primary network and the DN 7100

The interfaces between the primary network and the communications computer are the levels 'link control' and 'physical link'.

The connections may be

- fixed point-to-point
- circuit switching (X.21)
- packet switching (X.25).

For all these, the HDLC protocol is used as 'link control layer'. All exchanges of messages between host computer/secondary network and the primary network are handled by the DSA 'Communications Management Layer' (see Chapter 7 in the Section on Transport Station).

Secondary networks

Networks between terminals and concentrators or between terminals and communications computers are called secondary networks. Figure 12.12 shows which DNS modules are involved in passing messages on the network.

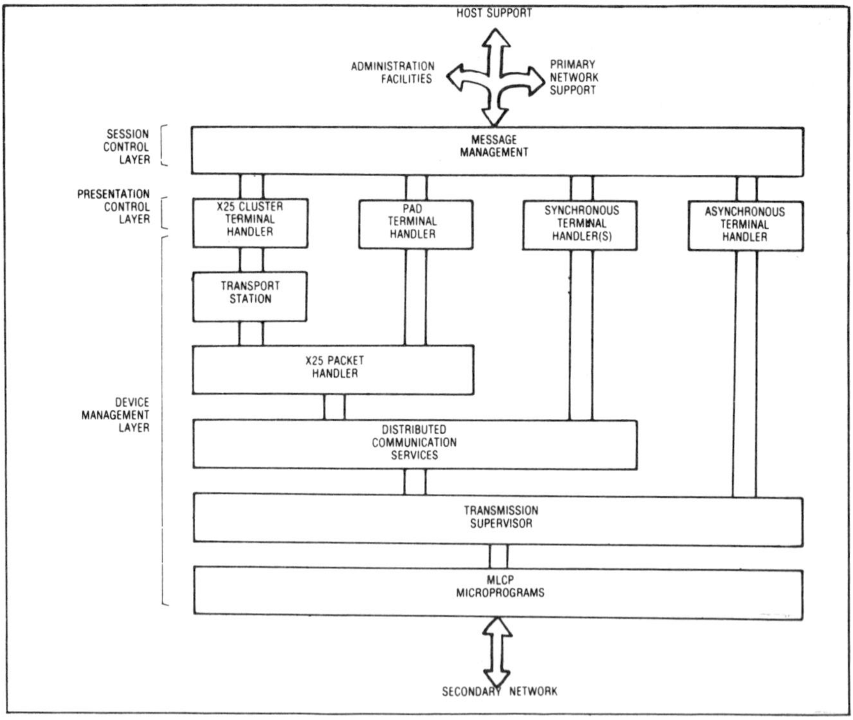

Figure 12.12 Secondary networks on the DN 7100

In contrast to the primary networks, it is the 'Device Management Layer' which forms the interface with the secondary network (compare Figures 12.11 and 12.12).

Several of the components of a secondary network are also to be found in a primary network.

Examples of these are

- physical lines
- logical lines
- communication control
- virtual circuits.

The software modules for the functioning of the primary network can be used to manage many of the functions of the secondary network.

One important difference, however, is that for the latter function there are modules for controlling the terminals which are connected to the network (terminal handlers).

Administrative functions

In order to be able to use a network effectively, functions are required which make it possible for the user to control and maintain it. There are special program modules for this purpose, which offer various service functions. Out in the node computers or concentrators there are programs which collect statistics on accessibility, charging information, retransmissions, etc. The user is also able to make dynamic changes in the network through the functions for network monitoring.

All the statistics collected (into a disc-memory file or log file) contain historic information on how the network is functioning. Analysis of this yields information on

- use of resources
- error statistics
- basis for further planning and development
- bottlenecks in the network
- charging
- the amount of data transferred
- transmission errors
- waiting times
- buffer utilisation
- statistics on how the lines are used.

In all the larger installations, a terminal monitoring function is usually installed. This was also hinted at in the introduction "It is essential that data communication works in today's advanced systems".

This chapter ends with diagrams which relate back to Chapter 7, and which also summarizes this chapter. Figure 12.13 shows the DN 7100 and its functions, and Figure 12.14 shows the DSA levels.

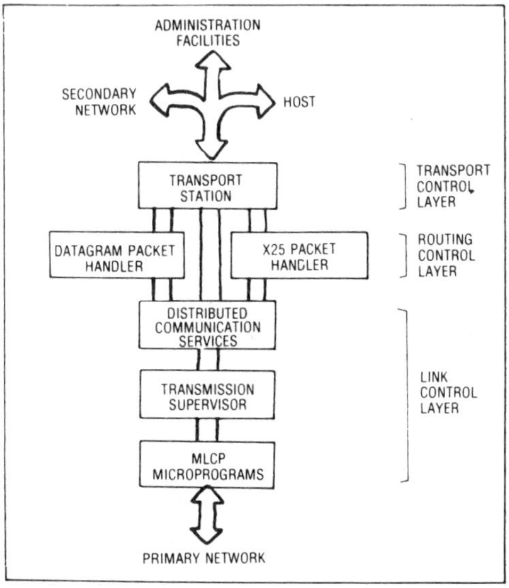

Figure 12.13 The DN 7100 and its functions

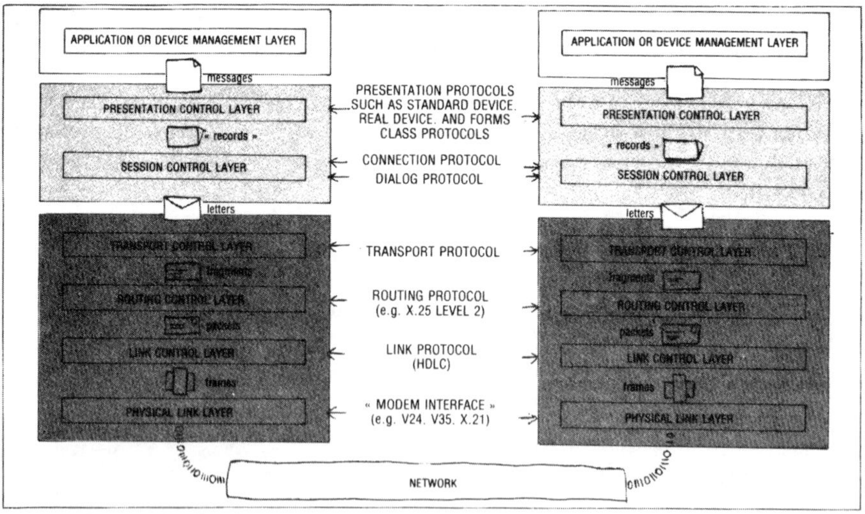

Figure 12.14 DSA levels

13 Modems and modulation

13.1 Introduction

One of the problems of data transmission over telephone lines is the conversion of digital data into a satisfactory form for transmission over an analogue line which was designed for transferring speech signals and not data.

A physical telephone channel works like a bandpass filter with a passband between 300–3400 Hz, which looks roughly like that shown in Figure 13.1.

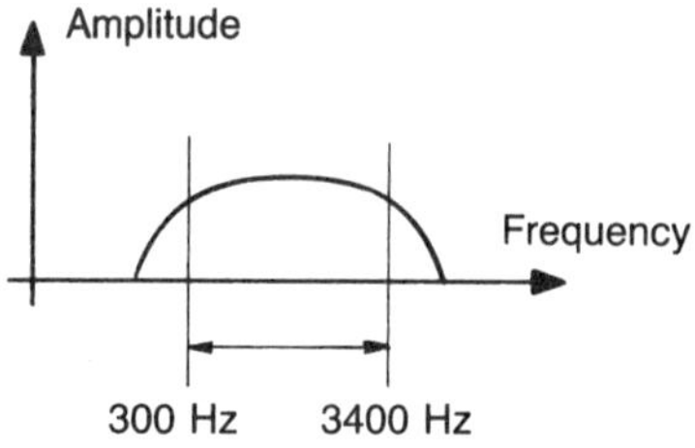

Figure 13.1 Passband for a telephony channel

The digital information which is to be transmitted, however, has the appearance of a random sequence of rectangular pulses, sent continuously (see Figure 13.1). The frequency spectrum for the digital information is shown in Figure 13.3. The spectrum has a considerable low-frequency content which the speech channel cannot transmit.

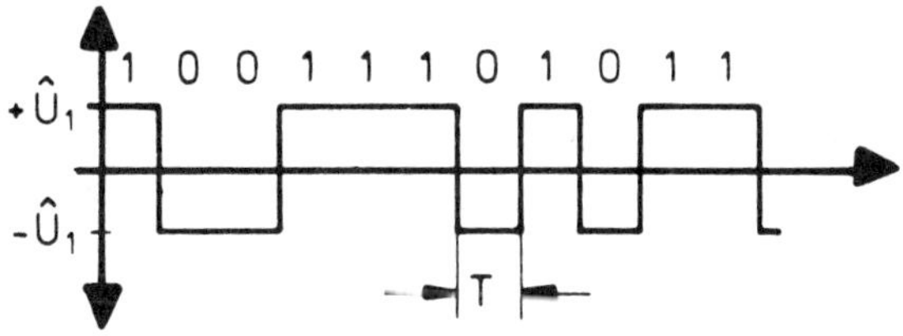

Figure 13.2 Digital information waveform (square wave)

The telephone channel cannot cope with the high frequency components of the spectrum either. In order to get over this problem, a carrier wave is modulated with the digital information at the transmitter's end, and the modulated signal is transmitted to the receiver. There the signal is demodulated and the digital information is regained.

The equipment used for this purpose is called a modem (MOdulator-DEModulator), an internationally-recognised name.

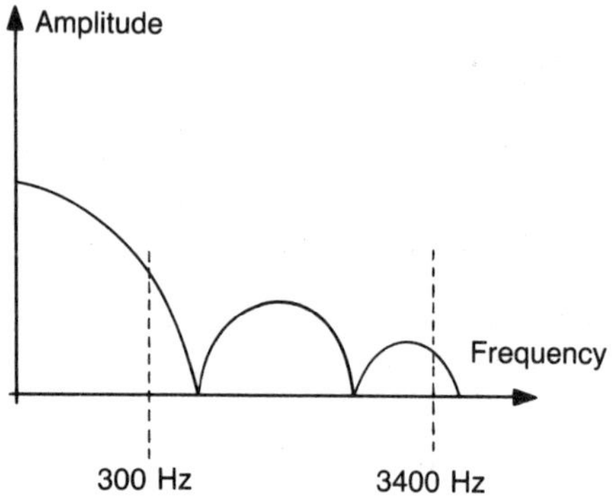

Figure 13.3 Frequency spectrum of a digital information wave

13.2 Modulation methods

The carrier wave in an information system does not in itself convey any information; this must be superimposed on the carrier in one way or another. If we look at a sine wave (the carrier), as shown in Figure 13.4, this can be described mathematically as

$$U_b = \hat{U}_b \sin(\omega t + \phi)$$

where

$\hat{U}_b$ = amplitude
ω = angular frequency
ϕ = phase

There are therefore three quantities which one can vary in time with a modulation voltage, and thereby superimpose information on the carrier wave. All three methods are used, and are called respectively

- amplitude modulation
- frequency modulation
- phase modulation

The most often used are frequency and phase modulation. For high transmission speeds, a combination of phase and amplitude modulation is used.

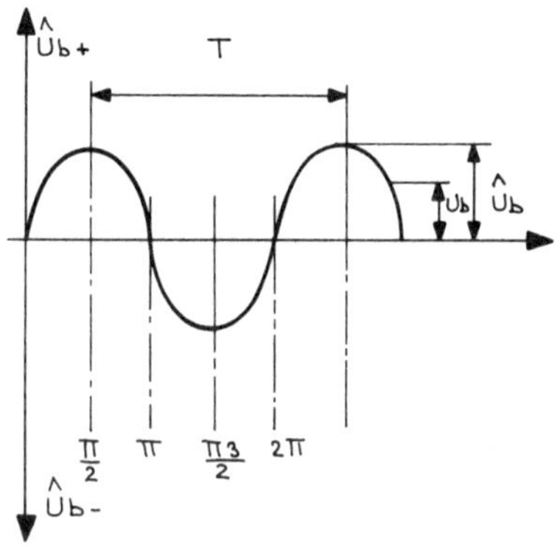

Figure 13.4 Carrier wave (sine wave)

Modulation and transmission speeds have been standardised under the auspices of CCITT.

13.3 Amplitude modulation

In amplitude modulation, the amplitude Ub of a carrier wave is varied in the expression

$$Ub = \hat{U}b \cdot \sin(\omega t + \phi)$$

The modulation voltage consists of a low frequency with the equation

$$Um = \hat{U}m \cdot \cos pt$$

The modulated signal Ûs will then appear as in Figure 13.5, where m is the degree of modulation.

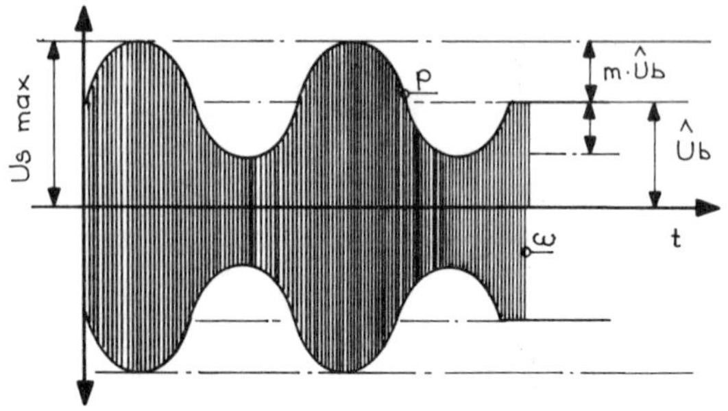

Figure 13.5. Amplitude-modulated signal

The expression for the modulated signal (assuming the phase of the carrier is zero) becomes

$$Us=\hat{U}b \cdot \sin \omega t+\frac{m \cdot \hat{U}b}{2} \sin(\omega+p)t+\frac{m \cdot \hat{U}b}{2} (\omega-p)t$$

Carrier Upper sideband Lower sideband

From the expression, one can see that the modulation signal Us consists of three components. Ûb is equal to the original carrier wave, and $\frac{m \cdot \hat{U}b}{2}$ is two signals lying p radians/second higher and lower than the carrier. The latter are called sidebands. Figure 13.6 shows the frequency spectrum of the amplitude modulated signal.

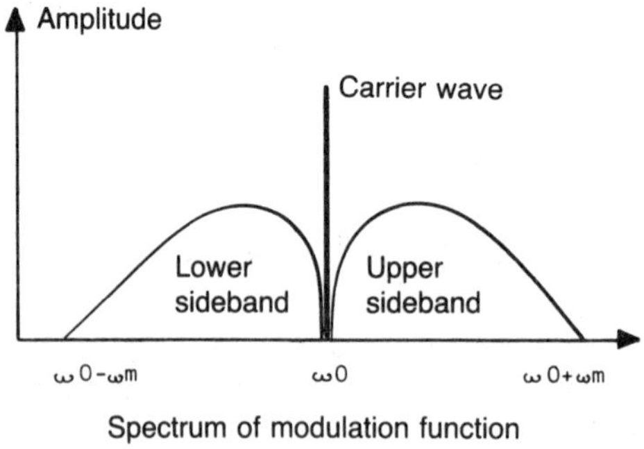

Figure 13.6 Frequency spectrum of an amplitude modulated signal

The degree of modulation m usually lies between 0 and 1, or 0–100%. If m equals 1, $\hat{U}m=\hat{U}b$ and the signal is fully modulated. In Figure 13.5, the signal is modulated to 50%. In full modulation, the power in one sideband is 25% of that in the carrier. The sideband power is reduced with lower degrees of modulation, so the idea is to keep the degree of modulation as high as possible without overmodulating the signal.

13.4 Frequency modulation

In frequency modulation, the frequency ω is varied in time with the modulating signal. The frequency varies around the carrier frequency in time with a low frequency signal according to the expression

$$Um=\hat{U}m \cdot \cos pt$$

The instantaneous frequency ω_i is defined as the speed of change of the total phase angle θ, i e derivative of θ with respect to time t

$$\omega i=\frac{d\theta}{dt}$$

If θ is constant, the instantaneous frequency is

$$\omega i=\frac{d\theta}{dt}=\frac{d}{dt} \cdot (\omega t+\phi)=\omega$$

i e $\omega=\omega i$.

Where the frequency varies around the carrier frequency in time to a low frequency signal,

$$Um=\hat{U}m \cdot \cos pt$$

where

$$(k \cdot \hat{U}m)=\Delta\omega$$

which is called the angular frequency deviation, and in this case is expressed in radians/second. The expression for the frequency-modulated signal becomes

$$Us-\hat{U}s \cdot \sin(\omega t \mid \frac{\Delta\omega}{p} \sin pt)$$

The relation between ωi and θ is best shown in Figure 13.7. The independence of θ from time when ϕ varies can be seen. Variation in ϕ also means a variation in the frequency of the signal. The momentary or instantaneous frequency is also defined as the slope of a tangent to the line at the corresponding point, a slope which varies with time. The instantaneous frequency equals the angular coefficient of the tangent, or as mentioned earlier, $\frac{d\theta}{dt}$

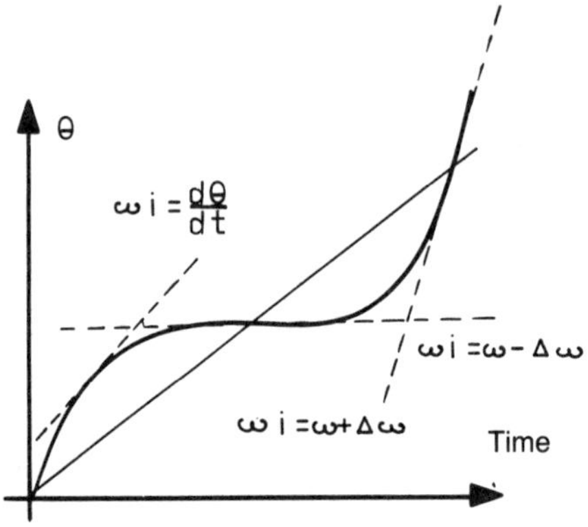

Figure 13.7 θ as a function of time for varying ϕ

The angular frequency

$$\omega = 2\pi \cdot f$$

and

$$p = 2\pi \cdot fm$$

where f equals the carrier frequency and fm equals the modulation frequency, giving

$$Us = \hat{U}s \cdot \sin(2\pi ft + \frac{\Delta f}{fm} \cdot \sin pt)$$

where Δf is called the frequency swing, and is the difference between the highest and lowest frequencies.

$\frac{\Delta f}{fm}$ is known as the modulation index.

Looking at the frequency spectrum for the frequency modulated signal, side frequencies are found in the same way as for amplitude modulation. On the other hand, the FM signal has a much broader spectrum than the AM signal. The higher the modulation index used, the more side frequencies there are, and the lower the amplitude of the carrier wave. For radio transmissions on the FM bands, a common value for the modulation index is 5, and the highest modulation frequency is 15 kHz.

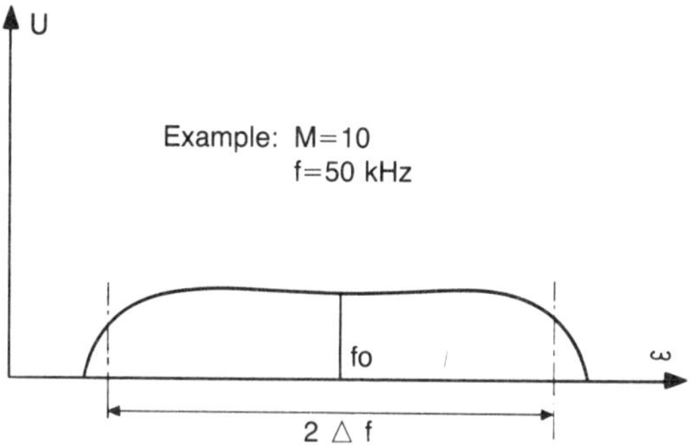

Figure 13.8 Spectrum of frequency modulated signal

13.5 Phase modulation

In phase modulation the phase (or phase angle) is varied in time with the modulated signal. However, a variation of frequency also involves a variation of phase angle. A phase modulated signal is the same as a frequency modulated signal where the swing is proportional both to the modulation voltage and to the modulation frequency. Phase and frequency modulation therefore have much in common. The expression for the unmodulated signal is as follows

$$Ub = \hat{U}b \cdot \sin(\omega t + \phi)$$

If ϕ varies with a low frequency wave according to the expression

$$Um = \hat{U}m \cdot \cos pt$$

Ub can be stated to be modulated by this low frequency wave. The expression for the phase modulated signal becomes

$$Uf = \hat{U}f \cdot \sin(\omega t + k \cdot \hat{U}m \cdot \cos pt)$$

where

$$\Delta\phi = k \cdot Um$$

is the phase deviation in radians/second.

13.6 Plugs and circuits for interface connection

We shall now connect a terminal to a computer via a modem link. At the terminal and computer ends, the modems are connected by cables of standardised lengths (3, 5 or 15 metres) and plugs. The modems are connected to the telephone lines using the standard telephone plugs and sockets.

CCITT recommendation V.24 deals with the circuits which are used in the interface between the data terminal (DTE) and the data circuit-terminating equipment (DCE).

These circuits transfer binary data, control and timing signals.

In the recommendation, each circuit has been given a 3-figure number. The 100 series is for general signals and the 200 series for automatic dialling.

Connection to the modem is via a 25-pin CANNON plug, which screws firmly into the socket on the back of the modem.

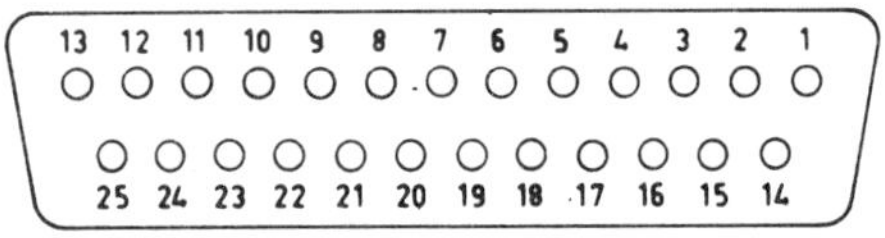

Figure 13.9 25-pin CANNON plug

Each pin number in the plug or socket has a corresponding CCITT circuit number. Pins and circuits are shown in Table 13.1.

Circuit 101 – protective ground

This circuit is to be electrically connected to the equipment box or stand. It can be connected to further earth points according to regulations.

Circuit 102 – signal ground

This circuit forms the reference voltage against which all other interface cirucits in the 100 series (except 101) are measured. In the DCE this circuit must be connected to a single connection point, and it must be possible to connect this point to circuit 101 via a strap. On installation this strap may be connected or removed in order to fulfil the relevant regulations or to reduce the noise in the circuit.

Table 13.1 Pins and circuits on the V.24 interface

CCITT No	Pin No	Direction Term – Mod	Description
102	7	↔	Signal ground
103	2	→	Transmitted data
104	3	←	Received data
105	4	→	Request to send (on 103)
106	5	←	Ready to send
107	6	←	Data Set ready
108.1	20	→	Connect data set to line
108.2		→	Data terminal ready
109	8	←	Data channel received line signal detector (carrier detect)
111	23	→	Change of data rate (transmission speed)
113	24 (15)	→	Transmitter signal element timing (sender to modem)
114	15	←	Transmitter signal element timing (sender from modem)
115	17	←	Receiver signal element timing (sender to modem)
118	14	→	Transmitted data, reverse channel
119	16	→	Received data, reverse channel
120	19	→	Request to send (on 118)
121	13	←	Reverse channel ready to send
122	12	←	Data channel received line signal detector, reverse channel
125	22	←	Call indication
140	21	→	Remote control
141	18	→	Local test control
142	25	←	Test indication
—	9*	←	+12 V
—	10*	←	−12 V

* Not CCITT standard

Circuit 103 – transmitted data

Direction: TO modem.

Data signals produced in the data terminal to be sent via the data channel to one or more receiving stations are transmitted on this circuit to the modem.

The data terminal has to hold Circuit 103 in the ON condition (negative) during each time interval between characters and on all other occasions where on information is to be sent via the data channel. The data terminal must not transmit data signals on circuit 103 if any of the following four circuits, where they are present, are in the ON condition

1	Circuit 105	– request to send, data channel
2	Circuit 106	– ready for sending
3	Circuit 107	– data set (modem) ready
4	Circuits 108.1/108.2	– connect modem/data terminal ready

Circuit 104 – received data

Direction: FROM modem.

Data signals produced by the modem's demodulator when line signals are received from a receiving station are transmitted on this line to the data terminal.

Circuit 105 – request to send, data channel

Direction: TO modem.

This circuit is necessary in half-duplex modems and in branching networks where the terminals decide which modem can send and when it can send. An alternative connection method for four-wire point-to-point networks allows the modem to send continuously.

The ON condition causes the data channel modulator in the modem to prepare to send. In this connection condition, the line signals required for setting the data channel running (e g equalisation, synchronisation, unlocking, etc) can also be transmitted, as long as Circuit 107 (data set ready) is in the ON condition.

The ON condition must be maintained as long as the data terminal is sending or transmitting data signals on Circuit 103 (transmitted data).

The OFF condition prevents the data channel's modulator in the modem from sending. When Circuit 105 has gone over to the OFF condition, it must not be restored to the ON condition before Circuit 106 (ready for sending) has been switched OFF.

Circuit 106 – ready for sending

Direction: FROM modem.

The condition of the signal on this circuit determines whether the data channel modulator in the modem is connected for sending or not, and forms an acknowledgement to Circuit 105 (request to send).

An ON condition means that the data channel modulator in the modem is ready to send.

An OFF condition means that the data channel modulator in the modem is prevented from sending.

105 or 107	**Delay on 106**			
	Note 1	**Note 2**	**Note 3**	**Note 4**
	ms	**ms**	**ms**	**ms**
OFF – ON	25. . .40	65. . .100	200. . .275	750. . .1400
ON – OFF	<2	<2	<2	<2

Note 1: These values are applied where Circuit 105 is in use frequently (e g in multipoint networks).

Note 2: These values are applied only at 2400 bits/s where Circuit 105 is rarely used (e g in point-to-point connections).

Note 3: These values are applied in general networks to protect the receiver from echo effects on the line and from reflections caused by mismatching on change of direction.

Note 4: These values are only applied at the connection stage with automatic calling and answering.

Circuit 107 – data set (modem) ready

Direction: FROM modem.

The condition of the signal on this circuit states whether the modem is ready to run or not.

The ON condition means that the modem is connected to the long distance line, and that it is ready to exchange further control signals with the data terminal to start data transmission.

The OFF condition means that the modem is not ready to run. The OFF condition on this circuit must not affect the function of Circuit 125 (call-up indication)

Circuit 108

Circuit 108 has two alternative meanings. The choice between these is made with the help of a two-way switch at installation. Circuit 108 can also be replaced completely by a switch.

Circuit 108.1 – connect data set (modem) to line

Direction: TO modem.

Signals on this circuit control the connection of the modem or corresponding equipment to the remote line.

An ON condition means that the modem or equivalent equipment is connected to the line regardless of the condition of the other interface circuits.

An OFF condition means that the modem or other equipment is disconnected from the line when the transmission of all data signals, previously sent on Circuit 103 (transmitted data), is complete. The OFF condition must not disallow use of Circuit 125 (call-up indicator).

When Circuit 108.1 has gone over to the OFF condition, it must not revert to the ON condition again before Circuit 107 (data set ready) has gone to OFF. *Note*: Using a strap in the modem, one may connect either Circuit 108.1 or 108.2.

Circuit 108.2 – data terminal ready

Direction: TO modem.

Signals on this circuit prepare for connection of the modem or equivalent equipment to the distant line.

An ON condition means that the data terminal is ready to run; it also prepares the modem (etc) for connection to the line, and where connection has been carried out externally, it maintains the running condition.

Where the modem contains automatic answering equipment, connection to the line only occurs with a combination of conditions ON on Circuit 125 (call-up indication) and ON on Circuit 108.2.

The data terminal can put an ON condition onto Circuit 108.2 whenever it is ready to send or receive data signals.

The OFF condition means that the modem (or other equipment) is disconnected from the line on completion of transmission of all data signals which were transmitted on Circuit 103 (transmit data). An OFF condition must not disallow the functioning of Circuit 125 (call-up indication).

Where Circuit 108.2 has gone over to the OFF condition, it must not return to the ON condition before Circuit 108 (data set ready) has gone to the OFF condition.

Circuit 109 – data channel received line signal detector (carrier detect)

Direction: FROM modem.

Signals on this circuit tell whether the received signal from the data channel lies within predetermined limits, which are specified in recommendations applicable to the modem.

The ON condition indicates that the signal is within the limits.

The OFF condition indicates no signal or that it does not lie within the specified limits.

Circuit 110 – Signal quality indication, data channel

Direction: FROM modem.

Signals on this line indicate whether a certain level of probability of faults on signals received is present. This only takes account of the quality of the transmission channel.

ON indicates that there is no reason to suppose that errors are present.

OFF indicates that there is reason to suppose that errors are present.

Circuit 111 – speed selection (controlled by data terminal)

Direction: TO the modem.

Either Circuit 111 or Circuit 112 may be used.

Signals on this circuit are used for selection of transmission speed on synchronous modems with two possible speeds, or for selection of speed range on asynchronous modems with two speed ranges.

In the ON condition, the higher of the two data signalling speeds or ranges is chosen.

In the OFF condition the lower speed or range is selected.

Circuit 112 – speed selection (controlled by modem)

Direction: FROM the modem.

Either Circuit 111 or Circuit 112 may be used.

Signals on this circuit are used for choice of speed or speed range in the data terminal in agreement with the speed or speed range for synchronous or asynchronous modems with two speeds or speed ranges respectively.

In the ON condition, the higher of the two data signalling speeds or ranges in chosen.

In the OFF condition the lower speed or range is selected.

Circuit 113 – element speed, sender (controlled by data terminal)

Direction: TO the modem (external timing).

The sender's timing in synchronous traffic is determined either by the terminal via Circuit 113 or by the modem via Circuit 114. The actual circuit to be used is set on installation. The timing signal on 113-timing control must consist of a square-wave with a frequency of 600/1200/2400 ± 0.01%, and synchronised with the transmitted data in the same way as Circuit 114.

The condition on the 113 circuit must correspond to ON and OFF during nominally the same time periods. A transition from the ON condition to the OFF condition must mark the midpoint of every signal element on Circuit 103 (transmitted data).

Timing information must be transmitted on Circuit 113 as soon as Circuit 107 is in the ON condition. It is permitted to transmit timing information even when Circuit 107 is in the OFF condition.

When timing information is not being transmitted, Circuit 113 must be in the OFF condition.

Circuit 114 – element speed, sender (internal timing)

Direction: FROM the modem.

Signals on this circuit provide the data terminal with timing information on the signal elements.

The condition of this circuit must correspond to ON and OFF conditions under nominally the same time periods. The data terminal must transmit data signals on Circuit 103 (transmitted data) whose timing of changes between signal elements corresponds nominally with the times of switching from OFF to ON conditions on Circuit 114.

Information is transmitted on Circuit 114 as soon as Circuit 107 (data set ready) is in the ON condition. Information may be sent even when Circuit 107 is in the OFF condition.

When information is to be transferred, Circuit 114 must be in the OFF condition.

Circuit 115 – element timing, receiver's side (controlled by the modem)

Direction: FROM modem (receiver timing controls the transmission).

Either Circuit 115 or Circuit 128 may be used.

Circuit 115 is kept in the same phase as the data signal received from a synchronised unit. Signal 115 is a square-wave synchronised so that it switches from OFF to ON at the same time as the received data changes state.

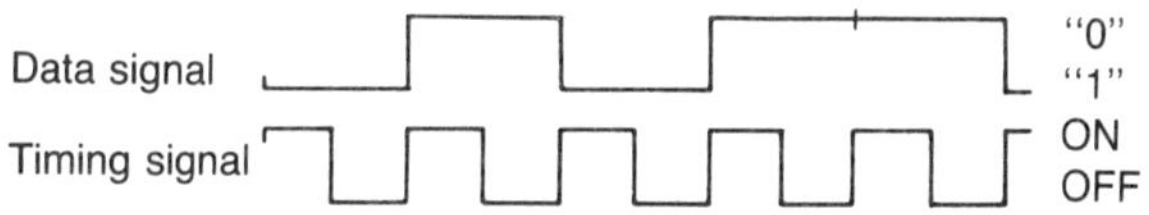

Figure 13.10 Synchronisation

The condition on this circuit must correspond to ON and OFF for nominally the same time periods. The switchover from ON to OFF must nominally mark the midpoint of every signal element on Circuit 104 (received data).

Clock pulses have to be transmitted on Circuit 115 as soon as Circuit 109 (carrier indication, data channel) is in the ON condition. After the changeover from ON to OFF on Circuit 109, this information can remain for a period whose length is dependent on the stability of the modem's timing circuits.

When information is not being transmitted, Circuit 115 goes to the OFF condition.

Circuit 116 – select standby

Direction: TO modem.

Signals on this circuit are used to select between normal and reserve running within the data communication equipment.

An ON condition shows that the reserve alternative has been selected, which means that the normal equipment in the data communication device has been replaced by the reserve device.

An OFF condition means that the reserve device in the data communication equipment has been replaced by the normal one. The OFF condition on this circuit is to be maintained as long as the reserve equiment does not need to be used.

Circuit 117 – standby indicator

Direction: FROM modem.

Signals on this circuit indicate whether the data communication equipment is in the reserve condition, with the normal devices having been replaced by the reserve ones.

An ON condition means that the data communication equipment is in the reserve running condition.

An OFF condition means that the data communication equipment is in the normal mode.

Circuit 118 – transmitted data, back channel

Direction: TO modem.

This circuit is equivalent to Circuit 103 (transmitted data), except that it is used to send data via the reserve channel.

The data terminal has to hold Circuit 118 in the ON condition (negative) during each time interval between characters or words and on all other occasions where no information is to be sent on the reverse channel. The data terminal must not transmit data signals on Circuit 118 unless all the folowing circuits, where they are used, are in the ON condition

1 Circuit 120 – request to send, reverse channel
2 Circuit 121 – back channel ready
3 Circuit 107 – data set (modem) ready
4 Circuit 108.1/108.2 – connect remote line/data terminal ready

Circuit 119 – received data, back channel

Direction: FROM modem.

This circuit is equivalent to Circuit 104 (received data), but is used for receiving data on the reverse channel.

Circuit 120 – request to send, back channel

Direction: TO modem.

This circuit is equivalent to Circuit 105 (request to send, data channel), except that it is used to control the reverse channel transmission part of the modem.

An ON condition makes the reverse channel modulator in the modem ready to send. In this state, the line signals required to get the back channel running can also be transmitted, as long as Circuit 107 (data set ready) is in the ON condition.

The ON condition must be maintained as long as the data terminal is transmitting via the back channel or transmitting data signals on Circuit 118 (transmitted data, back channel).

An OFF condition prevents the back channel modulator in the modem from sending. When Circuit 120 has gone to the OFF condition, it must not be returned to ON before Circuit 121 (back channel ready) has gone to OFF.

Circuit 121 – back channel ready

Direction: FROM modem.

This circuit is equivalent to Circuit 106 (data channel ready), except that it is used to tell whether the back channel modulator in the modem is ready to send or not.

The ON condition means that the back channel modulator in the modem is ready to transmit.

An OFF condition means that the back channel modulator in the modem is prevented from transmitting.

When Circuit 120 (request to send, back channel) is used, conditions of ON and OFF on Circuit 121 are used as responses to conditions ON and OFF respectively on Circuit 120.

Circuit 122 – carrier indication, back channel

Direction: FROM modem.

This circuit is equivalent to Circuit 109 (carrier indication, data channel), except that it is used to tell whether the level of the signal received via the reverse channel falls within specified limits; these are specified in the relevant recommendation for the modem.

Circuit 123 – signal quality indication, back channel

Direction: FROM modem.

This circuit is equivalent to Circuit 110 (signal quality indication, data channel), except that it is used to indicate the quality of the signal received on the reserve channel. Only the quality of the transmission channel itself is taken into account.

Circuit 125 – call-up indication

Direction: FROM modem.

Signals on this circuit indicate whether a call-up signal has been received by the modem.

ON means a call-up signal has been received.

OFF means that no call-up signal has been received, and it must also coincide approximately with each interval for a pulse-modulated call-up signal.

Circuit 126 – selected frequency, sender

Direction: TO modem.

Signals on this circuit are used to select one of two transmitting frequencies in the modem.

ON selects the higher transmission frequency.

OFF selects the lower transmission frequency.

Circuit 127 – selected frequency, receiver

Direction: TO modem.

Signals on this circuit are used to select one of two receiving frequencies in the modem.

ON selects the higher receiving frequency.

OFF selects the lower receiving frequency.

Circuit 128 – element timing, receiver (controlled by data terminal)

Direction: TO modem.

Either Circuit 128 or 115 may be used.

Signals on this circuit provide the modem with information on the signal elements.

The condition on this circuit must correspond to ON and OFF for nominally equal time periods. Transition from ON to OFF nominally marks the midpoint of every signal element on Circuit 104 (received data).

When information is not being transmitted, Circuit 128 must be OFF.

Circuit 130 – carrier, back channel

Direction: TO modem.

Signals on this control the sending out of the carrier signal on the reverse channel.

ON means that the modem is giving out a carrier signal on the reverse channel.

OFF means that the modem is blocking the transmission of the carrier on the reverse channel.

Circuit 131 – character timing, receiver

Direction: FROM modem.

Signals on this line supply the data terminal with the information on the received character signals which are required by the relevant specification for the modem.

Circuit 132 – changeover to non-data running

Direction: TO modem.

Signals on this line are used when a changeover to other types of information than data is required as far as the data communication equipment is concerned, without losing the connection with the receiving station.

The ON condition causes the data communication equipment to change over to non-data running.

When non-data running has been established, the circuit must be switched OFF.

Circuit 133 – ready to receive

Direction: TO modem.

Signals on this circuit control transmission of data on Circuit 104 (received data), and indicate whether the data terminal can receive a certain specified amount of data (e g a data block) in accordance with the relevant recommendation for the intermediate equipment, such as that for error monitoring.

An ON condition must occur and be held as soon as the data terminal can receive a data block, and it causes the intermediate equipment to transmit data received to the terminal.

The OFF condition means that the data terminal cannot receive a data block, and causes the intermediate equipment to hold this block back.

Circuit 134 – informational data is being transmitted

Direction: FROM modem.

Signals on this circuit are used to differentiate between informational data and monitoring data on Circuit 104 (received data).

ON means that the data transmitted is informational data.

The OFF condition must be maintained on all other occasions.

13.7 Modems

Introduction

Trying to describe how a modem works is rather like trying to describe how a car works. There are many different makes and models, incorporating different principles.

There are low and high speed modems, special purpose modems, short-haul modems, different methods of modulation, and different techniques for limiting interference and evening out the levels. In Section 13.6 the circuits in the V.24 interface between modem and terminal were described; we shall now look at the way some of the different modems work and how they are connected up.

13.8 Asynchronous modems

Asynchronous modems on dialled-up lines work in the speed range 110 bits/s to 1200 bits/s in full duplex. The modulation principle is frequency shift (frequency modulation, FSK), where two passbands (channels) are used within the permitted transmission spectrum of 300–3400 Hz. In practice only the frequency band between 900–2400 Hz is used for speeds up to 1200 bits/s, when the effect of group delay distortion and damping limit the available passband.

The ITT type 1161 modem works according to CCITT recomendation V.21. Both passbands lie between 980–1180 Hz and 1650–1850 Hz, where the higher frequency in the respective bands represents a 'zero' and the lower a 'one'.

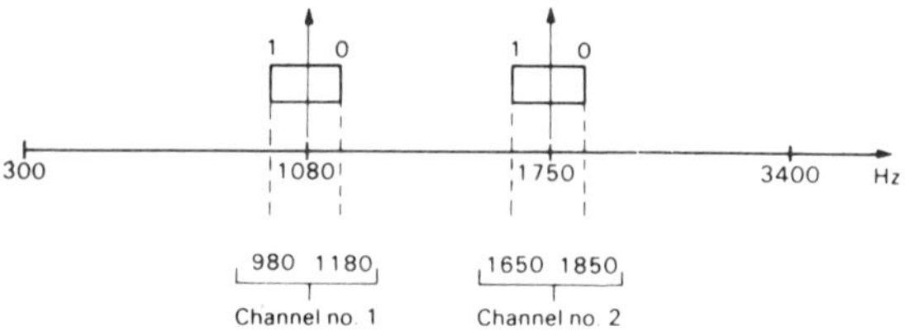

Figure 13.11 Passband for a modem according to CCITT recommendation V.21

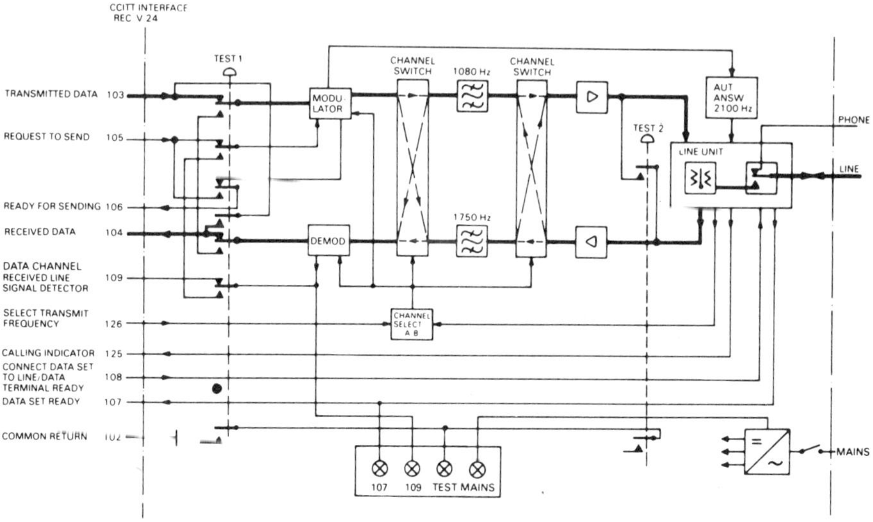

Figure 13.12 Block diagram of the ITT 1161 modem

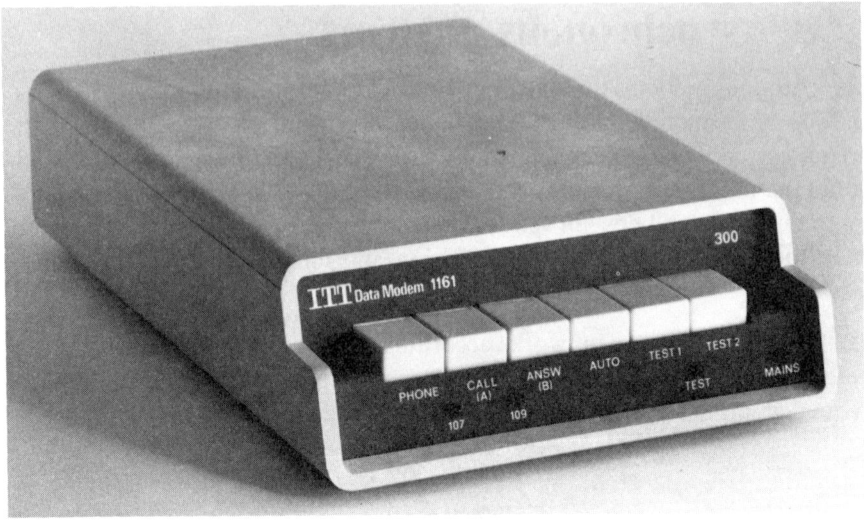

Figure 13.13 ITT modem type 1161

The called-up modem sends in the higher passband and receives in the lower band. At least 8 connections are required in the interface, apart from the earth lines, between the modem and the terminal for the transfer of signal and data information. The important difference between asynchronous and synchronous transfer is of course that the asynchronous modem does not contain a clock for timing generation. The clock timing is generated by the terminal when sending characters.

In a modem which works according to CCITT recommendation V.23, a 'zero' is represented by a frequency of 2100 Hz, and a 'one' by 1300 Hz, which means frequency limits of 1100 and 2300 Hz. In practice, transmission speeds obtained are 1 bit/s per 1 Hz channel bandwidth on frequency shift

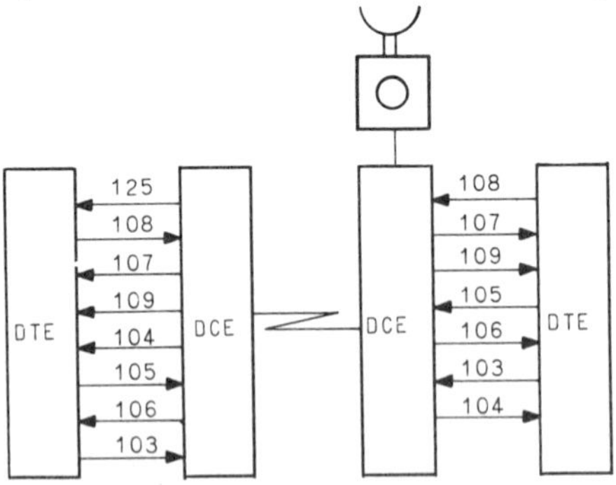

Figure 13.14 Circuits in the interface for dialled-through 300–1200 bits/s asynchronous connections

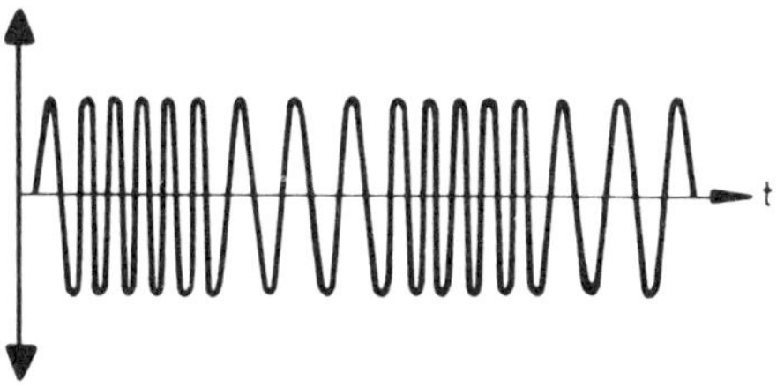

Figure 13.15 Frequency-modulated signal with a 010101 sequence

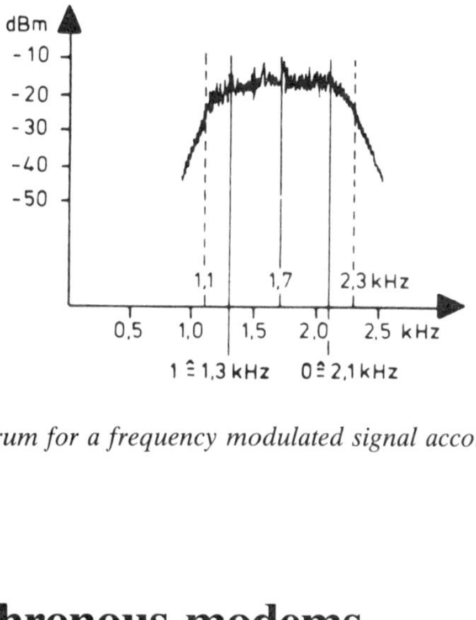

Figure 13.16 Spectrum for a frequency modulated signal according to CCITT V.23

13.9 Synchronous modems

At least 11 circuits are required for transmitting signal and data information in the digital interface. On dialled up connections, analogue signal transfer takes place over a single pair of wires. Sending can take place from one modem at a time.

Figure 13.7 Dialled up synchronous 1200/2400 connection

Circuit 107 is switched to 'on' as soon as the power is switched on to the modem. When the terminal's modem telephone 'rings up' the computer, this

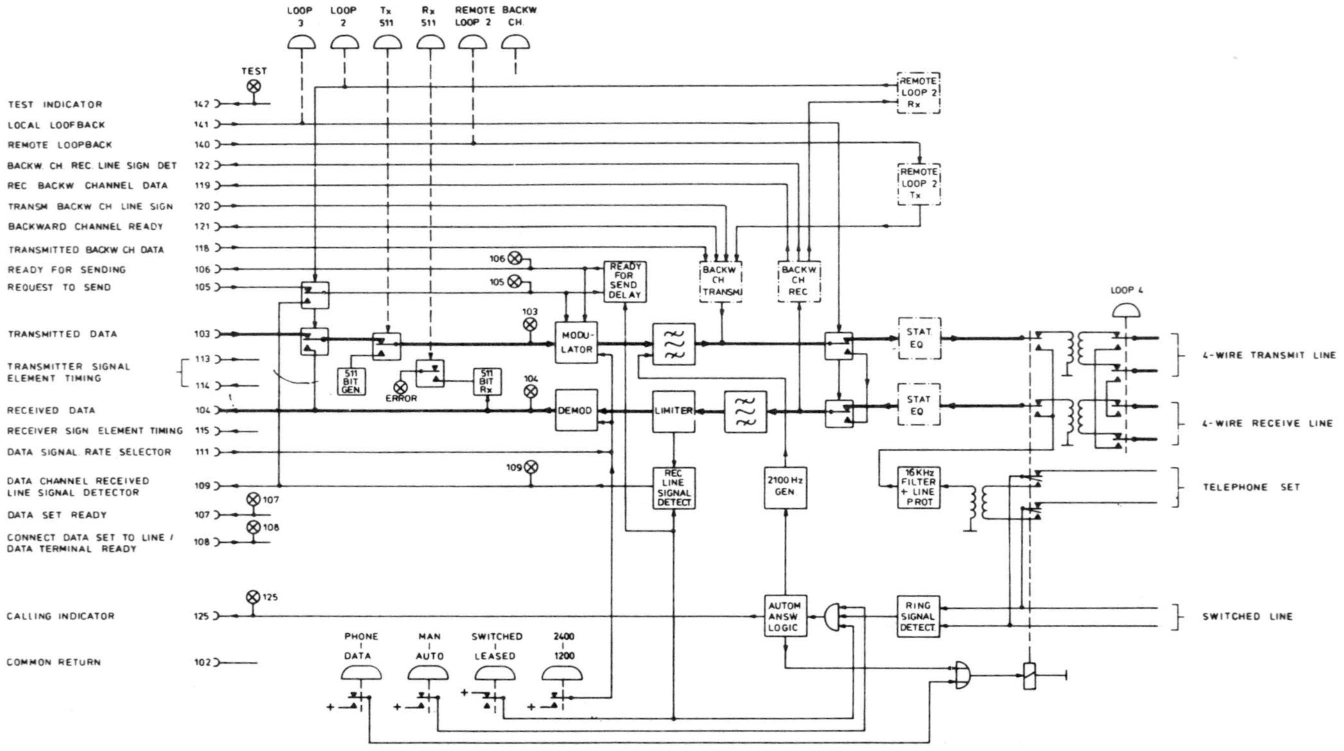

Figur 13.18 Block diagram for synchronous 1200/2400 bit/s modem type ITT 2084

is indicated at the computer's end by Circuit 125 going 'on' and signalling that connection is to take place. The computer acknowledges by setting Circuit 108 'on'. The modem at the computer end now 'tells' the operator of the terminal modem that the connection is established, which is done by sending a tone signal of 2100 Hz. The operator acknowledges this by pressing the 'data' button on the modem telephone. Circuit 108 at the terminal end is now turned 'on', and data transmission is now possible. As soon as the power is switched on to the modem, the sender's clock starts to send square-wave pulses to the terminal and the computer. It is now ready for data transmission, and we will assume that the computer starts sending a poll signal to the terminal. Circuit 105 at the computer end is switched 'on', whereupon the modem starts sending an unmodulated sine-wave signal over the analogue connection. When the transmission first starts, the sine wave is disorted; it takes a short time before the signal achieves its correct sinusoid form at the receiving end. This is called the settling time and during this time data transmission is not possible.

Figure 13.19 ITT modem 2084, 1200/2400 bits/s

When the carrier wave is perceived by the receiving modem as lying above a certain satisfactory level, this is indicated by switching Circuit 109 to 'on'. A common value for carrier wave indication is −42 dB. After a suitable delay, the computer modem signals that sending can begin by setting Circuit 106 to 'on'. This time delay before 106 goes 'on' can vary on dialled-up lines between 150–300 ms. On fixes lines the delay is shorter, from 40 ms down to none at all.

The logic circuits in the computer are now prepared for data transmission by putting the first data character into a 'send' register or a buffer.

The modem's transmit clock now indicates on Circuit 114 the speed with which data bits are 'plucked out' on lead 103. Modulation of the sine wave occurs according to the pattern of changes of the data bits. In the terminal end modem, the modulated signal is demodulated, and the recreated bit stream is sent into the terminal on the receiving modem's Circuit 104 to a timing given by the clock signal on Circuit 115 which is synchronised with the modulated data. When the message is ended the computer drops Circuit 105, and 106 then goes immediately to 'off' and the carrier stops. At the terminal end Circuit 109 goes 'off'. We have now sent a message to the terminal. The process is now repeated, with the difference that the terminal sends a response to the poll signal to the computer; this is shown in Figure 13.20, where times given are nominal.

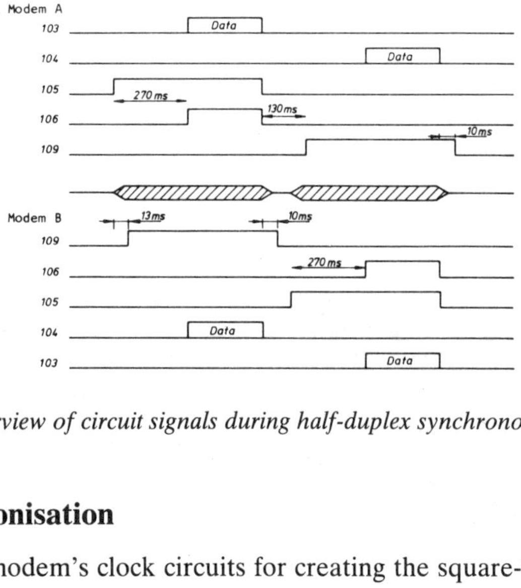

Figure 13.20 Overview of circuit signals during half-duplex synchronous transmission

Clock synchronisation

Control of the modem's clock circuits for creating the square-wave pulses is done in the oscillators. These are crystal-controlled, to obtain as accurate a frequency as possible. Despite this, it is impossible to get the oscillators to synchronise exactly, because of differences in circuits, voltage variations, etc. The transmit clock in modem A must therefore be adjusted to be exactly in time with the receive clock in modem B, otherwise data bits will be lost or corrupted. Synchronisation is carried out in the time period before Circuit 106 goes 'on'. When the sine wave reaches the modem, the receiver clock is synchronised in the same phase as the sine wave. Only when the transmit and receive clocks are completely synchronised can the sending begin. During the course of transmission, the receiver clock is synchronised automatically by what is known as timing regeneration.

Synchronous leased lines

If we now look at a four-wire line for synchronous transmission, it is usual to connect Circuit 105 in a permanent 'on' state by alternative connections in terminal or modem. The effect of this will be that 106 is always in the 'on' state, and therefore that a carrier is always sent to the other modem; 'constant carrier' is another term used for this connection method. The advantage of having Circuit 105 'on' all the time that there is no delay while Circuit 106 goes 'on'. When sending a large number of data blocks with the carrier being switched on and off each time, the total time delay can be considerable.

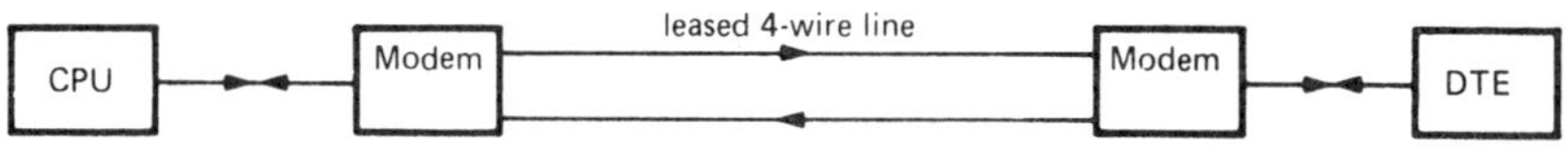

Figure 13.21 Permanently-connected point-to-point connection, synchronous transmission

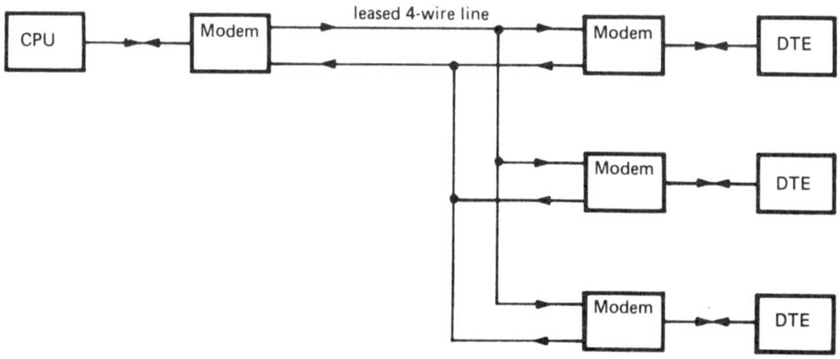

Figure 13.22 Permanently-connected multipoint connections, synchronous transmission

We have mentioned synchronisation of modems, and how the clock pulses on Circuit 114 'pluck' out data on Circuit 103, whose information content is used to modulate the carrier. In the receiving modem, demodulated data is 'plucked' in on Circuit 104 according to the timing on Circuit 115. From the element timing of the modulated data, the terminal or computer gets its information on when the demodulated character is to be read. The timing given by Circuit 115 is in turn controlled by the carrier, and therefore by the clock in the transmitting modem. This is shown in a simplified diagram (Figure 13.23) where only the timing lines are drawn in; this is known as the internal clock.

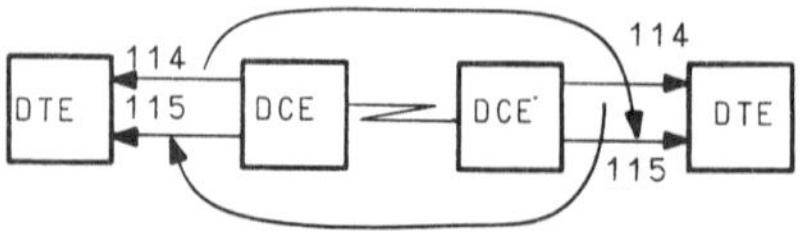

Figure 13.23 Internal clock, 114 timing

There are other types of clock synchronisation. In extension connections with more than two modems in series, or in 'tapping off' on multichannel functions, an external clock is used for controlling the modems. The clock timing is taken from one of the modems in the chain.

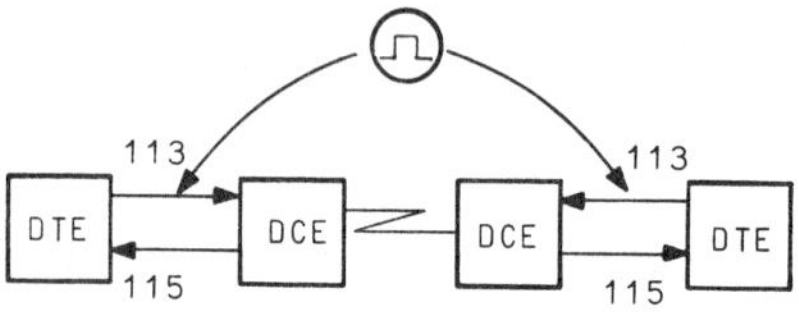

Figure 13.24 External clock, 113 timing

A variant on the internal clock is where the receiving timing on Circuit 115 controls the transmission on Circuit 114 of the opposite modem. The modems' own transmit clocks are not used by the other modem. Cross-connection is done in the modem or modem cable.

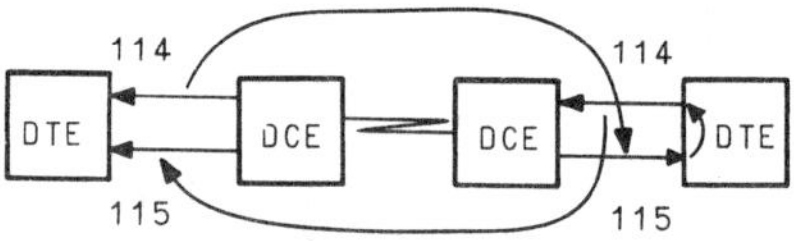

Figure 13.25 Receiver timing controls transmission, 115 timing

13.10 Modulation methods for high-speed modems

Synchronous transmission is most commonly used for transmission speeds of 2400 bits/s and upwards. As we cannot use the whole of the speech channel between 300 and 3400 Hz, which theoretically should allow a transmission rate of 3000 bits/s using frequency shift, other modulation methods must be used.

Two common methods are phase modulation and differential phase modulation (PSK, DPSK). These methods work by changing the instantaneous phase ϕ of a carrier suddenly by $\Delta\phi$ which is determined by the bit pattern transferred. The terms 'dibit' and 'tribit' transmission are used, where two or three bits respectively are transferred for every new modulation status.

Note that "Baud rate" and "bit speed" must not be confused or interchanged. The "Baud rate" is the number of changes per second which the modulated signal makes. On each modulation change, however, several "bits" can be transferred.

In phase shift modulation (PSK), the phase jump is determined by comparing the phase-modulated signal with a reference signal from an oscillator in the other modem.

In differential phase modulation (DPSK), the instantaneous phase angle is compared with the phase angle corresponding to the previous two or three bits.

Table 13.2 Four-stage differential phase-shift modulation; CCITT V.26

Dibit		**Phase-shift $\Delta\phi$**
A_i	**B_i**	**0°**
0	0	0°
0	1	90°
1	1	180°
1	0	270°

Table 13.3 Eight-stage differential phase-shift modulation; CCITT V.27

Tribit			**Phase-shift**
A_i	**B_i**	**C_i**	**$\Delta\phi$**
0	0	1	0°
0	0	0	45°
0	1	0	90°
0	1	1	135°
1	1	1	180°
1	1	0	225°
1	0	0	270°
1	0	1	315°

The principle of DPSK modulation is as follows. Data in serial form is transmitted to the modem's transmitter via Circuit 103 as usual. The transmission is checked by the modem's clock on Circuit 114. Serial data is transmitted to a parallel converter, where it is decoded. The decoder determines the bit pattern for every newly arriving bit pair. The previous bit pair and the bit pair which is to be sent determine the phase shift Δφ by which the carrier is to be modulated.

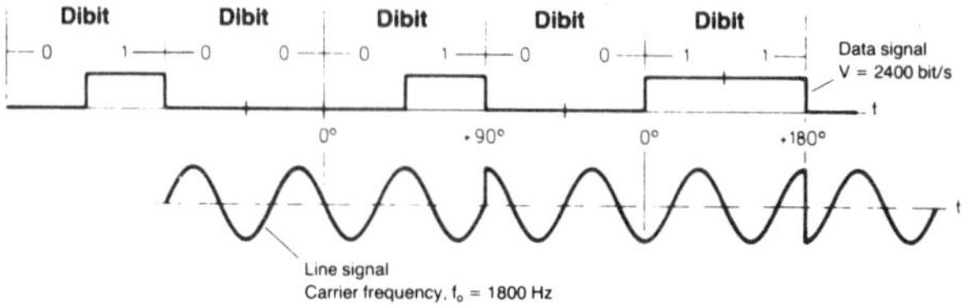

Figure 13.26 Relationship between transmitted data and phase shift for differential four-phase

Assume a random bit pattern where bit pair 0 0 has just been sent (compare Table 13.2 and Figure 13.26). The next bit pair to be sent is 0 1. After the last bit (a one) has been decoded, this new status must change the carrier, which is done by a phase shift Δφ of 90°. The next bit pair to be sent is 0 0, and we see from the Table that no phase shift occurs for this combination. The last bit pair is 1 1, and after the last one we get a phase shift of 180°. It can be seen that if no shift Δφ occurs, a constant stream of zeroes is transmitted.

13.11 Amplitude/Phase modulation (QAM)

If still greater transmission speed is required, other modulation methods must be used. One method, known as combined multistage amplitude and phase shift modulation (Quadrature Amplitude Modulation, QAM), is specified in CCITT recommendation V.29 for 9600 bits/s transmission speed. Given the eight-stage differential phase modulation, a further stage of modulation is applied, that of varying its amplitude. At 9600 bits/s, four bits are transmitted for every modulation status. Phase and amplitude changes are shown in Table 13.4.

One common method of QAM modulation is, after decoding of the digital information via two channels x and y, to get these to vary (modulate) the sum of two carrier signals (cos ωt and sin ωt) of the same frequency but 90° out of phase (see Figure 13.28). This sum is passed to a digital/analogue converter where the line signal is generated digitally. The signal put out onto the line is first put through a low-pass filter to eliminate parts of the spectra lying above the permitted 3400 Hz.

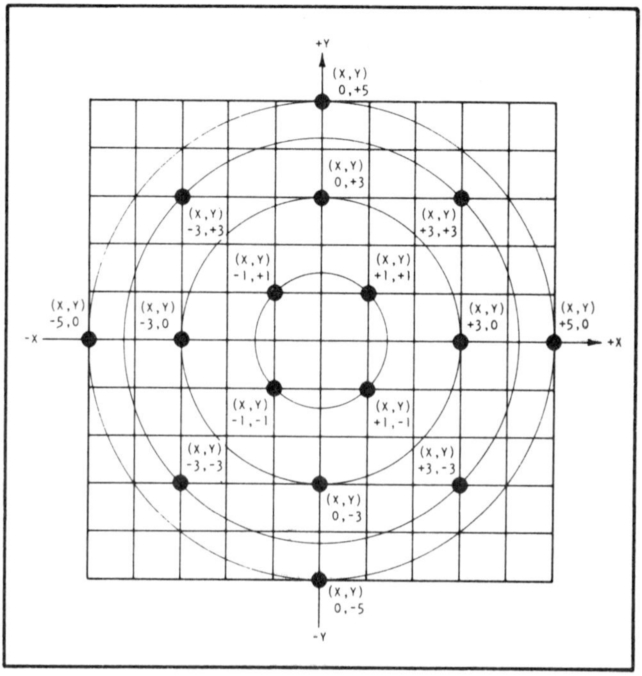

Figure 13.27 Polar diagram for 9600 bits/s according to CCITT recommendation V.29

The course of events for generating the coordinates described in Table 13.4 can be presented graphically, as shown in Figure 13.27.

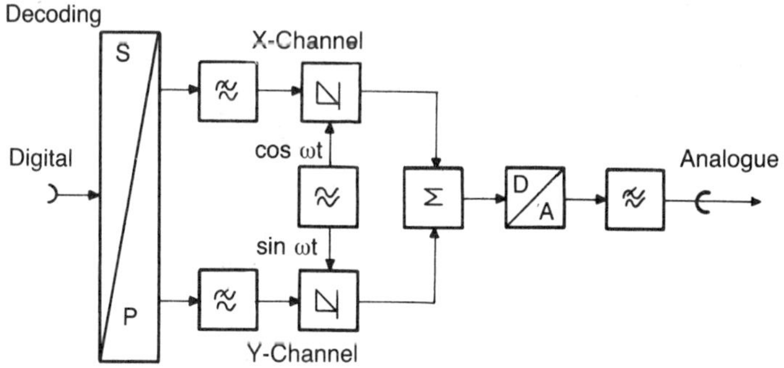

Figure 13.28 Example of block diagram for QAM modulation

The coordinate diagram has 16 points situated on four different rings. The points are positioned at 90° from each other on each ring. During transmission, the first two bits denote one of the four rings, and the next two bits denote the quadrant on the ring chosen.

Demodulation of the received line signal is done after amplification, passing through a bandpass filter and an analogue/digital converter. The signal is added to cos ωt and to sin ωt, phase-shifted by 90°, where ωt equals the carrier frequency.

The signal is then sampled and transferred to a series/parallel converter; the recreated data is sent to the terminal via Circuit 115.

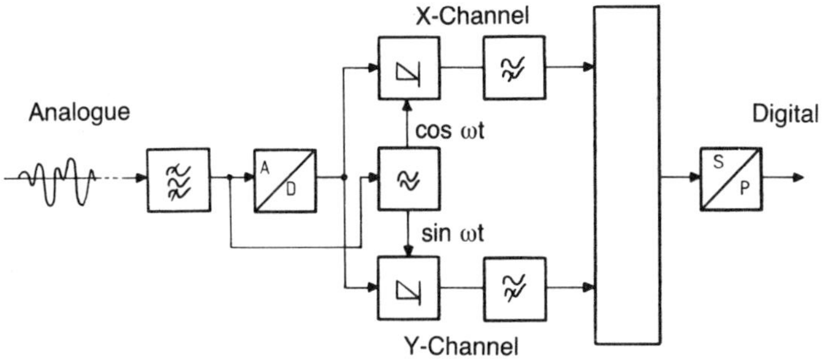

Figure 13.29 Example of a block diagram for demodulating QAM

Bit 2	Bit 3	Bit 4	Phase shift
0	0	1	0°
0	0	0	45°
0	1	0	90°
0	1	1	135°
1	1	1	180°
1	1	0	225°
1	0	0	270°
1	0	1	315°

Bit 1	Phase shift	Relative amplitude
0	0°, 90°, 180°, 270°	3
1		5
0	45°, 135°, 225°, 315°	$\sqrt{2}$
1		$3\sqrt{2}$

Table 13.4 a and b. Phase and amplitude changes in combined amplitude/phase-shift modulation

13.12 Reverse channel

Certain modems may be provided with what are known as reverse channels, or back channels, where a lower passband is used for a slower transmission than the main channel's passband. Using a back channel, one can use the full duplex facility in such a way that a terminal can send 'keyed-in' data on the slow back channel, and let the computer send the response text on the faster main channel. Previously, the back channel was also used in synchronous transmission, where the terminal or the computer sent the ACK-NAK sequences, ie only a few characters. The advantage was to avoid using line-switching modems on dialled-up two-wire connections, and thereby save time.

For the reverse channel, a 'second set' of control signals is used on circuits 118-123.

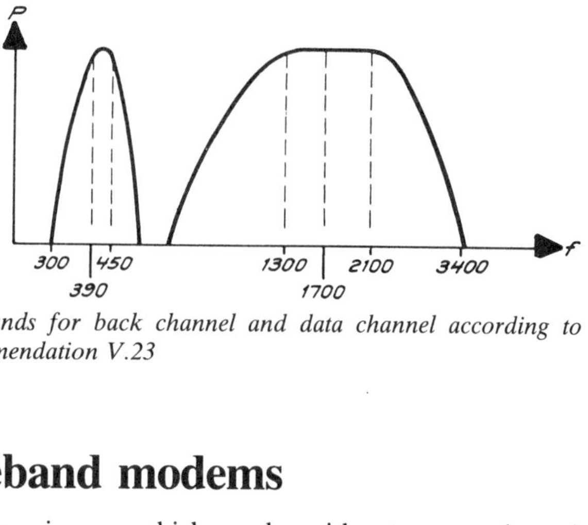

Figure 13.30 Passbands for back channel and data channel according to CCITT recommendation V.23

13.13 Baseband modems

A baseband modem is one which works without any real modulation. Square-waves are transferred on the physical link between modems. This means that, like the short-haul modems, one is limited as to distance and type of connection. Several types of signal transmission may be used:

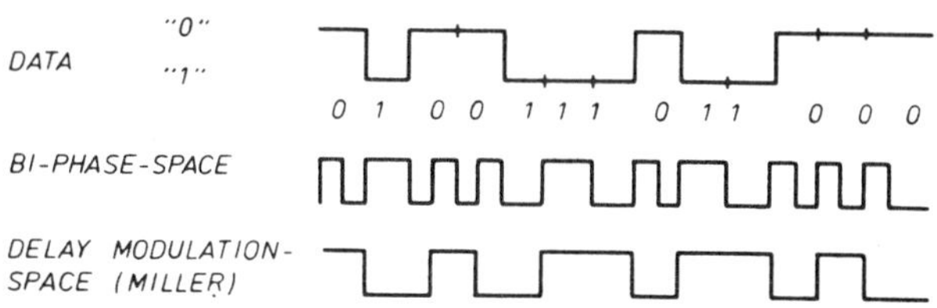

Figure 13.31 Signal transmission between baseband modems; biphase-space and delay modulation (Miller)

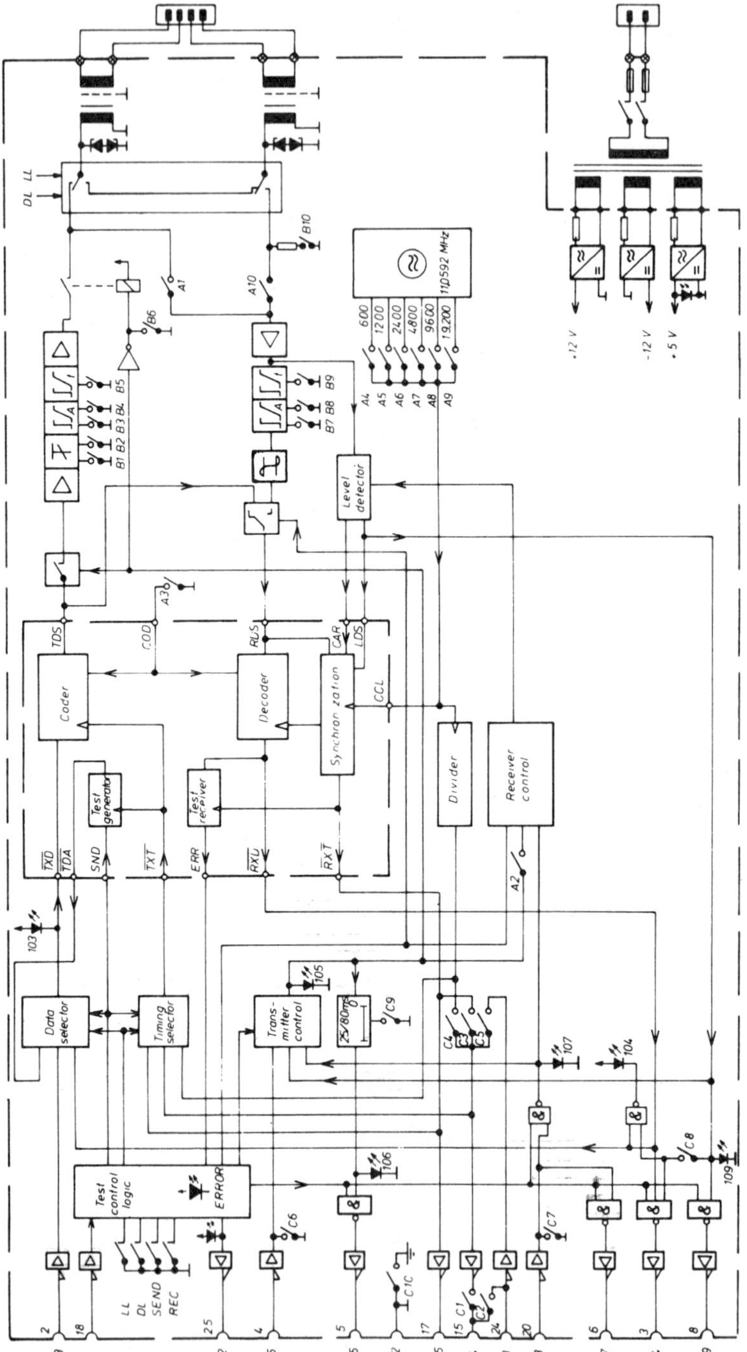

Figure 13.32 Block diagram of the NOKIA 2856 baseband modem

Transmission speeds lie between 600 bits/s and 19,200 bits/s. A certain amount of pupinisation is generally tolerated on the line, but the distance is limited; up to 20 km is a common distance.

13.14 Short-distance modems

Short-distance or short-haul modems are, as their name suggests, designed for data connections of limited length, and they come in many different makes and types. Modems may be synchronous, asynchronous or combined. The interface is V.24 (EIA RS232C), and the practical transmission distance is generally up to 5 km. At higher transmission speeds, the distance is correspondingly reduced.

It is usual for short-haul modems not to have the same ability to control or to transmit control signals over the V.24 interface as frequency modulating modems. Short-haul modems may be used for connection between terminal and computer in order to obtain electrical isolation between units. Connection between modems is via ordinary four-way 0.5 mm^2 wires. In conditions of high interference it may be necessary to screen the cable.

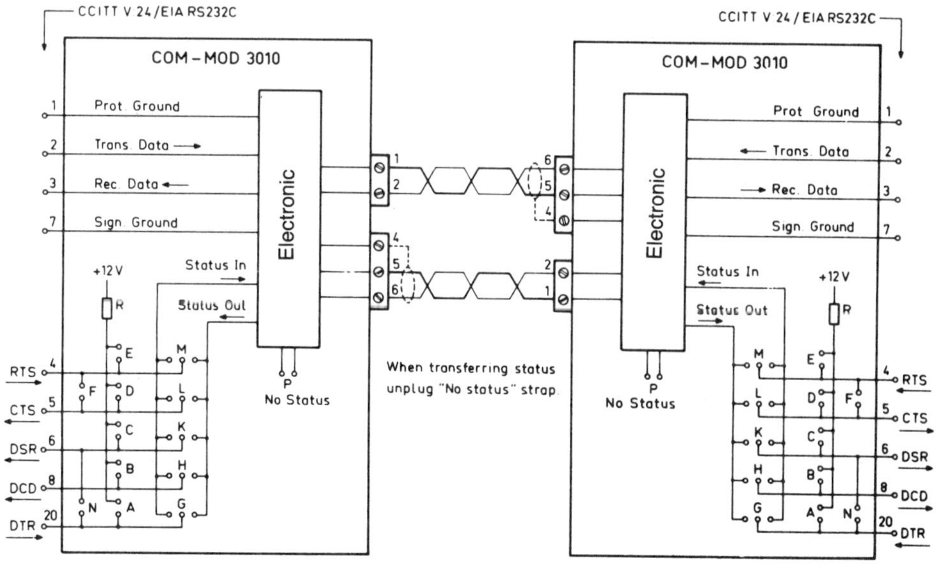

Figure 13.33 Asynchronous short-haul COMEX 3010 modem, interface and connections

The digital information wave is transferred directly over the physical connection, which is the reason why an electrical connection is necessary between modems. Pupinised or phantomised lines cannot therefore be used. This type of modem is most used in industry and business complexes with private telephone networks.

Figure 13.33 shows the interface for an asynchronous short-haul modem, the COMEX 3010. The modem can transmit a signal status on circuit 105, 106, 107, 108 or 109 to the receiving modem.

13.15 Current loop

Current loop is a transmission method suitable for use where the data is to go some distance without a modem being used. Current loop is, as its name implies, a current-controlled transmission method. Usually, current means a '1' and no current means '0'. There are also balanced current loops. Current loops are usually used to isolate computer and terminal electrically. The maximum distance is limited, up to a few kilometers. The current loop is not as well-defined as the V.24 interface, and the respective information sheets must therefore be studied to see whether different pieces of equipment can be connected together.

20 mA is the most commonly used current in the loop, but there are also 40 or 60 mA loops. Another parameter of importance in selecting current loops is whether the computer or the terminal is to provide the current for the loop. This varies between different manufacturers. It is not certain that the unit which is active in the sending loop will also provide current for the receiving loop.

13.16 Equaliser

The effect of delay distortion is that different frequencies 'arrive' at different times at the far end of a connection. This has no practical significance in a normal telephone conversation, but in data transmissions at higher speeds (>2400 bits/s) it can have a destructive effect. Using an equaliser, the signal received is corrected so that the various frequencies are 'lifted up' to a more even level.

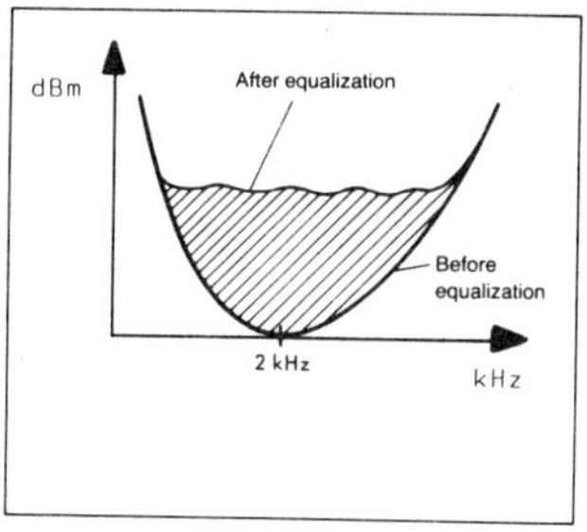

Figure 13.34 Equalisation of group delay disortion

13.17 Test switches and indicator lamps

Most modern modems are nowadays fitted with test switches and indicator lamps for fault-testing purposes. Using a switch, the connection with the receiving modem can be tested. The tests which can be used are 'analogue loops' and 'digital loops'. The terminal and computer are disconnected for the test, so that they do not affect the modem's transmitting circuits. For the test, a bit pattern generated in the modem is sent, and received in the other modem, which has circuits to analyse the bit pattern.

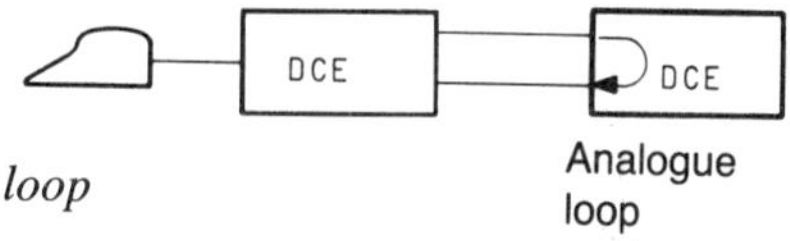

Figure 13.35 Analogue loop

The analogue loop is used for testing nearby modems and connections. The other modem's transmitting and receiving circuits are not connected in.

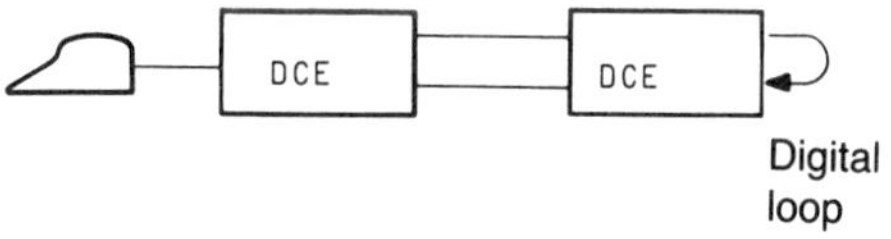

Figure 13.36 Digital loop

Using a digital loop, the modem's transmit and receive circuits are tested by operating the test switch several times. After a little practice, one can quickly see from the indicator lamps whether the modem is working as it should. The circuits which are connected to the LED's are generally 105, 106, 103, 104 or 109.

13.18 Eye pattern

Polarised relays are used in telex communication for transmitting characters. 'Double current' is used, where the relay switches between −60 V and +60 V. Proper equalisation is required on long telegraph lines in order that the distortion doesn't destroy the transmitted characters too much. When equalising a line, the telegraphist sends RYRYRYRY continuously, while the telegraphist at the other end has an oscilloscope attached to the line. He then adjusts the equaliser until an 'open eye' is obtained on the oscilloscope. At this point, the line is optimally equalised.

The expression 'eye pattern' is retained today in data communication for lines with modems connected.

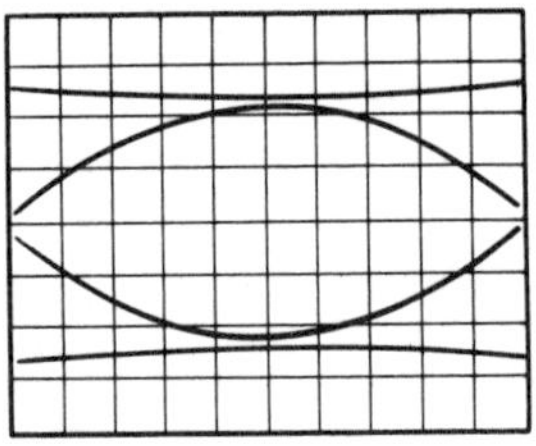

Figure 13.37 "Eye pattern" for telegraph connections

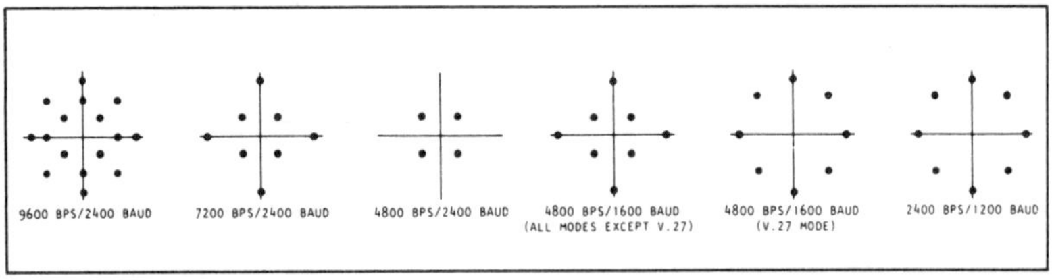

Figure 13.38 "Eye pattern" for different transmission speeds

If an oscilloscope is connected to the X and Y channels as shown in Figure 13.29, and the scope is triggered at the same speed as the bit frequency, a different appearance of 'eye pattern' is obtained for different transmission frequencies and methods of modulation. Each point on the scope shows a modulation status, and each set of points should be as close-lying as possible. If a point 'wanders' out of its sector, bit errors will occur during transmission.

Different types of interference give rise to characteristic 'eye patterns' on the oscilloscope.

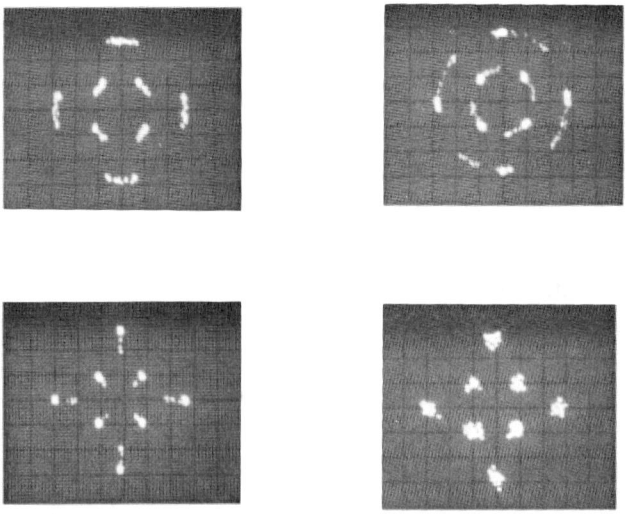

Figure 13.39 a) *Phase jitter disortion has the effect of rotating all points around a sector of the circles.*
b) *Phase hits cause all points momentarily to rotate around the centre.*
c) *Harmonic distortion tends to spread all points outwards from the centre.*
d) *White noise on the data channel has the effect of spreading the points out around their normal positions.*

13.19 Summary

There are at least 20 makes of modem on the Swedish market. Both Swedish and foreign makes are represented. If one wishes to subscribe to dialled up or fixed data lines in Sweden a modem may be obtained on a subscription basis from the Swedish telephone company, who in their turn buy modems from the manufacturers.

The recommendations produced by CCITT for how modems work are so comprehensive that different makes and models can always be used together. If, however, one still wishes to be completely sure that transmissions will be as error-free as possible, one should use modems of the same make and type at both ends of the line. There are of course exceptions to this rule. When ordering a modem from the Swedish telephone company, one can always specify a certain type of which one has had good experience.

On the other hand, for local connections, ie not hired from the Swedish telephone company, one is free to buy any modem one likes. One should of course choose modems which experience has shown to work well, and where good maintenance can be obtained. If a 'private' modem is to be connected to lines hired from the telephone company, on the other hand, it must be approved by them.

The LKD union (Union of Office and Data Equipment Suppliers) have for a long time criticised the Swedish telephone company's monopolistic stance in the area of modems. They have been trying to bring about complete freedom in direct selling from supplier to computer customer.

It is not only the idea that the computer customer shall have a wider choice. The motive is of course to sell more equipment. One of the arguments has thus been that many terminals and computers have modem equipment built into them.

It must not be forgotten how many different types of short-haul, baseband and frequency modulation modems there are, which can hardly be run together. More new problems are thus shifted over onto the computer customer. An advanced customer will certainly have the resources and knowledge to evaluate suitable modems, while the inexperienced can find it expensive to buy the experience. Another problem will be that of service.

A small supplier will naturally not be able to offer fast and efficient service, which means that the customer has to maintain a 'private' stock of modems himself.

Modem development is moving forward very rapidly. Transmission speeds increase and the size of modems is being reduced by the introduction of LSI technology. Modern high speed modems are provided with microprocessors for controlling the transmission. Numerous active filters which work on digital principles are available for eliminating undesired frequencies.

For those interested to read more about modems, technical specifications and service handbooks may be obtained from modem manufacturers.

14 DCE and DATEX

14.1 Introduction

The DCE (Data Circuit-terminating Equipment) unit is used for connecting data terminals to DATEX. The DCE is sited at the subscriber's data terminal and forms the connection point between the terminal and the data network.

The DCE is specially designed for the circuit-coupled data network, with data transmission in the form of 10-bit envelopes (envelope structure 8+2). The transmission method is full-duplex on 4-wire lines.

The data terminal is connected via an interface according to CCITT X- or V-type recommendations.

The electrical and mechanical construction of the DCE is based on a modular system, which means that different operating conditions can be accommodated by combining different circuit boards. The DCE can thereby be adapted to a number of different terminals of X and V types.

There are the following types of DCE's, DCE-X, DCE-VP and DCE-VPC.

Figure 14.1 DCE-X

DCE-X

- For connection of synchronous data terminals according to CCITT X.21.
- For transmission speeds of 600, 2400, 4800 and 9600 bits/s.
- Signalling for connection and disconnection of the terminal in accordance with CCITT X.21.

Figure 14.2 DCE-VP or DCE-VPC (marked DCE-V)

DCE-VP

- For connection of synchronous data terminals accordng to CCITT V.24.
- For transmission speeds of 600, 2400, 4800 and 9600 bits/s.
- Signalling for connection and disconnection of the terminal in accordance with CCITT X.21 bis (direct call), or alternatively by using the press-buttons and STATUS indicator on the DCE.

DCE-VPC

- For connection of synchronous data terminals according to CCITT V.21
- For transmission speeds of 50, 100, 110, 134.5, 200, 300, 600, 1200, 2400 and 4800 bits/s.
- Signalling for connection and disconnection of the terminal in accordance with CCITT X.20 bis (direct call), or alternatively by using the press-buttons and STATUS indicator on the DCE.

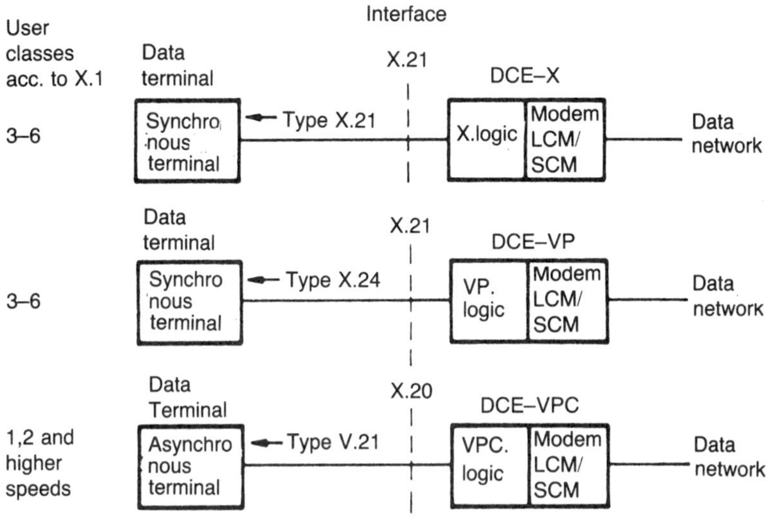

Figure 14.3 Main types of DCE

14.2 Main functional sections

Logic section

The logic section forms the connection point for the data terminal. The terminal's data is converted by this logic into envelope format. This is done by collecting the terminal's data into 8-bit groups, to which are added two bits for status indication and synchronisation. In the opposite direction, in from the data network, the logic reconverts the envelopes received into terminal data. See Figure 14.4.

As the logic section forms the data network's interface with the terminal, certain test and maintenance functions are included in it.

The logic section comes in two main forms, known as X logic and VP logic. The type of terminal determines which of these shall be used. These apart, there is a third form known as VPC logic. This is VP logic with an asynchronous/synchronous converter added. VPC logic is used when the terminal is run asynchronously. Figure 14.3 shows diagrammatically the different cases. The applicable CCITT recommendations are given.

X logic has an interface for terminals which are fitted out for signalling according to CCITT recommendation X.21. Signals are sent directly between terminal and data network, and the X logic is therefore transparent for data and status signals even during the connection time. The transparency is only broken for testing and under fault conditions.

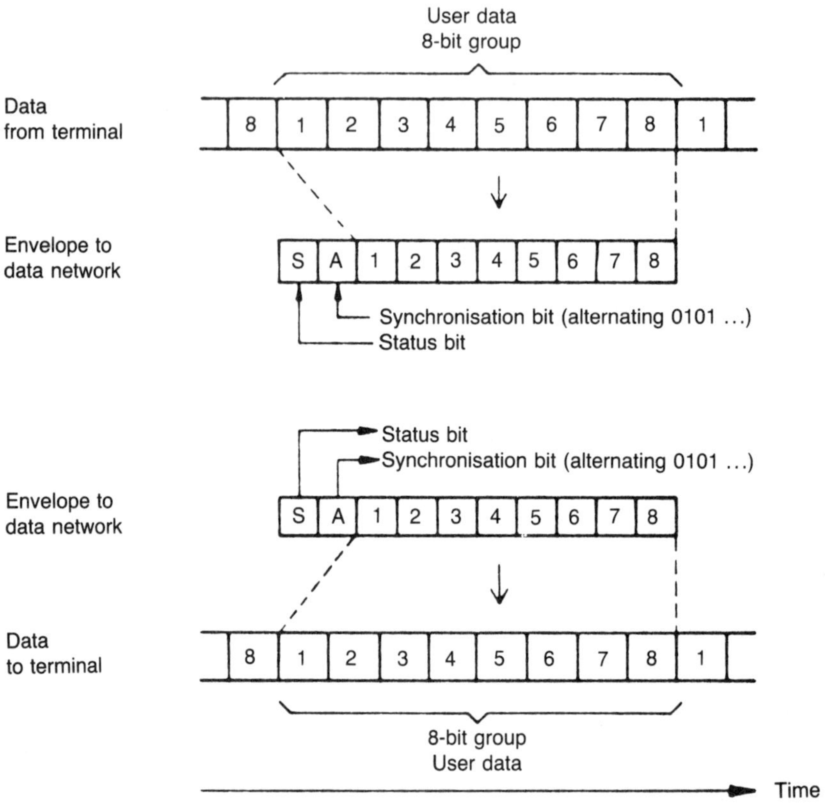

Figure 14.4 Envelope formatting in the logic section

VP logic has an interface of the CCITT V.24 type. This interface in its basic form is not designed for transferring connecting-up signals. The VP logic therefore carries out independent signalling during the connecting-up phase. It also has a keypad to allow number dialling.

The VP logic section also takes care of the protocol for connection and disconnection of lines on data terminals with a V-type interface.

Modem section

The job of the modem section is to give the data stream which is formatted into envelopes by the logic section a signal form which is suitable for transmission over the telephone line. The type and length of line vary. It may be a physical line in a multi-line cable, or a single-core type. The line may also be combined with pupinised sections. For the longer transmission distances, channels in the carrier frequency and PCM systems are used.

4-wire cables are used throughout, and the method used is full-duplex.

- SCM (Short-haul Customer Modem)
- LCM (Long-haul Customer Modem)

The modem sections in their turn come in four different variations, SCM Biphase, SCM AMI, LCM 750 and LCM 3000. The type used depends on type of line, length of line and data transmission speed. In addition there is a modem adaptor, LCMA (Long-haul Customer Modem Adaptor), which is used when the DCE is driven from an external modem. LCMA contains circuits for connection and interfacing the external modem to the DCE.

LINE		**MODEM** at data transmission speeds (bits/s)			
Type	**Total length**	**750**	**3000**	**6000**	**12000**
Unpupinised cable	<15 km	SCM Biphase	SCM Biphase	SCM Biphase	SCM Biphase
Unpupinised+ pupinised cable	<20	SCM Biphase	SCM Biphase	SCM AMI	–
Other lines	–	LCM 750	LCM 3000	LCMA	–

Table 14.1 Summary of suitable modem variants according to line type, length and data transmission speed

The baseband modems (SCM) have greater bandwidth requirements than carrier frequency modems (LCM). These pose special demands on transmission of low frequencies. Baseband modems are equipped with switchable equalisers. Carrier frequency modems must be used where the channels have limited bands. The range of the carrier frequency modems is limited only by the line characteristics in the speech spectrum. Approximately three carrier frequency sections can be bridged. For data transmission speeds of 3000 bits/s, switchable equalisers are used.

The timing of the DCE is looked after from the data network. This timing is obtained from the line signal received by the modem. The timing signal is connected in a loop, and can also control the transmit circuits in the DCE. When the connection is broken with the data network, an internal timing signal is maintained which is sufficiently stable for short breaks to be bridged without the need for re-synchronisation.

The modem section also contains a mains power failure generator which comes into action when the mains voltage to the DCE disappears, and this gives a signal on the condition which has arisen.

14.3 X logic

Introduction

The logic section is defined as the link between the DTE and the transmission circuits, i e the modem.

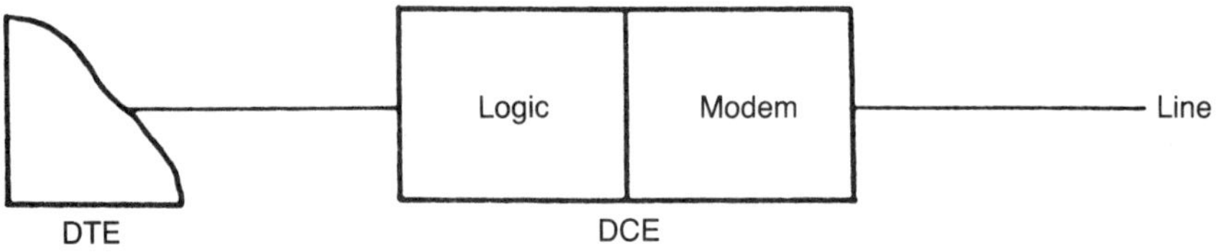

Figure 14.5 Definition of the X logic section

The X logic, which has a CCITT X.21 interface with the data terminal, has the following main tasks

- Establish and maintain envelope synchronisation
- Establish character synchronisation from the data terminal when setting up a data dialogue
- Input and decode envelopes from data on the X.21 interface
- Carry out loop connections and generate a test call from the DCE under manual control
- Recognise test calls from the data network and cary out loop connections in accordance with these
- Accept the following synchronous user speeds: 600, 2400, 4800 and 9600 bits/s.

Interface

The CCITT X.21 recommendation includes details of the leads to be used in the interface between the data terminal (DTE) and the modem (DCE). Connection is via a 15-pin D-plug screwed onto the back of the DCE.

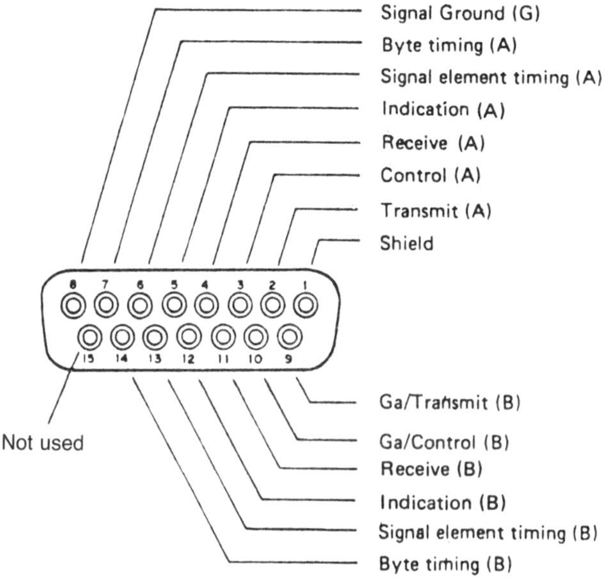

Figure 14.6 15-pin plug for connection to DCE-X

Circuit G: Signal ground or common return

This circuit forms a common voltage reference point for unbalanced two-way current with electrical characteristics according to V.28. This has to be connected to a single earthing point in the DCE.

Circuit Ga: DTE common return

This circuit is connected to the DTE and forms the voltage reference point for unbalanced circuits in the DCE according to recommendation X.26.

Circuit T: Transmit

Data signals send by the terminal (DTE) are transmitted on this line to the DCE.

Connection information is also sent on this line.

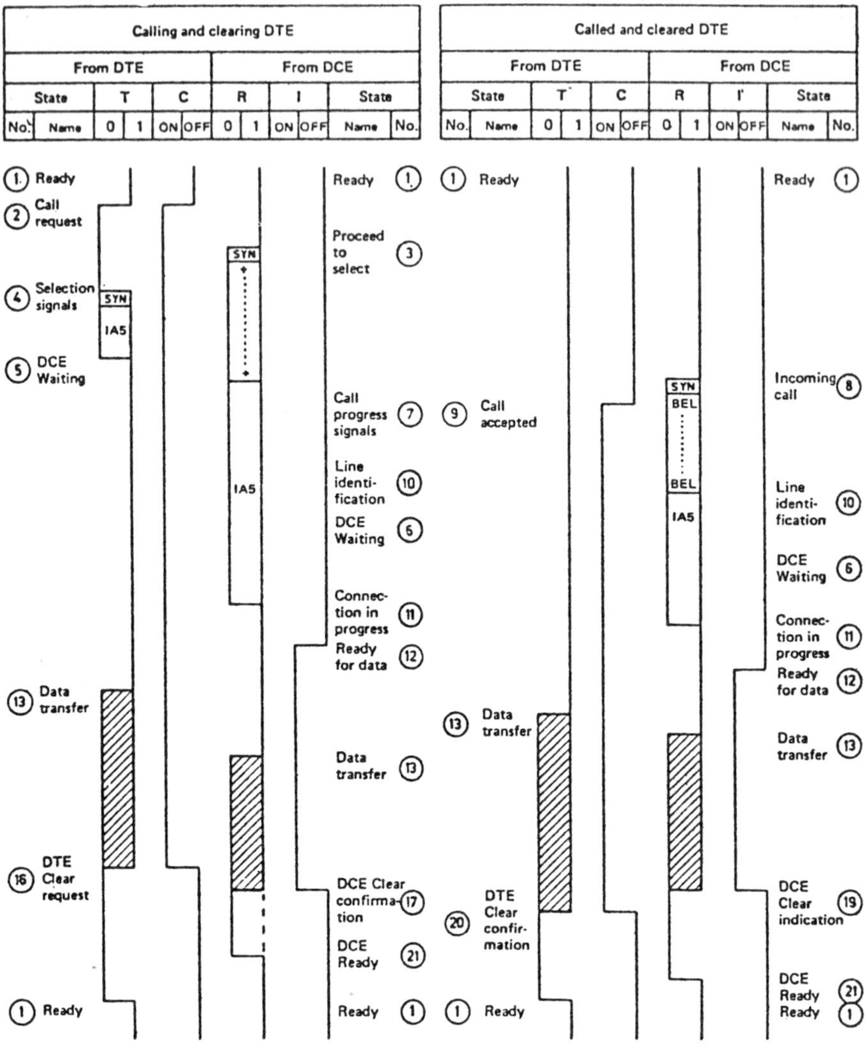

Figure 14.7 CCITT recommendation X.21; signal diagram

Circuit R: Received data

Data signals produced in the DCE and sent by the corresponding DTE are transmitted to the nearby DCE on this line. Control signals are also sent on this line during the connecting-up phase.

Circuit C: Control (Status bit sent)

This circuit must be in the 'on' state during the connection and data transmission phases.

Circuit I: Indication (status bit received)

This circuit goes into the 'on' state after the connection is established with the corresponding DCE or DTE. "I" goes 'off' after data transmission and disconnection.

Circuit S: Signal element timing

Signals on this line provide the DTE with timing information (square wave pulses) about the signal element. The DTE has to send binary data at the rate at which circuit S changes over. Circuit C must be in the 'on' state in order for the information on the "S" circuit to be transmitted.

Circuit B: Byte timing

Signals on this circuit provide 8-bit (byte) clocking information to the DTE. During transmission the state of this circuit must be 'off', but must change to 'on' during the sending of the last bit in each 8-bit group (byte). The 'on' state must be synchronous with the timing from circuit S of the last bit in the 8-bit group.

14.4 Summary

After a sluggish start, the DATEX network has been brought into commercial use. It was previously known as the Nordic Public Data Network (NPDN).

The network will be a good replacement or complement to existing alternatives (see also Chapter 6). There are as yet few terminals which are completely X.21 compatible, but leading manufacturers have products in this area. The policy of the Swedish telephone company in the area of DCE's, as for modems, is to buy in DCE's from manufacturers under contract, and then to hire them out to customers on a subscription basis.

15 Test instruments

15.1 Introduction

There do not need to be many terminals and modems in a data installation before it is realised that some form of technical aid is required in order to be able to set up the equipment, to diagnose faults and to put them right. Apart from the tools required for the job, a number of different types of instrument may be needed.

A suitable set of instruments may include

- interface tester
- multimeter
- frequency counter
- oscilloscope
- modem test instrument
- line listener
- mains interference analyser
- instrument for analogue lines.

15.2 Interface tester

The first instrument which should be obtained as soon as the terminals and connections are planned is what is known as an interface tester. The tester has several names, such as 'break-up box', and is sold by several electronics firms. It appeared in one variant called the 'blue box', followed by the 'red box'. The tester is a portable instrument which runs on batteries. It is used to isolate faults between modem and terminal, and is designed for systems with connections according to CCITT V.24.

The controls and indicators are mounted on the front of the instrument. They comprise

- connection points and LED's
- two CANNON plugs/sockets for connection to terminal and modem
- microswitches for each circuit in the interface
- batteries

All 25 circuits between the data equipment pass through the instrument at the same time. Seven of the LED's indicate continuously the state of the line. There are two LED's for indication of positive or negative pulse-edge. All circuits are accessible from pins on the front of the box. Each pin in the interface is also connected to a corresponding microswitch (except pin 1). Using the pins and the microswitches, any connection in the V.24 interface can be broken or short-circuited. Other types of instrument can be connected to the front pins, such as an oscilloscope.

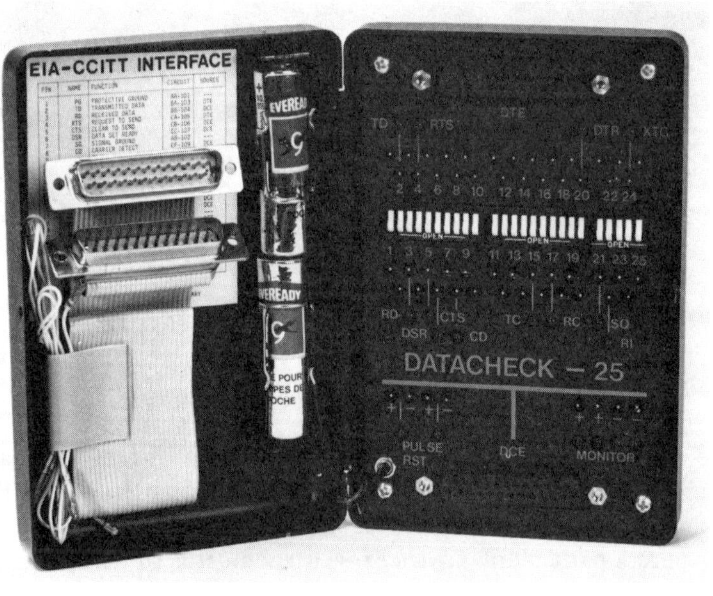

Figure 15.1 Interface tester

15.3 Multimeter

Analogue pointer-type instruments have largely been displaced by digital ones, known as multimeters. There are many different makes and models of multimeters; there are advanced programmable measuring systems and there are simple instruments.

In contrast to the older analogue instruments, which only give the effective value of a sine wave in AC measurements, the digital instrument can also give effective values for other forms of curve such as saw-tooth or square waveforms. Some instruments can accept probes for temperature measurement. Others again can 'freeze' a measurement value in cases where one has to see when the test pins are connected to what is being measured.

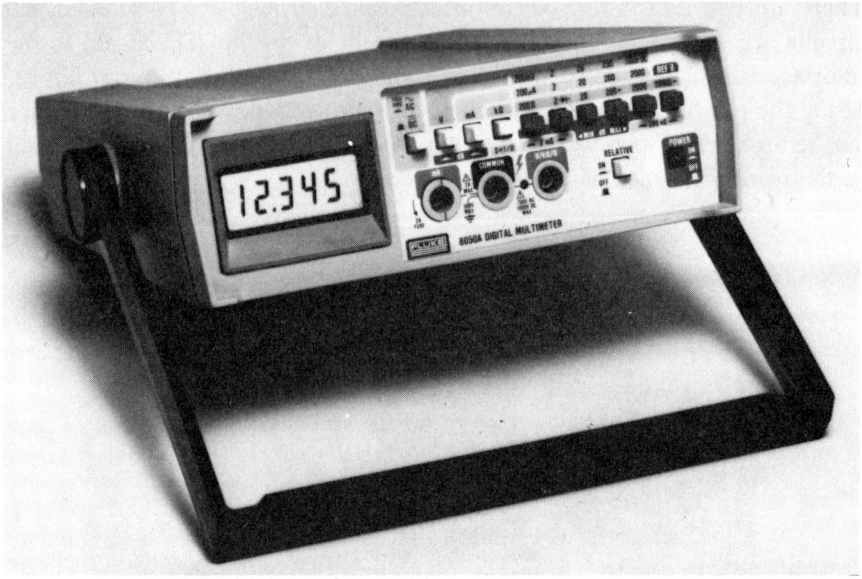

Figure 15.2 FLUKE 8050A Multimeter

There are built-in automatic protection devices in case of overload of the instrument. In most cases they use rechargeable batteries, but there are instruments solely for mains use. General use within data communication does not require a particularly advanced instrument. It is sufficient to be able to measure current, voltage and resistance to four-figure accuracy. Instruments in this class lie in the £200–300 price bracket.

15.4 Frequency counter

It may not be absolutely necessary to have a frequency counter on site. There are occasions where it can be useful, such as in checking the modem's timing pulse or the mains frequency. As with multimeters, frequency counters come in a range of makes and models. The counter has various frequency ranges, from a few Hz up to GHz. For communications applications, an instrument with ranges from 10 HZ to 100 MHz will suffice. The instrument has different 'gate' times and different damping in the measurement probes. As with multimeters, one should study the information sheets in order to find a suitable instrument.

15.5 Oscilloscope

The oscilloscope is an instrument which has been in use for many years for the most varied of technical measurement applications. The instrument has become highly developed in the last few years, and provided with microprocessors with the aid of which it can run complex measurement programs. One can get memory oscilloscopes where one trace can be stored or 'enlarged'. Oscilloscopes for data communication work usually have two channels. The screen does not need to be very large, as the traces from both channels can be superimposed on the screen. Suitable oscilloscopes can be bought for £240–500.

The use of the 'scope is to examine the square-wave pulses between the terminal and the modem. The oscilloscope can also be connected to a so-called 'eye pattern' – the generator for checking that transmission from the corresponding modem is acceptable. Analogue sine waves can also be studied when sent from the far end of the line. An oscilloscope is an essential instrument for anyone working on repair and setting-up of modems in data installations.

15.6 Data transmission test set

There are several instruments designed for testing modems. The instruments are connected to the Cannon plugs on the modem and the terminal and data lines are disconnected. The instrument is then used as a computer-terminal simulator. Test patterns are sent between instruments and analysed by the corresponding instrument at the far end.

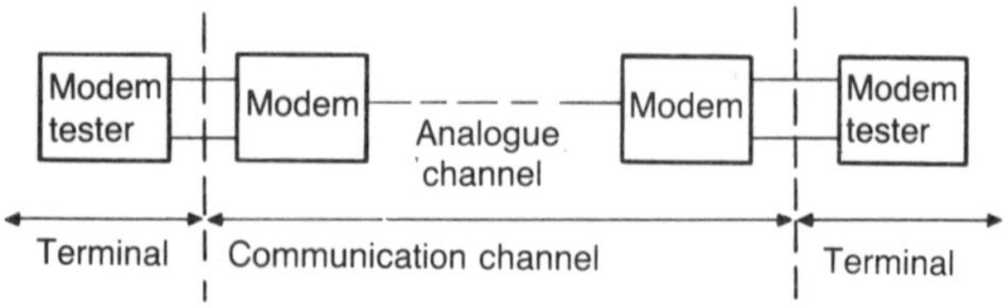

Figure 15.3 Connection of the modem test instruments

During measurement, both the instrument and the analogue line are of course connected and measured together. It may be difficult in some cases to isolate a fault. In practice one can change the modem over and see whether the result is any different. Different loop connections on the modem can also be made.

Among the several makes of instrument on the market are the Siemens DTS 500 and the Trend Data Transmission Test Set.

Figure 15.4 Siemens DTS 500 modem test instrument

The Siemens instrument is only designed for synchronous modems. It can, however, be used on multipoint configurations, where one instrument is connected as master and polls the other 'slaves' which are connected. A maximum of 16 'slaves' can be connected at the same time. During a test session, the instrument sends a 511-bit pattern as specified in CCITT V.52. The number of blocks received by both the near and far instruments can be read off on a display. Errors at block and bit level can be detected. On continuous transmission, so-called 'clock-slip' can be detected at the 8-bit (byte) level.

The Trend data transmission test set is a combined one for synchronous and asynchronous use. Synchronous tests can be carried out in the same way as for the Siemens instrument, but only for point-to-point connections.

Certain coded messages can be sent, for example the well-known 'quick brown fox'. Measurements of analogue disortion within the interval 50–9600 bits/s can be read off directly on a display. Disortion is expressed as a percentage, and is defined as the difference between the largest and smallest time delay for the pulse length in question.

$$\text{Dist } \% = \frac{(\text{Tmax}=\text{Tmin})}{\text{pulse length}}$$

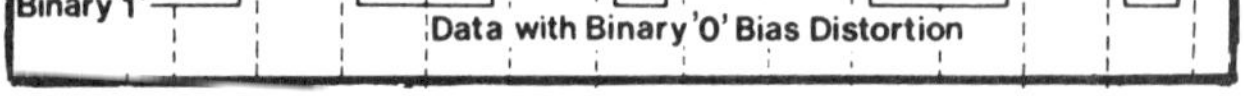

Figure 15.5 Measurement of disortion on asynchronous transmission

Figure 15.6 Trend data transmission test set

15.7 Line listener/analyser

A line listener is an interactive instrument with which one can listen continuously to the traffic on the selected line, or send a previously-programmed message to a terminal or a computer.

There are several suppliers on the Swedish market of this sort of equipment. Examples are the DATASCOPE from the Spectron Corporation and INTERVIEW from Atlantic Research.

The instrument is connected to the modem-terminal via a T-piece. In the monitor mode the ordinary data traffic is not affected. In the interactive mode, when the terminal or the computer is to be simulated, the ordinary traffic is interrupted. DATASCOPE can be connected to a tape recorder to play in a data flow or a program. INTERVIEW has a built-in tape recorder for the same purpose. Both instruments have an array of LED's on the front panel, one for each circuit in the V.24 interface (apart from circuit 1).

DATASCOPE is provided with a number of keys for use when monitoring, with which the desired type of traffic can be set up. On INTERVIEW, the corresponding functions are controlled by means of a menu technique, where the operator responds to a questionnaire.

DATASCOPE has a 5" screen, and INTERVIEW a 7" screen, where the current data is presented continuously. A built-in 4 K memory means that the monitoring can be suspended and the data received can be 'leafed through'. Larger volumes of data can be recorded onto tape for later analysis. In the interactive mode, DATASCOPE has 40 or so instructions.

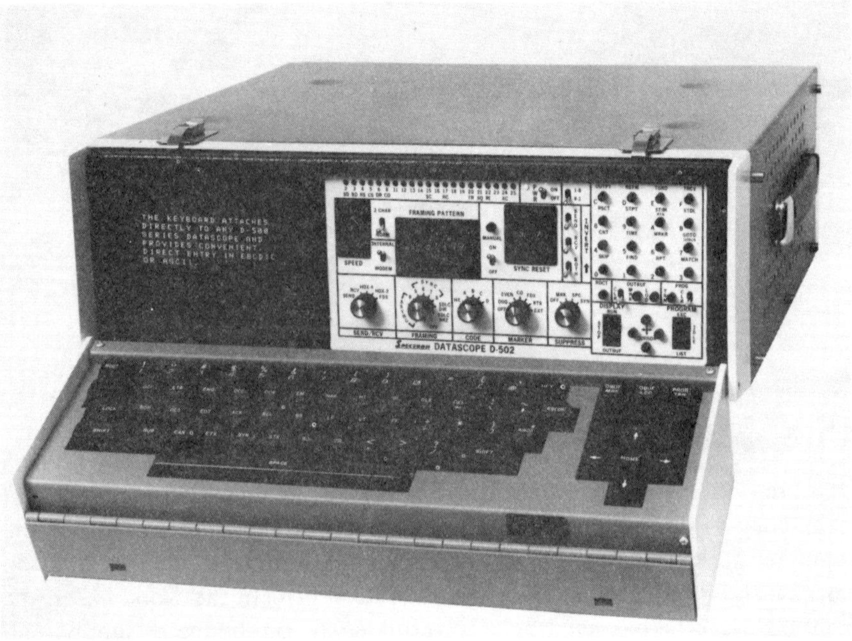

Figure 15.7 DATASCOPE Model 502

The instrument has clocks and counters which can be controlled from the program coded in. Using these clocks and counters, the line loading, error rates, etc, can be determined.

For general and advanced use, a line listener is a most useful instrument. Installations with terminals should not be without one.

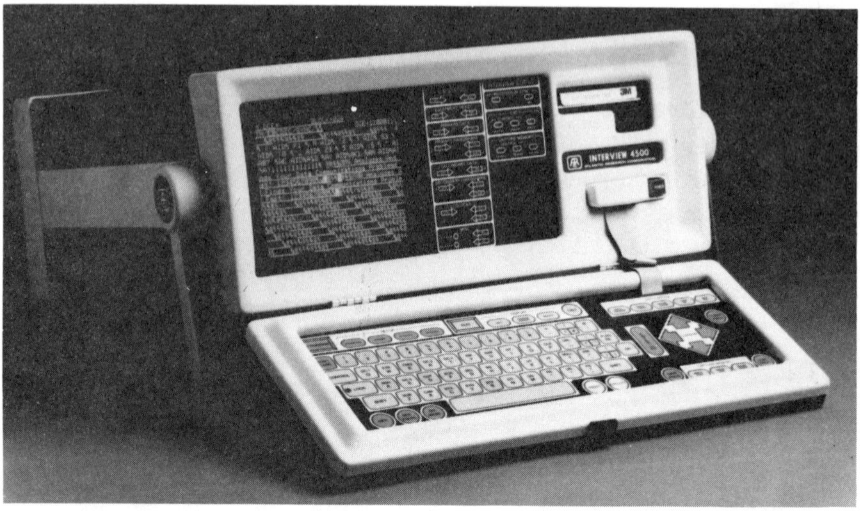

Figure 15.8 INTERVIEW Model 4500

15.8 Mains interference analyser

One area often forgotten about within data communication measurement technology is the mains power supply to the modem, terminals and the computer itself. Any modems and terminals connected to the mains will stop working the instant the mains voltage varies much. In the worst cases, the equipment can be damaged by a powerful ‘spike’ on the mains supply.

One method of examining disurbances of this nature is with an analyser, which is connected to the power supply which one suspects of causing faults. One instrument for this purpose is the DRANETZ Model 606, which is connected to 220 volts and which can monitor one to three phases. The type of interference and the time when it occurred are printed on a paper strip. The voltages and frequencies commonly found in data equipment, e g 208 volts, 60 Hz, can also be monitored.

If the interference level is much too high, one must try to trace the source of this, and if necessary connect magnetic stabilisers into the affected equipment. Mains voltage variations occur when machines taking a lot of power are switched on and off.

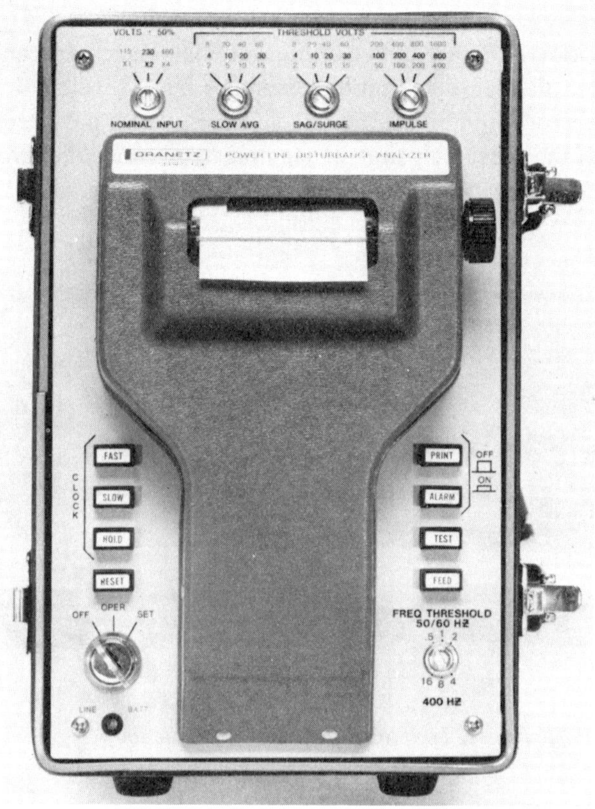

Figure 15.9 DRANETZ mains disurbance analyser

15.9 Analogue test instruments

There are only a few computer installations which would have a need for testing analogue connections. Apart from the telephone companies, there may be some, such as the military, who also need to carry out measurements on their private networks. When carrying out analogue measurements, it is definitely a question of 'knowing what you are doing'.

Measurements on the analogue side previously required a number of instruments. For example, one device would be needed for measuring group delay time, and another for measurement of short breaks and interference pulses.

More recently such instruments have been digitalised and provided with microprocessors, and a number of measurement functions can be combined into one and the same instrument. Siemens have developed an instrument based on microcomputer and FFT techniques, which have reduced the time required for the previously time-consuming measurement of group delay time and frequency to about one second.

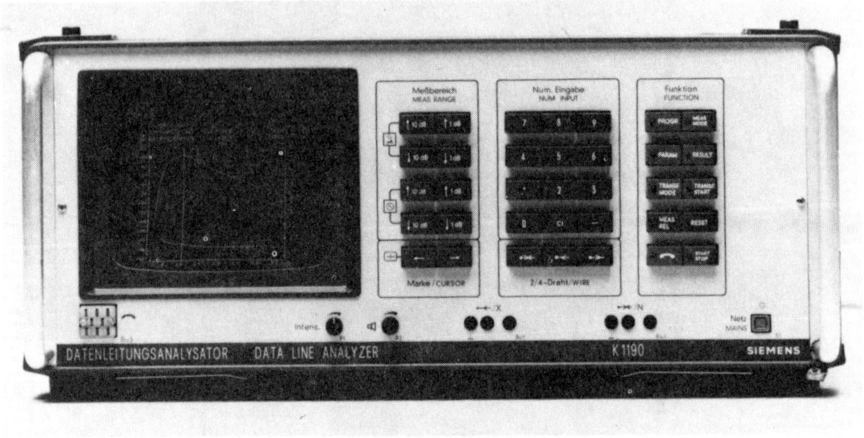

Figure 15.10 Siemens K 1190 instrument for analogue lines

The instrument is provided with dialogue-controlled setting-up, with the aid of a screen. The following tests can be carried out within the frequency range 200–3600 Hz

- level
- group delay disortion
- disortion and overtone damping
- reflection damping
- impedance
- interference level, weighted or unweighted
- phase jitter
- level change relative to a reference
- frequency shift
- event counting: – interference pulse
  – amplitude jumps
  – phase jumps

15.10 Digital switch and patch modules

When the number of modems and lines has grown beyond a certain level, the need to be able to connect a line listener rapidly soon becomes apparent. Using what are known as 'patch modules', which are connected in series with modem and computer, instruments can be connected in quickly without having to break the connection.

With the aid of the module, one can also break the connection and simulate the terminal or computer using interactive equipment.

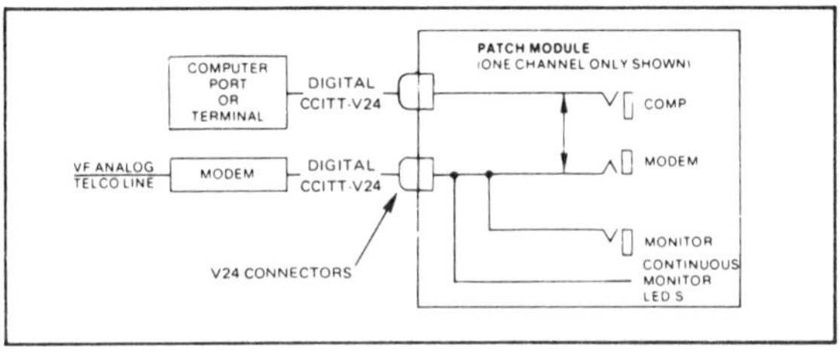

Figure 15.11 Diagram of the principles of the digital patch module

There are also analogue patch modules which are connected in series with the telephone connection and the modem. As mentioned earlier, there should be a special reason for making such a connection.

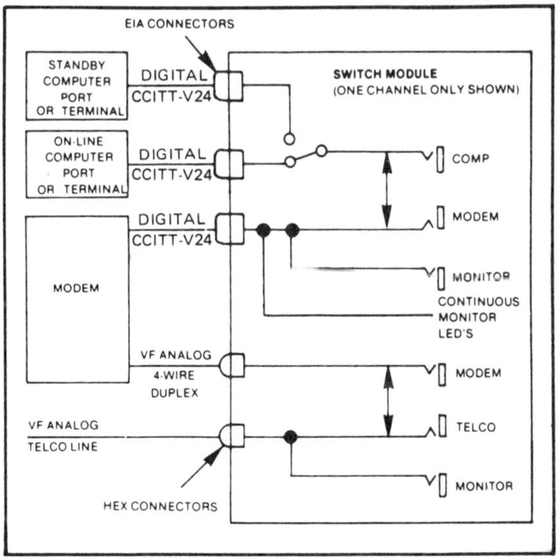

Figure 15.12 Diagram of the principles of the switch module

There are also modules with alarm functions, where selectable circuits in the interface can be connected to an audio-visual signal. Circuit 109 (carrier detect) is the usual one to be connected to the alarm function. If the carrier is lost within a set time period, the alarm sounds.

Switch modules are used for switching two incoming lines (modems) between two computer inputs, for example to the front-end computer for back-up reasons. Switch modules can also be cascade-coupled, and patch and switch modules can also be combined.

With the aid of a 'master switch', all circuits can be connected over to a reserve computer at the same time.

15.11 Processor-controlled monitoring

When all circuits in the V.24 interface are taken out into patch and switch modules, it isn't a big step to connecting a microprocessor to the interface for a more comprehensive monitoring of modem, terminal and line.

Figure 15.13 The LAS system for control and monitoring

Some suppliers have designed monitoring systems using this method. Two different techniques for interface monitoring may be distinguished. One method monitors the V.24 interface using programmable or plug-in equipment, which determines how the alarm functions will be set off.

A second method is based on following the line procedure itself continously. In this case the monitoring equipment must 'understand' the line procedure, which characters mean SYN, ETX, STX etc.

The Atlantic Research LAS (Line Access Switch) system is based on the first method. Altogether, 1024 lines can be connected to the system processor. Patch and switch modules connected in are controlled from the system's console.

Another system based on the same principles in Spectron Corporation's RASP (Remote Access Switching and Patching).

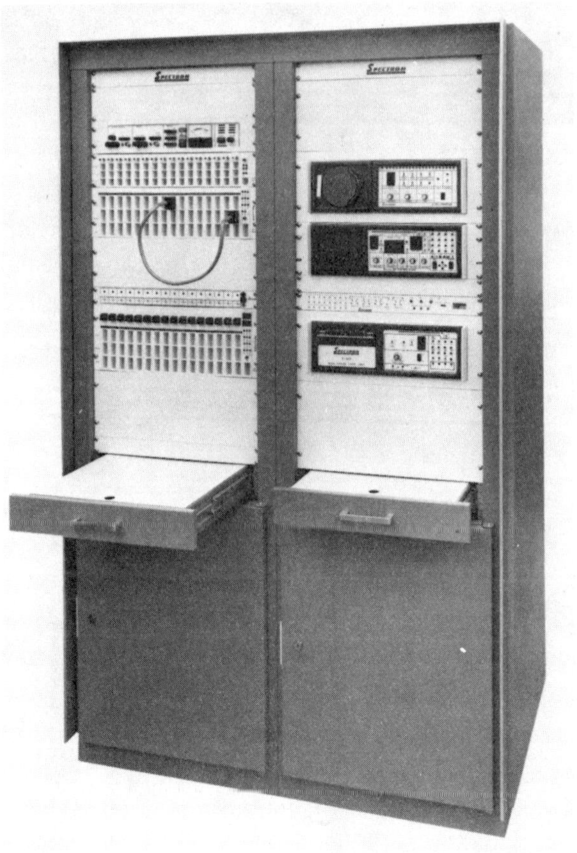

Figure 15.14 a and b. The RASP system for network monitoring

The system's console receives alarm messages if the status of the interface circuits differs from the status set in advance. One can, for example, monitor whether the carrier (circuit 109) is 'lost' from the modem on a fixed line.

Both systems can be expanded for monitoring lines to several computers in the network.

15.12 Summary

Instruments for installation and fault-finding are necessary in a data communication installation. It should however be made clear that it is not the instruments which do the job automatically. You need a person to do it as well.

Developments on the instrument side are accelerating. In recent years, more and more instruments have been 'digitalised' and provided with microprocessors. As in the computer area, the relative cost of such instruments is falling.

16 Glossary

A

Additional bit — A bit which is not an information bit.

Amplitude modulation
1. Modulation where the amplitude of the alternating current is changed.
2. Modulation where the significant condition is represented by currents of different amplitudes.

Analogue transmission — Transmission of a continuously changing signal.

Architecture — The framework for the relationship between systems within which services, functions and protocols are specified.

ARQ system (error detection system with automatic repeat request) — A system designed so that every error detected in the signal automatically triggers a repeat transmission of the signal in which the error was detected.

Asynchronous transmission — Transmission where both:
- the number of unit intervals between two randomly selected significant time intervals from one and the same character or block in the order transmitted are a whole number, and
- the number of unit intervals between two randomly selected significant time intervals from different characters or blocks in transmission order need not be a whole number.

B

Back channel — A channel generally used for transmission of help or monitoring information, and which is coordinated with the forward channel (the main information signal).

Base band signal — A limited-band base signal which mainly comprises the frequency components required for restoring the original information.

Base signal	Signal containing only those frequency components originally used for representing the information.
Basic mode	The generally standardised protocol for synchronous terminals. It is a character-orientated protocol in which control data is included in the transmission in the form of special control characters.
Baud (rate)	A unit for modulation speed.
Bidirectional transmission	Transmission allowing traffic in both directions.
Binary numbers	Number symbols in the binary arithmetic system, e g 0 or 1.
Bit	Abbreviation for Binary digIT. A bit represents only a 1 or a 0 in the binary number system.
Bit (element, character, block) error rate	The relationship between the number of incorrect bits (elements, characters, blocks) received and the total number transmitted.
Block	A group of binary numbers sent as a unit.
Block check	A means of monitoring blocks based on the fulfilling of certain rules for block construction.
Block start signal	Signal indicating the start of a block.

C

Character	Element (letter, number etc) used to form, control or represent data.
Character control	Measures for monitoring of characters based on the fulfilling of certain predetermined rules for the construction of characters.
Character signal	A group of signal elements corresponding to a character.
Code (telegraph or data)	A collection of rules according to which the telegraph or data signals which make up a message or a block are to be organised, sent, received and processed.
Code element	The signal elements which are included in an isometric code with several unit elements per character.
Code transformation	Automatic transformation of character signals or groups of character signals on one code to character signals or groups of character signals in another code.

Control bit	An additional bit on a character or block which allows the character or block to be checked.
Control character	A character used for controlling a peripheral, e g so that the terminal will go on to the next line.
Circuit connection	A method of connecting two parties together where one lead is used by them exclusively until the connection is broken. The common telephone is a well-known example.
Cyclic disortion	Disortion caused by events of a periodic nature.

D

DC transmission	A method of transmission where the transmission cable is fed from a source of direct current, and where this current is modulated in respect of amplitude, and maybe also polarity.
Data receiver	Equipment which receives data signals after transmission.
Data signal	Signal corresponding to a succession of binary numbers which are used for transmitting information and carrying out service functions.
Data source	Equipment which delivers data signals for transmission.
Data speed	The average number of bits, characters or blocks which are transferred between the equipment in a data transmission system per unit time.
Data transmission	Every transfer of data from one piece of quipment to another.
Defect modulation (restitution)	Modulation (restitution) containing one or more elements, whose significant state differs from that prescribed in the applicable code.
Differential modulation (DPSK)	Modulation in which the significant state of each signal element depends on the state of a previous signal element (usually the one immediately preceding).
Digital transmission	Transmission of data by means of discrete pulses or different signal levels.
Diplex	Transmission of two messages at the same time in the same direction.

Distributed system
: Computer systems in which a number of computers at different sites handle their own applications, but which are also connected so that they can work together.

Duplex, full duplex
: Transmission in both directions at the same time.

E

Element error rate
: See Bit error rate.

Error bit
: A bit which does not agree with what should have been received.

Error block
: A block which contains one or more faulty bits.

Error burst
: A group of bits within which two error bits in succession always have correct bits between them whose number is less than a certain fixed quantity.

Error-correcting code
: Code in which every telegraph or data signal follows certain rules, so that deviations from these in the signals received can not just be detected, but may also allow some or all of the errors detected to be corrected at the receiving end.

Error-correction system
: A system using digital or analogue error-detection, or error-detection code which is so designed that certain or all signals indicated as being in error are automatically corrected at the receiver's end before they are transferred to the collector or telegraph receiver.

Error detection code
: A code by which every telegraph or data signal follows such rules that deviations from these can be detected automatically in the received signals.

Error detection system
: Systems which use an error detection code (digital error detection) and/or a quality detector (analogue error detection), and which acts so that every signal which is indicated as in error is:
a either omitted from the data flow transmitted to the receiver (in which case the fact that such an omission has taken place is marked),
b or is transferred to the data collector with a marker to show that the signal has been found to have errors.

Exchanging
: The process in communications networks for directing data to the intended user(s).

F

FEP (Front-end processor) Communications computer.

Five-unit code Isometric code in which the modulation is binary and the character signals are composed of five unit elements.

Forward channel The main information channel.

Frequency-derived channel Each of the channels obtained through frequency multiplexing of a transmission channel.

Frequency modulation
1 Modulation where it is the frequency of an alternating current which is altered.
2 Modulation where each of two predetermined frequencies corresponds to one of the significant states.

Frequency multiplexing The method whereby the frequency range available for transmission is divided up into narrow bands, each of which is used as a separate channel.

Frequency shift modulation (keying) – FSK Frequency modulation where the frequency changes at the significant time-points.

G

Gateway An exchange in a network which gives access to and from another network.

General data network Communications network designed for transferring digital signals available to all who wish to subscribe to it.

H

Half duplex Transmission in both directions, but not at the same time.

IIDLC (High-level Data Link Control) A protocol for synchronous simplex, half duplex or full duplex transmission. HDLC is independent of data type, and in contrast to Basic Mode does not use control characters.

I

Information bit	One of the bits sent by the data source which transmits the main information, as distinct from start, stop and other control bits.
Insertion telegraphy	A form of transmission where a narrow band in a telephone channel is laid aside, so that the narrow-band telegraphy channel and the telephone channel can be used for traffic at the same time.
Interface	Specification of the conditions in the leads and circuits in the connection between two pieces of equipment.
Isochronous modulation (restitution)	Modulation (restitution) where the time interval between two random significant time points is theoretically equal to the unit interval or a multiple of it.
Isometric code	A code whose character signals consist of the same number of unit elements, which all have the same duration.

L

LAN	Local Area Network
Level, layer	A grouping of logically connected functions. The interface at one level can be standardised, but not the method for carrying out the internal functions of the level.
Local connection	A permanent connection between two sets of telephone apparatus, both in the same district (no switching in the connection).

M

Message monitoring by return transmission (message collation)	A method for testing the security of data transmission.
Minimum interval	The duration of the shortest significant interval in a system using a code such that the theoretical durations of the significant intervals are not all whole multiples of a unit interval.

Modem	Abbreviation for MOdulator-DEMdulator.
Modem (data transmission equipment)	The modem carries out one or both the following tasks: – modulation according to the signal to be transmitted, – demodulation of the received signals.
Modulation	A process whereby certain characteristics of one wave are modified in accordance with a characteristic of another wave or of a signal.
Modulation speed, telegraphy speed	The inverse of the unit interval measured in seconds (baud).
Multiplexing (Channelling multiplex)	Method whereby a broad channel is used to create two or more channels, or where these use shorter time divisions within the overall channel.
Multipoint line	Connections between three or more computers or terminals.

N

n-phase modulation	Phase modulation where the n significant states are phase-shifted (usually by $2\pi/n$ radians) in relation to each other.

O

Omnibus system	A transmission system where a number of stations are permanently connected together, so that when any station in the system transmits all the others receive the message.
Open system	A system (which may comprise people, terminals, computers, peripheral units, software, etc) which can be connected together and coordinated with other systems in accordance with general set standards.

P

Packet	A data block with a defined structure consisting partly of a header containing destination and control data, and partly of user data.
Packet switching	Data transmission in networks set up to transmit data in packets. The packets are transferred to the network, and the equipment in this uses the data in the header to send the packet to the specified destinations.
Parallel transmission	Simultaneous transmission of signal elements.
Parity check (odd or even parity)	Check that the number of digits (ONE's) in a group is odd (or even).
Phase modulation	Modulation where the phase angle of the carrier wave is the quantity changed.
Physical connection	Transmission medium between two or more users, usually consisting of electrical wires for transmission of the signal.
Pi-shift modulation (two-phase modulation)	Two-phase modulation where the two significant states are phase-shifted π radians in relation to each other.
Point-to-point connection	A connection consisting of a lead between two users.
Pre-correction	The deliberate addition of disortion.
Protocol	Rules for data communication.

R

Redundant code	Code using more signal elements than are required for representing the actual information.
Restitution	A series of significant states determined by the demodulation products.

S

Series transmission	Successive transmission of signal elements.
Service bit	An additional bit, which is not a control bit.

Signal element — Each of the parts of which a telegraph or data signal consists, and which differs from the others by its nature, size, duration and relative position (or at least by one or more of these characteristics).

Significant interval — The time interval between two successive significant time points.

Significant time point — The time point at which the significant state begins (after evaluation in the modulation or restitution equipment).

Simple error — A faulty bit, which is preceded and followed by at least one correct bit.

Simplex (connection) — A connection which allows transmission in both directions, but not at the same time.

Start signal (in a start-stop system) — A signal element whose job is to prepare the receiver mechanism for receipt and recording of a character, or for function monitoring.

Start-stop distortion —

1 The relationship a/b, where a is the maximum measured difference, regardless of character, between the actual and the theoretical time span between a randomly-chosen significant time point in a modulation (or a restitution) and the significant time point for the immediately preceding start element, and b is the unit interval.
2 The largest absolute value of the individual distortion of the significant time points in start-stop modulation.

Start-stop modulation (restitution) — Modulation (or restitution) characteristic for start-stop systems.

Stop signal (in a start-stop system) — A signal element whose job it is to return the receiving apparatus to a resting state, where the mechanism is prepared for receiving the next character.

Subcontrol station (on a line) — A station on a line.

Synchronous transmission — Transmission where the number of unit intervals between two significant time points chosen at random from anywhere in the transmission is a whole number.

T

Time-derivative channel	Each of the channels obtained by time multiplexing of a transmission channel.
Timer	Part of the timing equipment.
Timing equipment	Equipment used as the overall timing provider for the transmission system.
Timing follower, synchroniser	Part of the receiver's timing equipment which adjusts its timing to that of the sender.
Transmission with asymmetrical sidebands	A transmission method where one of the two sidebands is partially suppressed.
Transmission with reduced sidebands	A transmission technique where one of the two sidebands is modified somewhat nearest the carrier. Only a rudiment of the other near the carrier remains.
Transparent	A communications link which does not alter the data it transmits in any way.
Two-way simplex	This implies two single-direction channels or installations, one for each direction, grouped into a single lead.

U

Unidirectional (transmission)	Transmission from a sender to a receiver.
Unit element	Element in a character signal.
Unit interval	The time interval in a system which uses isometric code or isochronous modulation, such that the theoretical duration for the significant intervals in modulation or restitution are whole multiples of this time interval.

V

V series	CCITT's recommendations for data communication via telephone (i e analogue) networks.

X

X series	CCITT's recommendations for data transmission via digital networks.

Index